D1648944

Real Analog

An Introduction to Electrical Circuits

Author:

Tim Hanshaw

Edited and Updated By:

Kaitlyn Franz, Martha Migliacio, Ian Etheridge, and Norman MacDonald

Digilent Inc.
1300 NE Henley Court, Ste 3, Pullman, WA 99163, USA
Email: sales@digilentinc.com

ISBN: 978-1-791-94343-1

Contents

Chapter 1:
Circuit Analysis Fundamentals

In this chapter, we introduce all fundamental concepts associated with circuit analysis. Electrical circuits are constructed in order to direct the flow of electrons to perform a specific task. In other words, in circuit analysis and design, we are concerned with transferring electrical energy in order to accomplish a desired objective. For example, we may wish to use electrical energy to pump water into a reservoir; we can adjust the amount of electrical energy applied to the pump to vary the rate at which water is added to the reservoir. The electrical circuit, then, might be designed to provide the necessary electrical energy to the pump to create the desired water flow rate.

This chapter begins with introduction to the basic parameters which describe the energy in an electrical circuit: *charge*, *voltage*, and *current*. Movement of charge is associated with electrical energy transfer. The energy associated with charge motion is reflected by two parameters: voltage and current. Voltage is indicative of an electrical energy change resulting from moving a charge from one point to another in an electric field. Current indicates the rate at which charge is moving, which is associated with the energy of a magnetic field. We will not be directly concerned with charge, electrical fields, or magnetic fields in this course, we will work almost exclusively with voltages and currents. Since *power* quantifies the rate of energy transfer, we will also introduce power in this chapter.

Electrical circuits are composed of interconnected *components*. In this chapter, we will introduce two basic types of components: *power supplies* and *resistors*. Power supplies are used to provide power to our electrical circuits, and resistors dissipate electrical power by converting it to heat. These two types of components will allow us to introduce and exercise virtually all available circuit analysis techniques. Electrical components are described in terms of the relationships between the voltages and currents at their terminals, these relationships are called the *voltage-current characteristics* of the device. In this chapter, we will introduce voltage-current characteristics for power supplies and resistors. In later chapters, we will introduce additional circuit components, but our circuit analysis approaches will not change – we will simply substitute voltage-current characteristics for these components as appropriate to model future circuits.

Finally, we introduce the two fundamental rules of circuit analysis: *Kirchhoff's Current Law* and *Kirchhoff's Voltage Law*. These rules form the basis of all circuit analysis techniques used throughout this textbook.

Please pay special attention to the *passive sign convention* introduced in this chapter. Voltages and currents have signs – they can be positive or negative – and these signs are crucial to understanding the effect of these parameters on the energy transferred by the circuit. No useful circuit analysis can be performed without following the passive sign convention.

In summary, this chapter introduces virtually all the basic concepts which will be used throughout this textbook. After this chapter, little information specific to electrical circuit analysis remains to be learned – the remainder of the textbook is devoted to developing analysis methods used to increase the efficiency of our circuit analysis and introducing additional circuit components such as capacitors, inductors, and operational amplifiers. The student should be aware, however, that all of our circuit analysis is based on energy transfer among circuit components; this energy transfer is governed by Kirchhoff's Current Law and Kirchhoff's Voltage Law and the circuit components are modeled by their voltage-current relationships.

After Completing this Chapter, You Should be Able to:

- Define voltage and current in terms of electrical charge
- State common prefixes and the symbols used in scientific notation
- State the passive sign convention from memory
- Determine the power absorbed or generated by a circuit element, based on the current and voltage provided to it
- Write symbols for independent voltage and current sources
- State from memory the function of independent voltage and current sources
- Write symbols for dependent voltage and current sources
- State governing equations for the four types of dependent sources
- State Ohm's Law from memory
- Use Ohm's Law to perform voltage and current calculations for resistive circuit elements
- Identify nodes in an electrical circuit
- Identify loops in an electrical circuit
- State Kirchhoff's current law from memory, both in words and as a mathematical expression
- State Kirchhoff's voltage law from memory, both in words and as a mathematical expression
- Apply Kirchhoff's voltage and current laws to electrical circuits

1.1   Basic Circuit Parameters and Sign Conventions

This section introduces the basic engineering parameters for electric circuits: *voltage*, *current*, and *power*. The international system of units is commonly used to describe the units of these parameters; this system as it relates to electrical circuit analysis is briefly discussed in this section.

This section also introduces the *passive sign convention*. It is extremely important when analyzing electrical circuits to use the correct sign convention between the voltage across a circuit element and the current going through the element. Some of the most common errors of beginning students are associated with applying incorrect sign conventions when analyzing circuits.

1.1.1   Electrical Charge

Electron flow is fundamental to operation of electric circuits; the concept of *charge* can be used to describe the distribution of electrons in the circuit. Charge can be represented as either positive or negative – generally relative to some reference level. Charge is represented by the variable q and is measured in *coulombs*, abbreviated as *C*.

The charge of one electron corresponds to -1.6022×10⁻¹⁹ C. Charge can only exist in integer multiples of the charge of a single electron. Charge, however, is not widely used in electrical circuit analysis; voltage and current are more convenient ways to represent the electric charge in a system.

1.1.2 Voltage

Voltage is energy per unit charge. Energy is specified relative to some reference level; thus, voltages are more accurately specified as voltage *differences* between two points in a circuit. The voltage difference between two points can be thought of as a difference in potential energy between charges placed at those two points. Units of voltage are volts, abbreviated V. The voltage difference between two points indicates the energy necessary to move a unit charge from one of the points to the other. Voltage differences can be either positive or negative.

Mathematically, voltage is expressed in differential form as:

$$v = \frac{dw}{dq}$$

Eq. 1.1

Where v is the voltage difference (in volts), w is the energy (in joules), and q is the charge (in coulombs). The differences in equation (1.1) are all defined relative to different spatial positions; thus, the differentials dw and dq are between <u>two different points in space</u>, and the voltage is defined as being between these same two spatial points.

1.1.3 Current

Current is the rate at which charge is passing a given point. Current is specified at a particular point in the circuit, and is not relative to a reference. Since current is caused by charge in motion, it can be thought of as indicating *kinetic* energy.

Mathematically, current is represented as:

$$i = \frac{dq}{dt}$$

Eq. 1.2

Where i is the current in amperes, q is the charge in coulombs, and t is the time in seconds. Thus, current is the time rate of change of charge and units of charge are coulombs per second, or *amperes* (abbreviated as A).

1.1.4 Power

An electrical system is often used to drive a non-electrical system (in an electric stove burner, for example, electric energy is converted to heat). Interactions between electrical and non-electrical systems are generally described in terms of *power*. Electrical power associated with a particular circuit element is the product of the current passing through the element and the voltage difference across the element. This is often written as:

$$p(t) = v(t) \cdot i(t)$$

Eq. 1.3

Where $p(t)$ is the *instantaneous* power <u>at time</u> t, $v(t)$ is the voltage difference at time t, and $i(t)$ is the current at time t. Power can either be absorbed by a circuit element or generated by a circuit element; the determination as to whether the element is absorbing or generating power can be made by the relative signs of the values of voltage and current. These sign conventions are an important issue, and will be addressed separately in the next chapter. Units of power are watts, abbreviated W.

1.1.5 International System of Units and Prefixes

We will use the international system of units (SI). The scales of parameters that are of interest to engineers can vary over many orders of magnitudes. For example, voltages experienced during lightning strikes can be on the order of 10^7V, while voltages measured from an electroencephalograph (EEG) can be on the order of 10^{-4}V. For this reason, numbers represented in SI units are often associated with a prefix, which helps account for the order-of-magnitude variations in numbers. Table 1 below provides a list of common prefixes and the symbols used to represent them.

Multiple	Prefix	Symbol
10^9	giga	G
10^6	mega	M
10^3	kilo	k
10^{-3}	milli	m
10^{-6}	micro	μ
10^{-9}	nano	n
10^{-12}	pico	p

Table 1.1. SI prefixes.

1.1.6 Passive Sign Convention

A general two-terminal electrical circuit element is shown in Fig. 1.1. In general, there will be some current, i, flowing through the element and some voltage difference, v, across its terminals. Note that we are currently representing both voltage and current as constants, but none of the assertions made in this chapter change if they are functions of time.

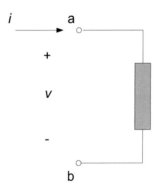

Figure 1.1. General circuit element and passive sign convention.

The assumed direction of the current, i, passing through the element is shown by the arrow on Fig. 1.1. In Fig. 1.1, i is assumed to be positive if it is going into node a. A negative value of i simply indicates a change in direction of the current – if i is negative, the current is going into node b (or, equivalently, out of node a). We will assume that our circuit elements do not accumulate charge, so any current entering node a must leave node b.

Example 1.1:

Three amperes (3 A) of current is passing through a circuit element connecting nodes a and b. The current is flowing from node a to node b. The physical situation can be represented schematically by any of the figures shown below – all four figures represent the same current flow and direction.

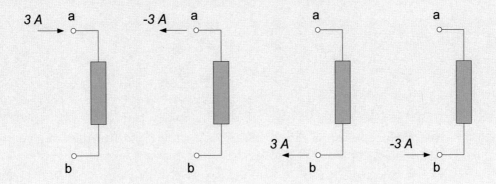

The <u>assumed</u> polarity of the voltage difference v across the element is shown by the + and - signs on Fig. 1.1. The polarity shown in Fig. 1.1 indicates that a positive value for v indicates that the voltage at the terminal marked with a + sign is higher than the voltage at the terminal marked with a - sign (that is, the voltage at node a is higher than the voltage at node b). A negative value for v simply reverses this polarity (negative voltage means that the voltage at node b is higher than the voltage at node a).

Example 1.2:

A 5 volt (5 V) voltage potential difference is applied across a circuit element connecting nodes a and b. The voltage at node a is positive relative to the voltage at node b. The physical situation can be represented schematically by either of the figures shown below – both figures represent the same voltage potential difference.

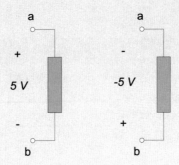

The assumed voltage polarity and current direction are not individually significant - the assumed direction of voltage polarity <u>relative</u> to current direction is important. To satisfy our sign convention, we will assume that positive current enters the node at which the positive voltage polarity is defined. This sign convention is called the *passive sign convention*. In the passive sign convention, the relative assumed sign convention between voltage and current is as shown in Fig. 1.1.

Example 1.3:

The passive sign convention is satisfied for either of the two voltage-current definitions shown below - the current is assumed to enter the positive voltage node.

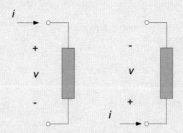

The passive sign convention is <u>not</u> satisfied for either of the two voltage current definitions shown below – the current is assumed to enter the negative voltage node.

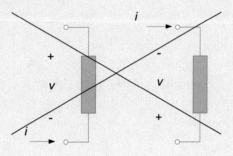

Note: Many students attempt to choose current directions and voltage polarities so that their calculations result in positive values for voltages and currents. In general, this is a waste of time - it is best to arbitrarily assume <u>either</u> a voltage polarity or current direction for each circuit element.

Choice of a positive direction for current dictates the choice of positive voltage polarity, per Fig. 1.1. Choice of a positive voltage polarity dictates the choice of positive current direction, per Fig. 1.1.

Analysis of the circuit is performed using the above assumed signs for voltage and current. The sign of the results indicates whether the assumed choice of voltage polarity and current direction was correct. A positive magnitude of a calculated voltage indicates that the assumed sign convention is correct; a negative magnitude indicates that the actual voltage polarity is opposite to the assumed polarity. Likewise, a positive magnitude of a calculated current indicates that the assumed current direction is correct; a negative magnitude indicates that the current direction is opposite to that assumed.

1.1.7   Voltage Subscript and Sign Conventions

The assumed sign convention for voltage potentials is sometimes expressed by using subscripts. The first subscript denotes the node at which the <u>positive</u> voltage polarity is assumed and the second subscript is the <u>negative</u> voltage polarity. For example, v_{ab} denotes the voltage difference between nodes a and b, for node a assumed to have a positive voltage relative to node b. Switching the order of the subscripts changes the assumed polarity of the voltage difference and this the sign of the voltage, so $v_{ab}=-v_{ba}$. Since our passive sign convention dictates the direction of current relative to voltage polarity, a circuit element whose voltage difference is denoted as v_{ab} will have positive current entering node a.

1.1.8 Reference Voltages and Ground

For convenience, voltage differences are often not explicitly stated as being differences between two potential levels - a node will simply be referred to as having some "voltage". This voltage must still be interpreted as a voltage difference, however. The difference in this case is assumed to be relative to come reference voltage, with the reference generally assumed to be 0V. The reference voltage is often referred to as *ground*. The symbol, displayed below, is used to denote the ground or reference voltage from which all other voltages are measured. When this convention is used, voltages at a node are often identified with a single subscript. For example, v_a would be the voltage at node a, relative to ground. It is assumed that positive voltages are positive relative to ground and negative voltages are negative relative to ground.

Example 1.4:

The two figures below show identical ways of specifying the voltage across a circuit element. In the circuit to the left, the voltage v is the voltage potential between nodes a and b, with the voltage at node a being assumed positive relative to voltage at node b. This can be equivalently specified as v_{ab}. In the figure to the right below, node b has been specified as our ground with the use of the ground symbol. In this figure, the voltage at node a can be specified simply as v_a, with the polarity being assumed positive relative to ground which is implied to be 0V. Thus, for the figures below:

$$v = v_{ab} = v_a \qquad \text{Eq. 1.3}$$

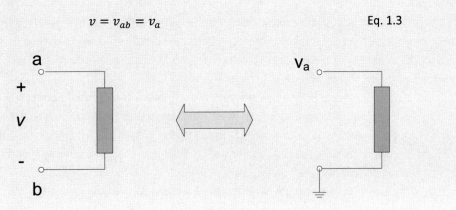

1.1.9 Power and Sign Conventions

The sign of the voltage across an element relative to the sign of the current through the element governs the sign of the power. Equation (1.3) above defines power as the product of the voltage times current:

$$P = vi \qquad \text{Eq. 1.4}$$

The power is *positive* if the signs of voltage and current agree with the passive sign convention - that is, if a positive current enters the positive voltage polarity node. If the power is positive, the element is said to be absorbing power. The power is *negative* if the signs of voltage and current disagree with the passive sign convention - that is, if positive current enters the negative voltage polarity node. If the power is negative, the element is said to be *generating* power.

Example 1.5:

In Fig. (a) below, the element agrees with the passive sign convention since a positive current is entering the positive voltage node. Thus, the element of Fig. (a) is absorbing energy. In Fig. (b), the element is absorbing power - positive current is leaving the negative voltage node, which implies that positive current enters the positive voltage node. The element of Fig. (c) generates power; negative current enters the positive voltage node, which disagrees with the passive sign convention. Fig. (d) also illustrates an element which is generating power, since positive current is entering a negative voltage node.

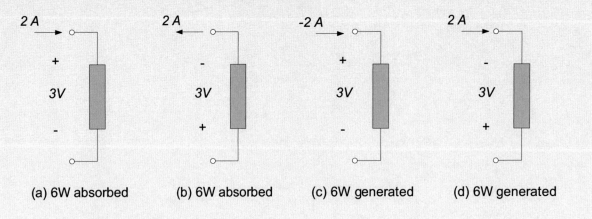

(a) 6W absorbed   (b) 6W absorbed   (c) 6W generated   (d) 6W generated

Section Summary

- In this text, we will be primarily concerned with the movement of electrical charge. Electrical charge motion is represented by voltage and current. Voltage indicates the energy change associated with the movement of a charge from one location to another, while current is indicative of the rate of current motion past a particular point.
  - Voltage is an energy difference between two physically separated points. The polarity of a voltage is used to indicate which point is to be assumed to be at the higher energy level. The positive terminal (+) is assumed to be at a higher voltage than the negative terminal (-). A negative voltage value simply indicates that the actual voltage polarity is opposite to the assumed polarity.
  - The sign of the current indicates the assumed direction of charge motion past a point. A change in the sign of the current value indicates that the current direction is opposite to the assumed direction.
- The assumed polarity of the voltage across a passive circuit element must be consistent with the <u>assumed</u> current direction through the element. The assumed positive direction for current must be such that positive current enters the positive voltage terminal of the element. Since this sign convention is applied only to passive elements, it is known as the *passive sign convention*.
  - The assumed current direction <u>or</u> the assumed voltage polarity can be chosen arbitrarily, but once one parameter is chosen, the other must be chosen to agree with the passive sign convention.
- The power absorbed or generated by an electrical circuit component is the product of the voltage difference across the element and the current through the element: $p=iv$. The relative sign of the voltage and current are set according to the passive sign convention. Positive power implies that the voltage and current are consistent with the passive sign convention (the element absorbs or dissipates energy) while negative power indicates that the relative signs between voltage and current are opposite to the passive sign convention (the element generates or supplies energy to the circuit).

1. Assign reference voltage and current directions to the circuit elements represented by the shaded boxes in the circuits below.

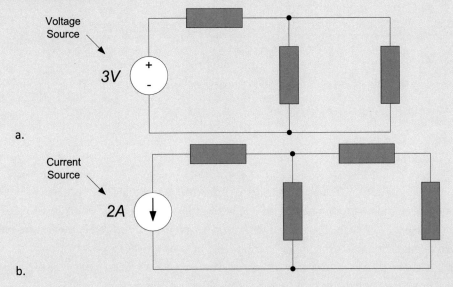

a.

b.

2. Either the reference voltage polarity or the reference current direction is provided for the circuit elements below. Provide the appropriate sign convention for the missing parameters.

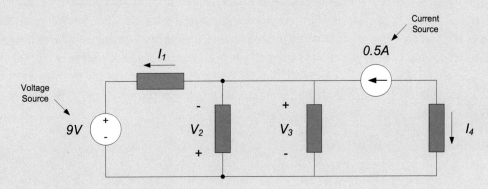

3. Determine the magnitude and direction of the current in the circuit element below if the element absorbs 10W.

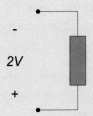

4. Determine the power absorbed or supplied by the circuit element below. State whether the power is absorbed or supplied.

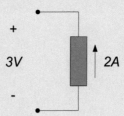

Solutions can be found at digilent.com/real-analog.

1.2 Power Sources

Circuit elements are commonly categorized as either *passive* or *active*. A circuit element is passive if the <u>total</u> amount of energy it delivers to the rest of the circuit (over all time) is non-positive (passive elements can <u>temporarily</u> deliver energy to a circuit, but only if the energy was previously stored in the passive element by the circuit). An active circuit element has the ability to create and provide power to a circuit from mechanisms <u>external</u> to the circuit. Examples of active circuit elements are batteries (which create electrical energy from chemical processes) and generators (which create electrical energy from mechanical processes, such as spinning a turbine).

In this section we consider some very important active circuit elements: voltage and current sources. We will discuss two basic types of sources: *independent sources* and *dependent sources*. Independent sources provide a specified voltage or current, regardless of what is happening elsewhere in the circuit to which they are connected - batteries and generators are generally considered to be independent sources. Dependent sources provide a voltage or current based on a voltage or current elsewhere in the circuit (the source voltage or current is <u>dependent</u> upon some other voltage or current). Dependent sources are often used in the mathematical modeling of common devices such as metal-oxide semiconductor field-effect transistors (MOSFETs) and bipolar junction transistors (BJTs).

1.2.1 Independent Voltage Sources

An independent voltage source maintains a specified voltage across its terminals. The symbol used to indicate a voltage source delivering a voltage $v_s(t)$ is shown in Fig. 1.2. As indicated in Fig. 1.2, the voltage supplied by the source can be time-varying or constant (a constant voltage is a special case of a time-varying voltage). An alternate symbol that is often used to denote a constant voltage source is shown in Fig. 1.3; we, however, will generally use the symbol of Fig. 1.2 for both time-varying and constant voltages.

Note that the sign of the voltage being applied by the source is provided on the source symbol - there is no need to assume a voltage polarity for voltage sources. The current direction, however, is unknown and must be determined (if necessary) from an analysis of the overall circuit.

Ideal voltage sources provide a specified voltage regardless of the current flowing through the device. Ideal sources can provide infinite power; all real sources will provide only limited power to the circuit. We will discuss approaches for modeling non-ideal sources in later chapters.

| Figure 1.2. Independent voltage source. | Figure 1.3. Constant voltage source. |

1.2.2 Independent Current Sources

An independent current source maintains a specified current. This current is maintained regardless of the voltage differences across the terminals. The symbol used to indicate a current source delivering a current $i_s(t)$ is shown in Fig. 1.4. The current supplied by the source can be time-varying or constant.

Note that the sign of the current being applied by the source is provided on the source symbol - there is no need to assume a current direction. The voltage polarity, however, is unknown and must be determined (if necessary) from an analysis of the overall circuit.

Ideal current sources provide a specified current regardless of the voltage difference across the device. Ideal current sources can, like ideal voltage sources, provide infinite power; all real sources will provide only limited power to the circuit. We will discuss approaches for modeling non-ideal current sources in later chapters.

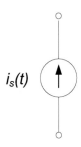

Figure 1.4. Independent current source.

1.2.3 Dependent Sources

Dependent sources can be either voltage or current sources; Fig. 1.5(a) shows the symbol for a dependent voltage source and Fig. 1.5(b) shows the symbol for a dependent current source. Since each type of source can be controlled by either a voltage or current, there are four types of dependent current sources:

- Voltage-controlled voltage source (VCVS)
- Current-controlled voltage source (CCVS)
- Voltage-controlled current source (VCCS)
- Current-controlled current source (CCCS)

(a) Dependent voltage source   (b) Dependent current source

Figure 1.5. Symbols for dependent sources.

Figure 1.6 illustrates the voltage-controlled dependent sources, and Fig. 1.7 illustrates the current-controlled dependent sources. In all cases, some electrical circuit exists which has some voltage and current combination at its terminals. Either the voltage or current at these terminals is used to set the voltage or current of the dependent source. The parameters μ and β in Figs. 1.6 and 1.7 are dimensionless constants. μ is the *voltage gain* of a VCVS and β is the *current gain* of a CCCS. The parameter r is the voltage-to-current ratio of a CCVS and has units of volts/ampere, or *ohms*. The parameter g is the current-to-voltage ratio of a VCCS and has units of amperes/volt, or *siemens*. The units of ohms and siemens will be discussed in more depth in section 1.3.

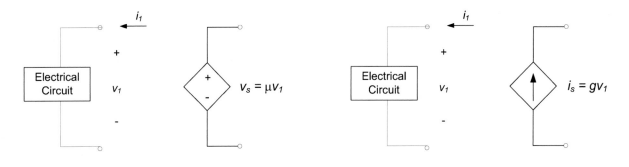

(a) Voltage controlled voltage source   (b) Voltage controlled current source

Figure 1.6. Voltage-controlled dependent sources

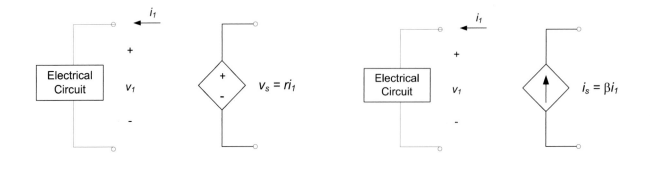

(a) Current controlled voltage source   (b) Current controlled current source

Figure 1.7. Current-controlled dependent sources

Section Summary

- Circuit elements can be either active or passive. Active elements provide electrical energy from a circuit from sources outside the circuit; active elements can be considered to create energy (from the standpoint of the circuit, anyway). Passive elements will be discussed in section 1.3, when we introduce resistors. Active circuit elements introduced in this section are ideal independent and dependent voltage and current sources.
  - Ideal independent sources presented in this section are voltage and current sources. Independent voltage sources deliver the specified voltage, regardless of the current demanded of them. Independent current sources provide the specified current, regardless of the voltage levels required to provide this current. Devices such as batteries are often modeled as independent sources.
  - Dependent sources provide a voltage or current which is controlled by a voltage or current elsewhere in the circuit. Devices such as operational amplifiers and transistors are often modeled as dependent sources. We will revisit the subject of dependent sources in chapter 5 of this text, when we discuss operational amplifier circuits.

1.2   Exercises:

1. The ideal voltage source shown in the circuit below delivers 12V to the circuit element shown. What is the current I through the circuit element?

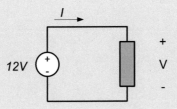

2. The ideal current source shown in the circuit below delivers 2A to the circuit element shown. What is the voltage difference V across the circuit element?

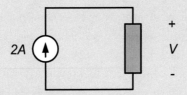

Solutions can be found at digilent.com/real-analog.

1.3   Resistors and Ohm's Law

Resistance is a property of all materials - this property characterizes the loss of energy associated with passing an electrical current through some conductive element. Resistors are circuit elements whose characteristics are dominated by this energy loss. Since energy is always lost when current is passed through an electrical circuit element, all electrical elements exhibit resistive properties which are characteristic of resistors. Resistors are probably the simplest and most commonly used circuit elements.

All materials impede the flow of current through them to come extent. Essentially, this corresponds to a statement that energy is always lost when transferring charge from one point in a circuit to another - this energy loss is generally due to heat generation and dissipation. The amount of energy required to transfer current in a particular element is characterized by the *resistance* of the element. When modeling a circuit, this resistance is represented by *resistors*. The circuit symbol for a resistor is shown in Fig. 1.8. The value of resistance is labeled in Fig. 1.8 as *R*. *i(t)* in Fig. 1.8 is the current flowing through the resistor and *v(t)* is the voltage drop across the resistor, caused by the energy dissipation induced by the resistor. The units of resistance are ohms (Ω).

The relationship between voltage and current for a resistor is given by *Ohm's Law*:

$$v(t) = Ri(t)$$ Eq. 1.5

Where voltage and current are explicitly denoted as functions of time. Note that in Fig. 1.8, the current is flowing from a higher voltage potential to a lower potential, as indicated by the polarity (+ and -) of the voltage and the arrow indicating direction of the current flow. The relative polarity between voltage and current for a resistor <u>must</u> be as shown in Fig. 1.8; the current enters the node at which the voltage potential is highest. Values of resistance, *R* are <u>always</u> positive, and resistors <u>always</u> absorb power.

Note: The voltage-current relationship for resistors always agrees with the passive sign convention. Resistors always absorb power.

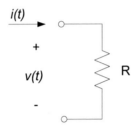

Figure 1.8. Circuit symbol for resistor.

Figure 1.9 shows a graph of *v* vs. *i* according to equation (1.5); the resulting plot is a straight line with slope *R*. Equation (1.5) thus describes the voltage-current relationship for a *linear* resistor. Linear resistors do not exist in reality - all resistors are *nonlinear,* to some extent. That is, the voltage-current relationship is not exactly a straight line for all values of current (for example, <u>all</u> electrical devices will fail if enough current is passed through them). Fig. 1.10 shows a typical nonlinear voltage-current relationship; however, many nonlinear resistors exhibit an approximately linear voltage-current characteristic over some <u>range</u> of voltages and currents; this is illustrated in Fig. 1.10. We will assume for now that any resistor we use is operating within a range of voltages and currents over which is voltage-current characteristic is linear and can be approximated by equation (1.5).

Note: For the most part, we will consider only linear resistors in this text. These resistors obey the linear voltage-current relationship shown in equation (1.5). All real resistors are nonlinear to some extent, but can often be assumed to operate as linear resistors over some range of voltages and currents.

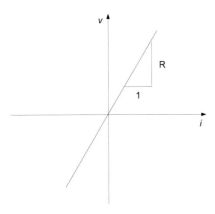

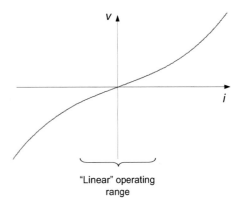

Figure 1.9. Linear resistor voltage vs. current characteristic.   Figure 1.10. Typical nonlinear resistor voltage vs. current characteristic.

1.3.1 Conductance

Conductance is an important quantity in circuit design and analysis. Conductance is simply the reciprocal of resistance, defined as:

$$G = \frac{1}{R}$$

Eq. 1.6

The unit for conductance is siemens (S). Ohm's law, written in terms of conductance, is:

$$i(t) = Gv(t)$$

Eq. 1.7

Some circuit analyses can be performed more easily and interpreted more readily if the elements' resistance is characterized in terms of conductance.

Note: In section 1.2, we characterized a current-controlled voltage source in terms of a parameter with units of ohms, since it had units of volts/amp. We characterized a voltage-controlled current source in terms of a parameter with units of siemens, since it had units of amps/volts.

1.3.2 Power Dissipation

Instantaneous power was defined by equation (1.3) in section 1.1 as:

$$P(t) = v(t) \cdot i(t)$$

For the special case of a resistor, we can re-write this (by substituting equation (1.5) into the above) as:

$$P(t) = Ri^2(t) = \frac{v^2(t)}{R}$$

Eq. 1.8

Likewise, we can write the power dissipation in terms of the conductance of a resistor as:

$$P(t) = \frac{i^2(t)}{G} = Gv^2(t)$$

Eq. 1.9

Note: We can write the power dissipation from a resistor in terms of the resistance or conductance of the resistor and <u>either</u> the current through the resistor <u>or</u> the voltage drop across the resistor.

1.3.3 Practical Resistors

All materials have some resistance, so all electrical components have non-zero resistance. However, circuit design often relies on implementing a specific, desired resistance at certain locations in a circuit; resistors are often placed in the circuit at these points to provide the necessary resistance. Resistors can be purchased in certain standard values. Resistors are manufactured in a variety of ways, though most commonly available commercial resistors are carbon composition or wire-wound. Resistors can have either a fixed or variable resistance.

Fixed resistors provide a single specified resistance value and have two terminals, as shown in Fig. 1.5 above. *Variable* resistors or *potentiometers* (commonly called "pots") have three terminals, two are "fixed" and one is "movable". The symbol for a variable resistor is shown in Fig. 1.11. The resistance between two of the terminals - R_{23} in Fig. 1.11 - of a variable resistor can be set as some fraction of the overall resistance of the device - R_{13} in Fig. 1.11. The ratio of R_{23} to $R_{13}$is generally set by a dial or screw on the side of the device.

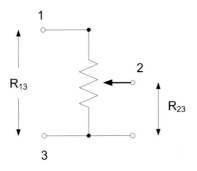

Figure 1.11. Schematic for variable resistor.

Resistors, which are physically large enough, will generally have their resistance value printed directly on them. Smaller resistors generally will use a color code to identify their resistance value. The color coding scheme is provided in Fig. 1.12. The resistance values indicated on the resistor will provide a *nominal* resistance value for the component; the actual resistance value for the component will vary from this by some amount. The expected tolerance between the allowable actual resistance values and the nominal resistance is also provided on the resistor, either printed directly on the resistor or provided as an additional color band. The color-coding scheme for resistor tolerances is also provided in Fig. 1.12.

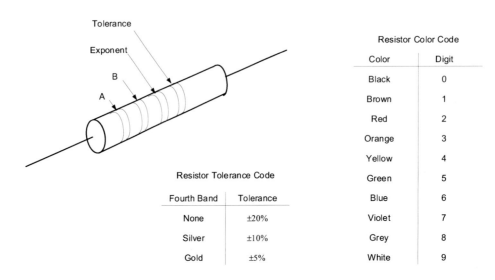

$$\text{Resistance} = ((10 \times A) + B) \times 10^{\text{Exponent}} \pm \text{Tolerance}$$

Figure 1.12. Resistor color code.

Example 1.6:

A resistor has the following color bands below. Determine the resistance value and tolerance.

- First band (A): Red
- Second band (B): Black
- Exponent: Orange
- Tolerance: Gold

Resistance = $(20+0) \times 10^3 \pm 5\%$ = 20 kΩ $\pm$ 1 kΩ

Section Summary

- The relationship between voltage and current for a resistor is Ohm's Law: $v = iR$. Since a resistor only dissipates energy, the voltage and current for a resistor must always agree with the passive sign convention.
- As noted in section 1.2, circuit elements can be either active or passive. Resistors are passive circuit elements. Passive elements can store or dissipate electrical energy provided to them by the circuit; they can subsequently return energy to the circuit which they have previously stored, but they cannot create energy. Resistors cannot store electrical energy; they can only dissipate energy by converting it to heat.

1.3 Exercises

1. The ideal voltage source shown in the circuit below delivers 18V to the resistor shown. What is the current I through the resistor?

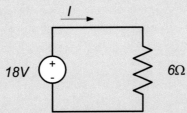

2. The ideal current source shown in the circuit below delivers 4mA to the resistor shown. What is the voltage difference V across the resistor?

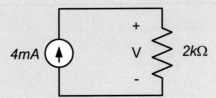

3. The ideal voltage source shown in the circuit below delivers 10V to the resistor shown. What is the current I in the direction shown?

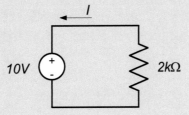

Solutions can be found at digilent.com/real-analog.

1.4   Kirchhoff's Laws

This section provides some basic definitions and background information for two important circuit analysis tools: Kirchhoff's Current Law and Kirchhoff's Voltage Law. These laws, together with the voltage-current characteristics of the circuit elements in the system, provide us with the ability to perform a systematic analysis of any electrical network.

We will use a *lumped-parameters* approach to a circuit analysis. This means that the circuit will consist of a number of discrete elements, connected by *perfect conductors*. Perfect conductors have no resistance, thus there is no voltage drop across a perfect conductor regardless of how much current flows through it. There is no energy stored or dissipated by a perfect conductor. All energy dissipation and energy storage is thus assumed to reside (or is *lumped*) in the circuit elements connected by the perfect conductors.

The lumped parameters approach toward modeling circuits is appropriate if the voltages and currents in the circuit change slowly relative to the rate with which information can be transmitted through the circuit. Since information propagates in an electrical circuit at a rate comparable to the speed of light and circuit dimensions are relatively small, this modeling approach if often appropriate.

An alternate approach to circuit analysis is a *distributed-parameters* approach. This approach is considerably more mathematically complicated than the lumped parameters approach, but is necessary when dimensions become very large (and in cross-country power transmission) or when signals are varying extremely rapidly (such as the rate of bit transmission in modern computers).

1.4.1   Nodes

Identification of circuit nodes will be extremely important to the application of Kirchhoff's Laws. A *node* is a point of connection of two or more circuit elements. A node has a single, unique voltage. Since there is no voltage drop across a perfect conductor, any points in a circuit which are connected by perfect conductors will be at the same voltage and will thus be part of the same node.

Example 1.7

The circuit below has four nodes, as shown. A common error for beginning students is to identify points a, b, and c as being separate nodes, since they appear as separate points on the circuit diagram. However, these points are connected by perfect connectors (no circuit elements are between points a, b, and c) and thus the points are at the same voltage and are considered electrically to be at the same point. Likewise, points d, e, f, and g are at the same voltage potential and are considered to be the same node. Node 2 interconnects two circuit elements (a resistor and a source) and must be considered as a separate node. Likewise, node 4 interconnects two circuit elements and qualifies as a node.

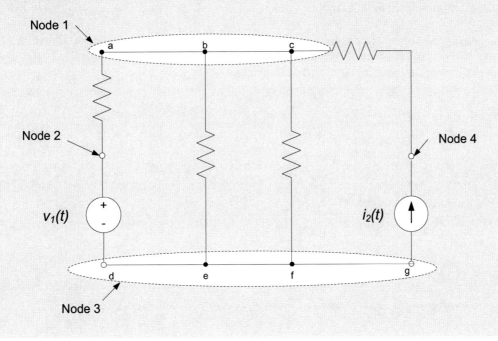

1.4.2 Loops

A *loop* is any closed path through the circuit which encounters no node more than once.

Example 1.8

There are six possible ways to loop through the circuit of the previous example. These loops are shown below.

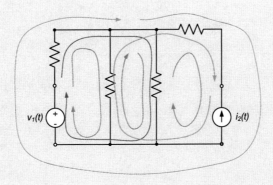

1.4.3 Kirchhoff's Current Law

Kirchhoff's Current Law is one of the two principle approaches we will use for generating the governing equations for an electrical circuit. Kirchhoff's Current Law is based upon our assumption that charges cannot accumulate at a node.

Kirchhoff's Current Law (commonly abbreviated in these chapters as KCL) states:

The algebraic sum of all currents entering (or leaving) a node is zero.

A common alternate statement for KCL is:

The sum of the currents entering any node equals the sum of the currents leaving the node.

A general mathematical statement for Kirchhoff's Current Law is:

$$\sum_{k=1}^{N} i_k(t) = 0$$

Eq. 1.10

Note: Current directions (entering or leaving the node) are based on <u>assumed</u> directions of currents in the circuit. As long as the assumed directions of the currents are consistent from node to node, the final result of the analysis will reflect the <u>actual</u> current directions in the circuit.

Example 1.9:

In the figure below, the assumed directions of $i_1(t)$, $i_2(t)$ and $i_3(t)$ are as shown.

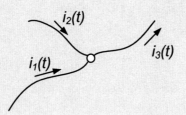

If we (arbitrarily) choose a sign convention such that currents entering the node are positive then currents leaving the node are negative and KCL applied at this node results in:

$i_1(t) + i_2(t) - i_3(t) = 0$

If, on the other hand, we choose a sign convention that currents entering the node are negative, then currents leaving the node are positive and KCL applied at this node results in:

$-i_1(t) - i_2(t) + i_3(t) = 0$

These two equations are the same; the second equation is simply the negative of the first equation. Both of the above equations are equivalent to the statement:

$i_1(t) + i_2(t) = i_3(t)$

Example 1.10:

Use KCL to determine the value of the current *i* in the figure below.

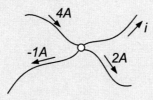

Summing the currents entering the node results in:

$$4A - (-1A) - 2A - i = 0 \implies i = 4A + 1A - 2A = 3A$$

and *i* = 3A, <u>leaving</u> the node.

In the figure below, we have reversed our assumed direction of *i* in the above circuit:

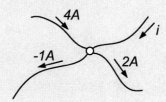

Now, if we sum currents entering the node:

$$4A - (-1A) - 2A + i = 0 \implies i = -4A - 1A + 2A = -3A$$

So now *i* = -3A, <u>entering</u> the node. The negative sign corresponds to a change in direction, so we can interpret this result to a +3A current <u>leaving</u> the node, which is consistent with our previous result. Thus, the assumed current direction has not affected our results.

We can generalize Kirchhoff's Current Law to include any enclosed portion of a circuit. To illustrate this concept, consider the portion of a larger circuit enclosed by a surface as shown in Fig. 1.13 below. Since none of the circuit elements within the surface store charge, the total charge which can be stored within any enclosed surface is zero. Thus, the net charge entering an enclosed surface must be zero. This leads to a generalization of our previous statement of KCL:

The algebraic sum of all currents entering (or leaving) any enclosed surface is zero.

Applying this statement to the circuit of Fig. 1 results in:

$$i_1 + i_2 + i_3 = 0$$

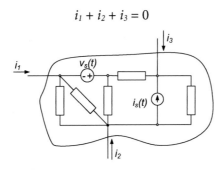

Figure 1.13 KCL applied to closed surface.

1.4.4 Kirchhoff's Voltage Law

Kirchhoff's Voltage Law is the second of two principle approaches we will use for generating the governing equations for an electrical circuit. Kirchhoff's Voltage Law is based upon the observation that the voltage at a node is unique.

Kirchhoff's Voltage Law (commonly abbreviated in these chapters as KVL) states:

The algebraic sum of all voltage differences around any closed loop is zero.

An alternate statement of this law is:

The sum of the voltage rises around a closed loop must equal the sum of the voltage drops around the loop.

A general mathematical statement for Kirchhoff's Voltage Law is:

$$\sum_{k=1}^{N} v_k(t) = 0$$

Eq. 1.11

Where V_k is the kth voltage difference in the loop and N is the total number of voltage differences in the loop.

Note: Voltage polarities are based on <u>assumed</u> polarities of the voltage differences in the loop. As long as the assumed directions of the voltages are consistent from loop to loop, the final result of the analysis will reflect the <u>actual</u> voltage polarities in the circuit.

Example 1.11:

In the figure below, the assumed (or previously known) polarities of the voltages v_1, v_2, v_3, v_4, v_5, and v_6 are as shown. There are three possible loops in the circuit: a-b-e-d-a, a-b-c-e-d-a, and b-c-e-b. We will apply KVL to each of these loops.

Our sign convention for applying signs to the voltage polarities in our KVL equations will be as follows: when traversing the loop, if the positive terminal of a voltage difference is encountered before the negative terminal, the voltage difference will be interpreted as <u>positive</u> in the KVL equation. If the negative terminal is encountered first, the voltage difference will be interpreted as <u>negative</u> in the KVL equation. We use this sign convention for convenience; it is not required for proper application of KVL, as long as the signs on the voltage differences are treated consistently.

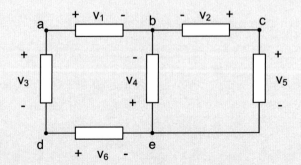

Applying KVL to the loop a-b-e-d-a, and using our sign convention as above results in:

$v_1 - v_4 - v_6 - v_3 = 0$

Chapter 1: Circuit Analysis Fundamentals

The starting point of the loop and the direction that we loop in is arbitrary; we could equivalently write the same loop equation as loop d-e-b-a-d, in which case our equation would become:

$$v_6 + v_4 - v_1 + v_3 = 0$$

This equation is identical to the previous equation, the only difference is that the signs of all variables has changed and the variables appear in a different order in the equation.

We now apply KVL to the loop b-c-e-b, which results in:

$$-v_2 + v_5 + v_4 = 0$$

Finally, application of KVL to the loop a-b-c-e-d-a provides:

$$v_1 - v_2 + v_5 - v_6 - v_3 = 0$$

Application Examples: Solving for Circuit Element Variables

Typically, when analyzing a circuit, we will need to determine voltages and/or currents in one or more elements in the circuit. In this section, we discuss use of the tools presented in previous sections for circuit analysis.

The complete solution of a circuit consists of determining the voltages and currents for _every_ element in the circuit. A complete solution of a circuit can be obtained by:

4. Writing a voltage-current relationship for each element in the circuit (e.g. write Ohm's Law for the resistors).
5. Applying KCL at all but one of the nodes in the circuit.
6. Applying KVL for all but one of the loops in the circuit.

This approach will typically result in a set of N equations in N unknowns, the unknowns consisting of the voltages and currents for each element in the circuit. Methods exist for defining a reduced set of equations or a complete analysis of a circuit; these approaches will be presented in later chapters.

If KCL is written for _every_ node in the circuit and KVL written for _every_ loop in the circuit, the resulting set of equations will typically be over-determined and the resulting equations will, in general, not be independent. That is, there will be more than N equations in N unknowns and some of the equations will carry redundant information.

Generally, we do not need to determine all the variables in a circuit. This often means that we can write fewer equations than those listed above. The equations to be written will, in these cases, be problem dependent and are often at the discretion of the person doing the analysis.

Examples of using Ohm's Law, KVL, and KCL for circuit analysis are provided next.

Example 1.12:

For the circuit below, determine v_{ab}.

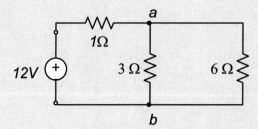

We are free to arbitrarily choose either the voltage polarity or the current direction in each element. Our choices are shown below:

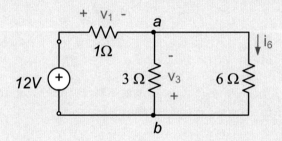

Once the above voltage polarities and current directions are chosen, we must choose all other parameters in a way that satisfies the passive sign convention. (Current must enter the positive voltage polarity node.) Our complete definition of all circuit parameters is shown below:

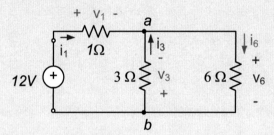

We now apply the steps outlined above for an exhaustive circuit analysis.

1. Ohm's law, applied for each resistor, results in:
    $v_1 = (1\Omega)i_1$; $v_3 = (3\Omega)i_3$; $v_6 = (6\Omega)i_6$

2. KCL, applied at node a:
    $i_1 + i_3 - i_6 = 0$

3. KVL, applied over any two of the three loops in the circuit:
    $-12V + v_1 - v_3 = 0$
    $v_3 + v_6 = 0$

The above provide six equations in six unknowns. Solving these for v_3 results in $v_3 = -8V$. Since $v_3 = -v_{ab}$, $v_{ab} = 8V$

Determine v_3 in the circuit shown below.

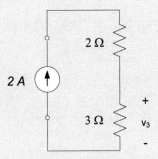

We choose voltages and currents as shown below. Since v_3 is defined in the problem statement, we define it to be consistent with the problem statement.

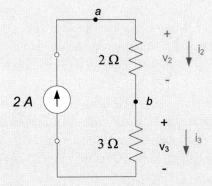

KVL around the single loop in the circuit does not help us – the voltage across the current source is unknown, so inclusion of this parameter in a KVL equation simply introduces an additional unknown to go with the equation we write. KVL would, however, be useful if we wished to determine the voltage across the current source.

KCL at node a tells us that $i_2 = 2A$. Likewise, KCL at node b tells us that $i_2 - i_3 = 0$, so $i_3 = i_2 = 2A$. Ohms law tells us that $v_3 = (3\Omega)(i_3) = (3\Omega)(2A) = 6V$.

Section Summary

- Kirchhoff's Current Law (KCL) and Kirchhoff's Voltage Law (KVL) govern the interactions between circuit elements. Governing equations for a circuit are created by applying KVL and KCL and applying the circuit element governing equations, such as Ohm's Law.
- Kirchhoff's current law states that the sum of the currents entering or leaving a node must be zero. A node in a circuit is an point which has a unique voltage.
  - A node is a point of interconnection between two or more circuit elements. A circuit node has a particular voltage. Nodes can be "spread out" with perfect conductors.
- Kirchhoff's voltage law states that the sum of the voltage differences around any closed loop in a circuit must sum to zero. A loop in a circuit is any path which ends at the same point at which it starts.
  - A loop is a closed path through a circuit. Loops end at the same node at which they start, and typically are chosen so that no node is encountered more than once.

1. For the circuit below, determine:
    a) The current through the 2Ω resistor
    b) The current through the 1Ω resistor
    c) The power (absorbed or generated) by the 4V power source

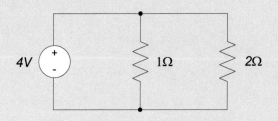

Solutions can be found at digilent.com/real-analog.

Chapter Summary:

- In this text, we are primarily concerned with the movement of electrical charge. Electrical charge motion is represented by voltage and current. Voltage indicates the energy change associated with the movement of a charge from one location to another, while current is indicative of the rate of current motion past a particular point.
    - Voltage is an energy difference between two physically separated points. The polarity of a voltage is used to indicate which point is to be assumed to be at the higher energy level. The positive terminal (+) is assumed to be at a higher voltage than the negative terminal (-). A negative voltage value simply indicates that the actual voltage polarity is opposite to the assumed polarity.
    - The sign of the current indicates the assumed direction of charge motion past a point. A change in the sign of the current value indicates that the current direction is opposite to the assumed direction.
- Circuit elements can be either active or passive. Active elements provide electrical energy to a circuit, from sources outside the circuit; active elements can be considered to create energy (from the standpoint of the circuit, anyway). Passive elements can store or dissipate electrical energy provided to them by the circuit; they can subsequently return energy to the circuit which they have previously stored, but they cannot create energy.
    - Active circuit elements introduced in this section are independent voltage and current sources, and dependent voltage and current sources.
    - Resistors are the only passive circuit elements introduced in this chapter. Resistors cannot store electrical energy, they can only dissipate energy energy by converting it to heat.
- The <u>assumed</u> polarity of the voltage across a passive circuit element must be consistent with the <u>assumed</u> current direction through the element. The assumed positive direction for current must be such that positive current enters the positive voltage terminal of the element. Since this sign convention is applied only to passive elements, it is known as the *passive sign convention*.
    - The assumed current direction <u>or</u> the assumed voltage polarity can be chosen arbitrarily, but once one parameter is chosen, the other must be chosen to agree with the passive sign convention.
- The power absorbed or generated by an electrical circuit component is the product of the voltage difference across the element and the current through the element: $p = iv$. The relative sign of the voltage and current are set according to the passive sign convention. Positive power implies that the

voltage and current are consistent with the passive sign convention (the element absorbs or dissipates energy) while negative power indicates that the relative signs between voltage and current are opposite to the passive sign convention (the element generates or supplies energy to the circuit).

- The relationship between voltage and current for a resistor is Ohm's Law: $v = iR$. Since a resistor only dissipates energy, the voltage and current for a resistor must always agree with the passive sign convention.

- Kirchoff's voltage law states that the sum of the voltage differences around any close loop in a circuit must sum to zero. A loop in a circuit is any path which ends at the same point at which it starts.

- Kirchoff's current law states that the sum of the currents entering or leaving a node must be zero. A node in a circuit is a point which has a unique voltage.

Real Analog Chapter 1: Homework

1.1 For the circuit below, determine
   a) the voltage, V_1
   b) the resistance, R
   c) the current, I_s
   d) the power (absorbed or supplied) by the current source
   e) the power (absorbed or supplied) by the 3V voltage source

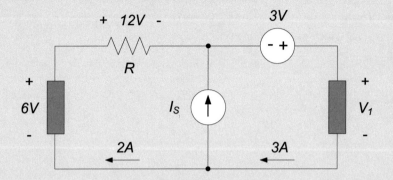

1.2 Find I_1 and V_1 in the circuit below.

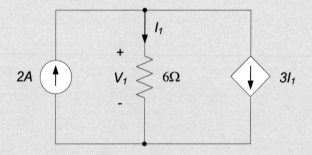

1.3 In the circuit below, determine V_{ab}, V_{ac}, and V_{cb}.

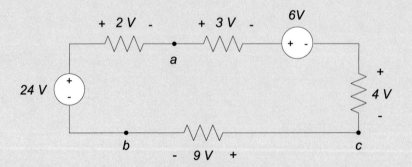

1.4 For the circuit shown, find:
a) Vs
b) R₁
c) Power absorbed or generated by the 10V source. State whether the power is absorbed or generated.

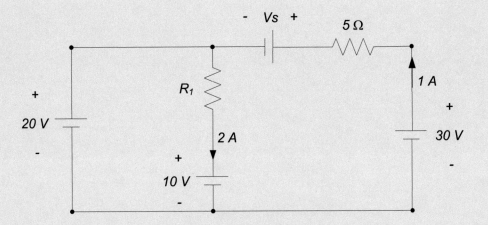

1.5 Find Vab and V1 in the circuit below.

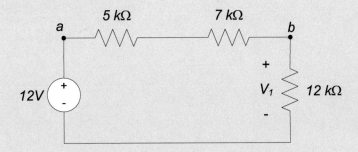

1.6 For the circuit below, determine
a) the power dissipated by the 6Ω resistor
b) the voltage across the 4Ω resistor
c) the current through the 2Ω resistor

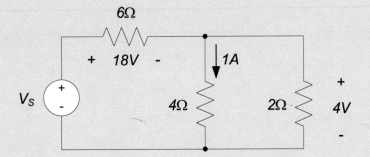

1.7 For the circuit elements below, determine the power generated or absorbed by the element. State whether the power is generated or absorbed.

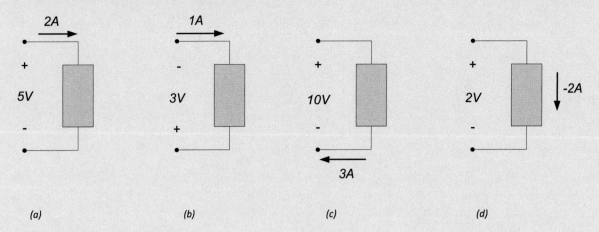

(a)   (b)   (c)   (d)

1.8 For the circuit below, determine
   a) the power dissipated by the 6Ω resistor
   b) the voltage across the 3Ω resistor
   c) the current through the 4Ω resistor

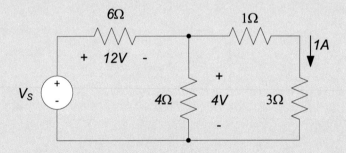

1.9 For the circuit elements below, determine the power generated or absorbed by the element. State whether the power is generated or absorbed.

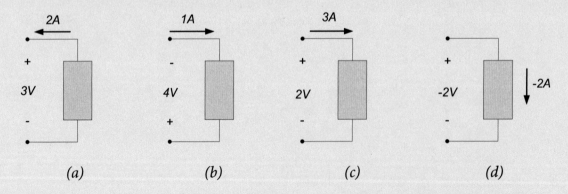

(a)   (b)   (c)   (d)

1.10 In the circuit below, determine v_{ab}, v_{ac}, and v_{cb}.

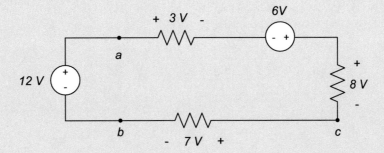

1.11 In the circuit below, determine the power (absorbed or generated) by the voltage source V_S.

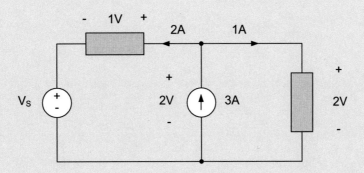

1.12 For the circuit shown, find:
a) V_1
b) R_1
c) The power (generated or absorbed) by the 1A source

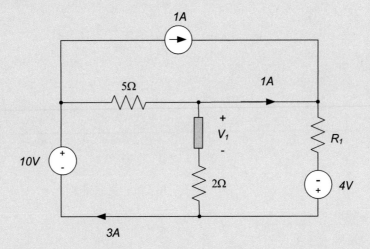

1.13 For the circuit shown, find:
   a) V$_S$
   b) R
   c) The power (generated or absorbed) by the 2A source

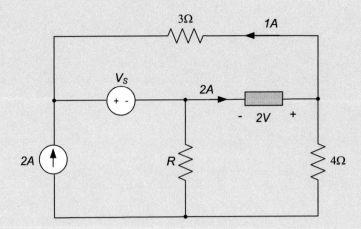

1.14 Write a set of equations from which you can determine the voltage V_1 in the circuit below. You do not need to solve the equations.

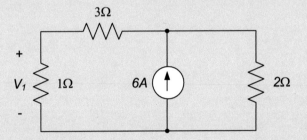

1.15 For the circuit below, determine the voltage v_x, the voltage v_{ab}, and the power (generated or absorbed) by the 3A source.

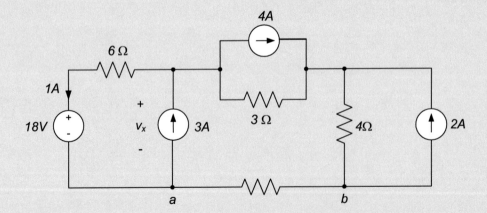

1.16 For the circuit shown, find the voltage v_x and the current i_4.

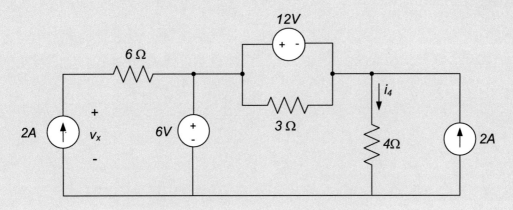

Solutions can be found at digilent.com/real-analog.

Chapter 2:
Circuit Reduction

In Chapter 1, we presented Kirchhoff's laws (which govern the interaction between circuit elements) and Ohm's law (which governs the voltage-current relationships for resistors). These analytical tools provide us with the ability to analyze any circuit containing only resistors and ideal power supplies. However, we also saw in Chapter 1 that a circuit analysis, which relies strictly on a brute-force application of these tools can become complex rapidly - we essentially must use as our unknowns the voltage differences across <u>all</u> resistors and the currents through <u>all</u> resistors. This generally results in a large number of unknowns and a correspondingly large number of equations, which must be written and solved in order to analyze any but the simplest circuit.

In the next few chapters, we will still apply Kirchhoff's laws and Ohm's law in our circuit analysis, but we will focus on improving the efficiency of our analyses. Typically, this improvement in efficiency is achieved by reducing the number of unknowns in the circuit, which reduces the number of equations, which must be written to describe the circuit's operation.

In this chapter, we introduce analysis methods based on *circuit reduction*. Circuit reduction consists of combining resistances in a circuit to a smaller number of resistors, which are (in some sense) equivalent to the original resistive network. Reducing the number of resistors, of course, reduces the number of unknowns in a circuit.

We begin our discussion of circuit reduction techniques by presenting two specific, but very useful, concepts: *Series* and *parallel* resistors. These concepts will lead us to *voltage* and *current divider* formulas. We then consider reduction of more general circuits, which typically corresponds to identifying multiple sets of series and parallel resistances in a complex resistive network. This chapter then concludes with two important examples of the application of circuit reduction techniques: the analysis of *non-ideal power sources* and *non-ideal measurement* devices; without an understanding of these devices, it is impossible to build practical circuits or understand the consequences of a voltage or current measurement.

After Completing this Chapter, You Should be Able to:

- Identify series and parallel combinations of circuit elements

- Determine the equivalent resistance of series resistor combinations
- Determine the equivalent resistance of parallel resistor combinations
- State voltage and current divider relationships from memory
- Determine the equivalent resistance of electrical circuits consisting of series and parallel combinations of resistors
- Sketch equivalent circuits for non-ideal voltage and current meters
- Analyze circuits containing non-ideal voltage or current sources
- Determine the effect of non-ideal meters on the parameter being measured

2.1   Series Circuit Elements and Voltage Division

There are a number of common circuit element combinations that are quite easily analyzed. These "special cases" are worth noting since many complicated circuits contain these circuit combinations as sub-circuits. Recognizing these sub-circuits and analyzing them appropriately can significantly simplify the analysis of a circuit.

This chapter emphasizes two important circuit element combinations: elements in series and elements in parallel. Also discussed is the use of these circuit element combinations to reduce the complexity of a circuit's analysis.

2.1.1   Series Connections

Circuit elements are said to be connected in *series* if all of the elements carry the same current. An example of two circuit elements connected in series is shown in Fig. 2.1. Applying KCL at node a and taking currents out of the node as positive we see that:

$$-i_1 + i_2 = 0$$

Or

$$i_1 = i_2$$

Eq. 2.1

Equation (2.1) is a direct outcome of the fact that the (single) node a in Fig. 2.1 interconnects only two elements - there are no other elements connected to this node through which current can be diverted. This observation is so apparent (in many cases[1]) that equation (2.1) is generally written by inspection for series elements such as those shown in Fig. 2.1 <u>without</u> explicitly writing KCL.

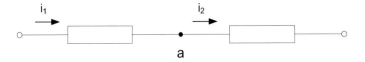

Figure 2.1. Circuit elements connected in series.

When resistors are connected in series, a simplification of the circuit is possible. Consider the resistive circuit shown in Fig. 2.2(a). Since the resistors are in series, they both carry the same current. Ohm's law gives:

$$v_1 = R_1 i$$

$$v_2 = R_2 i$$

Eq. 2.2

---

[1] If there is any doubt whether the elements are in series, apply KCL! Assuming elements are in series which are not in series can have disastrous consequences.

Applying KVL around the loop:

$$-v + v_1 + v_2 = 0 \Rightarrow v = v_1 + v_2$$

Eq. 2.3

Substituting equations (2.2) into equation (2.3) and solving for the current *i* results in:

$$i = \frac{v}{R_1 + R_2}$$

Eq. 2.4

Now consider the circuit of Fig. 2.2(b). Application of Ohm's law to this circuit and solution for the current *i* gives:

$$i = \frac{v}{R_{eq}}$$

Eq. 2.5

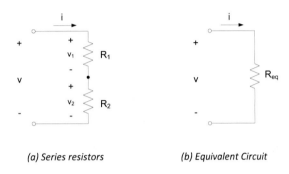

(a) Series resistors   (b) Equivalent Circuit

Figure 2.2. Series resistors and equivalent circuit.

Comparing equation (2.4) with equation (2.5), we can see that the circuits of Figs. 2.2(a) and 2.2(b) are indistinguishable if we select:

$$R_{eq} = R_1 + R_2$$

Eq. 2.6

Figures 2.2(a) and 2.2(b) are called *equivalent circuits* if the equivalent resistance of Fig. 2.2(b) is chosen as shown in equation (2.6). R_eq of equation (2.6) is called the equivalent resistance of the series combination of resistors R₁ and R₂.

This result can be generalized to a series combination of *N* resistances as follows:

A series combination of *N* resistors $R_1, R_2, \cdots, R_N$ can be replaced with a single equivalent resistance $R_{eq} = R_1 + R_2 + \cdots + R_N$. The equivalent circuit can be analyzed to determine the current through the series combination of resistors.

2.1.2 Voltage Division

Combining equations (2.2) with equation (2.4) results in the following expressions for v_1 and v_2:

$$v_1 = \frac{R_1}{R_1 + R_2} v$$

Eq. 2.7

$$v_2 = \frac{R_2}{R_1 + R_2} v$$

Eq. 2.8

These results are commonly called *voltage divider* relationships, because they state that the total voltage drop across a series combination of resistors is divided among the individual resistors in the combination. The ratio of each individual resistor's voltage drop to the overall voltage drop is the same as the ratio of the individual resistance to the total resistance.

The above results can be generalized for a series combination of *N* resistance as follows:

The voltage drop across any resistor in a series combination of N resistances is proportional to the total voltage drop across the combination of resistors. The constant of proportionality is the same as the ratio of the individual resistor value to the total resistance of the series combination. For example, the voltage drop of the kth resistance in a series combination of resistors given by:

$$v_k = \frac{R_k}{R_1 + R_2 + \cdots + R_N} v$$

Eq. 2.9

Example 2.1

For the circuit below, determine the voltage across the 5Ω resistor, *v*, the current supplied by the source, *i*, and the power supplied by the source.

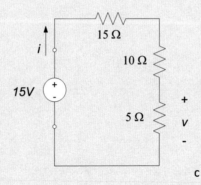

The voltage across the 5Ω resistor can be determined from our voltage divider relationship:

$$v = \left[\frac{5\Omega}{5\Omega + 15\Omega + 10\Omega}\right] \cdot 15V = \frac{5}{30} \cdot 15V = 2.5V$$

The current supplied by the source can be determined by dividing the total voltage by the equivalent resistance:

$$i = \frac{15V}{R_{eq}} = \frac{15V}{5\Omega + 15\Omega + 10\Omega} = \frac{15V}{30\Omega} = 0.5A$$

The power supplied by the source is the product of the source voltage and the source current:

$$P = iv = (0.5A)(15V) = 7.5W$$

We can double-check the consistency between the voltage *v* and the current *i* with Ohm's law. Applying Ohm's law to the 5Ω resistor, with a 0.5A current, results in $v = (5\Omega)(0.5A) = 2.5V$, which agrees with the result obtained using the voltage divider relationship.

Section Summary:

- If only two elements connect at a single node, the two elements are in *series*. A more general definition, however, is that circuit elements in series all share the same current - this definition allows us to determine series combinations that contain more than two elements. Identification of series circuit elements allows us to simplify our analysis, since there is a reduction in the number of unknowns: there is only a single unknown current for all series elements.

- A series combination of resistors can be replaced by a single *equivalent resistance*, if desired. The equivalent resistance is simply the sum of the individual resistances in the series combination. Therefore, a series combination of *N* resistors $R_1, R_2, \cdots, R_N$ can be replaced with a single equivalent resistance $R_{eq} = R_1 + R_2 + \cdots + R_N$.
- If the total voltage difference across a set of series is known, the voltage differences across any individual resistor can be determined by the concept of *voltage division*. The term voltage division comes from the fact that the voltage drop across a series combination of resistors is divided among the individual resistors. The ratio between the voltage difference across a particular resistor and the total voltage difference is the same as the ratio between the resistance of that resistor and the total resistance of the combination. If v_k is the voltage across the kth resistor, and R_{TOT} is the total resistance of the series combination, the mathematical statement of this concept is:

$$\frac{v_k}{v_{TOT}} = \frac{R_k}{R_{TOT}}$$

1.1 Exercises

1. Determine the voltage V_1 in the circuit below.

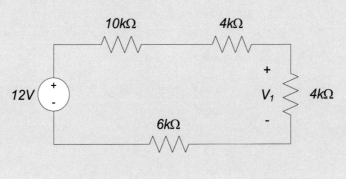

Solutions can be found at digilent.com/real-analog.

2.2 Parallel Circuit Elements and Current Division

Circuit elements are said to be connected in *parallel* if all of the elements share the same pair of nodes. An example of two circuit elements connected in parallel is shown in Fig. 2.3. Applying KVL around the loop of Fig. 2.3 results in:

$$v_1 = v_2$$ Eq. 2.10

Figure 2.3. Parallel connection of circuit elements.

We can simplify circuits, which consist of resistors connected in parallel. Consider the resistive circuit shown in Fig. 2.4(a). The resistors are connected in parallel, so both resistors have a voltage difference of *v*. Ohm's law applied to each resistor results in:

$$i_1 = \frac{v}{R_1}$$

$$i_2 = \frac{v}{R_2}$$

Eq. 2.11

Applying KCL at node a:

$$i = i_1 + i_2$$

Eq. 2.12

Substituting equations (2.11) into equation (2.12):

$$i = \left[\frac{1}{R_1} + \frac{1}{R_2}\right] v$$

Eq. 2.13

Or

$$v = \frac{1}{\frac{1}{R_1} + \frac{1}{R_2}} \cdot i$$

Eq. 2.14

If we set $R_{eq} = \frac{1}{\frac{1}{R_1} + \frac{1}{R_2}}$, we can draw Fig. 2.4(b) as being equivalent to Fig. 2.4(b).

We can generalize this result for *N* parallel resistances:

A parallel combination of *N* resistors $R_1, R_2, \cdots, R_N$ can be replaced with a single equivalent resistance:

$$R_{eq} = \frac{1}{\frac{1}{R_1} + \frac{1}{R_2} + \cdots \frac{1}{R_N}}$$

Eq. 2.15

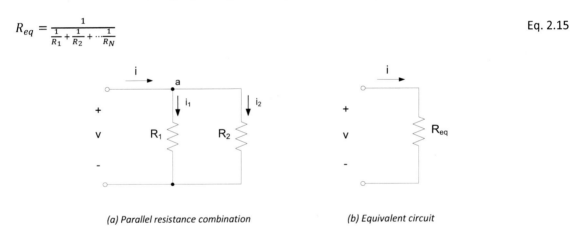

(a) Parallel resistance combination   (b) Equivalent circuit

Figure 2.4. Parallel resistances and equivalent circuit.

For the special case of two parallel resistances, R_1 and R_2, the equivalent resistance is commonly written as:

$$R_{eq} = \frac{R_1 R_2}{R_1 + R_2}$$

Eq. 2.16

This alternative way to calculate R_{eq} can be also used to calculate R_{eq} for larger numbers of parallel resistors since any number of resistors could be combined two at a time.

2.2.1 Current Division

Substituting equation (2.14) into equations (2.11) results in:

$$i_1 = \frac{1}{R_1} \cdot \frac{i}{\frac{1}{R_1} + \frac{1}{R_2}}$$

Eq. 2.17

Simplifying:

$$i_1 = i \cdot \frac{R_2}{R_1 + R_2}$$

Eq. 2.18

Likewise, for the current i_2:

$$i_2 = i \cdot \frac{R_1}{R_1 + R_2}$$

Eq. 2.19

Equations (2.18) and (2.19) are the current *divider relationships* for two parallel resistances, so called because the current into the parallel resistance combination is divided between the two resistors. The ratio of one resistor's current to the overall current in the same as the ratio of the <u>other</u> resistance to the total resistance.

The above results can be generalized for a series combination of N resistances. By Ohm's law, $v = R_{eq}i$. Substituting our previous result for the equivalent resistance for a parallel combination of N resistors results in:

$$v = \frac{1}{\frac{1}{R_1} + \frac{1}{R_2} + \cdots \frac{1}{R_N}} \cdot i$$

Eq. 2.20

Since the voltage difference across all resistors is the same, the current through the kth resistor is, by Ohm's law:

$$i_k \frac{v}{R_k}$$

Eq. 2.21

Where R_k is the resistance of the kth resistor. Combining equations (2.20) and (2.21) gives:

$$i_k = \frac{\frac{1}{R_k}}{\frac{1}{R_1} + \frac{1}{R_2} + \cdots \frac{1}{R_N}} \cdot i$$

Eq. 2.22

It is often more convenient to provide the generalized result of equation (2.20) in terms of the conductance of the individual resistors. Recall that the conductance is the reciprocal of the resistance, $G = \frac{1}{R}$. Thus, equation (2.22) can be re-expressed as follows:

The current through any resistor in a parallel combination of N resistances is proportional to the total current into the combination of resistors. The constant of proportionality is the same as the ratio of the conductance of the individual resistor value to the total conductance of the parallel combination. For example, the current through the kth resistance in a parallel combination of resistors is given by:

$$i_k = \frac{G_k}{G_1 + G_2 + \cdots + G_N} i$$

Eq. 2.23

Where *i* is the total current through the parallel combination of resistors.

One final comment about notation: two parallel bars are commonly used as shorthand notation to indicate that two circuit elements are in parallel. For example, the notation $R_1 \parallel R_2$ indicates that the resistors R_1 and R_2 are in parallel. The notation $R_1 \parallel R_2$ is often used as shorthand notation for the <u>equivalent resistance</u> of the parallel resistance combination, in lieu of equation (2.16).

Double-checking results for parallel resistances:

- The equivalent resistance for a parallel combination of N resistors will always be less than the smallest resistance in the combination. In fact, the equivalent resistance will always obey the following inequalities:

$$\frac{R_{min}}{N} \leq R_{eq} \leq R_{min}$$

- Where R_{min} is the smallest resistance value in the parallel combination.
- In a parallel combination of resistances, the resistor with the <u>smallest</u> resistance will have the <u>largest</u> current and the resistor with the <u>largest</u> resistance will have the <u>smallest</u> current.

Section Summary

- If several elements interconnect the same two nodes, the two elements are in *parallel*. A more general definition, however, is that circuit elements in parallel all share the same voltage difference. As with series circuit elements, identification of parallel circuit elements allows us to simplify our analysis, since there is a reduction in the number of unknowns: there is only a single unknown voltage difference for all of the parallel elements.
- A parallel combination of resistors can be replaced by a single *equivalent resistance*, if desired. The conductance of the parallel combination is simply the sum of the individual conductance of the parallel resistors. Therefore, a parallel combination of N resistors $R_1, R_2, \cdots, R_N$ can be replaced with a single equivalent resistance:

$$R_{eq} = \frac{1}{\dfrac{1}{R_1} + \dfrac{1}{R_2} + \cdots \dfrac{1}{R_N}}$$

- If the total current through a set of parallel resistors is known, the current through any individual resistor can be determined by the concept of *current division*. The term current division comes form the fact that the current through a parallel combination of resistors is divided among the individual resistors. The ratio between the current through a particular resistor and the total current is the same as the ratio between the conductance of that resistor and the total conductance of the combination. If i_k is the voltage across the kth resistor, i_{TOT}, is the total current through the parallel combination, G_k is the conductance of the kth resistor, and G_{TOT} is the total conductance of the parallel combination, the mathematical statement of this concept is:

$$\frac{v_k}{i_{TOT}} = \frac{G_k}{G_{TOT}}$$

1.2 Exercises

1. Determine the value of *I* in the circuit below.

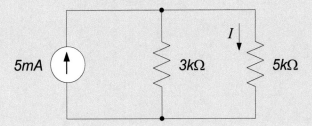

2. Determine the value of *R* in the circuit below which makes I=2mA.

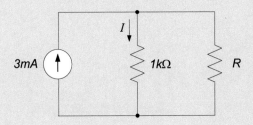

Solutions can be found at digilent.com/real-analog.

2.3 Circuit Reduction and Analysis

The previous results give us an ability to potentially simplify the analysis of some circuits. This simplification results if we can use *circuit reduction* techniques to convert a complicated circuit to a simpler, but equivalent, circuit which we can use to perform the necessary analysis. Circuit reduction is not always possible, but when it is applicable it can significantly simplify the analysis of a circuit.

Circuit reduction relies upon identification of parallel and series combinations of circuit elements. The parallel and series elements are then combined into equivalent elements and the resulting *reduced* circuit is analyzed. The principles of circuit reduction are illustrated below in a series of examples.

Example 2.2

Determine the equivalent resistance seen by the terminals of the resistive network shown below.

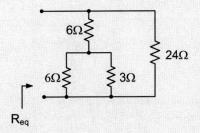

The sequence of operations performed is illustrated below. The 6Ω and 3Ω resistances are combined in parallel to obtain an equivalent 2Ω resistance. This 2Ω resistance and the remaining 6Ω resistance are in series, these are combined into an equivalent 8Ω resistance. Finally, this 8Ω resistor and the 24Ω resistor are combined in parallel to obtain an equivalent 6Ω resistance. Thus, the equivalent resistance of the overall network is 6Ω.

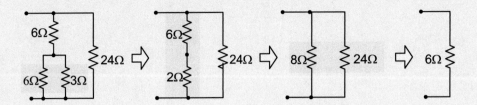

Example 2.3

In the circuit below, determine the power delivered by the source.

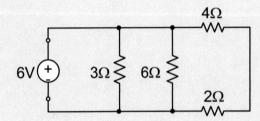

In order to determine power delivery, we need to determine the total current provided by the source to the rest of the circuit. We can determine current easily if we convert the resistor network to a single, equivalent resistance. A set of step for doing this are outlined below.

Step 1: The 4-ohm and 2-ohm resistors, highlighted in the figure to the left in blue, are in series. Series resistances add directly, so these can be replaced with a single 6-ohm resistor, as shown on the figure to the right below.

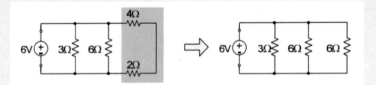

Step 2: The 3-ohm resistor and the two 6-ohm resistors are now all in parallel, as indicated on the figure to the left below. These resistances can be combined into a single equivalent resistor $R_{eq} = \frac{1}{\frac{1}{3}+\frac{1}{6}+\frac{1}{6}} = 1.5\Omega$. The resulting equivalent circuit is shown to the right below.

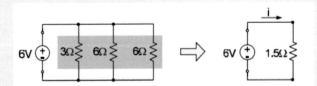

The current out of the source can now be readily determined from the figure to the right above. The voltage drop across the 1.5Ω resistor is 6V, so Ohm's law gives $i = \frac{6V}{1.5\Omega} = 4A$. Thus, the power delivered by the source is $P = (4A)(6V) = 24W$. Since the sign of the current relative to the current does <u>not</u> agree with the passive sign convention, the power is <u>generated</u> by the source.

Example 2.4

For the circuit shown below, determine the voltage, v_s, across the 2A source.

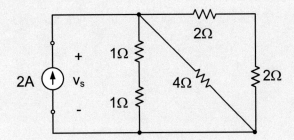

The two 1Ω resistors and the two 2Ω resistors are in series with one another, as indicated on the figure to the left below. These can be combined by simply adding the series resistances, leading to the equivalent circuit shown to the right below.

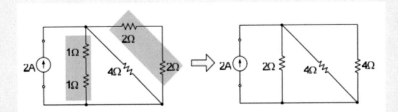

The three remaining resistors are all in parallel (they all share the same nodes) so they can be combined using the relation $R_{eq} = \frac{1}{\frac{1}{2}+\frac{1}{4}+\frac{1}{4}}$. Note that it is not necessary to combine all three simultaneously, the same result is obtained by successive combinations of two resistances. For example, the two 4Ω resistors can be combined using equation (2.16) to obtain: $R_{eq1} = \frac{4 \cdot 4}{4+4} = 2\Omega$. The total equivalent resistance can then be determined by a parallel combination of R_{eq1} and the 2Ω resistor: $R_{eq} = \frac{2 \cdot 2}{2+2} = 1\Omega$.

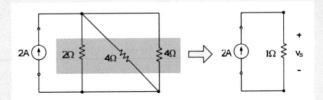

The voltage across the source can now be determined from Ohm's law: $v_s = (1\Omega)(2A) = 2V$. The assumed polarity of the source voltage is correct.

Example 2.5: Wheatstone Bridge

A Wheatstone bridge circuit is shown below. The bridge is generally presented as shown in the figure to the left; we will generally use the equivalent circuit shown to the right. A Wheatstone bridge is commonly used to convert a variation in resistance to a variation in voltage. A constant supply voltage V_s is applies to the circuit. The resistors in the circuit all have a nominal resistance of R; the variable resistor has a variation ΔR from this nominal value. The output voltage v_{ab} indicates the variation ΔR in the variable resistor. The variable resistor in the network is often a transducer whose resistance varies dependent upon some external variable such as temperature.

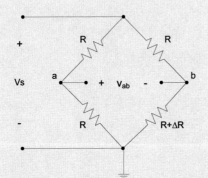 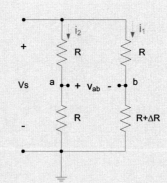

By voltage division, the voltages v_b and v_a (relative to ground) are:

$$v_b = \frac{(R + \Delta R)}{2R + \Delta R} V_s$$

And

$$v_a = R i_2 = \frac{V_s \cdot R}{2R} = \frac{V_s}{2}$$

The voltage v_{ab} is then:

$$v_{ab} = v_a - v_b = \left(\frac{1}{2} - \frac{R + \Delta R}{2R + \Delta R}\right) V_s = \left(\frac{(2R + \Delta R) - 2(R + \Delta R)}{2(2R + \Delta R)}\right) V_s = -\frac{\Delta R}{2(2R + \Delta R)} \cdot V_s$$

For the case in which $\Delta R \ll 2R$, this simplifies to:

$$v_{ab} \approx -\frac{V_s}{4R} \Delta R$$

And the output voltage is proportional to the change in resistance of the variable resistor.

Practical applications:

A number of common sensors result in a resistance variation resulting from some external influence. *Thermistors* change resistance as a result of temperature changes; *strain gages* change resistance as a result of deformation, generally due to application of a load to the part to which the gage is bonded; *photoconductive transducers*, or *photoresistors*, change resistance as a result of changes in light intensity. Wheatstone bridges are commonly used in conjunction with these types of sensors.

Section Summary

- In a circuit, which contains obvious series and/or parallel combinations of resistors, analysis can be simplified by combining these resistances into equivalent resistances. The reduction in the overall number of resistances reduces the number of unknowns in the circuit, with a corresponding reduction in the number of governing equations. Reducing the number of equations and unknowns typically simplifies the analysis of the circuit.
- Not all circuits are reducible.

1.3   Exercises

1. For the circuit shown, determine:
    a. R_{eq} (the equivalent resistance seen by the source)
    b.   The currents I_1 and I_2

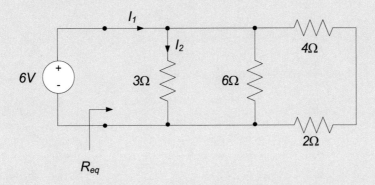

Solutions can be found at digilent.com/real-analog.

2.4   Non-ideal Power Supplies

In section 1.2, we discussed ideal power sources. In that section, an ideal voltage supply was characterized as providing a specified voltage <u>regardless of the current requirements made upon the device</u>. Likewise, an ideal current source was defined as providing a specified voltage <u>regardless of the voltage potential difference across the source</u>. These models are not realistic - since an ideal voltage source can provide infinite current with non-zero voltage difference and an ideal current source can provide infinite voltage difference with non-zero current, either device is capable of delivering infinite power. In many cases, the ideal voltage and current source models will be adequate, but in cases where we need to more accurately replicate the operation of realistic power supplies, we will need to modify our models of these devices.

In this section, we present simple models for voltage and current sources which incorporate more realistic assumptions as to the behavior of these devices.

2.4.1   Non-ideal Voltage Sources

An ideal voltage source was defined in section 1.2 as providing a specified voltage, regardless of the current flow out of the device. For example, an <u>ideal</u> 12V battery will provide 12V across its terminals, regardless of the load connected to the terminals. A real 12V battery, however, provides 12V across its terminals only when its terminals are open-circuited. As we draw current from the terminals, the battery will provide less than 12V - the voltage will decrease as more and more current is drawn from the battery. The real battery thus appears to have an internal voltage drop which increases with increased current.

We will model a real or *practical* voltage source as a series connection of an ideal voltage source and an *internal resistance*. This model is depicted schematically in Fig. 2.5, in which the non-ideal voltage source contains an ideal voltage source providing voltage V_s and an internal resistance R_s . The non-ideal voltage source delivers a voltage V and a current *i*, where:

$$V = V_s - i \cdot R_s$$

Eq. 2.24

Equation (2.24) indicates that the voltage delivered by our non-ideal voltage source model decreases as the current out of the voltage source increases, which agrees with expectations.

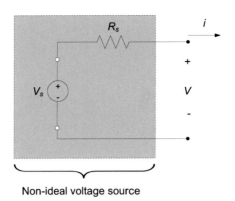

Non-ideal voltage source

Example 2.6

Consider the case in which we connect a resistive load to the non-ideal voltage source. The figure below provides a schematic of the overall system; R_L is the load resistance, V_L is the voltage delivered to the load, and i_L is the current delivered to the load.

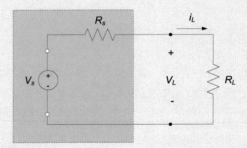

In the case above, the current delivered to the load is $i = \frac{V_S}{R_S + R_L}$ and the load voltage is $V_L = V_S \frac{R_L}{R_S + R_L}$. Thus, if the load resistance is infinite (the load is an open circuit), $V_L = V_S$, but the power supply delivers no current and hence no power to the load. If the load resistance is zero (the load is a short circuit), $V_L = 0$ and the power supply delivers current $i_L = \frac{V_S}{R_S}$ to the load; the power delivered to the load, however, is still zero.

Example 2.7: Charging a Battery

We have a "dead" car battery which is providing only 4V across its terminals. We want to charge the battery using a spare battery which is providing 12V across its terminals. To do this, we connect the two batteries as shown below:

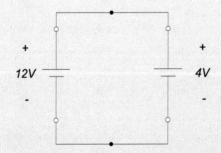

If we attempt to analyze this circuit by applying KVL around the loop, we obtain 12V=4V. This is obviously incorrect and we cannot proceed with our analysis - our model disagrees with reality!

To resolve this issue, we will include the internal resistance of the batteries. Assuming a 3Ω internal resistance in each battery, we obtain the following model for the system:

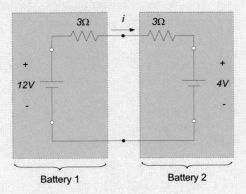

Applying KVL around the loop, and using Ohm's law to write the voltages across the battery internal resistances in terms of the current between the batteries results in:

$$-12V + (3\Omega)i + (3\Omega)i + 4V = 0$$

Which can be solved for the current i to obtain:

$$i = \frac{12V - 4V}{6\Omega} = 1.33A$$

Notice that as the voltage of the "dead" battery increases during the charging process, the current delivered to the "dead" battery decreases.

2.4.2 Non-ideal Current Sources

An ideal current source was defined in section 1.2 as providing a specified current, regardless of the voltage difference across the device. This model suffers from the same basic drawback as our ideal voltage source model - the model can deliver infinite power, which is inconsistent with the capabilities of a real current source.

We will use the circuit shown schematically in Fig. 2.6 to model a non-ideal current source. The non-ideal model consists of an ideal current source, i_s, placed in parallel with an internal resistance, R_s. The source delivers a voltage V and current i. The output current is given by:

$$i = i_s - \frac{V}{R_s}$$

Eq. 2.25

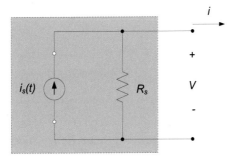

Figure 2.6. Non-ideal current source model.

Example 2.8

Consider the case in which we connect a resistive load to the non-ideal current source. The figure below provides a schematic of the overall system; R_L is the load resistance, V_L is the voltage delivered to the load, and i_L is the current delivered to the load.

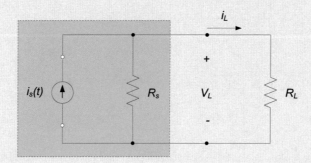

In the case above, the current delivered to the load can be determined from a current divider relation as $i_L = i_S \cdot \frac{R_S}{R_S + R_L}$ and the load voltage, by Ohm's law, is $V_L = i_L R_L = i_S \frac{R_S R_L}{R_S + R_L}$. If the load resistance is zero (the load is a short circuit), $i_L = i_S$, but the power supply delivers no voltage and hence no power to the load. In the case of infinite load resistance (the load is open circuit), $i_L = 0$. In this case, we can neglect R_S in the denominator of the load voltage equation to obtain $V_L \approx i_S \frac{R_S R_L}{R_L}$ so that $V_L \approx i_S R_S$. Since the current is zero, however, the power delivered to the load is still zero.

If we explicitly calculate the power delivered to the load, we obtain $V_L = i_S^2 \frac{R_S R_L}{R_S + R_L} \cdot \frac{R_S}{R_S + R_L}$. A plot of the power delivered to the load as a function of the load resistance is shown below; a logarithmic scale is used on the horizontal axis to make the plot more readable. As expected, the power is zero for high and low load resistances. The peak of the curve occurs when the load resistance is equal to the source resistance, $R_L = R_S$.

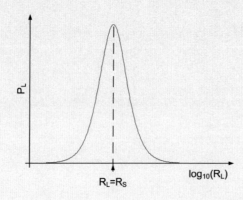

Section Summary

- In many cases, power supplies can be modeled as ideal power supplies, as presented in section 1.2. However, in some cases representation of a power supply as ideal results in unacceptable errors. For example, ideal power supplies can deliver infinite power, which is obviously unrealistic.
- In this section, we present a simple model for a non-ideal power supply.
    - Our non-ideal voltage source consists of an ideal voltage source in series with a resistance which is internal to the power supply.

- o Our non-ideal current supply consists of an ideal current source in parallel with a resistance which is internal to the power supply.
- Voltage and current divider formulas allow us to easily quantify the effects of the internal resistances of the non-ideal power supplies. Our analysis indicates that the non-ideal effects are negligible, as long as the resistance of the load is large relative to the internal resistance of the power supply.

1.4   Exercises

1. A voltage source with an internal resistance of 2Ω as shown below is used to apply power to a 3Ω resistor. What voltage would you measure across the 3Ω resistor?

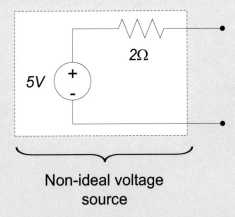

Non-ideal voltage source

2. The voltage source of exercise 1 above is used to apply power to a 2kΩ resistor. What voltage would you measure across the 2kΩ resistor?

Solutions can be found at digilent.com/real-analog.

2.5   Practical Voltage and Current Measurement

The process of measuring a physical parameter will almost invariably change the parameter being measured. This effect is both undesirable and, in general, unavoidable. One goal of any measurement is to affect the parameter being measured <u>as little as possible</u>.

The above statement is true of voltage and current measurements. An <u>ideal</u> voltmeter, connected in parallel with some circuit element, will measure the voltage across the element without affecting the current flowing through the element. Unfortunately, any real or practical voltmeter will draw some current from the circuit it is connected to; this *loading effect* will change the circuit's operating conditions, causing some difference between the measured voltage and the corresponding voltage without the voltmeter present in the circuit. Likewise, an ideal ammeter, connected in series with some circuit element, will measure current without affecting the voltage in the circuit. A practical ammeter, like a practical voltmeter, will introduce loading effects which change the operation of the circuit on which the measurement is being made.

In this section, we introduce some effects of measuring voltages and currents with practical meters.

2.5.1 Voltmeter and Ammeter Models

We will model both voltmeters and ammeters as having some internal resistance and a method for displaying the measured voltage difference or current. Fig. 2.7 shows schematic representations of voltmeters and ammeters.

The ammeter in Fig. 2.7(a) has an internal resistance R_M; the current through the ammeter is i_A and the voltage difference across the ammeter is V_a. The ammeter's voltage difference should be as small as possible - an ammeter, therefore, should have an extremely small internal resistance.

The voltmeter in Fig. 2.7(b) is also represented as having an internal resistance R_M; the current through the meter is i_A and the voltage difference across the meter is V_v. The current through the voltmeter should be as small as possible - the voltmeter should have an extremely high internal resistance.

The effects of non-zero ammeter voltages and non-zero voltmeter currents are explored in more detail in the following subsections.

2.5.2 Voltage Measurement

Consider the circuit shown in Fig. 2.8(a). A current source, i_s, provides current to a circuit element with resistance, R. We want to measure the voltage drop, V, across the circuit element. We do this by attaching a voltmeter across the circuit element as shown in Fig. 2.8(b).

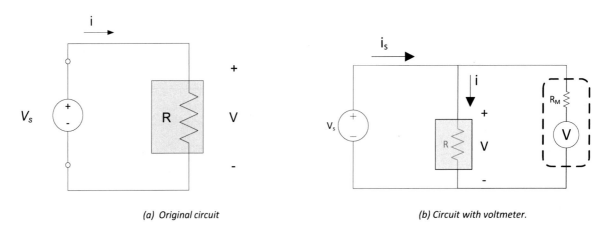

(a) Original circuit   (b) Circuit with voltmeter.

In Fig. 2.8(b) the voltmeter resistance is in parallel to the circuit element we wish to measure the voltage across and the combination of the circuit element and the voltmeter becomes a current divider. The current through the resistor R then becomes:

$$i = i_s \frac{R_M}{R+R_M}$$

Eq. 2.26

The voltage across the resistor R is then, by Ohm's law:

$$V = i_s \frac{R \cdot R_M}{R+R_M}$$

Eq. 2.27

If $R_M \gg R$, this expression simplifies to:

$$V \approx i_s \frac{R \cdot R_M}{R_M} = R \cdot i_s$$

Eq. 2.28

And negligible error is introduced into the measurement - the measured voltage is approximately the same as the voltage without the voltmeter. If, however, the voltmeter resistance is comparable to the resistance R, the simplification of equation (2.28) is not appropriate and significant changes are made to the system by the presence of the voltmeter.

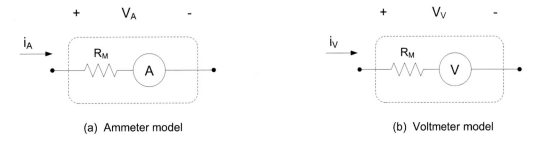

(a) Ammeter model　　　　　　　　　(b) Voltmeter model

Figure 2.7. Ammeter and voltmeter models.

2.5.3　Current Measurement

Consider the circuit shown in Fig. 2.9(a). A voltage source, V_s, provides power to a circuit element with resistance, R. We want to measure the current, i, through the circuit element. We do this by attaching an ammeter in series with the circuit element as shown in Fig. 2.9(b).

In Fig. 2.9(b) the series combination of the ammeter resistance and the circuit element whose current we wish to measure creates a voltage divider. KVL around the single circuit loop provides:

$$V_s = i(R_M + R)$$

Eq. 2.29

Solving for the current results in:

$$i = \frac{V_s}{R_M + R}$$

Eq. 2.30

If $R_M << R$, this simplifies to:

$$i \approx \frac{V_s}{R}$$

Eq. 2.31

And the measured current is a good approximation to current in the circuit of Fig. 2.9(a). However, if the ammeter resistance is not small compared to the resistance R, the approximation of equation (2.31) is not appropriate and the measured current is no longer representative of the circuit's operation without the ammeter.

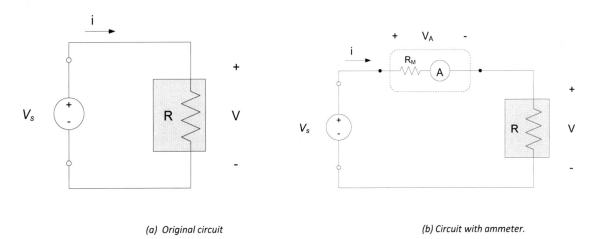

(a) Original circuit　　　　　　　　(b) Circuit with ammeter.

Figure 2.9.　Current measurement.

Caution

Incorrect connections of ammeters or voltmeters can cause damage to the meter. For example, consider the connection of an ammeter in <u>parallel</u> with a relatively large resistance, as shown below.

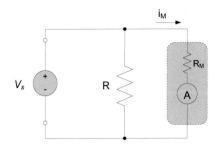

In this configuration, the ammeter current, $i_M = \dfrac{V_S}{R_M}$. Since the ammeter resistance is typically very small, this can result in high currents being provided to the ammeter. This, in turn, may result in excessive power being provided to the ammeter and resulting damage to the device.

Ammeters are generally intended to be connected in <u>series</u> with the circuit element(s) whose current is being measured. Voltmeters are generally intended to be connected in <u>parallel</u> with the circuit element(s) whose voltage is being measured. Alternate connections can result in damage to the meter.

Section Summary

- Measurement of voltage and/or current in a circuit will always result in some effect on the circuit's behavior - that is, our measurement will always change the parameter being measured. One goal when measuring a voltage or current is to ensure that the measurement effects are negligible.
- In this section, we present simple models for voltmeters and ammeters (voltage and current measurement devices, respectively).
  - Our non-ideal voltmeter consists of an ideal voltmeter (which had infinite resistance, and thus draws no current from the circuit) in parallel with a resistance which is internal to the voltmeter. This model replicates the finite current which is necessarily drawn from the circuit by a real voltmeter.
  - Our non-ideal ammeter consists of an ideal ammeter (which has zero resistance, and thus introduces no voltage drop in the circuit) in series with a resistance which is internal to the ammeter. This resistance allows us to model the finite voltage drop which is introduced into the circuit by a real current measurement.
- Voltage and current divider formulas allow us to easily quantify the effects of the internal resistances of voltage and current meters. Our analysis indicates that the non-ideal effects are negligible, as long as:
  - The resistance of the voltmeter is large relative to the resistance across which the voltage measurement is being made.
  - The resistance of the ammeter is small compared to the overall circuit resistance.

2.5   Exercises

A voltmeter with an internal resistance of 10MΩ is used to measure the voltage v_{ab} in the circuit below. What is the measured voltage? What voltage measurement would you expect from an ideal voltmeter?

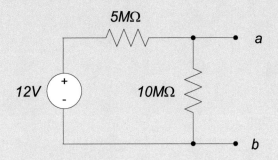

Solutions can be found at digilent.com/real-analog.

Chapter 3:
Nodal and Mesh Analysis

In Chapters 1 & 2, we introduced several tools in circuit analysis:

- Ohm's Law
- Kirchhoff's laws
- Circuit reduction

Circuit reduction, it should be noted, is not fundamentally different from direct application of Ohm's and Kirchhoff's laws - it is simply a convenient re-statement of these laws for specific combinations of circuit elements.

In Chapter 1, we saw that direct application of Ohm's law and Kirchhoff's laws to a specific circuit using the *exhaustive method* often results in a large number of unknowns - even if the circuit is relatively simple. A correspondingly large number of equations must be solved to determine these unknowns. Circuit reduction allows us, in some cases, to simplify the circuit to reduce the number of unknowns in the system. Unfortunately, not all circuits are reducible and even analysis of circuits that are reducible depends upon the engineer "noticing" certain resistance combinations and combining them appropriately.

In cases where circuit reduction is not feasible, approaches are still available to reduce the total number of unknowns in the system. *Nodal analysis* and *mesh analysis* are two of these. Nodal and mesh analysis approaches still rely upon application of Ohm's law and Kirchhoff's laws - we are just applying these laws in a very specific way in order to simplify the analysis of the circuit. One attractive aspect of nodal and mesh analysis is that the approaches are relatively rigorous - we are assured of identifying a reduced set of variables, if we apply the analysis rules correctly. Nodal and mesh analysis are also more general than circuit reduction methods - virtually any circuit can be analyzed using nodal or mesh analysis.

Since nodal and mesh analysis approaches are fairly closely related, section 3.1 introduces the basic ideas and terminology associated with <u>both</u> approaches. Section 3.2 provides details of nodal analysis, and mesh analysis is presented in section 3.3.

After Completing this Chapter, You Should be Able to:

- Use nodal analysis techniques to analyze electrical circuits
- Use mesh analysis techniques to analyze electrical circuits

3.1   Introduction and Terminology

As noted in the introduction, both nodal and mesh analysis involve identification of a "minimum" number of unknowns, which completely describe the circuit behavior. That is, the unknowns themselves may not directly provide the parameter of interest, but <u>any</u> voltage or current in the circuit can be determined from these unknowns. In nodal analysis, the unknowns are the *node voltages*. In mesh analysis, the unknowns are the *mesh currents*. We introduce the concept of these unknowns via an example below.

Consider the circuit shown in Fig. 3.1(a). The circuit nodes are labeled in Fig. 3.1(a), for later convenience. The circuit is not readily analyzed by circuit reduction methods. If the exhaustive approach toward applying KCL and KVL is taken, the circuit has 10 unknowns (the voltages and currents of each of the five resistors), as shown in Fig. 3.1(b). Ten circuit equations must be written to solve for the ten unknowns. Nodal analysis and mesh analysis provide approaches for defining a <u>reduced</u> number of unknowns and solving for these unknowns. If desired, any other desired circuit parameters can subsequently be determined from the reduced set of unknowns.

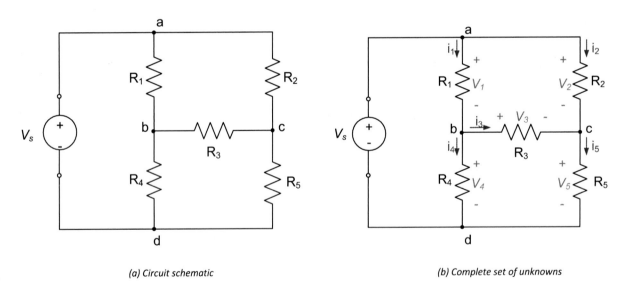

(a) Circuit schematic   (b) Complete set of unknowns

Figure 3.1. Non-reducible circuit.

In nodal analysis, the unknowns will be *node voltages*. Node voltages, in this context, are the *independent voltages* in the circuit. It will be seen later that the circuit of Fig. 3.1 contains only two independent voltages - the voltages at nodes b and c[1]. Only two equations need be written and solved to determine these voltages! Any other circuit parameters can be determined from these two voltages.

---

[1] The voltages at nodes a and d are <u>not</u> independent; the voltage source v_s *constrains* the voltage at node a relative to the voltage at node d (KVL around the leftmost loop indicates the $v_{ad} = V_S$)

Basic Idea

In nodal analysis, Kirchhoff's current law is written at each independent voltage node; Ohm's law is used to write the currents in terms of the node voltages in the circuit.

In mesh analysis, the unknowns will be *mesh currents*. Mesh currents are defined only for *planar circuits*; planar circuits are circuits which can be drawn in a single plane such that no elements overlap one another. When a circuit is drawn in a single plane, the circuit will be divided into a number of distinct areas; the boundary of each area is a *mesh* of the circuit. A *mesh current* is the current flowing around a mesh of the circuit. The circuit of Fig. 3.1 has three meshes:

- The mesh bounded by V_s, node a, and node d
- The mesh bounded by node a, node c, and node b
- The mesh bounded by node b, node c, and node d

These three meshes are illustrated schematically in Fig. 3.2. Thus, in a mesh analysis of the circuit of Fig. 3.1, three equations must be solved in three unknowns (the mesh currents). Any other desired circuit parameters can be determined from the mesh currents.

Basic Idea

In mesh analysis, Kirchhoff's voltage law is written around each mesh loop; Ohm's law is used to write the voltage in terms of the mesh currents in the circuit. Since KVL is written around closed loops in the circuit, mesh analysis is sometimes known as *loop analysis*.

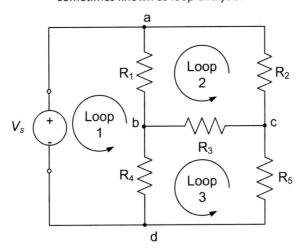

Figure 3.2. Meshes for circuit of Figure 3.1.

Section Summary

1. In nodal analysis:
   - Unknowns in the analysis are called the *node voltages*
   - Node voltages are the voltages at the <u>independent</u> nodes in the circuit
   - Two nodes connected by a voltage source are <u>not independent</u>. The voltage source constrains the voltages at the nodes relative to one another. A node which is not independent is also called dependent.
2. In mesh analysis:
   - Unknowns in the analysis are called *mesh currents*.

o Mesh currents are defined as flowing through the circuit elements which form the perimeter of the circuit meshes. A mesh is any enclosed, non-overlapping region in the circuit (when the circuit schematic is drawn on a piece of paper).

Exercises

1. The circuit below has three nodes, A, B, and C. Which two nodes are dependent? Why?

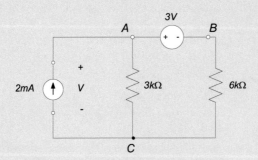

2. Identify meshes in the circuit below.

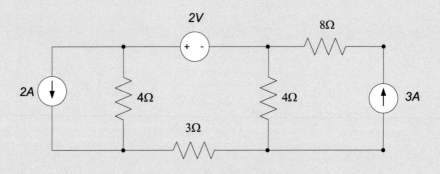

Solutions can be found at digilent.com/real-analog.

3.2 Nodal Analysis

As noted in section 3.1, in nodal analysis we will define a set of node voltages and use Ohm's law to write Kirchhoff's current law in terms of these voltages. The resulting set of equations can be solved to determine the node voltages; and other circuit parameters (e.g. currents) can be determined from these voltages.

The steps used in nodal analysis are provided below. The steps are illustrated in terms of the circuit of Fig. 3.3.

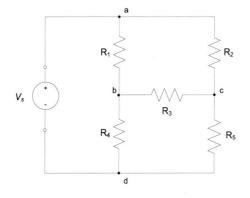

Figure 3.3. Example circuit.

Step 1: Define Reference Voltage

One node will be arbitrarily chosen as a *reference node* or *datum node*. The voltages of all other nodes in the circuit will be defined to be <u>relative</u> to the voltage of this node. Thus, for convenience, it will be assumed that the reference node voltage is zero volts. It should be emphasized that this definition is arbitrary - since voltages are actually potential differences, choosing the reference voltage as zero is primarily a convenience.

For our example circuit, we will choose node *d* as our reference node and define the voltage at this node to be 0V, as shown in Fig. 3.4.

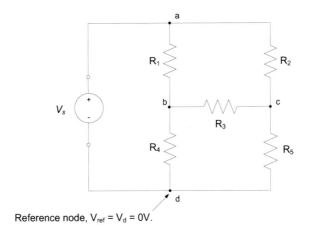

Reference node, $V_{ref} = V_d = 0V$.

Figure 3.4. Definition of reference node and reference voltage.

Step 2: Determine Independent Nodes

We now define the voltages at the *independent* nodes. These voltages will be the unknowns in our circuit equations. In order to define independent nodes:

- "Short-circuit" all voltage sources
- "Open-circuit" all current sources

After removal of the sources, the remaining nodes (with the exception of the reference node) are defined as *independent* nodes (the nodes which were removed in this process are *dependent* nodes. The voltages at these nodes are sometimes said to be *constrained*). Label the voltages at these nodes - they are the unknowns for which we will solve.

For our example circuit of Fig. 3.3, removal of the voltage source (replacing it with a short circuit) results in nodes remaining only at nodes b and c. This is illustrated in Fig. 3.

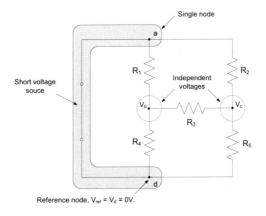

Reference node, $V_{ref} = V_d = 0V$.

Figure 3.5. Independent voltages V_b and V_c.

Step 3: Replace Sources in the Circuit and Identify Constrained Voltages

With the independent voltages defined as in Step 2, replace the sources and define the voltages at the dependent nodes in terms of the independent voltages and the known voltage difference.

For our example, the voltage at node a can be written as a known voltage V_S above the reference voltage, as shown in Fig. 3.6.

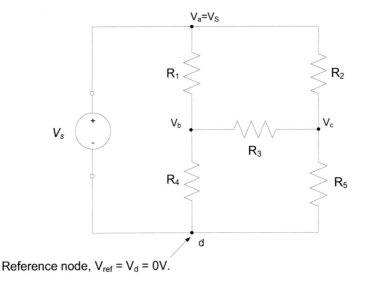

Reference node, $V_{ref} = V_d = 0V$.

Figure 3.6. Dependent voltages defined.

Step 4: Applying KCL at Independent Nodes

Define currents and write Kirchhoff's current law at all independent nodes. Currents for our example are shown in Fig. 3.7 below. The defined currents include the assumed direction of positive current - this defines the sign convention for our currents. To avoid confusion, these currents are defined consistently with those shown in Fig. 3.1(b). The resulting equations are (<u>assuming that currents leaving the node are defined as positive</u>):

Node b:

$$-i_1 + i_3 + i_4 = 0$$

Eq. 3.1

Node c:

$$-i_2 + i_3 + i_5 = 0$$

Eq. 3.2

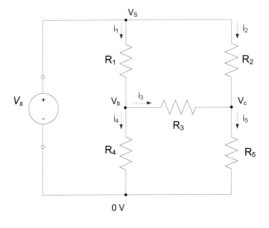

Figure 3.7. Current definitions and sign conventions.

Step 5: Use Ohm's Law to Write the Equations From Step 4 in Terms of Voltages

The currents defined in Step 4 can be written in terms of the node voltages defined previously. For example, from Fig. 3.7: $i_1 = \frac{V_S - V_b}{R_1}$, $i_3 = \frac{V_b - V_c}{R_3}$, and $i_4 = \frac{V_b - 0}{R_4}$, so equation (3.1) can be written as:

So the KCL equation for node b becomes:

$$\left(\frac{1}{R_1} + \frac{1}{R_3} + \frac{1}{R_4}\right) V_b - \frac{1}{R_3} V_c = \frac{1}{R_1} V_S \qquad \text{Eq. 3.3}$$

Likewise, the KCL equation for node c can be written as:

$$-\frac{1}{R_3} V_b + \left(\frac{1}{R_3} + \frac{1}{R_2} + \frac{1}{R_5}\right) V_c = \frac{1}{R_2} V_S \qquad \text{Eq. 3.4}$$

Double-checking Results

If the circuit being analyzed contains only <u>independent sources</u>, and the sign convention used in KCL equations is the same as used above (<u>currents leaving nodes are assumed positive</u>), the equations written at each node will have the following form:

- The term multiplying the voltage at that node will be the sum of the conductances connected to that node. For the example above, the term multiplying V_b in the equation for node b is $\frac{1}{R_1} + \frac{1}{R_3} + \frac{1}{R_4}$ while the term multiplying V_c in the equation for node c is $\frac{1}{R_3} + \frac{1}{R_2} + \frac{1}{R_5}$.
- The term multiplying the voltages adjacent to the node will be the negative of the conductance connecting the two nodes. For the example above, the term multiplying V_c in the equation for node b is $-\frac{1}{R_3}$, and the term multiplying V_b in the equation for node c is $-\frac{1}{R_3}$.

If the circuit contains dependent sources, or a different sign convention is used when writing the KCL equations, the resulting equations will not necessarily have the above form.

Step 6: Solve the System of Equations Resulting from Step 5

Step 5 will always result in N equations in N unknowns, where N is the number of independent nodes identified in Step 2. These equations can be solved for the independent voltages. Any other desired circuit parameters can be determined from these voltages.

The example below illustrates the above approach.

Example 3.1

Find the voltage V for the circuit shown below:

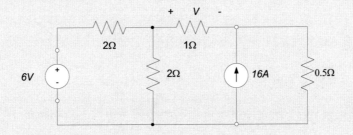

Steps 1, 2, and 3: Choosing the reference voltage as shown below, identifying voltages at dependent nodes, and defining voltages V_A and V_B at the independent nodes results in the circuit schematic shown below:

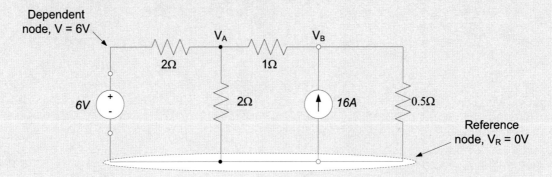

Steps 4 and 5: Writing KCL at nodes A and B and converting currents to voltages using Ohm's law results in the following two equations:

Node A:

$$\frac{V_A - 6}{2\Omega} + \frac{V_A - 0}{2\Omega} + \frac{V_A - V_B}{1\Omega} = 0 \Rightarrow \left(\frac{1}{2} + \frac{1}{2} + \frac{1}{1}\right) V_A - V_B = 3 \Rightarrow 2V_A - V_B = 3$$

Node B:

$$\frac{V_B - V_A}{1} + \frac{V_B - 0}{0.5} - 16 = 0 \Rightarrow \left(\frac{1}{1} + \frac{1}{0.5}\right) V_B - V_A = +16 \Rightarrow 3V_B = 16 + V_A$$

Step 6: Solving the above equations results in $V_A = 5V$ and $V_B = 7V$. The voltage V is:

$$V = V_A - V_B = -2V$$

Several comments should be made relative to the above example:

1. Steps 4 and 5 (applying KCL at each independent node and using Ohm's law to write these equations in terms of voltages) have been combined into a single step. This approach is fairly common, and can provide a significant savings in time.
2. There may be a perceived inconsistency between the two node equations, in the assumption of positive current direction in the 1Ω resistor. In the equation for node A, the current is apparently assumed to be positive from node A to node B, as shown below:

$$i_1$$
$$V_A \longrightarrow V_B$$
$$1\Omega$$

This leads to the corresponding term in the equation for node A becoming: $\frac{V_A - V_B}{1}$. In the equation for node B, however, the positive current direction appears to be from node B to node A, as shown below:

$$i_1$$
$$V_A \longleftarrow V_B$$
$$1\Omega$$

This definition leads to the corresponding term in the equation for node B becoming: $\frac{V_B - V_A}{1}$.

The above inconsistency in sign is, however, insignificant. Suppose that we had assumed (consistently with the equation for node A) that the direction of positive current for the node B equation is from Node A to B. Then, the corresponding term in the equation for node B would have been: $-\frac{V_A-V_B}{1}$ (note that a negative sign has been applied to this term to accommodate our assumption that <u>currents flowing into nodes are negative</u>). This is equal to $\frac{V_A-V_B}{1}$, which is exactly what our original result was.

3. The current source appears <u>directly</u> in the nodal equations.

Note

When we write nodal equations in these chapters, we will generally assume that any unknown currents are flowing away from the node for which we are writing the equation, <u>regardless of any previous assumptions we have made for the direction of that current</u>. The signs will work out, as long as we are consistent in our sign convention <u>between assumed voltage polarity and current direction</u> and our sign convention relative to <u>positive currents flowing out of nodes</u>.

The sign applied to currents induced by current sources must be consistent with the current direction assigned by the source.

3.2.1 Supernodes

In the previous examples, we identified <u>dependent</u> nodes and determined <u>constrained</u> voltages. Kirchhoff's current law was then only written at <u>independent</u> nodes. Many readers find this somewhat confusing, especially if the dependent voltages are not relative to the reference voltage. We will thus discuss these steps in more detail here in the context of an example, introducing the concept of a *supernode* in the process.

Example: for the circuit below, determine the voltage difference, V, across the 2mA source.

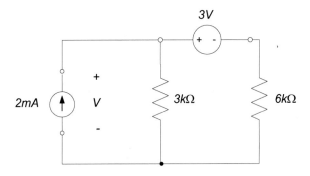

Step 1: define Reference Node

Choose reference node (somewhat arbitrarily) as shown below; label the reference node voltage, V_R, as zero volts.

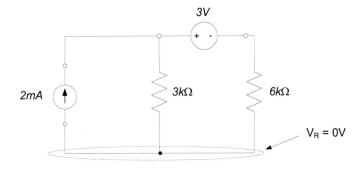

Step 2: Define Independent Nodes

Short circuit voltage sources, open circuit current sources as shown below and identify independent nodes/voltages. For our example, this result in only one independent voltage, labeled as V_A below.

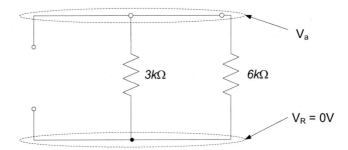

Step 3: Replace Sources and Label any Known Voltages

The known voltages are written in terms of node voltages identified above. There is some ambiguity in this step. For example, either of the representations below will work equally well - either side of the voltage source can be chosen as the node voltage, and the voltage on the other side of the source written in terms of this node voltage. Make sure, however, that the correct <u>polarity</u> of the voltage source is preserved. In our example, the left side of the source has a potential that is three volts higher than the potential of the right side of the source. This fact is represented correctly by both of the choices below.

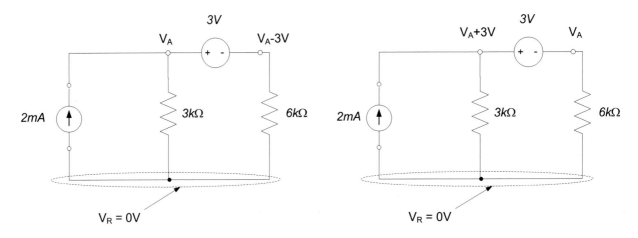

Step 4: Apply KCL at the Independent Nodes

It is this step that sometimes causes confusion among readers, particularly when voltage sources are present in the circuit. Conceptually, it is possible to think of two nodes connected by an ideal voltage source as forming a single *supernode* (some authors use the term *generalized node* rather than supernode). A node is rigorously defined as having a single, unique voltage. However, although the two nodes connected by a voltage source do not share the same voltage, they are not entirely independent - the two voltages are *constrained* by one another. This allows us to simplify the analysis somewhat.

For our example, we will arbitrarily choose the circuit to the left above to illustrate this approach. The supernode is chosen to include the voltage source and both nodes to which it is connected, as shown below. We define two currents leaving the supernode, i_1 and i_2, as shown. KCL, applied at the supernode, results in:

$$-2mA + i_1 + i_2 = 0$$

As before, currents leaving the node are assumed to be positive. This approach allows us to account for the current flowing through the voltage source without ever explicitly solving for it.

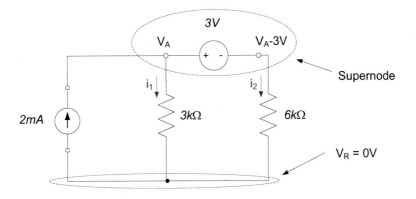

Step 5: Use Ohm's Law to Write the KCL Equations in Terms of Voltages

For the single KCL equation written above, this results in:

$$-2mA + \frac{V_A - 0}{3k\Omega} + \frac{(V_A - 3) - 0}{6k\Omega} = 0$$

Step 6: Solve the System of Equations to Determine the Nodal Voltages

Solution of the equation above results in $V_A = 5V$. Thus, the voltage difference across the current source is $V = 5V$.

3.2.2 Alternate Approach: Constraint Equations

The use of supernodes can be convenient, but is not a necessity. An alternate approach, for those who do not wish to identify supernodes, is to restrain separate nodes on either side of the voltage source and then write a constraint equation relating these voltages. Thus, in cases where the reader does not recognize a supernode, the analysis can proceed correctly. We now revisit the previous example, but use constraint equations rather than the previous supernode technique.

In this approach, Steps 2 and 3 (identification of independent nodes) are not necessary. One simply writes Kirchhoff's current law at all nodes and then writes constraints equations for the voltage sources. A disadvantage of this approach is that currents through voltage sources must be accounted for explicitly; this result in a greater number of unknowns (and equations to be solved) than the supernode technique.

Example (revisited): for the circuit below, determine the voltage difference, V, across the 2mA source.

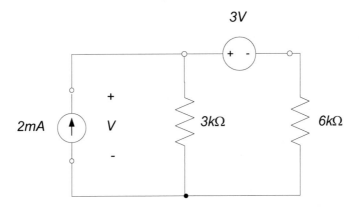

Choice of a reference voltage proceeds as previously. However, now we will not concern ourselves too much with identification of independent nodes. Instead, we will just make sure we account for voltages and currents everywhere in the circuit. For our circuit, this results in the node voltages and currents shown below. Notice that we have now identified two unknown voltages (V_A and V_B) and three unknown currents, one of which (i_3) is the current through the voltage source.

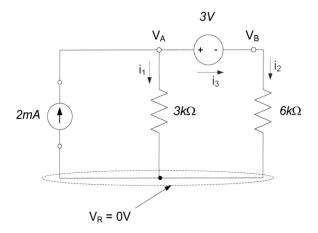

Now we write KCL at each of the identified nodes, making sure to account for the current through the voltage source. This results in the following equations (assuming currents leaving the node are positive):

Node A: $-2mA + i_1 + i_3 = 0$

Node B: $-i_3 + i_2 = 0$

Using Ohm's law to convert the currents i_1 and i_2 to voltages results in:

Node A: $-2mA + \frac{V_A - 0}{3k\Omega} + i_3 = 0$

Node B: $-i_3 + \frac{V_B - 0}{6k\Omega} = 0$

Notice that we cannot, by inspection, determine anything about the current i_3 from the voltages; <u>the voltage-current relationship for an ideal source is not known.</u>

The two equations above have three unknowns - we cannot solve for the node voltages from them without a third equation. This third equation is the <u>constraint</u> equation due to the presence of the voltage source. For our circuit, the voltage source causes a direct relationship between V_A and V_B:

$$V_B = V_A - 3$$

These thee equations (the two KCL equations, written in terms of the node voltages and the constraint equation) constitute three equations in three unknowns. Solving these for the node voltage V_A results in $V_A = 5V$, so the voltage across the current source is $V = 5V$.

Example 3.2

For the circuit below, find the power generated or absorbed by the 2V source <u>and</u> the power generated or absorbed by the 2A source.

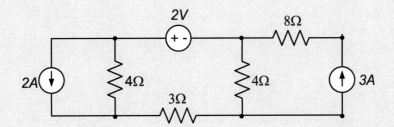

Steps 1, 2, and 3: we choose our reference node (arbitrarily) as shown below. Shorting voltage sources and open-circuiting current sources identifies three independent node voltages (labeled below as V_A, V_B, and V_C) and one dependent node, with voltage labeled below as $V_A - 2$.

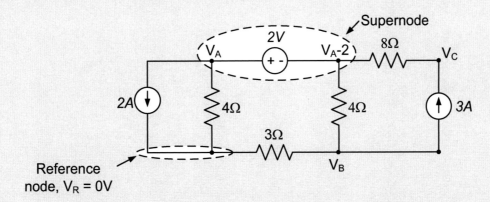

Steps 4 and 5: Writing KCL at nodes A, B, and C and converting the currents to voltages using Ohm's law results in the equations below. Note that we have (essentially) assumed that all unknown currents at a node are flowing out of the node, consistent with our node 2 for example 1 above.

Node A:

$$2A + \frac{V_A - 0V}{4\Omega} + \frac{(V_A - 2V) - V_B}{4\Omega} + \frac{(V_A - 2V) - V_C}{8\Omega} = 0 \Rightarrow 5V_A - 2V_B - V_C = -10$$

Node B:

$$\frac{V_B - 0V}{3\Omega} + \frac{(V_B - (V_A - 2V))}{4\Omega} + 3A = 0 \Rightarrow 7V_B - 3V_A = -42$$

Node C:

$$\frac{V_C - (V_A - 2)}{8\Omega} - 3A = 0 \Rightarrow V_C - V_A = 22$$

Step 6: Solving the above results in $V_A = 5V$, $V_B = -4V$, and $V_C = 27V$. Thus, the voltage difference across the 2A source is zero volts, and the <u>2A source delivers no power</u>. KCL at node A indicates that the current through the 2V source is 2A, and the <u>2V source generates 4W</u>.

3.2.3 Dependent Sources

In the presence of dependent sources, nodal analysis proceeds approximately as outlined above. The main difference is the presence of additional equations describing the dependent source. As before, we will discuss the treatment of dependent sources in the context of examples.

Example 3.3

Write the nodal equations for the circuit below. The dependent source is a voltage controlled voltage source. I_S is an independent current source.

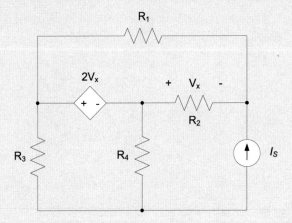

As always, the choice of reference node is arbitrary. To determine independent voltages, dependent voltage sources are short-circuited in the same way as independent voltage sources. Thus, the circuit below has two independent nodes; the dependent voltage source and the nodes on either side of it form a supernode. The reference voltage, independent voltages, supernode, and resulting dependent voltage are shown below.

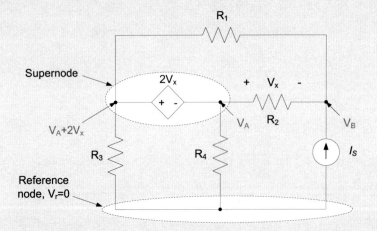

We now, as previously, write KCL for each independent node, taking into account the dependent voltage resulting from the presence of the supernode:

$$\frac{(V_A + 2V_X) - 0}{R_3} + \frac{V_A - 0}{R_4} + \frac{V_A - V_B}{R_2} = 0$$

$$\frac{V_B - V_A}{R_2} + \frac{V_B - (V_A + 2V_X)}{R_1} - I_S = 0$$

The above equations result in a system with two equations and three unknowns: V_A, V_B, and V_X (I_S is a known current). We now write any equations governing the dependent sources. Writing the controlling voltage in terms of the independent voltages results in:

$$V_X = V_A - V_B$$

Example 3.4

Write the nodal equations for the circuit below.

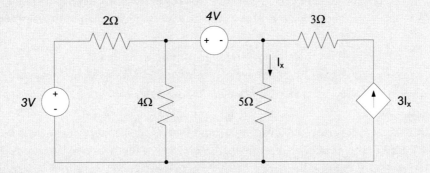

The reference node, independent voltages and dependent voltages are shown on the figure below. A supernode, consisting of the 4V source and the nodes on either side of it, exists but is not shown explicitly on the figure.

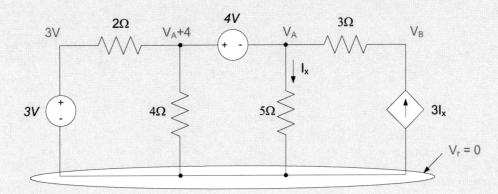

Applying KCL for each independent node results in:

$$\frac{(V_A + 4V) - 3V}{2\Omega} + \frac{(V_A + 4V) - 0}{4\Omega} + \frac{V_A - 0}{5\Omega} + \frac{V_A - V_B}{3\Omega} = 0$$

$$\frac{V_B - V_A}{3\Omega} - 3I_X = 0$$

This consists of two equations with three unknowns. The equation governing the dependent current source provides the third equation. Writing the controlling current in terms of independent voltages results in:

$$I_X = \frac{V_A - 0}{5\Omega}$$

- Basic steps in nodal analysis are:
    - Define a reference node. All node voltages will be relative to this reference voltage.
    - Identify independent nodes. This can be done by short-circuiting voltage sources, open-circuiting current sources, and identifying the remaining nodes in the circuit. The voltages at these nodes are the node voltages.
    - Determine dependent voltages. This can be done by replacing the sources in the circuit schematic, and writing voltage constraints introduced by voltage sources.
    - Use Ohm's law to write KCL at each independent node, in terms of the node voltages. This will result in N equations in N unknowns, where N is the number of node voltages. Independent "nodes" can be *supernodes;* supernodes typically contain a voltage source; this minimizes the number of equations being written by taking advantage of voltage constraints introduced in step 3.
    - Solve the equations of step 4 to determine the node voltages.
    - Use the node voltages to determine any other desired voltages/currents in the circuit.
- Modifications to the above approach are allowed. For example, it is not necessary to define supernodes in step 4 above. Once can define unknown voltages at either terminal of a voltage source and write KCL at each of these nodes. However, the unknown current through the voltage source must be accounted for when writing KCL - this introduces an additional unknown into the governing equations. This added unknown requires an additional equation. This equation is obtained by explicitly writing a constraint equation relating the voltages at the two terminals of the voltage source.

Exercises

1. Use nodal analysis to write a set of equations from which you can find I_1, the current through the 12Ω resistor. Do not solve the equations.

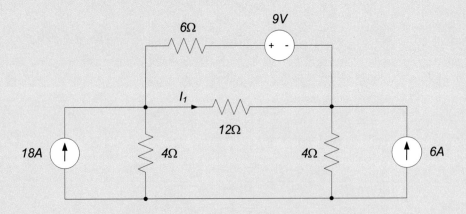

2. Use nodal analysis to find the current I flowing through the 10Ω resistor in the circuit below.

Solutions can be found at digilent.com/real-analog.

3.3   Mesh Analysis

In mesh analysis, we will define a set of mesh currents and use Ohm's law to write Kirchhoff's voltage law in terms of these voltages. The resulting set of equations can be solved to determine the mesh currents; any other circuit parameters (e.g. voltages) can be determined from these currents.

Mesh analysis is appropriate for *planar circuits*. Planar circuits can be drawn in a single plane[2] such that no elements overlap one another. Such circuits, when drawn in a single plane will be divided into a number of distinct areas; the boundary of each area is a *mesh* of the circuit. A *mesh current* is the current flowing around a mesh of the circuit.

The steps used in mesh analysis are provided below. The steps are illustrated in terms of the circuit of Fig. 3.8.

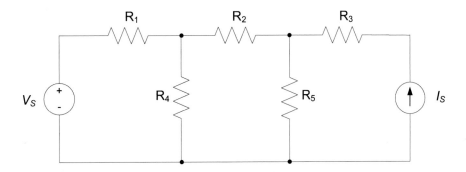

Figure 3.8. Example circuit.

Step 1: Define Mesh Currents

In order to identify our mesh loops, we will turn off all sources, much like what we did in nodal analysis. To do this, we:

- Short-circuit all voltage sources.
- Open-circuit all current sources.

Once the sources have been turned off, the circuit can be divided into a number of <u>non-overlapping</u> areas, each of which is completely enclosed by circuit elements. The circuit elements bounding each of these areas form the meshes of our circuit. The mesh currents flow around these meshes. Our example circuit has two meshes after removal of the sources, the resulting mesh currents are as shown in Fig. 3.9.

Note

We will always choose our mesh currents as flowing <u>clockwise</u> around the meshes. This assumption is not fundamental to the application of mesh analysis, but it will result in a special form for the resulting equations which will later allow us to do some checking of our results.

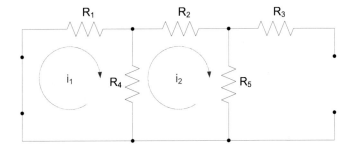

Figure 3.9. Example circuit meshes.

---

[2] Essentially, you can draw the schematic on a piece of paper without ambiguity.

Step 2: Replace Sources and Identify Constrained Loops

The presence of current sources in our circuit will result in the removal of some meshes during Step 1. We must now account for these meshes in our analysis by returning the sources to the circuit and identifying *constrained* loops.

We have two rules for constrained loops:

3. Each current must have <u>one and only one</u> constrained loop passing through it.
4. The <u>direction and magnitude</u> of the constrained loop current must agree with the direction and magnitude of the source current.

For our example circuit, we choose our constrained loop as shown below. It should be noted that constrained loops can, if desired, cross our mesh loops - we have, however, chosen the constrained loop so that is does not overlap any of our mesh loops.

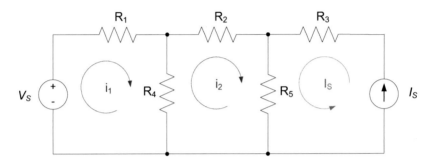

Step 3: Write KVL Around the Mesh Loops

We will apply Kirchhoff's voltage law around each mesh loop in order to determine the equations to be solved. Ohm's law will be used to write KVL in terms of the mesh currents and constrained loop currents as identified in Steps 1 & 2 above.

Note that more than one mesh current may pass through a circuit element. When determining voltage drops across individual elements, the <u>contributions from all mesh currents passing through that element must be included in the voltage drop</u>.

When we write KVL for a given mesh loop, we will base our sign convention for the voltage drops on the direction of the mesh current for that loop.

For example, when we write KVL for the mesh current i_1 in our example, we choose voltage polarities for resistors R_1 and R_4 as shown in the figure below - these polarities agree with the passive sign convention for voltages <u>relative to the direction of the mesh current i_1</u>.

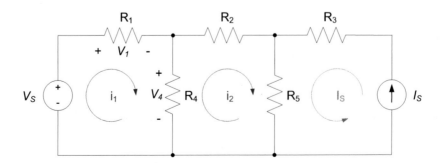

From the above figure, the voltage drops across the resistor R_1 can then be determined as:

$$V_1 = R_1 i_1$$

Since only mesh current i_1 passes through the resistor R_1. Likewise, the voltage drop for the resistor R_4 is:

$$V_4 = R_4(i_1 - i_2)$$

Since mesh currents i_1 and i_2 both pass through R_4 and the current i_2 is in the opposite direction to our assumed polarity for the voltage V_4.

Using the above expressions for V_1 and V_4, we can write KVL for the first mesh loop as:

$$-V_S + R_1 i_1 + R_4(i_1 - i_2) = 0$$

When we write KVL for the mesh current i_2 in our example, we choose voltage polarities for resistors R_4, R_2, and R_5 as shown in the figure below – these polarities agree with the passive sign convention for voltages relative to the direction of the mesh current i_2. Please note that these sign conventions do not need to agree with the sign conventions used in the equations for other mesh currents.

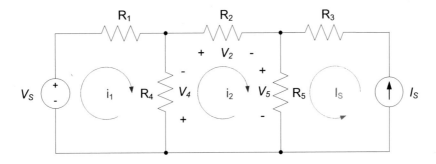

Using the above sign conventions, KVL for the second mesh loop becomes:

$$R_4(i_2 - i_1) + R_2 i_2 + R_5(i_2 + I_S) = 0$$

Please note that the currents i_2 and I_S are in the same direction in the resistor R_5, resulting in a summation of these currents in the term corresponding to the voltage drop across the resistor R_5.

Notes:

1. Assumed sign conventions on voltage drops for a particular mesh loop are based on the assumed direction of that loop's mesh current.
2. The current passing through an element is the <u>algebraic sum</u> of all mesh and constraint currents passing through that element. This algebraic sum of currents is used to determine the voltage drop of the element.

Step 4: Solve the System of Equations to Determine the Mesh Currents of the Circuit

Step 3 will always result in N equations in N unknowns, where N is the number of mesh currents identified in Step 1. These equations can be solved for the mesh currents. Any other desired circuit parameters can be determined from the mesh currents.

The following example illustrates the above approach.

Example 3.5

In the circuit below, determine the voltage drop, V, across the 3Ω resistor.

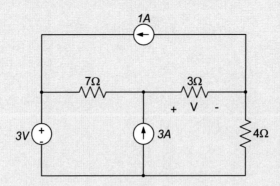

Removing the sources results in a single mesh loop with mesh current i_1, as shown below.

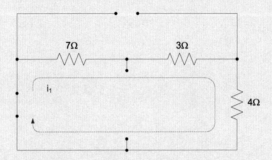

Replacing the sources and defining one constrained loop per source results in the loop definitions shown below (note that each constrained loop goes through only one source and that the amplitude and direction of the constrained currents agrees with source).

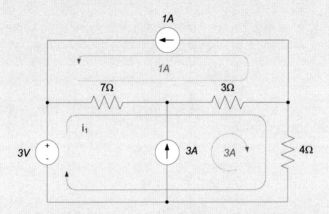

Applying KVL around the loop i_1 and using Ohm's law to write voltage drops in terms of currents:

$$-3V + 7\Omega(i_1 + 1A) + 3\Omega(i_1 + 1A + 3A) + 4\Omega(i_1 + 3A) = 0 \Rightarrow i_1 = -2A$$

Thus, the current i_1 is 2A, in the opposite direction to that shown. The voltage across the 3Ω resistor is $V = 3\Omega(i_1 + 3A + 1A) = 3\Omega(-2A + 3A + 1A) = 3(2A) = 6V$.

3.3.1 Alternate Approach to Constraint Loops: Constraint Equations

In the above examples, the presence of current sources resulted in a reduced number of meshes. Constraint loops were then used to account for current sources. An alternate approach, in which we retain additional mesh currents and then apply *constraint equations* to account for the current sources, is provided here. We use the circuit of the previous example to illustrate this approach.

Example: determine the voltage, V, in the circuit below.

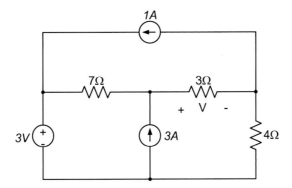

Define three mesh currents for each of the three meshes in the above circuit and define unknown voltages V_1 and V_3 across the two current sources as shown below.

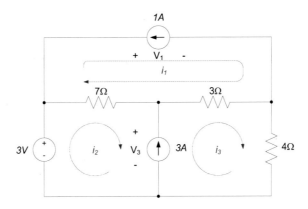

Applying KVL around the three mesh loops results in three equations with five unknowns:

$$V_1 + 3\Omega \cdot (i_1 - i_3) + 7\Omega \cdot (i_1 - i_2) = 0$$

$$-3V + 7\Omega \cdot (i_2 - i_1) + V_3 = 0$$

$$-V_3 + 3\Omega \cdot (i_3 - i_1) + 4\Omega \cdot i_3 = 0$$

Two additional *constrain equations* are necessary. These can be determined by the requirement that the algebraic sum of the mesh currents passing through a current source must equal the current provided by the source. Thus, we obtain:

$$-i_2 + i_3 = 3A$$

$$-i_1 = 1A$$

Solving the five simultaneous equations above results in the same answer determined previously.

3.3.2 Clarification: Constraint Loops

Previously, it was claimed that the choice of constraint loops is somewhat arbitrary. The requirements are that each source has only one constraint loop passing through it, and that the magnitude and direction of the constrained loop current be consistent with the source. Since constraint loops <u>can</u> overlap other mesh loops without invalidating the mesh analysis approach, the choice of constraint loops is not unique. The examples below illustrate the effect of different choices of constraint loops on the analysis of a particular circuit.

Example 3.6: Version 1

Using mesh analysis, determine the current, i, through the 4Ω resistor.

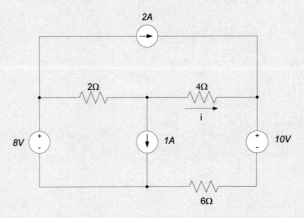

Step 1: Define mesh loops

Replacing the two current sources with open circuits and the two voltage sources with short circuits results in a single mesh current, i_1, as shown below.

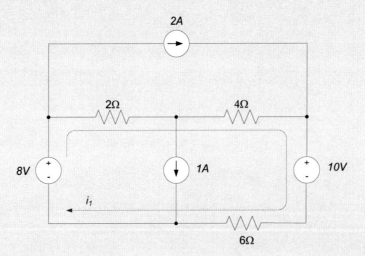

Step 2: Constrained loops, version 1

Initially, we choose the constrained loops shown below. Note that each loop passes through only one source and has the magnitude and direction imposed by the source.

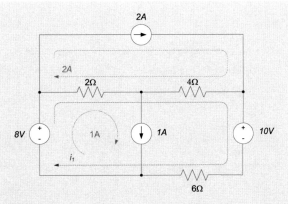

Step 3: Write KVL around the mesh loops

Our example has only one mesh current, so only one KVL equation is required. This equation is:

$$-8V + 2\Omega(i_1 + 1A - 2A) + 4\Omega(i_1 - 2A) + 10V + 6\Omega(i_1) = 0$$

Step 4: Solve the system of equations to determine the mesh currents of the circuit

Solving the above equation results in $i_1 = 0.667A$. The current through the 4Ω resistor is then, accounting for the 2A constrained loop passing through the resistor, $i = i_1 - 2A = -1.333A$.

Example 3.6: Version 2

In this version, we choose an alternate set of constraint loops. The alternate set of loops is shown below; all constraint loops still pass through only one current source, and retain the magnitude and direction of the source current.

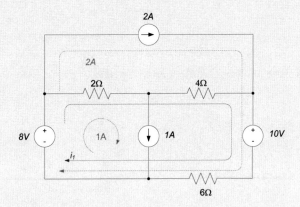

Now, writing KVL for the single mesh results in:

$$-8V + 2\Omega(i_1 + 1A) + 4\Omega \cdot i_1 + 10V + 6\Omega(i_1 + 2A) = 0$$

Solving for the mesh current results in i_1; note that this result is <u>different</u> than it previously was. However, we determine the current through the 4Ω resistor as $i = i_1 = -1.333A$, which <u>is</u> the same result as previously.

Note

Choice of alternate constrained loops may change the values obtained for the mesh currents. The currents through the circuit elements, however, do not vary with choice of constrained loops.

Example 3.6: Version 3

In this version, we choose yet another set of constrained loops. These loops are shown below. Again, each loop passes through one current source and retains that source's current direction and amplitude.

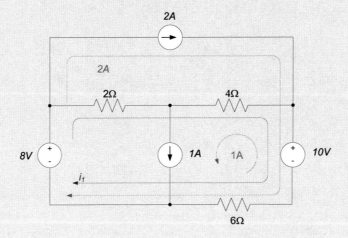

KVL around the mesh loop results in:

$$-8V + 2\Omega \cdot i_1 + 4\Omega(i_1 - 1A) + 10V + 6\Omega(i_1 - 1A + 2A) = 0$$

Which results in $i_1 = -0.333A$. Again, this is different from the result from our first two approaches. However, the current through the 4Ω resistor is $i = i_1 - 1A = -1.333A$, which is the same result as previously.

3.3.3 Dependent Sources

As with nodal analysis, the presence of dependent sources does not significantly alter the overall mesh analysis approach. The primary difference is simply the addition of the additional equations necessary to describe the dependent sources. We discuss the analysis with dependent sources in the context of the following examples.

Example 3.7

Determine the voltage V in the circuit below.

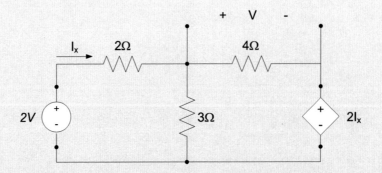

Shorting both of the voltage sources in the circuit above results in two mesh circuits. These are shown in the figure below.

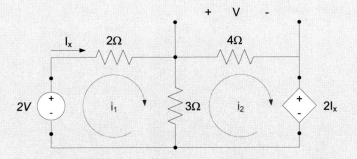

Writing KVL around the two mesh loops results in:

$$-2V + 2\Omega \cdot i_1 + 3\Omega(i_1 - i_2) = 0$$

$$2I_X + 3\Omega(i_2 - i_1) + 4\Omega \cdot i_2 = 0$$

We have two equations and three unknowns. We need an additional equation to solve the system of equations. The third equation is obtained by writing the dependent source's controlling current in terms of the mesh currents:

$$I_X = i_1$$

The above three equations can be solved to obtain $i_1 = 0.4375\Omega$ and $i_2 = 0.0625\Omega$. The desired voltage $V = 4i_2 = 0.25V$.

Example 3.8

Write mesh equations for the circuit shown below.

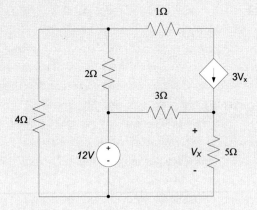

Mesh loops and constraint loops are identified as shown below:

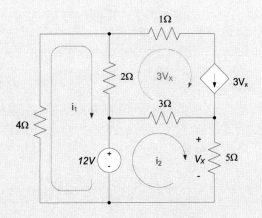

Writing KVL for the two mesh loops results in:

$$4\Omega \cdot i_1 + 2\Omega(i_1 - 3V_X) + 12V = 0$$

$$-12V + 3\Omega(i_2 - 3V_X) + 5\Omega \cdot i_2 = 0$$

Writing the controlling voltage V_X in terms of the mesh currents results in:

$$V_X = 5\Omega \cdot i_2$$

The above consists of three equations in three unknowns, which can be solved to determine the mesh currents. Any other desired circuit parameters can be determined from the mesh currents.

Section Summary

- Basic steps in mesh analysis are:
    - Identify mesh currents. This can be done by short-circuiting voltage sources, open-circuiting current sources, and identifying the enclosed, non-overlapping regions in the circuit. The perimeters of these areas are the circuit meshes. The mesh currents flow around the circuit meshes.
    - Determine constrained loops. The approach in Step 1 will ensure that no mesh currents will pass through the current sources. The current source currents can be accounted for by defining constrained loops. Constrained loops are defined as loop currents which pass through the current sources. Constrained loops are identified by replacing the sources in the circuit schematic, and defining mesh currents which pass through the current sources; these mesh currents form the constrained loops and must match both the magnitude and direction of the current in the current sources.
    - Use Ohm's law to write KVL around each mesh loop, in terms of the mesh currents. This results in N equations in N unknowns, where N is the number of mesh currents. Keep in mind that the voltage difference across each element must correspond to the voltage difference induced by <u>all</u> the mesh currents which pass through that element.
    - Solve the equations of Step 4 to determine the mesh currents.
    - Use the mesh currents to determine any other desired voltages/currents in the circuit.
- The constrained loops in Step 2 above are not unique. Their only requirement is that they must account for the currents through the current sources.
- Modifications to the above approach are allowed. For example, it is not necessary to define constrained loops in Step 3 above. One can define (unknown) mesh currents which pass through the current sources and write KVL for these additional mesh currents. However, the unknown voltage across the current source must be accounted for when writing KVL - this introduces an additional unknown into the governing equations. This added unknown requires an additional equation which is obtained by explicitly writing a constraint equation equating the algebraic sum of the mesh currents passing through a current source to the current provided by the source.

Exercises

1. Use mesh analysis to write a set of equations from which you can find I_1, the current through the 12Ω resistor. Do not solve the equations.

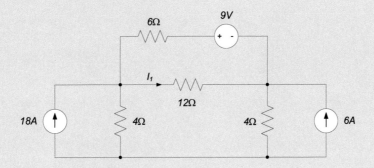

2. Use mesh analysis to find the current I flowing through the 10Ω resistor in the circuit below. Compare your result to your solution to exercise 2 of section 3.2.

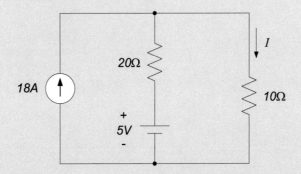

Solutions can be found at digilent.com/real-analog.

Chapter 4:
Systems and Network Theorems

In previous chapters, a number of approaches have been presented for analyzing electrical circuits. In these analysis approaches, we have been provided with a circuit consisting of a number of elements (resistors, power supplies, etc.) and determined some circuit variable of interest (a voltage or current, for example). In the process of determining this variable, we have written equations which allow us to determine <u>any and all</u> variables in the system. For a complex circuit, with many elements, this approach can result in a very large number of equations and a correspondingly large amount of effort expended in the solution of these equations. Unfortunately, much of the physical insight about the <u>overall</u> operation of the circuit may be lost in the detailed description of all of the individual circuit elements. This limitation becomes particularly serious when we attempt to <u>design</u> a circuit to perform some task.

In this chapter, we introduce the concept of a *systems level approach* to circuit analysis. In this type of approach, we represent the circuit as a *system* with some inputs and outputs. We then characterize the system by the mathematical relationship between the system inputs and the system outputs. This relationship is called the *input-output relation* for the system. This representation of a system leads to several network theorems whose use can simplify the analysis of these systems. The network theorems essentially allow us to model a portion of a complicated circuit as a much simpler (but equivalent) circuit. This simplified model can then be used to facilitate the design or analysis of the remainder of the circuit.

The above approach for representing circuits is particularly useful in circuit <u>design</u>; successful design approaches for large circuits typically use a *top-down strategy*. In this design approach, the overall system is broken down into a number of interconnected *subsystems*, each of which performs some specific task. This input-output relationships for these individual subsystems can be determined based on the task performed. The subsystems can then be designed to implement the desired input-output relation. An audio compact disc player, for example, will include subsystems to perform filtering, digital-to-analog conversion, and amplification processes. It is significantly easier to designate the subsystems based on their individual requirements than to attempt to design the entire system all at once. We will thus begin to think of the circuits we analyze as systems which perform some overall task, rather than as a collection of individual circuit elements.

After Completing this Chapter, You Should be Able to:

- Define signals and systems
- Represent systems in block diagram form
- Identify system inputs and outputs
- Write input-output equations for systems
- State the defining properties of linear systems
- Determine whether a system is linear
- State conditions under which superposition can be applied to circuit analysis
- Analyze electrical circuits using the principle of superposition
- Define the i-v characteristic for a circuit
- Represent a resistive circuit in terms of its i-v characteristic
- Represent a resistive circuit as a two-terminal network
- Determine Thévenin and Norton equivalent circuits for circuits containing power sources and resistors
- Relate Thévenin and Norton equivalent circuits to i-v characteristics of two-terminal networks
- Determine a load resistance which will maximize the power transfer from a circuit

4.1   Signals and Systems

In this section, we introduce basic concepts relative to systems-level descriptions of general physical systems. Later sections will address application of these concepts specifically to electrical circuits.

A system is commonly represented as shown in the block diagram of Fig. 4.1. The system has some input, $u(t)$, and some output, $y(t)$. In general, both the input and output can be functions of time; the case of constant values is a special case of a time-varying function. The output will be represented as some arbitrary function of the input:

$$y(t) = f\{u(t)\}$$

Eq. 4.1

Equation (4.1) is said to be the *input-output equation* governing the system. The above relationship has only one input and one output - the system is said to be a *single-input-single-output (SISO) system*. Systems can have multiple inputs and multiple outputs, in these cases there will be an input-output equation for each system output and each of these equations may be a function of several inputs. We will concern ourselves only with SISO systems for now.

Figure 4.1. Block diagram representation of a system.

Once important aspect of the systems-level approach represented by equation (4.1) and Fig. (4.1) is that we are representing our system as a "black box". We really have no idea what the system itself is, beyond a mathematical dependence of the output variable on the input variable. The physical system itself could be mechanical, thermal, electrical, or fluidic. In fact, it is fairly common to represent a mechanical system as an "equivalent" electrical system (or vice-versa), if doing so increases the physical insight into the system's operation.

The circuits we analyze can now be thought of as *systems* which perform some overall task, rather than as collections of individual circuit elements. We will also think of the inputs and outputs of the system as *signals*, rather than specific circuit parameters such as voltages or currents. This approach is somewhat more abstract than we are perhaps used to, so we will provide some additional discussion of what we mean by these terms.

Generally, most people think of a *system* as a group of interrelated "elements" which perform some task. This viewpoint, though intuitively correct, is not specific enough to be useful from an engineering standpoint. In these chapters, we will define a system as a collection of <u>elements which store and dissipate energy</u>. The system transfers the energy in the system inputs to the system outputs; the process of energy transfer is represented by the input-output equation for the system. Examples of the energy transfer can include mechanical systems (the kinetic energy resulting from using a force to accelerate a mass, or the potential energy resulting from using a force to compress a spring), thermal systems (applying heat to change a mass's temperature), and electrical systems (dissipating electrical power with the filament in a light bulb to produce light).

The task to be performed by the system of Fig. 4.1 is thus the transformation of some input *signal u(t)* into an output *signal y(t)*. Signals, for us, will be any waveform which can vary as a function of time. This is an extremely broad definition - examples of signals include:

- The force applied to mass.
- The velocity of the mass as it accelerates in response to the applied force.
- The current applied to a circuit by a power supply.
- The voltage difference across a resistor which is subjected to some current flow.
- The electrical power supplied to a heating element.
- The temperature of a mass which is being heated by an electric coil.

The transformation of the input signal to the output signal is performed by the input-output relation governing the system. The input-output relation can be a combination of algebraic, differential, and integral equations.

To provide some concrete examples of the above concepts, several examples of system-level representations of common processes are provided below.

Example 4.1: Mass Subjected to an External Force

Consider the mass-damper system shown in the figure below. The applied force *F(t)* pushes the mass to the right. The mass's velocity resulting from the applied force is *v(t)*. The mass slides on a surface with sliding coefficient of friction b, which induces a force $F_b = bv(t)$ which opposes the mass's motion. The mass is initially at rest and the applied force is zero for time before time *t=0*.

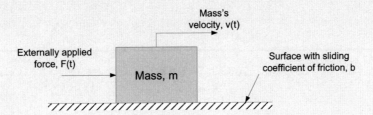

The governing equation for the system (obtained by drawing a free body diagram of the mass and applying $\sum F = ma$ is:

$$m\frac{dv(t)}{dt} + bv(t) = F(t)$$

The governing equation for the system is a first order differential equation. Knowledge of the externally applied force F(t) and the initial velocity of the mass allows us to determine the velocity of the mass at all subsequent times. Thus, we can model the system as having an input signal F(t) - which is known - and an output velocity v(t) which can be determined from the input signal and the properties of the system (the mass, *m*, and coefficient of fiction, *b*). The system can then be represented by the block diagram below:

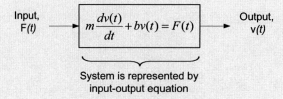

Input,
F(t) → $m \dfrac{dv(t)}{dt} + bv(t) = F(t)$ → Output, v(t)

System is represented by
input-output equation

(It is rather unusual to place the system governing equation directly in a block diagram; we do it here to illustrate a point.)

Example 4.2: Electrical Circuit

For the electrical circuit below, write the equations governing the input-output relationship for the circuit. The applied input to the circuit is the voltage source V_{in} and the output is the voltage V across the 2Ω resistor.

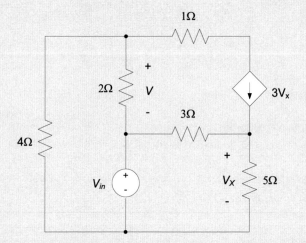

We previously wrote mesh equations for this circuit (for a specific value of V_{in}) in Chapter 3.2. We repeat these mesh equations here, along with our definitions of the mesh currents:

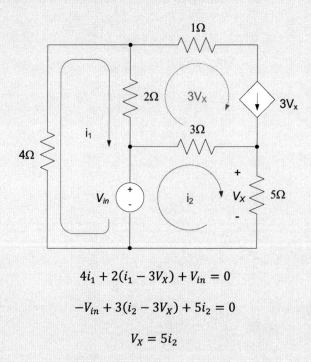

$$4i_1 + 2(i_1 - 3V_X) + V_{in} = 0$$

$$-V_{in} + 3(i_2 - 3V_X) + 5i_2 = 0$$

$$V_X = 5i_2$$

The output voltage *V* is related to the mesh currents by:

$$V = 2(i_1 - 3V_x)$$

The above four equations provide an input-output description of the circuit. If desired, they can be combined to eliminate all variables except V_{in} and V and re-written in the form V=f{V_{in}} per equation 4.1. <u>Note that all information about the original system, except the relationship between the input and output signals, is lost once we do this.</u>

The system-level block diagram for the circuit might then be drawn as:

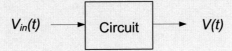

Example 4.3: Temperature Control System

Our final example is of a temperature control system. This example illustrates the representation of a complex system as a set of interacting subsystems.

A typical temperature control system for a building will have a thermostat which allows the occupants to set a desired temperature, a furnace (or air conditioner) which provides a means of adjusting the building's temperature, some way of measuring the actual building temperature, and a *controller* which decides whether to turn the furnace or air conditioner on or off, based on the difference between the desired and actual temperatures. The block diagram below provides one possible approach toward interconnecting these subsystems into an overall temperature control system. This block diagram can be used to identify individual subsystems, and provide specifications for the subsystems, which can allow the design to proceed efficiently. For example:

1. The temperature measurement system might be required to produce a voltage, which is a function of the temperature in the building. The thermistor-based temperature measurement systems we have designed and constructed in the lab are good examples of this type of system.
2. The controller might operate by comparing the desired temperature (generally represented by a voltage level) with the voltage indicating the actual temperature. For a heating system, if the actual temperature is lower than desired by some minimum amount, the controller will make a decision to switch the furnace on. Design decisions might be made to determine what minimum temperature difference is required to turn the furnace on, and whether to base the decision to turn on the furnace strictly upon a temperature difference or on a rate of change in temperature difference.
3. When the furnace turns on it will apply heat to the building, causing the building's temperature to increase. Once the building temperature is high enough, the controller will then typically turn the furnace back off. The furnace must be designed to provide appropriate heat input to the building, based on the building size and the anticipated heat losses to the building's surroundings. (For example, a larger building or a building in a colder climate will require a larger furnace.)
4. A model of the building's heat losses will generally be necessary in order to size the furnace correctly and choose an appropriate control scheme. Design choices for the building itself may include insulation requirements necessary to satisfy desired heating costs.

Designs for the above subsystems can now proceed somewhat independently, with proper coordination between the design activities.

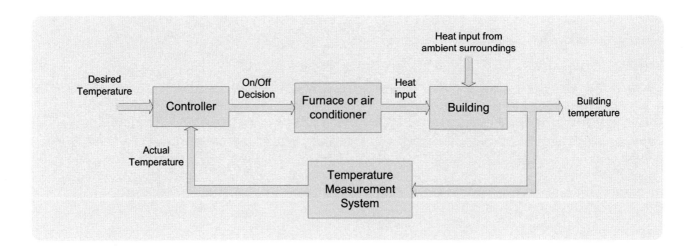

Section Summary

- *Systems* are a set of components which work together to perform some task. Systems are typically considered to have one or more inputs (which are provided to the system from the external environment) and one or more outputs (which the system provides to the environment).
- Generically, the inputs and outputs of systems are *signals*. Signals are simply time-varying functions. They can be voltages, currents, velocities, pressures, etc.
- Systems are often characterized by their *input-output equations*. The input-output equation for a system simply provides a mathematical relationship between the input to the system and the output from the system. Once the input is defined as a particular number or function of time, that value or function can be substituted into the input-output equation to determine the system's response to that input.

4.1 Exercises

1. The input to the circuit below is the current, *U*. The output is the current through the 10Ω resistor, *I*. Determine an input-output equation for the circuit.

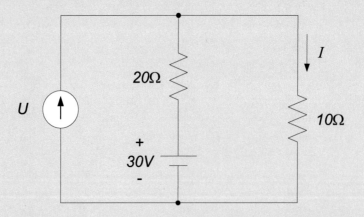

2. The input to the circuit is the voltage U. The output is the voltage V_1. Determine an input-output relation for the circuit.

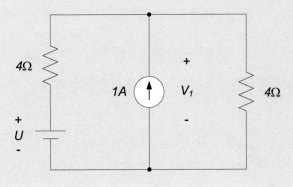

4.2 Linear Systems

We have so far introduced a number of approaches for analyzing electrical circuits, including: Kirchhoff's current law, Kirchhoff's voltage law, circuit reduction techniques, nodal analysis, and mesh analysis. When we have applied the above analysis methods, we have generally assumed that any circuit elements operate <u>linearly</u>. For example, we have used Ohm's law to model the voltage-current relationship for resistors. Ohm's law is applicable only for *linear* resistors - that is, for resistors whose voltage-current relationship is a straight line described by the equation v=Ri. Non-linear resistors have been mentioned briefly; in Lab Assignment 1, for example, we forced a resistor to dissipate an excessive amount of power, thereby causing the resistor to burn out and display nonlinear operating characteristics. <u>All circuit elements will display some degree of non-linearity, at least under extreme operating conditions.</u>

Unfortunately, the analysis of non-linear circuits is considerably more complicated than analysis of linear circuits. Additionally, in subsequent chapters we will introduce a number of analysis methods which are applicable <u>only</u> to linear circuits. The analysis of linear circuits is thus very pervasive - for example, designing linear circuits is <u>much</u> simpler than the design of non-linear circuits. For this reason, many non-linear circuits are assumed to operate linearly for design purposes; non-linear effects are accounted for subsequently during design validation and testing phases.

The concept of treating an electrical circuit as a *system* was introduced in section 4.1. In systems-level analysis of circuits, we are primarily interested in the relationship between the system's input and output *signals*. Circuits governed by nonlinear equations are considered to be *nonlinear systems*; circuits whose governing input-output relationship is linear are *linear systems*. In this chapter, we formally introduce the concept of linear systems. The analysis of linear systems is extremely common, for the reasons mentioned above: structural systems, fluid dynamic systems, and thermal systems are often analyzed as linear systems, even though the underlying processes are often inherently nonlinear. Linear *circuits* are a special case of linear systems; in which the system consists only of interconnected electrical circuit elements whose voltage-current relationships are linear.

Linear systems are described by linear relations between *dependent variables*. For example, the voltage-current characteristic of a linear resistor is provided by Ohm's law:

$$v = Ri$$

Where v is the voltage drop across the resistor, i is the current through the resistor, and R is the resistance of the resistor. Thus, the dependent variables – current and voltage – are linearly related. Likewise, the equations we have used to describe dependent sources (provided in section 1.2):

- Voltage controlled voltage source: $v_s = \mu v_1$
- Voltage controlled current source: $i_s = g v_1$
- Current controlled voltage source: $v_s = r i_1$
- Current controlled current source: $i_s = \beta i_1$

All describe linear relationships between the controlled and controlling variables.

All of the above relationships are of the form:

$$y(t) = Kx(t)$$

Eq. 4.2

Where x(t) and y(t) are voltages or currents in the above examples. More generally, x(t) and y(t) can be considered to be the *input* and *output signals*, respectively, of a linear *system*. Equation 4.2 is often represented in block diagram form as shown in Fig. 4.2.

Input,
x(t) → K → Output,
y(t) = Kx(t)

Figure 4.2. Linear system block diagram.

The output is sometimes called the *response* of the system to the input. The multiplicative factor K relating the input and output is often called the system's *gain*. Elements which are characterized by relationships of the form of equation 4.2 are sometimes called *linear elements*. The equation relating the system's input and output variables is called the *input-output relationship* of the system.

Aside: Many types of systems can be described by the relationship of equation (1). For example, Hooke's law, which relates the force applied to a spring to the spring's displacement, is:

$$F = k \cdot \Delta x$$

Where *k* is the spring constant, *F* is the applied force, and *Δx* is the resulting displacement as shown below. In this example, *F* is the input to the system and *Δx* is the system output.

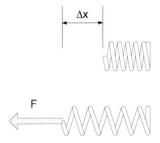

Notice that we have allowed the input and output of our system to vary as functions of time. Constant values are special cases of time-varying functions. We will assume that the system gain is <u>not</u> a time-varying quantity.

For our purposes, we will define linearity in somewhat more broad terms than equation (4.2). Specifically, we will define a system as linear if it satisfies the following requirements:

4.2.1 Linearity:

1. If the response of a system to some input $x_1(t)$ is $y_1(t)$ then the response of the system to some input $\alpha x_1(t)$ is $\alpha y_1(t)$, where α is some constant. This property is called homogeneity.
2. If the response of the same system to an input $x_2(t)$ is $y_2(t)$, then the response of the system to an input $x_1(t)+x_2(t)$ is $y_1(t)+y_2(t)$. This is called the additive property.

The above two properties defining a linear system can be combined into a single statement, as follows: if the response of a system to an input $x_1(t)$ is $y_1(t)$ and the system's response to an input $x_2(t)$ is $y_2(t)$, then the response of the system to an input $\alpha x_1(t)+\beta x_2(t)$ is $\alpha y_1(t)+\beta y_2(t)$. This property is illustrated by the block diagram of Fig. 4.3. The Sigma symbol in Fig. 4.3 denotes signal summation; the signs on the inputs to the summation block indicate the signs to be applied to the individual signals.

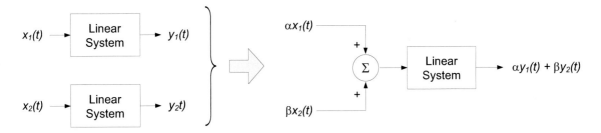

Figure 4.3. Block diagram representation of properties defining a linear system.

The above definition of linearity is more general than the expression of equation (4.2). For example, the processes of differentiation and integration are linear processes according to the above definition. Thus, systems with the input-output relations such as:

$$y = a \int a\,dt \qquad \text{and} \qquad y = b\frac{dx}{dt}$$

4.2.2 Dependent Variables and Linearity:

Linearity is based on the relationships between *dependent* variables, such as voltage and current. In order for a system to be linear, relationships between dependent variables must be linear – plots of one dependent variable against another are straight lines. This causes confusion among some readers when we begin to talk about *time varying* signals. Time is <u>not</u> a dependent variable, and plots of voltages or currents as a function of time for a linear system may <u>not</u> be straight lines.

Although the above definitions of linear systems are fundamental, we will not often use them directly. Kirchhoff's voltage law and Kirchhoff's current law rely upon summing multiples of voltages or currents. As long as the voltage-current relations for individual circuit elements are linear, application of KVL and KCL to the circuit will result in linear equations for the system. Therefore, rather than direct application of the above definitions of linear systems, we will simply claim that an electrical circuit containing only linear circuit elements will be linear and will have linear input-output relationships. All circuits we have analyzed so far have been linear.

4.2.3 Linearity:

If <u>all</u> elements in a circuit have linear voltage-current relationships, the overall circuit will be linear.

Important Note About Power:

A circuit's power is *not a linear* property, even if the voltage-current relations for all circuit elements are linear. Resistors which obey Ohm's law dissipate power according to $P = iv = \dfrac{v^2}{R} = i^2R$. Thus, the power dissipation of a linear resistor is not a linear combination of voltages or currents – the relationship between voltage or current and power is quadratic. Thus, if power is considered directly in the analysis of a linear circuit, the resulting system is nonlinear.

Section Summary

- *Linear systems* are characterized by linear relationships between dependent variables in the system. For electrical system, this typically means that the relationship between voltage and current for any circuit component is linear – in electrical circuits, for example, this means that a plot of voltage vs. current for every element in the system is a straight line. Ohm's law, for example, describes a linear voltage-current relationship.
- Linear systems have a very important property: the *additive principle* applies to them. Superposition essentially means that the response of a system to some combination of inputs $x_1 + x_2$ will be the same as the sum of the response to the individual inputs x_1 and x_2.

4.2   Exercises

1. The 20Ω resistor below obeys Ohm's law, so that $V=20I$. We will consider the input to be the current through the resistor and the output to be the voltage drop across the resistor. Determine:
   - The output V if the input $I = 2A$
   - The output V if the input $I = 3A$
   - The output V is the input $I = 2A + 3A = 5A$

   Do your answers above indicate that the additive property holds for this resistor? Why?

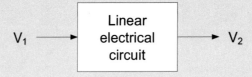

2. A linear electrical circuit has an input voltage V_1 and provides an output voltage V_2, as indicated in the block diagram below. If an input voltage $V_1=3V$ is applied to the circuit, the measured output voltage $V_2=2V$. What is the output voltage if an input voltage $V_1=6V$ is applied to the circuit?

$$V_1 \longrightarrow \boxed{\begin{array}{c}\text{Linear} \\ \text{electrical} \\ \text{circuit}\end{array}} \longrightarrow V_2$$

4.3   Superposition

In section 4.2, we stated that, by definition, the input-output relations for linear systems have an additive property. The additive property of linear systems states that:

- If the response of a system to an input $x_1(t)$ is $y_1(t)$ and the response of the system to an input $x_2(t)$ is $y_2(t)$, then the response of the system to an input $x_1(t)+x_2(t)$ is $y_1(t)+y_2(t)$.

Thus, if a system has multiple inputs, we can analyze the system's response to each input individually and then obtain the overall response by summing the individual contributions. This property can be useful in the analysis of circuits which have multiple sources. If we consider the sources in a circuit to be the inputs, linear circuits with multiple independent sources can be analyzed by determining the circuit's response to each source individually, and then summing, or *superimposing*, the contributions from each source to obtain the overall response of the circuit to all sources. In general, the approach is to analyze a complicated circuit with multiple sources by determining the responses of a number of simpler circuits – each of which contains only a single source.

We illustrate the overall approach graphically by the block diagram of Figure 4.4 (which is really just a reversed form of the block diagram of Figure 4.3).

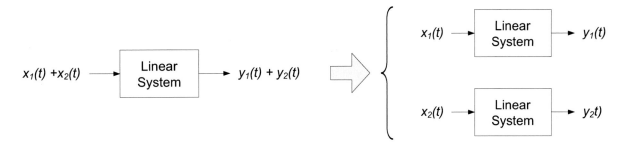

Figure 4.4. Additive property of linear systems.

In Figure 4.4, we have a linear system with two input signals which are applied by sources in the circuit. We can analyze this circuit by noting that each input signal corresponds to an <u>independent source</u> in the circuit. Thus, if the circuit's overall response to a source $x_1(t)$ is $y_1(t)$ and the circuit's response to a source $x_2(t)$ is $y_2(t)$, then the total circuit response will be the sum of the two individual responses, $y_1(t)+y_2(t)$. Thus, if we wish to determine the response of the circuit to both sources, $x_1(t)$ and $x_2(t)$, we can determine the individual responses of the circuit, $y_1(t)$ and $y_2(t)$ and then sum (or *superimpose*) the responses to obtain the circuit's overall response to both inputs. This analysis method is called *superposition*.

In order to determine a circuit's response to a single source, all other <u>independent</u> sources must be *turned off* (or, in more colorful terminology, *killed*, or made *dead*). To turn off a current source, we must make the input current zero, which corresponds to an open circuit. To turn off a voltage source, we must make the input voltage zero, which corresponds to a short circuit.

Killing Sources:

- To kill a voltage source, replace it with a short circuit
- To kill a current source, replace it with an open circuit

To apply the superposition method, then, the circuit's response to <u>each</u> source in the circuit is determined, with all other sources in the circuit dead. The individual responses are then algebraically summed to determine the total response to all inputs. To illustrate the method, we consider the examples below.

Example 4.4

Determine the voltage, V, in the circuit below, using superposition.

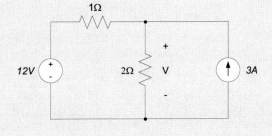

The circuit above can be considered to be the superposition of the two circuits shown below, each with a single source (the other source, in both cases, has been killed).

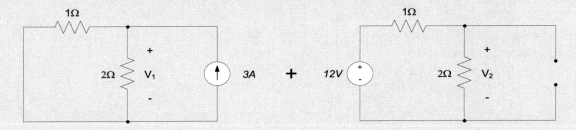

The voltage V_1 above can be determined to be the result of a current division: $V_1 = \left[\frac{1\Omega}{1\Omega+2\Omega} \cdot 3A\right] \times 2\Omega = 2V$.

V_2 can be determined to be the result of a voltage division: $V_1 = 12V \cdot \frac{2\Omega}{2\Omega+1\Omega} = 8V$. Thus, the voltage: $V = V_1 + V_2 = 10V$.

Example 4.5

Determine the voltage, V, in the circuit below, using superposition.

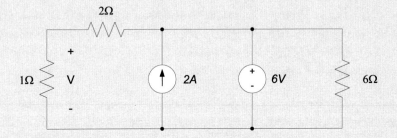

We begin by determining the response V_1 to the 6V source by killing the 2A source, as shown in the figure below.

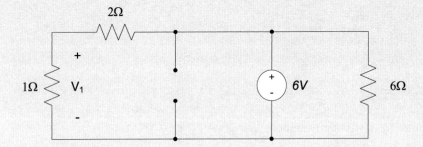

The voltage V_1 is simply the result of a voltage division: $V_1 = \frac{1}{3} \cdot 6V = 2V$. The response V_2 to the 2A source can be determined by killing the 6V source, resulting in the circuit below:

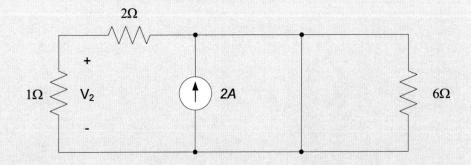

Killing the 6V source places a short circuit in parallel with the 2A source, so no voltage is induced in any of the resistors by the 2A source. Thus, $V_2 = 0V$.

The voltage V is the sum of the two individual voltages: $V = V_1 + V_2 = 2V + 0V = 2V$.

Notes on Superposition:

1. <u>Superposition cannot be used directly to determine power</u>. Previously, we noted that power is not governed by a linear relationship. Thus, you <u>cannot</u> determine the power dissipated by a resistor by determining the power dissipation due to each source and then summing the results. You can, however, use superposition to determine the <u>total</u> voltage or current for the resistor and then calculate the power from that voltage and/or current.
2. When using superposition to analyze circuits with dependent sources, <u>do not kill the dependent sources</u>. You must include the effects of the dependent sources in response to each independent source.
3. Superposition is a powerful circuit analysis tool, but its application <u>can</u> result in additional work. Before applying superposition, examine the circuit carefully to ensure that an alternate analysis approach is not more efficient. Circuits with dependent sources, in particular, tend to be difficult to analyze using superposition

Section Summary

- Superposition is a defining property of linear systems. It essentially means that, for linear systems, we can decompose any input to the system into a number of components, determine the system output resulting from each component of the input, and obtain the overall output by summing up these individual components of the output.
- Superposition can be used directly to analyze circuits which contain multiple independent sources. The responses of the circuit to each source (killing all other sources) are determined individually. The overall response of the circuit – due to all sources – is then obtained by summing (superimposing) these individual contributions.
- The principle of superposition is a fundamental property of linear systems and has very broad-ranging consequences. We will be invoking it throughout the remainder of this textbook, often without overtly stating that superposition is being used. The fact that superposition applies to linear circuits is the basic reason why engineers make every possible attempt to use linear models when analyzing and designing systems.

4.3   Exercises

1. Use superposition to determine the voltage V_1 in the circuit below.

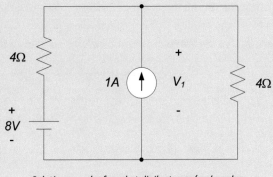

Solutions can be found at digilent.com/real-analog.

4.4   Two-terminal Networks

As noted in section 4.1, it is often desirable, especially during the design process, to isolate different portions of a complex system and treat them as individual subsystems. These isolated subsystems can then be designed or analyzed somewhat independently of one another and subsequently integrated into the overall system in a top-down design approach. In systems composed of electrical circuits, the subsystems can often be represented as *two-terminal networks*. As the name implies, two-terminal networks consist of a pair of terminals; the voltage potential across the terminals and the current flow into the terminals characterizes the network. This approach is consistent with our systems-level approach; we can characterize the behavior of what may be an extremely complex circuit by a relatively simple input-output relationship.

We already have some experience with two-terminal networks; when we determined equivalent resistances for series and parallel resistor combinations, we treated the resistive network as a two-terminal network. For analysis purposes, the network was then replaced with a single equivalent resistance which was indistinguishable from the original circuit by any external circuitry attached to the network terminals. In this chapter, we will formalize some two-terminal concepts and generalize our approach to include networks which contain both sources and resistors.

We will assume that the electrical circuit of interest can be subdivided into two sub-circuits, interconnected at two terminals, as shown in Fig. 4.5. Our goal is to replace circuit A in our overall system with a simpler circuit which is indistinguishable by circuit B from the original circuit. That is, if we disconnect circuit A from circuit B at the terminals and replace circuit A with its equivalent circuit, the voltage v and the current i seen at the terminals of the circuits will be unchanged and circuit B's operation will be unaffected. In order to make this substitution, we will need to use the principle of superposition in our analysis of circuit A – thus, circuit A must be a linear circuit. We are not changing circuit B in any way – circuit B can be either linear or nonlinear.

It should be emphasized that circuit A is not being physically changed. We are making the change conceptually in order to simplify our analysis of the overall system. For example, the design of circuit B can now proceed with a simplified model of circuit A's operation, perhaps before the detailed design of circuit A is even finalized. When the designs of the two circuits are complete, they can be integrated and the overall system has a high probability of functioning as expected.

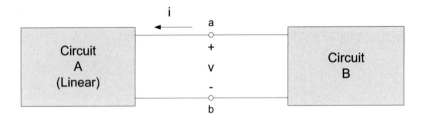

Figure 4.5. Circuit composed of two, two-terminal sub-circuits.

In order to perform the above analysis, we will disconnect the two sub-circuits in Fig. 4.5 at the terminals a – b and determine the current-voltage relationship at the terminals of circuit A. We will generally refer to circuit A's current-voltage relationship as its *i-v characteristic*. Our approach, therefore, is to look at circuit A alone, as shown in Fig. 4.6, and determine the functional relationship between a voltage applied to the terminals and the resulting current. (Equivalently, we could consider that a current is applied at the terminals and look at the resulting voltage.) Figure 4.6 is at first glance somewhat misleading – the terminals should not be considered to be open-circuited, as a cursory look at the figure might indicate; we are determining the relationship between a voltage difference applied to the circuit and the resulting current flow. (Figure 4.6 indicates a current I flowing into the circuit, which will, in general, not be zero.)

System-level Interpretation

When we determine the *i-v* characteristic for the circuit, we are determining the input-output relationship for a system. Either the voltage or the current at the terminals can be viewed as the input to a system; the other parameter is the output. The *i-v* characteristic then provides the output of the system as a function of the input.

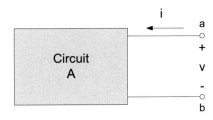

Figure 4.6. Two-terminal representation of circuit.

4.4.1 Resistive Networks

We have already (somewhat informally) treated purely resistive circuits as two-terminal networks when we determined equivalent resistances for series and parallel resistors. We will briefly review these concepts here in a systems context in terms of a simple example.

Example 4.6

Determine the i-v characteristic for the circuit below.

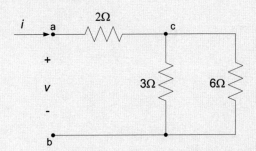

Previously, we would use circuit reduction techniques to solve this problem. The equivalent resistance is $R_{eq} = 2\Omega + \frac{(3\Omega)\cdot(6\Omega)}{3\Omega+6\Omega} = 4\Omega$. Since $v = R_{eq}i$, the circuit's *i-v* characteristic is $v = 4i$.

We would now, however, like to approach this problem in a slightly more general way and using a systems-level view to the problem. Therefore, we will choose the terminal voltage, *v*, to be viewed as the input to the circuit. By default, this means the current *i* will be our circuit's output. (We could, just as easily define the current as the input, in which case the voltage would become our output.) Thus, our circuit conceptually looks like a system as shown in the block diagram below.

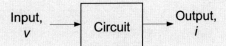

Applying KCL to node c in the above circuit results in $i = \frac{v_c}{6\Omega} + \frac{v_c}{3\Omega}$. Ohm's law, applied to the 2Ω resistor, results in $v - v_c = 2\Omega \cdot i$. Eliminating v_c from the above two equations results in $v = 4i$, which is the same result we obtained using circuit reduction. The i-v characteristic for the above circuit is shown graphically below; the slope of the line is simply the equivalent resistance of the network.

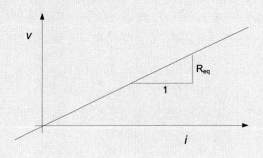

In the above example, viewing the circuit as a general two-terminal network and using a more general systems-level approach to the problem results in additional work relative to using our previous circuit reduction approach. Viewing the circuit as a more general two-terminal network is, however, very profitable if circuit reduction techniques are not applicable or if we allow the circuit to contain voltage or current sources. The latter topic is addressed in the following subsection.

4.4.2 Two-terminal Networks with Sources

When the network consists of resistive elements and independent sources, the circuit's i-v characteristic can be represented as a single equivalent resistance and a single source-like term. In general, however, we cannot determine this directly by using circuit reduction techniques. The overall approach and typical results are illustrated in the following examples.

Example 4.7

Determine the i-v characteristic of the circuit below.

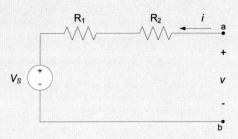

Although it is fairly apparent, by applying Ohm's law across the series combination of resistors, that $v = (R_1 + R_2)i + V_S$, we will (for practice) use superposition to approach this problem. The voltage source V_S will, of course, be one source in the circuit. We will use the voltage across the terminals a-b as a second source in the circuit.

Killing the voltage source V_S results in the circuit to the left below; the resulting current is $i_1 = \dfrac{v}{R_1 + R_2}$. Killing the "source" v results in the circuit to the right below; the resulting current is $i_2 = -\dfrac{V_S}{R_1 + R_2}$. The total current is, therefore, $i = \dfrac{v}{R_1 + R_2} - \dfrac{V_S}{R_1 + R_2}$ or $v = (R_1 + R_2)i + V_S$.

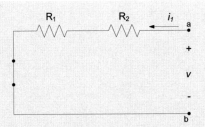
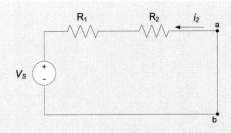

Plotting the above *i-v* characteristic results in the figure below.

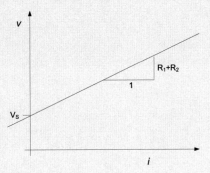

Example 4.8

Determine the i-v characteristic of the circuit below.

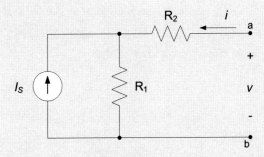

Although not the most efficient approach for this problem, we will again use superposition to approach the problem. One source will, of course, be the current source I_S. We will assume that our second source is the current i at node a. Killing the current source I_S results in the circuit to the left below; from this figure the voltage v_1 can be seen to be $v_1=i(R_1+R_2)$. Killing the current source i results in the figure to the right below; from this figure the voltage v_2 is seen to be $v_2=R_1I_S$ (the dead current source results in an open circuit, so no current flows through the resistor R_2). The total voltage across the terminals is, therefore, $v=(R_1+R_2)i+R_1I_S$.

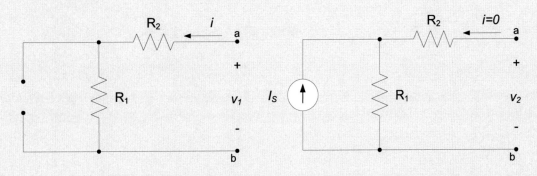

The i-v characteristic for the circuit is, therefore, as shown in the figure below.

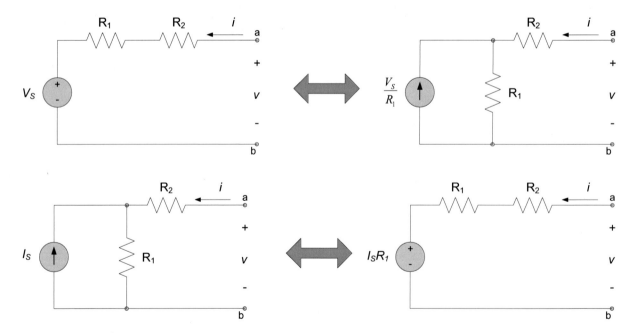

Notes on Linear Circuit i-v Characteristics:

1. All two-terminal networks which contain only sources and resistors will have i-v relationships of the form shown in examples 4.6, 4.7, and 4.8. That is, they will be straight lines of the form $v=m \cdot i+b$. The y-intercept term, b, is due to sources in the network; if there are no sources in the network, $b=0$ and the i-v characteristic will pass through the origin.

2. Due to the form of the i-v characteristic provided in note 1 above, any two-terminal network can be represented as a single source and a single resistor.

3. The form of the solution for examples 4.7 and 4.8 are the same. Thus, the circuit of example 4.7 is indistinguishable from a similar circuit with a current source $\frac{V_S}{R_1}$ in parallel with the resistor R_1. Likewise, the circuit of example 4.8 is indistinguishable from a similar circuit with a voltage source I_SR_1 in series with the resistor R_1. The equivalent circuits are shown below.

Section Summary

- Electrical circuits, sub-circuits, and components are often modeled by the relationship between voltage and current at their terminals. For example, we are familiar with modeling resistors by Ohm's law, which simply relates the voltage to the current at the resistor terminals. In Chapter 2, we used circuit reduction methods to extend this concept by replacing resistive networks with equivalent resistances which provided the same voltage-current relations across their terminals. In this section, we continue to extend this concept to circuits which include sources.

- For linear circuits, the voltage-current relationship across two terminals of the circuit can always be represented as a straight line of the form $v = m \cdot i + b$. If we plot this relationship with voltage on the vertical axis and current on the horizontal axis, the slope of the line corresponds to an equivalent resistance seen across the terminals, while the y-intercept of the line is the voltage across the terminals, if the terminals are open-circuited. We will formalize this important result in section 4.5.

4.4   Exercises

1. Determine the i-v characteristics of the circuit below, as seen at the terminals a-b.

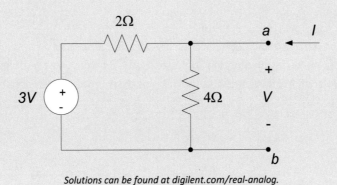

Solutions can be found at digilent.com/real-analog.

4.5   Thévenin's and Norton's Theorems

In section 4.4, we saw that it is possible to characterize a circuit consisting of sources and resistors by the voltage-current (or *i-v*) characteristic seen at a pair of terminals of the circuit. When we do this, we have essentially simplified our description of the circuit from a detailed model of the internal circuit parameters to a simpler model which describes the overall behavior of the circuit as seen at the terminals of the circuit. This simpler model can then be used to simplify the analysis and/or design of the overall system.

In this section, we will formalize the above result as *Thévenin's* and *Norton's theorems*. Using these theorems, we will be able to represent any linear circuit with an equivalent circuit consisting of a single resistor and a source. Thévenin's theorem replaces the linear circuit with a voltage source in series with a resistor, while Norton's theorem replaces the linear circuit with a current source in parallel with a resistor. In this section, we will apply Thévenin's and Norton's theorems only to purely resistive networks. However, these theorems can be used to represent any circuit made up of linear elements.

Consider the two interconnected circuits shown in Figure 4.7 below. The circuits are interconnected at the two terminals a and b, as shown. Our goal is to replace circuit A in the system of Figure 4.7 with a simpler circuit which has the same current-voltage characteristic as circuit A. That is, if we replace circuit A with its simpler equivalent circuit, the operation of circuit B will be unaffected. We will make the following assumptions about the overall system:

- Circuit A is linear
- Circuit A has no dependent sources which are controlled by parameters within circuit B
- Circuit B has no dependent sources which are controlled by parameters within circuit A

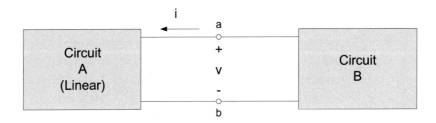

Figure 4.7. Interconnected two-terminal circuits.

In section 4.3, we determined i-v characteristics for several example two-terminal circuits, using the superposition principle. We will follow the same basic approach here, except for a general linear two-terminal circuit, in order to develop Thévenin's and Norton's theorems.

4.5.1 Thévenin's Theorem

First, we will kill all sources in circuit A and determine the voltage resulting from an applied current, as shown in Fig. 4.8 below. With the sources killed, circuit A will look strictly like an equivalent resistance to any external circuitry. This equivalent resistance is designated as R_{TH} in Fig. 4.8. The voltage resulting from an applied current, with circuit A dead is:

$$v_1 = R_{TH} \cdot i$$

Eq. 4.3

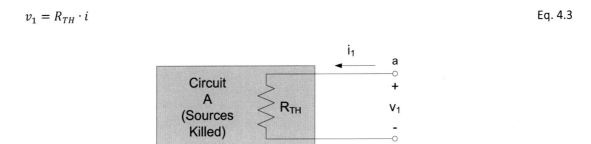

Figure 4.8. Circuit schematic with dead circuit.

Now we will determine the voltage resulting from re-activating circuit A's sources and open-circuiting terminals a and b. We open-circuit the terminals a-b here since we presented equation (4.3) as resulting from a current source, rather than a voltage source. The circuit being examined is as shown in Fig. 4.9. The voltage v_{OC} is the "open-circuit" voltage.

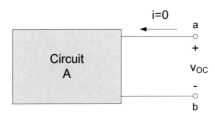

Figure 4.9. Open-circuit response.

Superimposing the two voltages above results in:

$$v = v_1 + v_{OC}$$

Eq. 4.4

Or

$$v = R_{TH} \cdot i + v_{OC}$$

Eq. 4.5

Equation (4.5) is Thévenin's theorem. It indicates that the voltage-current characteristic of any linear circuit (with the exception noted below) can be duplicated by an independent voltage source in series with a resistance R_{TH}, known as the *Thévenin resistance*. The voltage source has the magnitude v_{OC} and the resistance is R_{TH}, where v_{OC} is the voltage seen across the circuit's terminals if the terminals are open-circuited and R_{TH} is the equivalent resistance of the circuit seen from the two terminals, with all independent sources in the circuit killed. The equivalent Thévenin circuit is shown in Fig. 4.10.

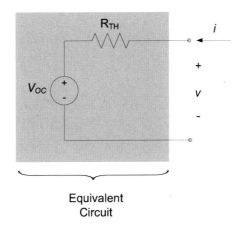

Figure 4.10. Thévenin equivalent circuit.

Procedure for Determining Thévenin Equivalent Circuit

1. Identify the circuit and terminals for which the Thévenin equivalent circuit is desired.
2. Kill the independent sources (do nothing to any dependent sources) in circuit and determine the equivalent resistance R_{TH} of the circuit. If there are no dependent sources, R_{TH} is simply the equivalent resistance of the resulting resistive network. Otherwise, one can apply an independent current source at the terminals and determine the resulting voltage across the terminals; the voltage-to-current ratio is R_{TH}.
3. Re-activate the sources and determine the open-circuit voltage V_{OC} across the circuit terminals. Use any analysis approach you choose to determine the open-circuit voltage.

Example 4.9

Determine the Thévenin equivalent of the circuit below, as seen by the load, R_L.

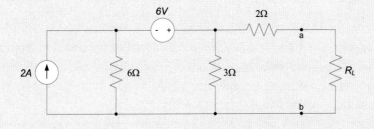

We want to create a Thévenin equivalent circuit of the circuit to the left of the terminals a-b. The load resistor, R_L, takes the place of "circuit B" in Fig. 4.7. The circuit has no dependent sources, so we kill the independent sources and determine the equivalent resistance seen by the load. The resulting circuit is shown below.

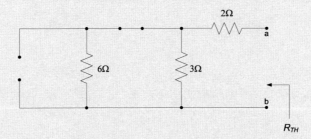

From the above figure, it can be seen that the Thévenin resistance R_{TH} is a parallel combination of a 3Ω resistor and a 6Ω resistor, in series with a 2Ω resistor. Thus, $R_{TH} = \frac{(6\Omega)(3\Omega)}{6\Omega+3\Omega} + 2\Omega = 4\Omega$.

The open-circuit voltage v_{OC} is determined from the circuit below. We (arbitrarily) choose nodal analysis to determine the open-circuit voltage. There is one independent voltage in the circuit; it is labeled as v_0 in the circuit below. Since there is no current through the 2Ω resistor, $v_{OC}=v_0$.

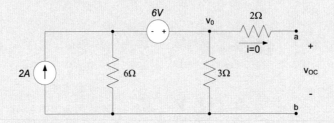

Applying KCL at v_0, we obtain: $-2A + \frac{v_0-6V}{6\Omega} + \frac{v_0}{3\Omega} = 0 \Rightarrow v_0 = v_{OC} = 6V$. Thus, the Thévenin equivalent circuit is on the left below. Re-introducing the load resistance, as shown on the right below, allows us to easily analyze the overall circuit.

4.5.2 Norton's Theorem

The approach toward generating Norton's theorem is almost identical to the development of Thévenin's theorem, except that we apply superposition slightly differently. In Thévenin's theorem, we looked at the voltage response to an input current; to develop Norton's theorem, we look at the current response to an applied voltage. The procedure is provided below.

Once again, we kill all sources in circuit A, as shown in Fig. 4.8 above but this time we determine the current resulting from an applied voltage. With the sources killed, circuit A still looks like an equivalent resistance to any external circuitry. This equivalent resistance is designated as R_{TH} in Fig. 4.8. The current resulting from an applied voltage, with circuit A dead is:

$$i_1 = \frac{v}{R_{TH}}$$

Eq. 4.6

Notice that equation (4.6) can be obtained by rearranging equation (4.3).

Now we will determine the current resulting from re-activating circuit A's sources and short-circuiting terminals a and b. We short-circuit the terminals a-b here since we presented equation (4.4) as resulting from a voltage source. The circuit being examined is as shown in Fig. 4.11. The current i_{sc} is the "short-circuit" current. It is typical to assume that under short-circuit conditions the short-circuit current enters the node at a; this is consistent with an assumption that circuit A is generating power under short-circuit conditions.

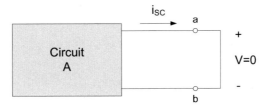

Figure 4.11. Short-circuit response.

Employing superposition, the current into the circuit is (notice the negative sign on the short-circuit current, resulting from the definition of the direction of the short-circuit current opposite to the direction of the current i).

$$i = i_1 - i_{SC}$$

Eq. 4.7

So

$$i = \frac{v}{R_{TH}} - i_{SC}$$

Eq. 4.8

Equation (4.8) is Norton's theorem. It indicates that the voltage-current characteristic of any linear circuit (with the exception noted below) can be duplicated by an independent current source in parallel with a resistance. The current source has the magnitude i_{sc} and the resistance is R_{TH}, where i_{sc} is the current seen at the circuit's terminals if the terminals are short-circuited and R_{TH} is the equivalent resistance of the circuit seen from the two terminals, with all independent sources in the circuit killed. The equivalent Norton circuit is shown in Fig. 4.12.

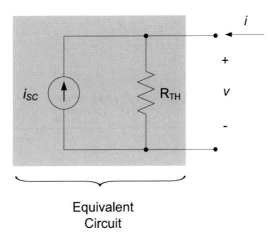

Equivalent
Circuit

Figure 4.12. Norton equivalent circuit.

Procedure for Determining Norton Equivalent Circuit:

1. Identify the circuit and terminals for which the Norton equivalent circuit is desired.
2. Determine the equivalent resistance R_{TH} of the circuit. The approach for determining R_{TH} is the same for Norton circuits as Thévenin circuits.
3. Re-activate the sources and determine the short-circuit current i_{sc} across the circuit terminals. Use any analysis approach you choose to determine the short-circuit current.

Example 4.10

Determine the Norton equivalent of the circuit seen by the load, R_L, in the circuit below.

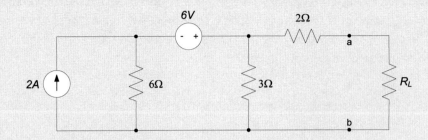

This is the same circuit as our previous example. The Thévenin resistance, R_{TH}, is thus the same as calculated previously: $R_{TH}=4\Omega$. Removing the load resistance and placing a short-circuit between the nodes a and b, as shown below, allows us to calculate the short-circuit current, i_{SC}.

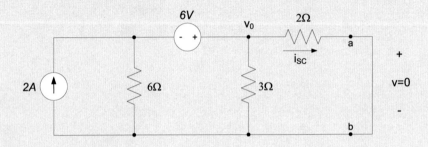

Performing KCL at the node v_0, results in:

$$\frac{v_0}{2\Omega} + \frac{v_0 - 6V}{6\Omega} + \frac{v_0}{3\Omega} = 2A$$

So

$$v_0 = 3V$$

Ohm's law can then be used to determine i_{SC}:

$$i_{SC} = \frac{3V}{2\Omega} = 1.5A$$

And the Norton equivalent circuit is shown on the left below. Replacing the load resistance in the equivalent overall circuit is shown to the right below.

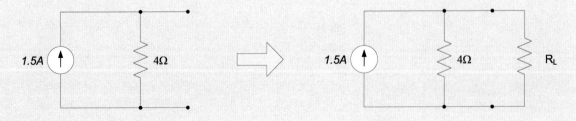

Exceptions:

Not all circuits have Thévenin and Norton equivalent circuits. Exceptions are:

1. An ideal current source does not have a Thévenin equivalent circuit. (It cannot be represented as a voltage source in series with a resistance.) It is, however, its own Norton equivalent circuit.

2. An ideal voltage source does not have a Norton equivalent circuit. (It cannot be represented as a current source in parallel with a resistance.) It is, however, its own Thévenin equivalent circuit.

4.5.3 Source Transformations

Circuit analysis can sometimes be simplified by the use of *source transformations*. Source transformations are performed by noting that Thévenin's and Norton's theorems provide two different circuits which provide essentially the same terminal characteristics. Thus, we can write a voltage source which is in series with a resistance as a current source in parallel with the same resistance, and vice-versa. This is done as follows.

Equations (4.5) and (4.8) are both representations of the *i-v* characteristic of the same circuit. Rearranging equation (4.5) to solve for the current *i* results in:

$$i = \frac{v}{R_{TH}} - \frac{v_{OC}}{R_{TH}}$$

Eq. 4.9

Equating equations (4.8) and (4.9) leads to the conclusion that:

$$i_{SC} = \frac{v_{OC}}{R_{TH}}$$

Eq. 4.10

Likewise, rearranging equation (4.8) to obtain an expression for *v* gives:

$$v = i \cdot R_{TH} + i_{SC} \cdot R_{TH}$$

Eq. 4.11

Equating equations (4.11) and (4.5) results in:

$$V_{OC} = i_{SC} \cdot R_{TH}$$

Eq. 4.12

Which is the same result as equation (4.10).

Equations (4.10) and (4.12) lead us to the conclusion that any circuit consisting of a voltage source in series with a resistor can be transformed into a current source in parallel with the same resistance. Likewise, a current source in parallel with a resistance can be transformed into a voltage source in series with the same resistance. The values of the transformed sources must be scaled by the resistance value according to equations (4.10) and (4.12). The transformations are depicted in Fig. 4.13.

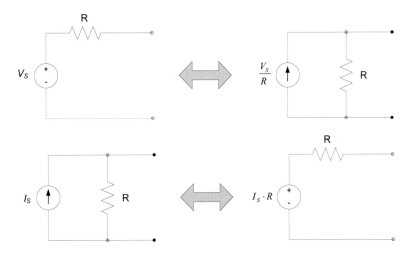

Figure 4.13. Source transformations.

Source transformations can simplify the analysis of some circuits significantly, especially circuits which consist of series and parallel combinations of resistors and independent sources. An example is provided below.

Example 4.11

Determine the current i in the circuit shown below.

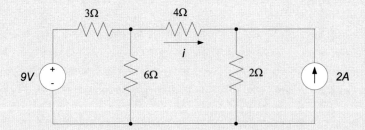

We can use a source transformation to replace the 9V source and 3Ω resistor series combination with a 3A source in parallel with a 3Ω resistor. Likewise, the 2A source and 2Ω resistor parallel combination can be replaced with a 4V source in series with a 2Ω resistor. After these transformations have been made, the parallel resistors can be combined as shown in the figure below.

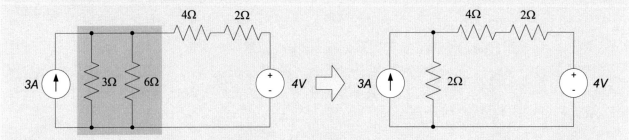

The 3A source and 2Ω resistor parallel combination can be combined to a 6V source in series with a 2Ω resistor, as shown below.

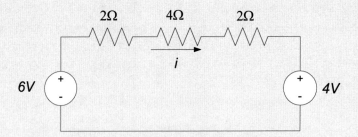

The current i can now be determined by direct application of Ohm's law to the three series resistors, so that $i = \frac{6V-4V}{2\Omega+4\Omega+2\Omega} = 0.25A$.

4.5.4 Voltage-current Characteristics of Thévenin and Norton Circuits

Previously, in section 4.4, we noted that the i-v characteristics of linear two-terminal networks containing only sources and resistors are straight lines. We now look at the voltage-current characteristics in terms of Thévenin and Norton equivalent circuits.

Equations (4.5) and (4.8) both provide a linear voltage-current characteristic as shown in Fig. 4.14. When the current into the circuit is zero (open-circuited conditions), the voltage across the terminals is the open-circuit voltage, v_{OC}. This is consistent with equation (4.5), evaluated at $i=0$:

$$v = R_{TH} \cdot i_{OC} + v_{OC} = R_{TH} \cdot 0 + v_{OC} = v_{OC}$$

Likewise, under short-circuited conditions, the voltage differential across the terminals is zero and equation (4.8) readily provides:

$$i = \frac{v_{SC}}{R_{TH}} - i_{SC} = \frac{0}{R_{TH}} - i_{SC} = -i_{SC}$$

Which is consistent with Fig. 4.14.

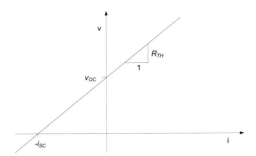

Figure 4.14. Voltage-current characteristic for Thévenin and Norton equivalent circuits.

Figure 4.14 is also consistent with equations (4.10) and (4.12) above, since graphically the slope of the line is $R_{TH} = \frac{v_{OC}}{i_{SC}}$.

Figure 4.14 also indicates that there are three simple ways to create Thévenin and Norton equivalent circuits:

1. Determine R_{TH} and v_{OC}. This provides the slope and y-intercept of the i-v characteristic. This approach is outlined above as the method for creating a Thévenin equivalent circuit.
2. Determine R_{TH} and i_{SC}. This provides the slope and x-intercept of the i-v characteristic. This approach is outlined above as the method for creating a Norton equivalent circuit.
3. Determine v_{OC} and i_{SC}. The equivalent resistance R_{TH} can then be calculated from $R_{TH} = \frac{v_{OC}}{i_{SC}}$ to determine the slope of the i-v characteristic. Either a Thévenin or Norton equivalent circuit can then be created. This approach is not commonly used, since determining R_{TH} – the equivalent resistance of the circuit – is usually easier than determining either v_{OC} or i_{SC}.

Note: It should be emphasized that the Thévenin and Norton circuits are not independent entities. One can always be determined from the other via a source transformation. Thévenin and Norton circuits are simply two different ways of expressing the same voltage-current characteristic.

Section Summary

- Thévenin's theorem allows us to replace any linear portion of a circuit with equivalent circuit consisting of a <u>voltage source in series with a resistance</u>. This circuit is called the Thévenin equivalent, and provides the same voltage-current relationship at the terminals as the original circuit. The voltage source in the equivalent circuit is the same as the voltage which would be measured across the terminals of the original circuit, if those terminals were open-circuited. The resistance in the equivalent circuit is called the Thévenin resistance, it is the resistance that would be seen across the terminals of the original circuit, if all sources in the circuit were killed.
- Norton's theorem allows us to replace any linear portion of a circuit with equivalent circuit consisting of a <u>current source in parallel with a resistance</u>. This circuit is called the Norton equivalent, and provides the same voltage-current relationship at the terminals as the original circuit. The current source in the equivalent circuit is the same as the current which would be measured across the terminals of the original circuit, if those terminals were short-circuited. The resistance in the equivalent circuit is the resistance

that would be seen across the terminals of the original circuit, if all sources in the circuit were killed; it is the same as the Thévenin resistance.

- Thevenin and Norton's theorems allow us to perform *source transformations* when analyzing circuits. This approach simply allows us to replace any voltage source which is in series with a resistance with a current source in parallel with the same resistance, and vice-versa. The relationship between the voltage and current sources used in these transformations are provided in equations (4.10) and (4.12).

4.5 Exercises

1. Replace everything except the 1A current source with its Thévenin equivalent circuit and use the result to find V_1.

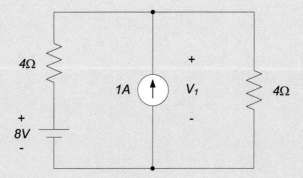

2. Replace everything except the 1A current source with its Norton equivalent circuit and use the result to find V_1.

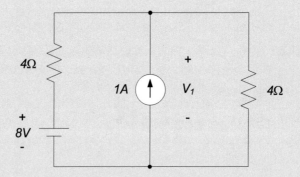

3. Determine a Norton equivalent circuit for the circuit below.

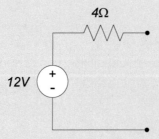

Solutions can be found at digilent.com/real-analog.

4.6 Maximum Power Transfer

It is often important for our electrical system to transfer as much power as possible to some related system. For example, in an audio system it is important that the amplifier transfer as much power as possible to the loudspeakers. Otherwise, the amplifier generates power which is not used for any productive purpose[1] and the efficiency of the overall system suffers.

In this section, we will develop design guidelines which will ensure that the maximum possible amount of power is transferred from our electrical circuit to the load that the circuit is driving. These guidelines will be based on Thevenin's theorem.

Consider the system shown in Fig. 4.15. The overall system consists of an electrical circuit which is being used to drive a load. Physically, the load can be either another electrical system or some electromechanical system such as an electric motor or a loudspeaker. We will model the load as an electrical resistance, R_L, though the principles presented here are applicable to more general loading conditions.

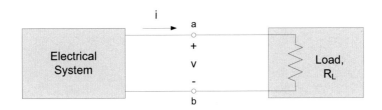

Figure 4.15. General electrical network – load combination.

We will replace our electrical system with its Thevenin equivalent in order to analyze the power delivered by the circuit to the load. The overall circuit that we are analyzing is now modeled as shown in Fig. 4.16.

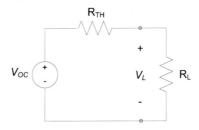

Figure 4.16. Electric circuit – load combination. Electric circuit modeled by its Thevenin equivalent.

From Fig. 4.16, the voltage delivered to the load can be readily determined from a voltage divider relation:

$$V_L = V_{OC} \frac{R_L}{R_L + R_{TH}}$$

Eq. 4.13

Thus, the power delivered to the load is:

$$P_L = \frac{V_L^2}{R_L} = \frac{V_{OC}^2}{R_L} \left(\frac{R_L}{R_L + R_{TH}} \right)^2$$

Eq. 4.14

Figure 4.17 shows a plot of the power delivered to the load, as a function of the load resistance. The power delivered to the load is zero when the load resistance is zero (since there is no voltage drop across the load under this condition) and goes to zero as the load resistance approaches infinity (since there is no current provided to the

---

[1] Other than, perhaps, heating the room it is in.

load under this condition). At some value of R_L the power transfer will be maximized – our goal will be to determine the value for R_L which maximizes the power delivered to the load.

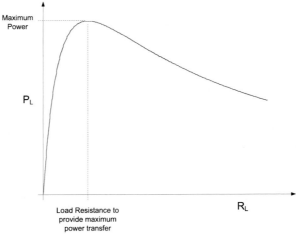

Figure 4.17. Delivered power vs. load resistance.

The maximum value of power on the curve shown in Fig. 4.17 can be determined by differentiating equation (4.14) with respect to the load resistance R_L and setting the result to zero. This leads to:

$$\frac{\partial P_L}{\partial P_L} = V_{OC}^2 \left[\frac{(R_L + R_{TH})^2 - 2R_L(R_{TH} + R_L)}{(R_L + R_{TH})^2} \right] = 0$$

Eq. 4.15

The above condition is satisfied if the numerator of equation (4.15) is zero, so our condition becomes:

$$(R_L + R_{TH})^2 = 2R_L(R_{TH} + R_L)$$

Dividing both sides by $R_{TH} + R_L$ results in:

$$R_L + R_{TH} = 2R_L$$

Or

$$R_L = R_{TH}$$

Eq. 4.16

Thus, maximum power transfer takes place when the load resistance and the Thevenin resistance of the circuit supplying the power are equal. The above result is sometimes called the *maximum power transfer theorem*. When the conditions of the maximum power transfer theorem are met, the total power delivered to the load is:

$$P_L = \frac{\left(\frac{V_{OC}}{2}\right)^2}{R_{TH}} = \frac{V_{OC}^2}{4R_{TH}}$$

Eq. 4.17

This is one half of the total power generated by the circuit, half the power is absorbed in the resistance R_{TH}.

Conclusion: The power delivered to the load is maximized if the load resistance is equal to the Thevenin resistance of the circuit supplying the power. When this condition is met, the circuit and the load are said to be matched. When the load and the circuit are matched, 50% of the power generated in the circuit can be delivered to the load – under any other circumstances, a smaller percentage of the generated power will be provided to the load.

4.6.1 Practical Power Supplies

Practical power supplies were discussed in section 2.4. It was seen that the presence of an internal resistance in a voltage or current source limited the power that could be delivered to a circuit connected to the source. Practical power supplies are a special case of the results presented above; we use them below as examples of the application of the above principles.

In section 2.4, practical voltage sources were modeled as an ideal voltage source V_S in series with some internal resistance R_S, as shown in Fig. 4.18. This corresponds exactly to a Thevenin circuit with $V_{OC}=V_S$ and $R_{TH}=R_S$. The practical voltage source provides maximum power to a circuit connected to it when the input resistance of the circuit (the equivalent resistance of the circuit, seen at the terminals to which the power source is connected) is equal to the internal resistance of the voltage source. Under these circumstances, the power delivered to the circuit is:

$$P = \frac{V_S^2}{4R_S}$$

The same amount of power is converted to heat within the power supply; this is the reason many power supplies contain a fan to actively disperse this heat to the atmosphere. If the circuit's input resistance is not equal to the source resistance, less power is transmitted to the circuit and a correspondingly greater amount is dissipated within the power supply.

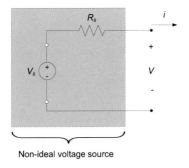

Figure 4.18. Practical voltage source model.

Practical current sources were modeled in section 2.4 as an ideal current source I_S in parallel with some internal resistance R_S, as shown in Fig. 4.19. This corresponds directly to a Norton equivalent circuit with $I_{SC}=I_S$ and $R_{TH}=R_S$. The current source provides maximum power to a circuit connected to it when the input resistance of the circuit is equal to the internal resistance of the source. A source transformation in conjunction with equation (5) indicates that the power delivered to the circuit by the current source is:

$$P = \frac{R_S I_S^2}{4}$$

Again, a reduced percentage of the power generated by the source will be delivered to the circuit when the circuit and source are not well matched.

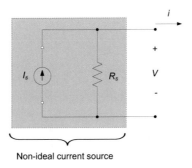

Figure 4.19. Non-ideal current source model.

Often, it may not be feasible to match the load with the power supply. For example, when we are testing circuits in our lab assignments we do not generally attempt to maximize the power delivered to the circuit – this is typical when prototype circuits are being tested. One simply recognizes that excessive power is being dissipated within the power supply and that the overall system is not functioning efficiently. If, however, the power supply and associated circuit are being designed as part of an integrated overall system one will generally attempt to match the power supply to the rest of the system.

One problem which can occur during circuit testing is that extremely poorly matched power supply-load combinations may result in so much power being dissipated within the power supply that insufficient power is available to drive the load. This can result in the load apparently behaving abnormally, <u>unless</u> power delivery effects are considered.

Section Summary

- The maximum power that a circuit can deliver to a load resistor occurs when the load resistance is equal to the Thévenin equivalent resistance of the circuit.

4.6 Exercises

1. Determine the resistance R which will absorb the maximum power from the 7V source.

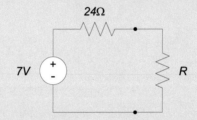

Solutions can be found at digilent.com/real-analog.

Chapter 5:
Operational Amplifiers

Operational amplifiers (commonly abbreviated as *op-amps*) are extremely useful electronic devices. Some argue, in fact, that operational amplifiers are the single most useful integrated circuit in analog circuit design. Operational amplifier-based circuits are commonly used for *signal conditioning*, performing *mathematical operations*, and *buffering*. These topics are discussed briefly below.

Signal conditioning is the process of manipulating a given signal (such as a voltage) to improve its properties or usefulness. Examples of common signal conditioning processes are:

- <u>Level adjustment</u>: the overall level of a signal may be too small to be usable. For example, the voltage output from a thermocouple (an electrical component used to measure temperature) may be only a few thousandths of a volt. It is often desirable to *amplify* the signal to increase the output voltage – this is often done using circuits containing operational amplifiers.
- <u>Noise reduction</u>: electrical signals are susceptible to noise; an undesirable component of a signal. (For example, static on a radio signal.) Operational amplifier circuits can be used to remove or filter out undesirable components of a voltage signal.
- <u>Signal manipulation</u>: Electrical signals are often used to transmit information. For example, the voltage output of a thermocouple changes as the temperature of the thermocouple changes. The sensitivity of the thermocouple output to temperature changes may be changed by an operational amplifier circuit to provide a more readily usable output voltage-to-temperature relationship.

A common use of electrical circuits is to perform <u>mathematical operations</u>. So far, we have focused on developing mathematical models of existing circuits – we have been performing <u>analysis</u> tasks. The <u>design</u> process, conversely, can be considered to consist of implementing an electrical circuit that will perform a desired mathematical operation. (Of course, a large part of the design process consists of determining what mathematical operation is to be performed by the circuit.) Operational amplifier circuits are readily developed to perform a wide range of mathematical operations, including addition, subtraction, multiplication, differentiation, and integration.

Buffers allow us to electrically isolate one section of an electrical circuit from another. For example, using an electrical circuit to supply power to a second electrical circuit may result in undesirable loading effects, in which the power requirements of the second circuit exceed the power that the first circuit can provide. In this case, a buffer can be used to isolate the two circuits and thus simplifying design problems associated with integrating the two circuits. Operational amplifier circuits are commonly used for this purpose.

Operational amplifiers (or *op-amps*) are active devices. This differs from *passive* devices, such as resistors, in that an external power source must be provided to the operational amplifier in order to make it function properly. Op-amps are rather complex devices, consisting of a number of interconnected transistors and resistors. We will not be interested at this point in a detailed description of the internal operation of operational amplifiers – instead, we will use an op-amp model which provides us with relatively simple input-output relations for the overall circuit. In fact, our op-amp model will most often take the form of a dependent source[1]. In their most basic form, operational amplifiers are most readily modeled as voltage-controlled voltage sources, but it can be used within other circuits to create devices which act as other types of dependent sources. This simplified model will be adequate for many analysis and design purposes.

The operational amplifier symbol which we will most often use is shown in Fig. 5.1. Operational amplifiers are essentially three-terminal devices (ignoring the power supply connections previously mentioned for the moment), having two input terminals and one output terminal. The inputs are called the inverting terminal (indicated by the – sign) and the non-inverting terminal (indicated by the + sign). We will use v_n and i_n to denote the voltage and current at the inverting terminal, and v_p and i_p to denote the voltage and current at the non-inverting terminal. The voltage and current at the output terminal are denoted as v_{OUT} and i_{OUT}. The voltages v_p, v_n, and v_{OUT} are all measured relative to some common reference voltage level, such as ground.

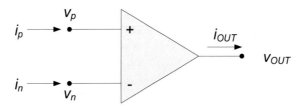

Figure 5.1. Operational amplifier symbol.

After Completing this Chapter, You Should be Able to:

- State ideal operational amplifier modeling rules
- State constraints on the operational amplifier output voltage
- Represent operational amplifiers as dependent voltage sources
- Be able to identify standard operational amplifier pin connections
- Analyze electrical circuits containing ideal operational amplifiers and resistors
- Sketch op-amp based circuits which perform the following operations:
    - Inverting voltage amplification
    - Non-inverting voltage amplification
    - Summation (addition)
    - Differencing (subtraction)
    - Buffering
- Describe the operation of a comparator

---

[1] Op-amp circuits will be our first exposure to physical devices which act as dependent sources.

- Briefly describe the effect of the following non-ideal op-amp parameters, relative to ideal op-amp performance:
  - Finite input resistance
  - Finite output resistance
  - Finite op-amp gain

5.1 Ideal Operational Amplifier Model

We will begin by summarizing the rules governing <u>ideal</u> operational amplifiers. In the following section, we will provide some background material relative to these rules and some additional criteria which the operational amplifier must satisfy. It should be emphasized that these rules govern ideal operational amplifiers; modeling of non-ideal operational amplifiers will most likely be presented in later electronics courses.

Ideal Op-amp Modeling Rules

1. No current flows into the input terminals: $i_n = i_p = 0$
2. The voltages at the input terminals are the same: $v_n = v_p$ (when sufficient negative feedback is applied).

<u>No requirements are placed on the output voltage and current</u>. One may <u>not</u> conclude that $i_{OUT} = 0$ simply because the input currents are zero. It may appear, from the input-output relations governing the op-amp, that the op-amp violates Kirchhoff's current law – this is because we are not examining the details of the internal operation of the op-amp. Since the op-amp is an active device with its own power supply, it can provide an output current with no input current. <u>Operational amplifiers, unlike passive devices, are capable of adding power to a signal</u>. The presence of the external power supplies raises some additional constraints relative to op-amp operation; we address these issues next.

A more complete schematic symbol for an operational amplifier, including the op-amp's external power supplies, is shown in Fig. 5.2. Figure 5.2 shows two additional op-amp terminals. One is connected to a voltage source V^+ and the other is connected to a voltage source V^-. These terminals are sometimes called the *positive* and *negative* *power supply terminals*. We must set the external voltage supplies so that the positive power supply voltage is greater than the negative power supply voltage: $V^+>V^-$. In our discussions, it will be assumed that the power supply voltages are relative to the same reference voltage as all other voltages on the schematic.

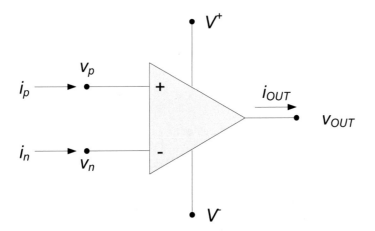

Figure 5.2. Operational amplifier schematic, including external power supplies.

The power supply voltages provide a constraint on the range of allowable output voltages, as provided below:

Output Voltage Constraint:

The output voltage is constrained to be between the positive and negative power supply voltages: $V^- < v_{OUT} < V^+$

The above constraint is based on pure inequalities – in general, the output voltage range will be somewhat less than the range specified by V- and V+. The margin between the output and the supply voltages will vary depending on the specific op-amp. Any attempt to drive the output voltage beyond the range specified by the supply voltages will cause the output to *saturate* at the appropriate supply voltage. Similarly, it makes sense that the power supply voltages will constrain the range of allowable input voltages, as provided below:

Input Voltage Constraint:

- The input voltages, v_p and v_n, are constrained to be between the positive and negative power supply voltages: $V^- < v_p, v_n < V^+$.

The above constraint is based on pure inequalities – in general, the input voltage range will be somewhat less than the range specified by V- and V+. The margin between the inputs and the supply voltages will vary depending on the specific op-amp. Any attempt to drive the input voltages beyond the range specified by the supply voltages will cause the op-amp to no longer operate as we describe in this simple ideal model.

It is important to keep in mind, when analyzing operational amplifier circuits, that all of the terminal voltages shown in Fig. 5.2 should be taken as having the same reference voltage[2]. Figure 5.3 provides an explicit illustration of what is implied by this statement.

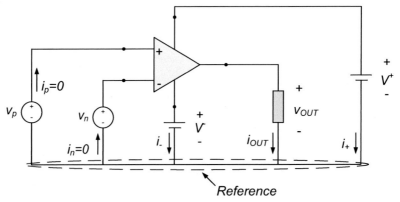

Figure 5.3. Op-amp voltages with reference node defined.

All voltages in Fig. 5.3, including the power supply voltages V+ and V−, have the same reference. It is clear from Fig. 5.3 that KCL at the reference node provides:

$$i_p + i_n = i_- + i_{OUT} + i_+ = 0$$

So that the positive and negative power supplies provide the current to the output. However, it is common to leave the power supply terminals off of the op-amp diagram (as in Fig. 5.1). If one interprets these types of diagrams literally, the figure corresponding to Fig. 5.3 will be as shown in Fig. 5.4.

---

[2] This can be difficult at times, since circuit schematics containing operational amplifiers often do not emphasize this point. It is common to assume that the person reading the schematic understands op-amp operation.

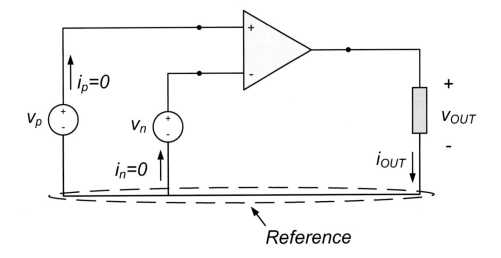

Figure 5.4. Op-amp voltages with reference node defined, but without supply voltages explicitly noted.

And it is tempting to infer that the current out of the op-amp must be zero. This is not true; it is a misconception based upon an attempt to literally interpret a somewhat incomplete schematic.

Section Summary

- The operational amplifier symbol is:

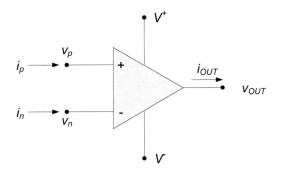

- The operation of ideal operational amplifiers follows the rules below:
    - No current flows into the input terminals: $i_n = i_p = 0$
    - The voltages at the input terminals are the same: $v_n = v_p$
    - The output voltage is constrained to be between the positive and negative power supply voltages: $V^- < v_{OUT} < V^+$
    - Nothing is known about the current out of the op-amp, i_{OUT}
- All voltages on the above diagram are relative to the same reference.

5.1 Exercises

1. The op-amp in the circuit with negative feedback below is ideal. Find:
   a. The current I_S
   b. The voltage V_p
   c. The voltage V_n

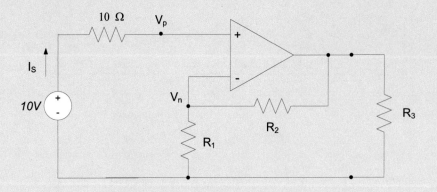

Solutions can be found at digilent.com/real-analog.

5.2 Operational Amplifier Model Background

The rules provided in section 5.1 governing our ideal operational amplifier model can be applied directly to operational amplifier circuits, but some background information will allow more insight into the basis for these rules. We will still treat the operational amplifier as a single circuit element with some input-output relationship, but our more complete description will model the op-amp as a dependent source. Certain assumptions relative to this dependent source allow us to recover the op-amp rules presented in section 5.2, but our more complete model will allow us to later introduce some basic non-ideal operational amplifier effects.

An operational amplifier operates as a differential amplifier with a very high gain. That is, the output of the amplifier is the <u>difference</u> between the input voltages, multiplied by a large <u>gain</u> factor, K. Figure 5.5 shows the operation of the op-amp, from a systems-level standpoint:

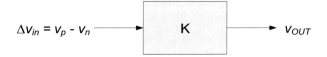

Figure 5.5. Block diagram of op-amp operation.

Thus, the input-output relation for an operational amplifier is:

$$V_{OUT} = K(v_p - v_n) = K \cdot \Delta v_{in}$$

Eq. 5.1

Where in Δv_{in} is the difference between the voltages at the input terminals and K is a very large number. (Values of K for typical commercially available operational amplifiers can be on the order of 10^6 or higher.) Since the output voltage is constrained to be less than the supply voltages,

$$V^- < K \cdot \Delta v_{in} < V^+$$

Chapter 5: Operational Amplifiers

So

$$\frac{V^-}{K} < \Delta v_{in} < \frac{V^+}{K}$$

Eq. 5.2

If the voltage supplies are finite and K is very large, the difference in the input voltages must be very small. Thus,

$$\Delta v_{in} \approx 0$$

And $\Delta v_p \approx \Delta v_{in}$. This is of course only true when $V^- < v_{OUT} < V^+$.

The second operational amplifier modeling rule is a result of the high input resistance of operational amplifiers. We assume that any difference in the input terminal voltages is due to the operational amplifier's input resistance, R_{in}, times the current at the input terminals. This is illustrated <u>conceptually</u> in Fig. 5.6.

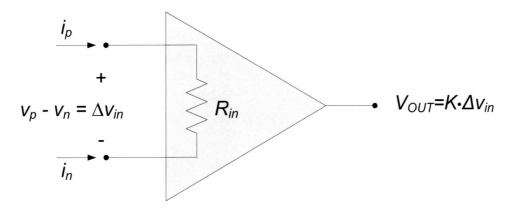

Figure 5.6. Operational amplifier symbol with "input resistance" indicated.

From Fig. 5.6, we see that the voltage difference between the input terminals can be considered to result from an input current passing through this input resistance.

$$v_p - v_n = R_{in} \cdot i_p$$

We will also assume that KCL applies across the input terminals of Fig. 5.6, so that:

$$i_p = -i_n$$

The above equations can be combined to give:

$$i_p = -i_n = \frac{v_p - v_n}{R_{in}}$$

Eq. 5.3

Since the input resistance of operational amplifiers is very large (commercial operational amplifiers have input resistances of several mega-ohms or higher) and the voltage difference across the input terminals is very small,

$$i_p = -i_n \approx 0$$

The above results suggest that an operational amplifier operates as a voltage-controlled-voltage source as shown in Fig. 5.7. Typically, commercially available operational amplifiers have very high gains, K, very high input resistances, R_{in}, and very low output resistances, R_{OUT}.

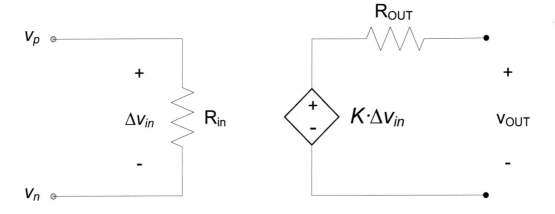

Figure 5.7. Equivalent circuit for operational amplifier model.

Combining the criteria provided by equations (5.1) and (5.2) results in the input-output relationship shown graphically in Fig. 5.8 below. The circuit operates linearly only when the output is between the supply voltages. When the output attempts to go outside this range, the circuit saturates and the output remains at the appropriate supply voltage. Notice that the negative supply voltage in Fig. 5.8 is indicated as a negative number; this is fairly typical, though not a requirement.

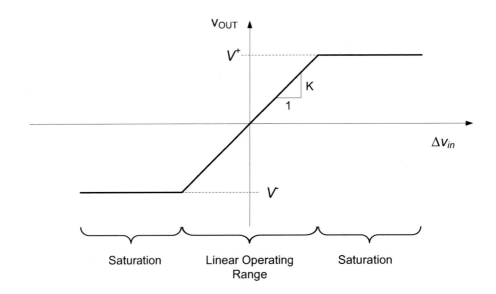

Figure 5.8. Op-amp input-output relationship.

Our ideal operational amplifier model rules are based on the above, more general, operational amplifier relationships. The assumptions relative to ideal operational amplifier operation, along with their associated conclusions, are provided below:

- The output voltage is bounded by the power supply voltages: $V^- < v_{OUT} < V^+$
- $K \to \infty$. This, in conjunction with equation (5.2) implies that $\Delta v_{in} = 0$ and $v_p = v_n$.
- $R_{in} \to \infty$. This, in conjunction with equation (5.3) implies that $i_p = -i_n = 0$.
- $R_{OUT} = 0$.

Section Summary

- A circuit modeling the behavior of an operational amplifier is:

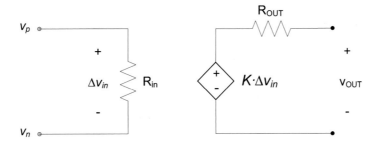

- For ideal operational amplifiers, the parameters in the circuit above are:
  - $K \to \infty$. This implies that $\Delta v_{in} = 0$ and $v_p = v_n$.
  - $R_{in} \to \infty$. This implies that $i_p = -i_n = 0$.
  - $R_{OUT} = 0$. This implies that the operational amplifier can provide infinite power as its output.
- In the operational amplifier model above, it is still assumed that $V^- < v_{OUT} < V^+$.

5.2 Exercises

1. An operational amplifier has a gain K = 10,000. The voltage supplies are $V+= 20V$ and $V-= -10V$. Determine the output voltage if the voltage difference between the input terminals $(v_p - v_n)$ is:
   a. 1mV
   b. 2mV
   c. 4mV
   d. -0.2mV
   e. -2mV

Solutions can be found at digilent.com/real-analog.

5.3 Commercially Available Operational Amplifiers

Operational amplifiers are available commercially as integrated circuits (ICs). They are generally implemented as *dual in-line packages (DIPs)*, so called because the terminals (pins) on the package are in pairs and line-up with one another. A typical DIP is shown in Fig. 5.9. The pins on DIPs are numbered; in order to correctly connect the DIP, pin 1 must be correctly oriented. Pin 1 is commonly located by looking for a notch at one end of the IC – pin 1 will be to the immediate left of this notch, if you are looking at the IC from the top. Alternate methods of indicating pin 1 are also used: sometimes the corner of the IC nearest pin 1 is shaved off or a small indentation or dot is located at the corner of the IC nearest pin 1.

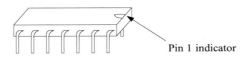

Figure 5.9. Dual in-line transistor package.

One common op-amp device is the 741 op-amp. The 741 is an eight-lead DIP; a top view of the package, with the leads labeled, is shown in Fig. 5.10. Key features of the package are as follows:

- Orientation of the pins is determined by the location of a semicircular notch on the package, as shown in Fig. 5.10. (Recall that Fig. 5.10 is a top view of the device.) Alternately, some packages place a circular indentation near pin 1 in order to provide the orientation of the pins.
- Inverting and non-inverting inputs are pins 2 and 3, respectively in Fig. 5.10
- The output terminal is pin 6 on the package.
- The positive and negative power supplies are labeled as $V_{CC}+$ and $V_{CC}-$ in Fig. 5.10. They are pins 7 and 4, respectively. $V_{CC}+$ should be less than +15 volts and $V_{CC}-$ should be more than -15 volts. A larger range of power supply voltages may destroy the device.
- The pins labeled OFFSET NULL 1, OFFSET NULL 2, and NC (pins 1, 5, and 8) will not be used for this class. The offset null pins are used to improve the op-amp's performance. The NC pin is never used. (NC stands for "not connected").

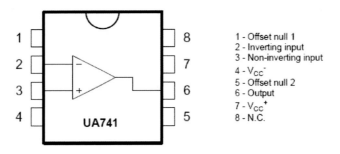

Figure 5.10. 741-type operational amplifier pin connections.

Most commercially available operational amplifiers will conform to a relatively standard pin connection layout. However, there will tend to be variations to one extent or another. For example, pin connections for an OP27 operational amplifier are shown in Fig. 5.11(a). Some operational amplifier chips will also contain more than one operational amplifier on the chip. For example, Fig. 5.11(b) provides pin connections for an OP282 package, in which two operational amplifiers are included. (A chip with two operational amplifiers is commonly called a "dual package". Chips with four operational amplifiers are also common; they are often called "quad packages".) In Fig. 5.11, V+ and V- are the positive and negative power supplies, respectively. (Both operational amplifiers on the OP282 chip share the same power supplies.) +IN and −IN are the positive and negative input terminals, and OUT is the output terminal. In the OP27 amplifier, the VOS TRIM terminals perform the same purpose as the Offset Null pins on the 741-type operational amplifier. The OP282 chip contains two amplifiers, "A" and "B". In Fig. 5.11(b), the inputs and outputs for the two amplifiers are identified as being associated with the "A" or "B" amplifier by appending the appropriate letter.

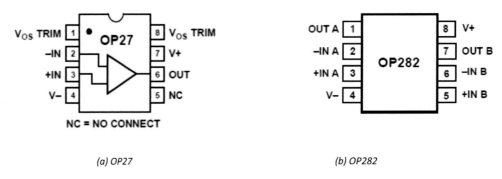

(a) OP27   (b) OP282

Figure 5.11. Additional operational amplifier pin connection examples.

Note: <u>Always</u> check the manufacturer's data sheet for the specific operational amplifier you are using. This can eliminate irritating and time-consuming errors when wiring your circuits!

5.3   Exercises:

1.   Go to the Analog Devices website, http://www.analog.com, and look up the pin connections for the OP482 operational amplifier package. Sketch the package and label the pin connections. Briefly describe your interpretation of the various pin connections.

Solutions can be found at digilent.com/real-analog.

5.4   Analysis of Op-amp Circuits

Operational amplifiers can be used as either linear or nonlinear circuit elements. When used as nonlinear circuit elements, the op-amp is deliberately operated so that the output voltage from the op-amp is driven to the power supply voltages. In this mode of operation, the output of the op-amp is said to be saturated and does not necessarily change as the input to the system changes. When the operational amplifier is used as a linear circuit element, the output is maintained within the range of the power supply voltages and the output voltage is a linear function of some input voltage or voltages.

In this chapter, we will be concerned with the use of operational amplifiers as linear circuit elements. When used in this mode, the overall circuit is generally constructed to provide *negative feedback* around the operational amplifier itself. When operated in a negative feedback mode, the output of the operational amplifier is connected to the <u>inverting</u> input terminal, generally through some other circuit elements. Negative feedback tends to make the overall circuit less sensitive to the specific value of the op-amp gain and reduces the likelihood of saturation at the op-amp output. We will not be concerned here with the details of why this is true, beyond noting that these devices will generally not operate linearly without feedback. (Later electronics courses will discuss why this is true.)

Nodal analysis is often the most efficient way to approach the analysis of an operational amplifier-based circuit. When applying nodal analysis to a circuit containing an ideal operational amplifier, the first step should be to apply the basic op-amp rules to the overall circuit. These were presented in the previous section, and are repeated here for convenience:

1.   The voltages at the input terminals of the operational amplifier are the same.
2.   The currents into the input terminals of the operational amplifier are zero.

It should be emphasized that application of rule 1 above does <u>not</u> imply that both of the op-amp input terminals can be treated as being part of the same node. <u>The op-amp input terminals should be treated as being two separate nodes, with the same voltage potential</u>. After applying the basic op-amp rules, it is generally appropriate to <u>apply Kirchhoff's current law at the input terminals of the operational amplifier</u>. Additional nodes in the circuit may necessitate application of KCL at other points, but the above approach is generally an extremely good starting point.

Important Tip: Applying KCL at the output node of an operational amplifier is often not productive. Since no information is available about the current out of an operational amplifier (due to the active nature of the device, as noted in the previous section), application of KCL at the output node generally provides an additional equation <u>at the expense of introducing an additional unknown</u>. Application of KCL at an op-amp output node is generally only productive if one must determine the current output of the op-amp.

When analyzing an operational amplifier as a linear circuit element, the external power supply voltages will generally be ignored. <u>We will assume that the output voltage is within the voltage range specified by the external power supplies.</u> If the output voltage is not within this range, the circuit will not behave linearly, and our analysis will be invalid. The final step of any analysis of an operational amplifier circuit is to determine whether the output voltage is within the external power supply voltage range; meeting this constraint often results on a constraint on the input voltages applied to the circuit.

Suggested Analysis Approach:

1. Apply ideal operational amplifier rules to circuit. (Voltage potentials at op-amp input terminals are the same; no current enters the op-amp input terminals.)
2. Apply KCL at op-amp input terminals.
3. Apply KCL at other circuit nodes, if necessary.
4. Check to ensure that output voltage remains within range specified by op-amp power supply voltages.

We illustrate the above analysis approach with several examples. The example circuits provided below illustrate the use of operational amplifier circuits to perform the mathematical operations of scaling (multiplication by a constant), addition, and subtraction. We also provide an example circuit which performs a buffering operation – this circuit can be useful for isolating different parts of a circuit from one another.

Example 5.1

Determine V_{OUT} as a function of V_{IN} for the circuit shown below.

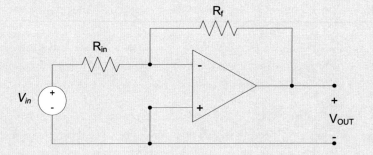

Choosing the non-inverting terminal voltage as our reference voltage and applying the ideal operational amplifier rules allows us to label the voltages and currents shown in red below.

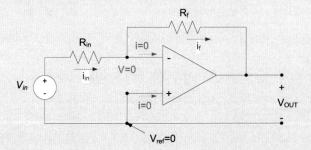

Applying KCL at the non-inverting input terminal provides no new information (we know the current and voltage at the non-inverting input). Applying KCL at the <u>inverting input terminal</u> results in:

$$i_{in} = i_f$$

Using Ohm's law to write these currents in terms of node voltages and taking advantage of the fact that the voltage at the inverting terminal of the op-amp is zero (because there is no voltage difference across the input terminals of the op-amp and we have chosen the non-inverting terminal voltage as our reference) results in:

$$\frac{V_{in} - 0}{R_{in}} = \frac{0 - V_{OUT}}{R_f}$$

Solving for V_{OUT} results in:

$$V_{OUT} = -\left(\frac{R_f}{R_{in}}\right) V_{in}$$

Comments:

- This circuit is called an *inverting voltage amplifier*. The output voltage is a scaled version of the input voltage, hence the term "voltage amplifier". The change in sign between the output and input voltage makes the amplifier "invert".
- The output voltage must be between the op-amp power supply voltages. Depending on the values of R_f and R_{in}, this sets limits on the magnitude of the input voltage to avoid saturation.

It is worthwhile at this point to make a few comments relative to some concepts presented sections 5.1 and 5.2, in the context of the op-amp circuit of Example 5.1.

- The input-output relationship governing the circuit of Example 5.1 can be represented conceptually as a dependent source-based circuit. The input-output relationship for the circuit, as determined in Example 5.1, is:

$$V_{OUT} = -\left(\frac{R_f}{R_{in}}\right) V_{in}$$

While the current provided by the source to the circuit is:

$$i_{in} = \frac{V_{in} - 0}{R_{in}}$$

These two relationships are satisfied by the voltage controlled voltage source (VCVS) shown in Fig. 5.12 below. The input resistance of this circuit is the resistance R_{in}; the input resistance governs the relationship between the voltage applied by the source and the source current necessary to maintain that voltage. Thus, increasing R_{in} reduces the power which the source must provide to maintain the output voltage V_{OUT}.

Note: The input resistance of the circuit of Example 5.1 is <u>not</u> the same as the input resistance of the operational amplifier itself, as shown in Figs. 5.6 and 5.7.

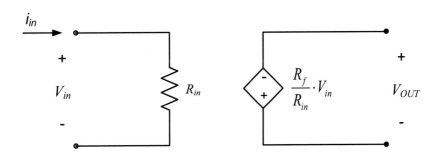

Figure 5.12. VCVS to model circuit of Example 5.1.

- The representation given in Fig. 5.12 of the circuit of Example 5.1 is not unique. For example, the current controlled voltage source (CCVS) model shown in Fig. 5.13 is also a valid model for the circuit.

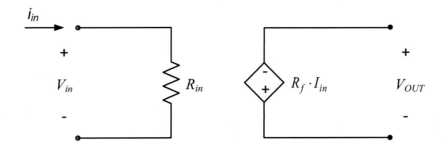

Figure 5.13. CCVS model for circuit of Example 5.1.

- The circuit of Example 5.1 has an open-circuit at the op-amp output terminal. Thus, no current is provided to the output. However, this does not imply that the current at the output terminal of the op- amp is zero! KCL at the op-amp output terminal indicates that the current through the feedback resistor goes into the op-amp output terminal, where (from our diagram) it seems to disappear! Recall, however, from our discussion in section 5.1 (Fig. 5.3 in particular) that this current will pass through the supply voltages and then to the reference node. <u>The supply voltages and their associated path to the reference node are not shown on the circuit diagram in Example 5.1, but they do exist.</u>
- If we apply a load resistor R_L to the output terminal of the operational amplifier in Exercise 5.1, we obtain the circuit shown in Fig. 5.14. The analysis of the circuit proceeds exactly as in Exercise 5.1, and we again obtain:

$$V_{OUT} = -\left(\frac{R_f}{R_{in}}\right)V_{in}$$

This result does not depend on the current through the load, i_L! This is because we made no assumptions relative to the current out of the operational amplifier output; the operational amplifier adjusts its output current as necessary to provide the current required to maintain the output voltage as in the above expression.

Note: Our ideal operational amplifier will draw power from the supply voltages to provide whatever output current is necessary to satisfy the rules governing operational amplifier provided in section 5.1. Real operational amplifiers, of course, have current limitations. We will discuss these limitations in section 5.6.

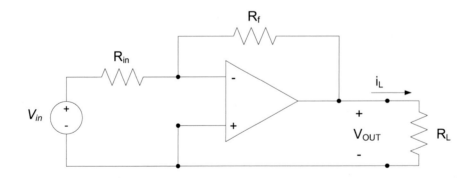

Figure 5.14. Inverting voltage amplifier with load resistor.

Example 5.2

Determine V_{OUT} as a function of V_{IN} for the circuit shown below.

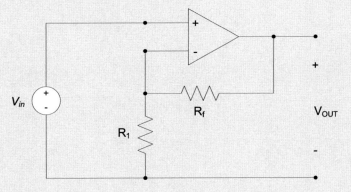

Choosing our reference voltage at the negative terminal of both V_{in} and V_{OUT} and applying the ideal operational amplifier rules allows us to label the voltages and currents shown in red below. (Note that since the input voltage sets the voltage of the non-inverting op-amp terminal, it also indirectly sets the voltage at the inverting terminal of the op-amp.)

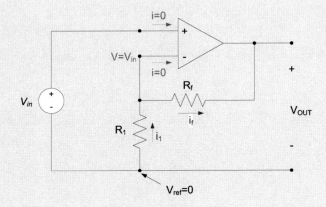

Applying KCL at the inverting terminal of the op-amp results in $i_1 = i_f$. Using Ohm's law to write these in terms of voltages provides:

$$\frac{0 - V_{in}}{R_1} = \frac{V_{in} - V_{OUT}}{R_f}$$

Solving this for V_{OUT} gives $V_{OUT} = \left(1 + \frac{R_f}{R_{in}}\right) V_{in}$

Comments:

- The output voltage can be expressed as a gain (a multiplicative factor) times the input voltage; the circuit is a "voltage amplifier". Since there is no sign change between the input and output voltage, the circuit is a *non-inverting voltage amplifier*.
- The output voltage must be between the op-amp power supply voltages. Depending on the values of R_f and R_1, this sets limits on the magnitude of the input voltage to avoid saturation.

Example 5.3

Determine V_{OUT} as a function of V_1 and V_2 for the circuit shown below.

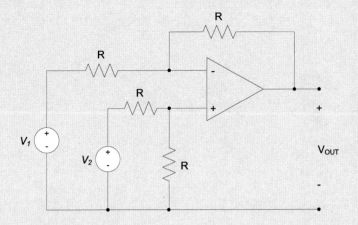

Denoting the non-inverting terminal of the op-amp as node a and the inverting terminal as node b, and applying the ideal op-amp rules results in the figure below:

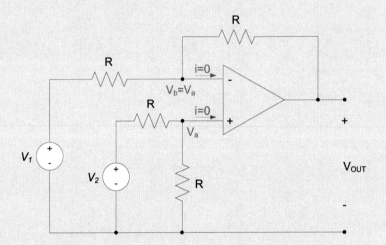

The voltage V_a can be determined from a voltage divider relation (or by applying KCL at node a) as $V_a = \frac{V_2}{2}$.

Thus, the voltage at the inverting terminal is $V_b = V_a = \frac{V_2}{2}$. Applying KCL at node b results in:

$$\frac{V_1 - V_b}{R} = \frac{V_b - V_{OUT}}{R} \Rightarrow \frac{V_1 - \frac{V_2}{2}}{R} = \frac{\frac{V_2}{2} - V_{OUT}}{R}$$

Simplification of the above results in $V_{OUT} = V_2 - V_1$.

Comments:

- The above circuit performs a subtraction operation. The voltage V_1 is subtracted from the voltage V_2.
- The inverting and non-inverting terminals of the op-amp are treated as separate nodes in this analysis, even though the op-amp constrains the voltages at these nodes to be the same. Thus, we apply KCL at <u>each</u> input terminal of the op-amp.

Example 5.4

Determine V_{OUT} as a function of V_1 and V_2 for the circuit shown below.

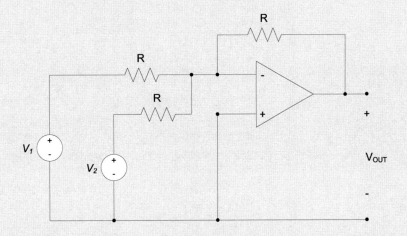

Choosing the non-inverting terminal voltage as our reference voltage and applying the ideal operational amplifier rules allows us to label the voltages and currents shown in red below:

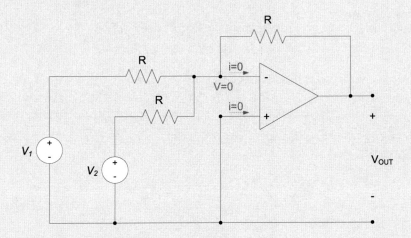

Applying KCL at the inverting terminal of the op-amp results in:

$$\frac{V_1 - 0}{R} + \frac{V_2 - 0}{R} = \frac{0 - V_{OUT}}{R}$$

Or

$$V_{OUT} = -(V_1 + V_2)$$

Comments:

- The circuit inverts the sum of the inputs. One can use an inverting amplifier with a gain of one in conjunction with the above circuit to obtain a non-inverted sum of the inputs.
- An arbitrary number of inputs can be summed, by simply increasing the number of input signals and resistors applied at the inverting terminal of the op-amp, which is often referred to as the "summing node".

Example 5.5

Determine V_OUT as a function of V_IN for the circuit shown below.

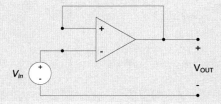

Since there is no circuit element in the feedback loop, the inverting terminal voltage is identical to the output voltage, V_{OUT}. The ideal op-amp rules require that the inverting and non-inverting terminal voltages are the same, so:

$$V_{OUT} = V_{in}$$

The circuit is called a *voltage follower*, since the output voltage simply "follows" the input voltage. This circuit, though it appears to do nothing, is actually extremely useful. Since the input voltage is applied directly to an op-amp input terminal, the input resistance to the circuit is infinite and no current is drawn from the source. Thus, the source provides no power in order to generate the output voltage - all power provided to the load comes from the op-amp power supplies. This can be extremely useful in isolating different portions of a circuit from one another.

Consider, as an example, the following case. We have a loading circuit with an equivalent resistance of 100Ω. We wish to apply 6V to the circuit, but only have access to a 12V source. It is decided that we will use a voltage divider containing two 100Ω resistors in series to reduce the supply voltage to the desired 6V level as shown in the circuit to the left below. However, adding the loading circuit to the voltage divider changes the voltage provided to the load, as shown to the right below.

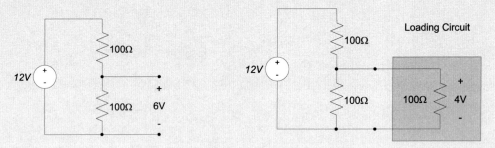

Addition of a voltage follower to the circuit isolates the voltage divider from the load, as shown below. Power to the op-amp can be provided by connecting the 12V source to V+ and grounding V−, as shown, since the desired op-amp output is between 0V and 12V.

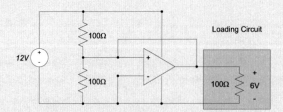

Section Summary

- Analysis of linear operational amplifier circuits typically consists of the following components:
    - Assume that the voltage difference across the input terminals is zero.
    - Assume that the currents into the input terminals are zero.
    - Apply KCL at op-amp input terminals.
    - Apply KCL at other circuit nodes, if necessary.
    - Check to ensure that output voltage remains within range specified by op-amp power supply voltages.
- Op-amp circuits which perform the following functions are presented in this section:
    - Inverting voltage amplification
    - Non-inverting voltage amplification
    - Summation (addition)
    - Differencing (subtraction)
    - Buffering

The reader should be able to sketch circuits, which perform the functions above.

5.4   Exercises

1. Represent the circuit of Example 5.2 as a voltage controlled voltage source.
2. Represent the circuit of Example 5.2 as a voltage controlled current source.
3. Find V$_{out}$ for the circuit below.

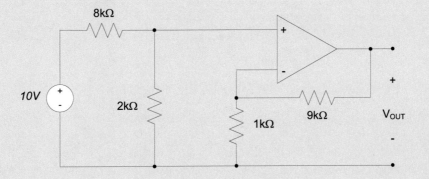

4. Find V in the circuit below.

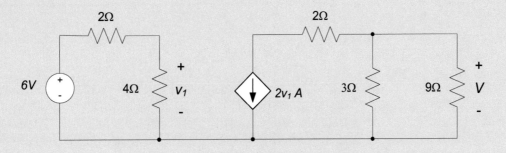

Solutions can be found at digilent.com/real-analog.

5.5   Comparators

Operational amplifiers are intended to be incorporated into circuits which *feeds back* the op-amp output to one or both of the input terminals. That is, the output voltage is connected in some way to the op-amp inputs. Typically, for stable operation, the output is fed back to the <u>inverting</u> input terminal (as in all of our circuit examples in section 5.4). If the output is not fed back to the input of the op-amp, the op-amp may not function as expected.

Comparators are operational amplifier–like devices which are intended to be operated without feedback from the output to the input. The circuit symbol for a comparator looks like an op-amp symbol, reflecting their similarities. Figure 5.15 provides a typical comparator symbol, with applicable voltages labeled.

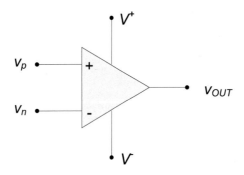

Figure 5.15. Comparator circuit symbol.

Operation of the comparator is simple: if v_p is greater than v_n, the output goes to the high supply voltage, V^+. If v_p is less than v_n, the output goes to the low supply voltage, V^-. The comparator is essentially checking the sign between the voltage at the inverting and non-inverting inputs, and adjusting the output voltage accordingly. Mathematically, the operation of a comparator can be expressed as:

$$V_{OUT} = \begin{cases} V^+, v_p - v_n > 0 \\ V^-, v_p - v_n < 0 \end{cases}$$

5.5   Exercises

1. A comparator like that shown in Fig. 5.14 has the sinusoidal signal below applied across the input terminals. (E.g. the plot below is v_p-v_n vs. time.) Sketch the output voltage $v_{out}(t)$.

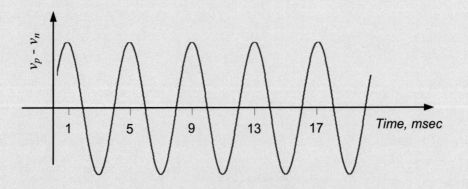

Solutions can be found at digilent.com/real-analog.

5.6   A Few Non-ideal Effects

In section 5.2, we indicated that operational amplifiers are designed to have high input resistances, low output resistances and high gains between the input voltage difference and the output voltage. Figure 5.7 of section 5.2 provided a model of an operational amplifier as a dependent source, including input and output resistances. This model is repeated below as Fig. 5.16 for convenience.

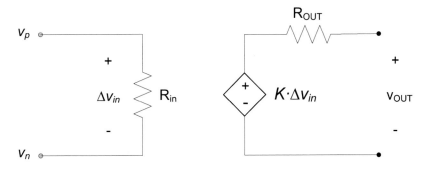

Figure 5.16. Operational Amplifier model.

In section 5.2, we also provided the assumptions applicable to ideal operational amplifier operation, along with their associated conclusions, and are provided below:

- The output voltage is bounded by the power supply voltages: $V^- < V_{OUT} < V^+$

- $K \rightarrow \infty$. Thus, $\Delta v_{in} = 0$ and $v_p = v_n$.

- $R_{in} \rightarrow \infty$. Thus, $i_p = -i_n = 0$, and the operational amplifier draws no power at its input.

- $R_{OUT} = 0$. Thus, there is no limit on the output current (or power) which can be provided by the op-amp.

Practical operational amplifiers have finite gains (K for most amplifiers is in the range $10^5 - 10^7$), finite input resistances (typical values are on the order of a few mega-ohms to hundreds or thousands of mega-ohms) and non-zero output resistances (generally on the order of 10 to 100 ohms). In this section, we will very briefly discuss a few of the ramifications of these non-ideal parameters.

5.6.1   Input Resistance Effects

The high input resistance of the operational amplifier means that circuits connected to the op-amp input do not have to provide much power to the op-amp circuit. This is the op-amp property that is employed in buffer amplifiers and instrumentation amplifiers. Instrumentation systems, for example, have very limited power output capabilities; these limitations are typically modeled as high output resistances in the instrumentation systems. Thermocouples, for example, provide low voltage levels, and very small power output – they can be modeled as a voltage source with a fairly high output resistance. When a system of this type is connected to the input terminals of an op-amp, the situation is as shown in Fig. 5.17.

It is apparent from Fig. 5.17 that the output resistance of the system, if it is large enough, can have an effect on the voltage difference across the op-amp input terminals, since:

$$\Delta v_{in} = V_S \left(\frac{R_{in}}{R_{in} + R_S} \right)$$

Since we generally want to amplify V_S directly, any difference between V_S and Δv_{in} will degrade our output voltage from its desired value.

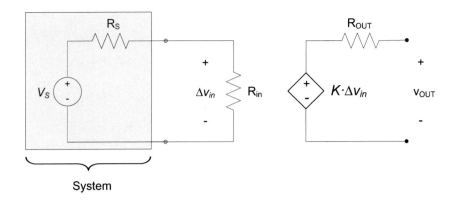

Figure 5.17. Effect of input resistance on output.

5.6.2 Output Resistance Effects

The op-amp output resistance essentially limits the amount of power the op-amp can provide at its output terminal. This can become a problem if we want to connect very low resistance loads to the output of an operational amplifier. For example, audio speakers commonly have an 8Ω resistance. Figure 5.18 shows an 8Ω speaker connected to the output of an operational amplifier which has an 80Ω output resistance. In this case, we expect the maximum output voltage to be:

$$v_{OUT} = K \cdot V_S \left(\frac{8\Omega}{8\Omega + 80\Omega} \right) = 0.09 K V_S$$

If the maximum output voltage of the op-amp is low, we may not have nearly enough power to operate the speaker.

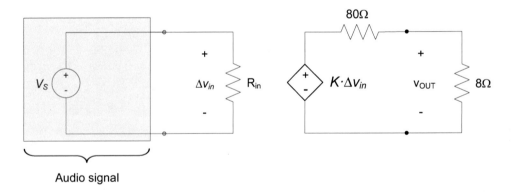

Figure 5.18. Audio amplifier.

5.6.3 Finite Gain Effects

As an example of the effects of a finite voltage gain, let us assume that an operational amplifier has a gain of K = 10,000 and supply voltages V⁺ = 10V and V⁻ = -10V. From equation (5.2), the linear operating range of the operational amplifier is over the range of input voltage differences:

$$\frac{V^-}{K} \leq \Delta V_{in} \leq \frac{V^+}{K}$$

The non-ideal operational amplifier of interest can then allow input terminal voltage differences of up to $-1mV \leq \Delta v_{in} \leq 1mV$. Although voltage differences of a millivolt will be considered to be essentially zero for any of the voltage levels we will deal with in this class, these voltages are definitely <u>not</u> zero for some applications.

Section Summary

- The effect of a finite input resistance on an operational amplifier's operation is that the current into the input terminals will not be identically zero. Thus, a real operational amplifier with finite input resistance will always draw some power from a circuit connected to it. Whether this has a significant effect on the overall circuit's operation is generally a function of the output resistance of the circuit to which the amplifier is connected.

- The effect of a non-zero output resistance on an operational amplifier's operation is that the power output of the amplifier is limited. Thus, a realistic operational amplifier will not be able to provide any arbitrary current to a load. Whether this has a significant effect on the overall circuit's operation is primarily dependent upon the value of the load resistance.

- The effect of a finite op-amp gain is that the voltage difference across the input terminals may not be identically zero.

Chapter 6:
Energy Storage Elements

So far, we have considered circuits that have been governed by algebraic relations. These circuits have, in general, contained only power sources and resistive elements. All elements in these circuits, therefore, have either <u>supplied power</u> from external sources or <u>dissipated</u> power. For these resistive circuits, we can apply either time-varying or constant signals to the circuit without really affecting our analysis approach. Ohm's law, for example, is equally applicable to time-varying or constant voltages and currents:

$$V = I \cdot R \Leftrightarrow v(t) = i(t) \cdot R$$

Since the governing equation is algebraic, it is applicable at every point in time – voltages and currents at a point in time are affected only by voltages and currents at the same point in time.

We will now begin to consider circuit elements, which are governed by differential equations. These circuit elements are called *dynamic circuit elements* or *energy storage elements*. Physically, these circuit elements store energy, which they can later release back to the circuit. The response, at a given time, of circuits that contain these elements is not only related to other circuit parameters at the same time; it may also depend upon the parameters at other times.

This chapter begins with an overview of the basic concepts associated with energy storage. This discussion focuses not on electrical systems, but instead introduces the topic qualitatively in the context of systems with which the reader is already familiar. The goal is to provide a basis for the mathematics, which will be introduced subsequently. Since we will now be concerned with time-varying signals, section 6.2 introduces the basic signals that we will be dealing with in the immediate future. This chapter concludes with presentations of the two electrical energy storage elements that we will be concerned with: capacitors and inductors. The method by which energy is stored in these elements is presented in sections 6.3 and 6.4, along with the governing equations relating voltage and current for these elements.

After completing this chapter, you should be able to:

- Qualitatively state the effect of energy storage on the type of mathematics governing a system
- Define transient response
- Define steady-state response
- Write the mathematical expression for a unit step function
- Sketch the unit step function
- Sketch shifted and scaled versions of the unit step function
- Write the mathematical expression for a decaying exponential function
- Define the time constant of an exponential function
- Sketch a decaying exponential function, given the function's initial value and time constant
- Use a unit step function to restrict an exponential function to times greater than zero
- Write the circuit symbol for a capacitor
- State the mechanism by which a capacitor stores energy
- State the voltage-current relationship for a capacitor in both differential and integral form
- State the response of a capacitor to constant voltages and instantaneous voltage changes
- Write the mathematical expression describing energy storage in a capacitor
- Determine the equivalent capacitance of series and parallel combinations of capacitors
- Sketch a circuit describing a non-ideal capacitor
- Write the circuit symbol for an inductor
- State the mechanism by which an inductor stores energy
- State the voltage-current relationship for an inductor in both differential and integral form
- State the response of an inductor to constant voltages and instantaneous current changes
- Write the mathematical expression describing energy storage in an inductor
- Determine the equivalent inductance of series and parallel combinations of inductors
- Sketch a circuit describing a non-ideal inductor

6.1   Fundamental Concepts

This section provides a brief overview of what is meant by energy storage in terms of a system-level description of some physical process. Several examples of energy storage elements are presented, for which the reader should have an intuitive understanding. These examples are intended to introduce the basic concepts in a qualitative manner; the mathematical analysis of dynamic systems will be provided in later chapters.

We have previously introduced the concept of representing a physical process as a *system*. In this viewpoint, the physical process has an input and an output. The input to the system is generated from sources external to the system – we will consider the input to the system to be a known function of time. The output of the system is the system's response to the input. The *input-output equation* governing the system provides the relationship between the system's input and output. A general input-output equation has the form:

$$y(t) = f\{u(t)\}$$

Eq. 6.1

The process is shown in block diagram form in Fig. 6.1.

Figure 6.1. Block diagram representation of a system.

The system of Fig. 6.1 transfers the energy in the system input to the system output. This process transforms the input signal *u(t)* into the output signal *y(t)*. In order to perform this energy transfer, the system will, in general, contain elements that both store and dissipate energy. To date, we have analyzed systems which contain only energy dissipation elements. We review these systems briefly below in a systems context. Subsequently, we introduce systems that store energy; our discussion of energy storage elements is mainly qualitative in this chapter and presents systems for which the reader should have an intuitive understanding.

6.1.1 Systems with no Energy Storage

In previous chapters, we considered cases in which the input-output equation is algebraic. This implies that the processes being performed by the system involve only sources and components which dissipate energy. For example, output voltage of the inverting voltage amplifier of Fig. 6.2 is:

$$V_{OUT} = -\left(\frac{R_f}{R_{in}} V_{in}\right)$$

Eq. 6.2

This circuit contains only resistors (in the form of R_f and R_{in}) and sources (in the form of V_{in} and the op-amp power supplies) and the equation relating the input and output is algebraic. Note that the op-amp power supplies do not appear in equation (6.2), since linear operation of the circuit of Fig. 6.2 implies that the output voltage is independent of the op-amp power supplies.

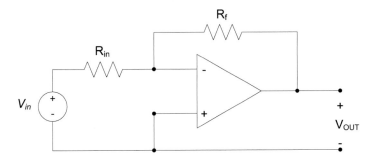

Figure 6.2. Inverting voltage amplifier.

One side effect of an algebraic input-output equation is that the output responds instantaneously to any changes in the input. For example, consider the circuit shown in Fig. 6.3. The input voltage is based on the position of a switch; when the switch closes, the input voltage applied to the circuit increases instantaneously from 0V to 2V. Fig. 6.3 indicates that the switch closes at time *t* = 5 seconds; thus, the input voltage as a function of time is as shown in Fig. 6.4(a). For the values of R_f and R_{in} shown in Fig. 6.3, the input-output equation becomes:

$$V_{OUT}(t) = -5V_{in}(t)$$

Eq. 6.3

And the output voltage as a function of time is as shown in Fig. 6.4(b). The output voltage responds immediately to the change in the input voltage.

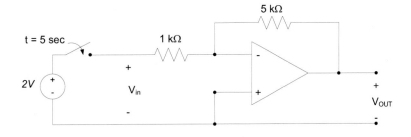

Figure 6.3. Switched voltage amplifier.

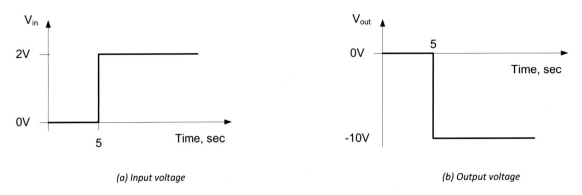

(a) Input voltage   (b) Output voltage

Figure 6.4. Input and output signals for circuit of Figure 3.

6.1.2 Systems with Energy Storage

We now consider systems, which contain energy storage elements. The inclusion of energy storage elements results in the input-output equation for the system, which is a differential equation. We present the concepts in terms of two examples for which the reader most likely has some expectations based on experience and intuition.

Example 6.1: Mass-damper system

As an example of a system, which includes energy storage elements, consider the mass-damper system shown in Fig. 6.5. The applied force *F(t)* pushes the mass to the right. The mass's velocity is *v(t)*. The mass slides on a surface with sliding coefficient of friction *b*, which induces a force, which opposes the mass's motion. We will consider the applied force to be the input to our system and the mass's velocity to be the output, as shown by the block diagram of Fig. 6.6. This system models, for example, pushing a stalled automobile.

The system of Fig. 6.5 contains both energy storage and energy dissipation elements. Kinetic energy is <u>stored</u> in the form of the velocity of the mass. The sliding coefficient of friction <u>dissipates</u> energy. Thus, the system has a single energy storage element (the mass) and a single energy dissipation element (the sliding friction). In section 4.1, we determined that the governing equation for the system was the first order differential equation:

$$m\frac{dv(t)}{dt} + bv(t) = F(t)$$

Eq. 6.4

The presence of the energy storage element causes the input-output equation to be a differential equation.

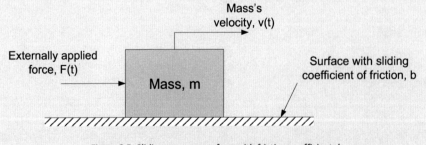

Figure 6.5. Sliding mass on surface with friction coefficient, b

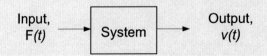

Figure 6.6. Mass-damper system represented as a block diagram.

We will examine the effect that the energy storage element has upon the system response in qualitative terms, rather than explicitly solving equation (6.4). If we increase the force applied to the mass, the mass will accelerate and the velocity of the mass increases. The system, therefore, is converting the energy in the input force to a kinetic energy of the mass. This energy transfer results in a change in the output variable, velocity.

The energy storage elements of the system of Fig. 6.5 <u>do not</u>, however, allow an instantaneous change in velocity to an instantaneous change in force. For example, say that before time t = 0 no force is applied to the mass and the mass is at rest. At time t = 0 we suddenly apply a force to the mass, as shown in Fig. 6.7(a) below. At time t = 0 the mass begins to accelerate but it takes time for the mass to approach its final velocity, as shown in Fig. 6.7(b). This transitory stage, when the system is in transition from one constant operating condition to another is called the *transient response*. After a time, the energy input from the external force is balanced by the energy dissipated by the sliding friction, and the velocity of the mass remains constant. When the operating conditions are constant, the energy input is exactly balanced by the energy dissipation, and the system's response is said to be in *steady-state*. We will discuss these terms in more depth in later chapters when we perform the mathematical analysis of dynamic systems.

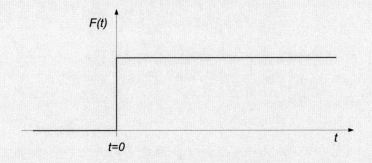

Figure 6.7(a). Force applied to mass.

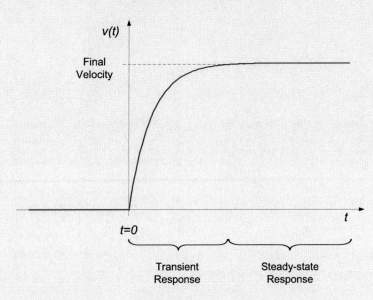

Figure 6.7(b). Velocity of mass.

Example 6.2

Our second example of a system, which includes energy storage elements, is a body that is subjected to some heat input. The overall system is shown in Figure 6.8. The body being heated has some mass m, specific heat C_p, and temperature T_B. Some heat input q_{in} is applied to the body from an external source, and the body transfers heat q_{out} to its surroundings. The surroundings are at some ambient temperature T_0. We will consider the input to our system to be the applied heat input q_{in} and the output to be the temperature of the body T_B, as shown in the block diagram of Fig. 6.9. This system is a model, for example, of the process of heating a frying pan on a stove. Heat input is applied by the stove burner and the pan dissipates heat by transferring it to the surroundings.

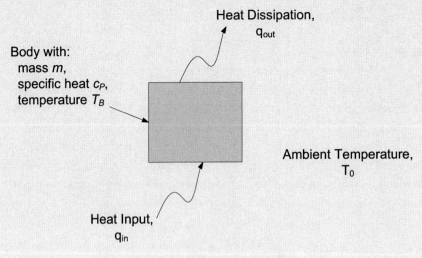

Figure 6.8. Body subjected to heating.

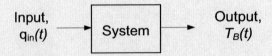

Figure 6.9. System block diagram.

The system of Fig. 6.8 contains both energy storage and energy dissipation elements. Energy is <u>stored</u> in the form of the temperature of the mass. Energy is dissipated in the form of heat transferred to the surroundings. Thus, the system has a single energy storage element (the mass) and a single energy dissipation element (the heat dissipation). The governing equation for the system is the first order differential equation:

$$mc_p \frac{d(T_B - T_0)}{dt} + q_{OUT} = q_{in}$$

Eq. 6.5

The presence of the energy storage element causes the input-output equation to be a differential equation.

We again examine the response of this system to some input in qualitative rather than quantitative terms in order to provide some insight into the overall process before immersing ourselves in the mathematics associated with analyzing the system quantitatively. If the heat input to the system is increased instantaneously (for example, if we suddenly turn up the heat setting on our stove burner) the mass's temperature will increase. As the mass's temperature increases, the heat transferred to the ambient surroundings will increase. When the heat input to the mass is exactly balanced by the heat transfer to the surroundings, the mass's temperature will no longer change and the system will be at a *steady-state* operating condition. Since the mass provides energy storage, the temperature of the mass will not respond instantaneously to a sudden change in heat input – the temperature will rise relatively slowly to its steady-state operating condition. (We know from experience that changing the burner setting on the stove does not immediately change the temperature of our pan, particularly if the pan is heavy.) The process of changing the body's temperature from one steady state operating condition to another is the system's *transient response*.

The process of changing the body's temperature by instantaneously increasing the heat input to the body is illustrated in Fig. 6.10. The signal corresponding to the heat input is shown in Fig. 6.10(a), while the resulting temperature response of the body is shown in Fig. 6.10(b).

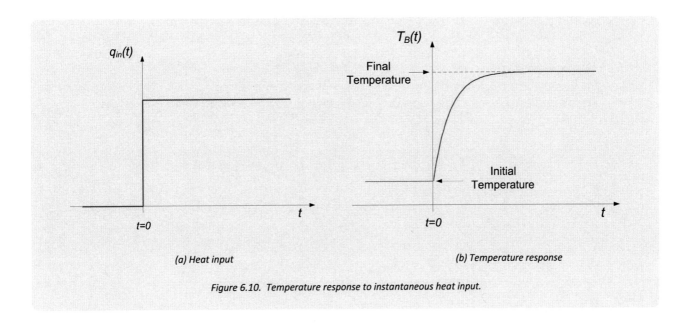

(a) Heat input

(b) Temperature response

Figure 6.10. Temperature response to instantaneous heat input.

Section Summary

- Systems with energy storage elements are governed by differential equations. Systems that contain only energy dissipation elements (such as resistors) are governed by algebraic equations.
- The responses of systems governed by algebraic equations will typically have the same "shape" as the input. The output at a given time is simply dependent upon the input at that same time – the system does not "remember" any previous conditions.
- The responses of systems governed by differential equations will not, in general, have the same "shape" as the forcing function applied to the system. The system "remembers" previous conditions – this is why the solution to a differential equation requires knowledge of initial conditions.
- The response of a system that stores energy is generally considered to consist of two parts: the *transient* response and the *steady-state* response. These are described as follows:
    - The transient response typically is shaped differently from the forcing function. It is due to initial energy levels stored in the system.
    - The steady-state response is the response of the system as $t \longrightarrow \infty$. It is the same "shape" as the forcing function applied to the system.

In differential equations courses, the transient response corresponds (approximately) to the homogeneous solution of the governing differential equation, while the steady-state response corresponds to the particular solution of the governing differential equation.

1. A mass is sliding on a surface with an initial velocity of 5 meters/seconds. All external forces (except for the friction force on the surface) are removed from the mass at time t = 0 seconds. The velocity of the mass as a function of time is shown below. What is the steady-state velocity of the mass?

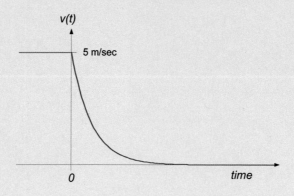

Solutions can be found at digilent.com/real-analog.

6.2   Basic Time-varying Signals

Since the analysis of dynamic systems relies upon time-varying phenomenon, this chapter section presents some common time-varying signals that will be used in our analyses. Specific signals that will be presented are step functions and exponential functions.

6.2.1   Step Function

We will use a *step function* to model a signal, which changes suddenly from one constant value to another. These types of signals can be very important. Examples include digital logic circuits (which switch between low and high voltage levels) and control systems (whose design specifications are often based on the system's response to a sudden change in input).

We define a *unit step function, $u_0(t)$* as follows:

$$u_0(t) = \begin{cases} 0, t < 0 \\ 1, t > 0 \end{cases}$$

Eq. 6.6

The unit step function is illustrated in Fig. 6.11 below. For now, it will not be necessary to define a value for the step function at time *t=0*.

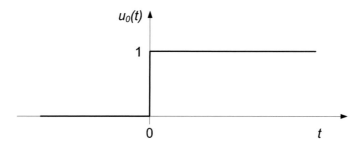

Figure 6.11. Unit step function.

Physically, the step function models a switching process. For example, the output voltage V_{out} of the circuit shown in Figure 6.12, in which a constant 1V source supplies voltage through a switch which closes at time $t=0$, is a unit step function.

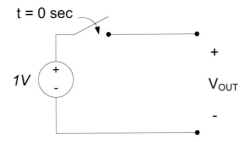

Figure 6.12. Circuit to realize a unit step function.

The unit step function can be *scaled* to provide different amplitudes. Multiplication of the unit step function by a constant K results in a signal which is zero for times less than zero and K for times greater than zero, as shown in Fig. 6.13.

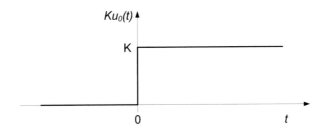

Figure 6.13. Scaled step function $Ku_0(t)$; $K>0$.

The step function can also be *shifted* to model processes which switch at times other than $t=0$. A step function with amplitude K which occurs at time $t=a$ can be written as $Ku_0(t-a)$:

$$Ku_0(t-a) = \begin{cases} 0, t < a \\ K, t > a \end{cases}$$

Eq. 6.7

The function is zero when the argument $t-a$ is less than zero and K when the argument t-a is greater than zero, as shown in Fig. 6.14. If $a>0$, the function is shifted to the right of the origin; if $a<0$, the function is shifted to the left of the origin.

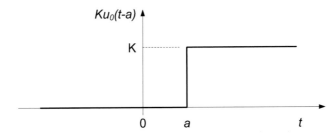

Figure 6.14. Shifted and scaled step function $Ku_0(t-a)$; $K>0$ and $a>0$.

Switching the sign of the above argument in equation (6.7) results in:

$$Ku_0(-t+a) = Ku_a(a-t) = \begin{cases} K, t < a \\ 0, t > a \end{cases}$$

Eq. 6.8

And the value of the function is K for $t<a$ and zero for $t>a$, as shown in Fig. 6.15. As above, the transition from K to zero is to the right of the origin if $a>0$ and to the left of the origin if $a<0$.

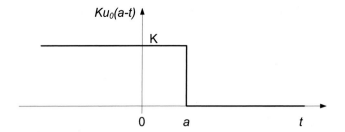

Figure 6.15. The function step function $Ku_0(a-t)$; K>0 and a>0.

Step functions can also be used to describe finite-duration signals. For example, the function:

$$f(t) = \begin{cases} 0, t < 0 \\ 1, 0 < t < 2 \\ 0, t > 2 \end{cases}$$

Illustrated in Fig. 6.16, can be written in terms of sums or products of unit step functions as follows:

$$f(t) = u_0(t) - u_0(t - 1)$$

Or

$$f(t) = u_0(t) \cdot u_0(2 - t)$$

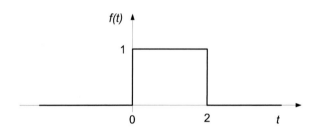

Figure 6.16. Finite-duration signal.

The step function can also be used to create other finite-duration functions. For example, the finite-duration *ramp* function:

$$f(t) = \begin{cases} 0, t < 0 \\ t, 0 < t < 1 \\ 0, t > 1 \end{cases}$$

Shown in Fig. 6.17, can be written as a single function over the entire range $-\infty < t < \infty$ by using unit step functions, as follows:

$$f(t) = t \cdot [u_0(t) - u_0(t - 1)]$$

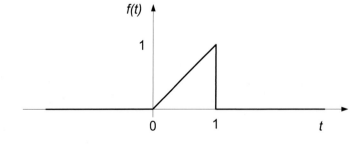

Figure 6.17. Finite-duration "ramp" signal.

Chapter 6: Energy Storage Elements

6.2.2 Exponential Functions

A function that appears commonly in the analysis of linear systems is the *decaying exponential*:

$$f(t) = Ae^{-at}$$

Where a>0. The function *f(t)* is illustrated in Fig. 6.18. The value of the function is *A* at *t=0* and decreases to zero as $t \rightarrow \infty$. As $t \rightarrow -\infty$ the function increases without bound. The constant *a* dictates the rate at which the function decreases as time increases.

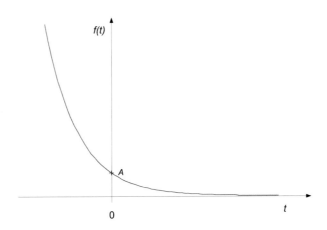

Figure 6.18. Decaying exponential function.

We will usually be interested in this function only for positive values of time. We will also commonly write our exponential function in terms of a time constant, τ, rather than the constant *a*. Thus, the decaying exponential function we will generally use is:

$$f(t) = \begin{cases} 0, t < 0 \\ Ae^{\frac{-1}{\tau}}, t > 0 \end{cases}$$
Eq. 6.10

Or, using the unit step function to limit the function to positive values of time:

$$f(t) = Ae^{\frac{-t}{\tau}} \cdot u_0(t)$$
Eq. 6.11

The function of equations (6.10) and (6.11) is illustrated in Fig. 6.19. The time constant, τ, is a positive number which dictates the rate at which the function will decay with time. When the time $t = \tau, f(t)Ae^{-1} = 0.368A$ and the function has decayed to 36.8% of its original value. In fact, <u>the function decreases by 36.8% every τ seconds</u>. Therefore, a signal with a small time constant decays more rapidly than a signal with a large time constant, as illustrated in Fig. 6.20.

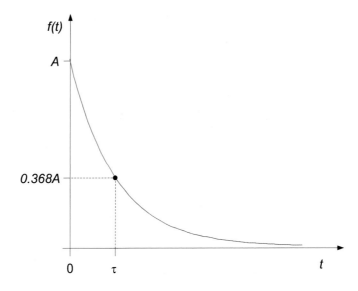

Figure 6.19. Exponential function $f(t) = Ae^{\frac{-t}{\tau}}u_0(t)$.

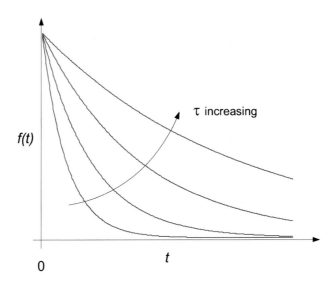

τ increasing

Figure 6.20. Exponential function variation with time cons.

Section Summary

- Step functions are useful for representing conditions (generally inputs), which change from one value to another instantaneously. In electrical engineering, they are commonly used to model the opening or closing of a switch that connects a circuit to a source, which provides a constant voltage or current. Mathematically, an arbitrary step function can be represented by:

$$Ku_0(-t + a) = Ku_0(a - t) = \begin{cases} K, t < a \\ 0, t > a \end{cases}$$

So that the step function turns "on" at time $t=a$, and has an amplitude K.

- An exponential function, defined for $t>0$, is mathematically defined as:

$$f(t) = Ae^{\frac{-t}{\tau}} \cdot u_0(t)$$

The function has an initial value, A, and a time constant, τ. The time constant indicates how quickly the function decays; the value of the function decreases by 63.2% every τ seconds. Exponential functions are important to use because the solutions of linear, constant coefficient, ordinary differential equations typically take the form of exponentials.

6.2   Exercises

1.   Express the signal below in terms of step functions.

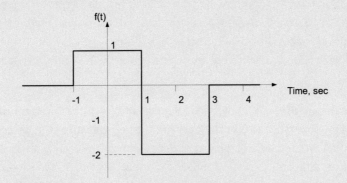

2.   The function shown below is a decaying exponential. Estimate the function from the given graph.

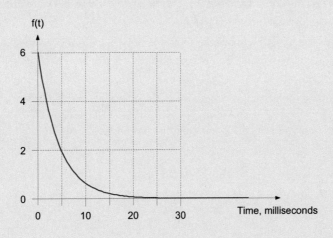

Solutions can be found at digilent.com/real-analog.

6.3   Capacitors

We begin our study of energy storage elements with a discussion of capacitors. Capacitors, like resistors, are passive two-terminal circuit elements. That is, no external power supply is necessary to make them function. Capacitors consist of a non-conductive material (or *dielectric*) which separates two electrical conductors; capacitors store energy in the form of an electric field set up in the dielectric material.

In this section, we describe physical properties of capacitors and provide a mathematical model for an <u>ideal</u> capacitor. Using this ideal capacitor model, we will develop mathematical relationships for the energy stored in a capacitor and governing relations for series and parallel connections of capacitors. The section concludes with a brief discussion of practical (non-ideal) capacitors.

6.3.1 Capacitors

Two electrically conductive bodies, when separated by a non-conductive (or *insulating*) material, will form a *capacitor*. Figure 6.21 illustrates the special case of a *parallel plate capacitor*. The non-conductive material between the plates is called a dielectric; the material property of the dielectric, which is currently important to us, is its *permittivity*, ε. When a voltage potential difference is applied across the two plates, as shown in Fig. 6.21, charge accumulates on the plates – the plate with the higher voltage potential will accumulate positive charge q, while the plate with the lower voltage potential will accumulate negative charge, $-q$. The charge difference between the plates induces an *electric field* in the dielectric material; the capacitor <u>stores energy</u> in this electric field. The *capacitance* of the capacitor is a quantity that tells us, essentially, how much energy can be stored by the capacitor. Higher capacitance means that more energy can be stored by the capacitor. Capacitance has units of *Farads*, abbreviated F.

The amount of capacitance a capacitor has is governed by the geometry of the capacitor (the shape of the conductors and their orientation relative to one another) and the permittivity of the dielectric between the conductors. These effects can be complex and difficult to quantify mathematically; rather than attempt a comprehensive discussion of these effects, we will simply claim that, in general, capacitance is dependent upon the following parameters:

- The spacing between the conductive bodies (the distance d in Fig. 6.21). As the separation between the bodies <u>increases</u>, the capacitance <u>decreases</u>.
- The surface area of the conductive bodies. As the surface area of the conductors <u>increases</u>, the capacitance <u>increases</u>. The surface area referred to here is the area over which both the conductors and the dielectric overlap.
- The permittivity of the dielectric. As the permittivity <u>increases</u>, the capacitance <u>increases</u>.

The parallel-plate capacitor shown in Fig. 6.21, for example, has capacitance:

$$C = \frac{\varepsilon \cdot A}{d}$$

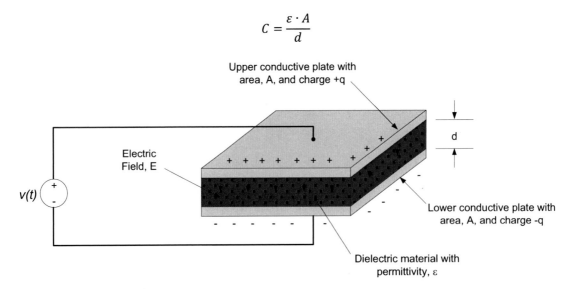

Figure 6.21. *Parallel plate capacitor with applied voltage across conductors.*

Mathematically, the capacitance of the device relates the voltage difference between the plates and the charge accumulation associated with this voltage:

$$q(t) = CV(t)$$

Eq. 6.12

Capacitors that obey the relationship of equation (6.12) are *linear capacitors*, since the potential difference between the conductive surfaces is linearly related to the charge on the surfaces. Please note that the charges on the upper and lower plate of the capacitor in Fig. 6.21 are equal and opposite – thus, if we increase the charge on one plate, the charge on the other plate must decrease by the same amount. This is consistent with our previous assumption electrical circuit elements cannot accumulate charge, and current entering one terminal of a capacitor must leave the other terminal of the capacitor.

Since current is defined as the time rate of change of charge, $i(t) = \frac{dq(t)}{dt}$, equation (6.12) can be re-written in terms of the current through the capacitor:

$$i(t) = \frac{d}{dt}[Cv(t)]$$
Eq. 6.13

Since the capacitance of a given capacitor is constant, equation (6.13) can be written as:

$$i(t) = C\frac{dv(t)}{dt}$$
Eq. 6.14

The circuit symbol for a capacitor is shown in Fig. 6.22, along with the sign conventions for the voltage-current relationship of equation (6.14). We use our passive sign convention for the voltage-current relationship – positive current is assumed to enter the terminal with positive voltage polarity.

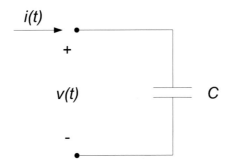

Figure 6.22. Capacitor circuit symbol and voltage-current sign convention.

Integrating both sides of equation (6.14) results in the following form for the capacitor's voltage-current relationship:

$$v(t) = \frac{1}{C}\int_{t_0}^{t} i(\xi)d\xi + v(t_0)$$
Eq. 6.15

Where $v(t_0)$ is a known voltage at some initial time, t_0. We use a dummy variable of integration, ξ, to emphasize that the only "t" which survives the integration process is the upper limit of the integral.

Important result: The voltage-current relationship for an ideal capacitor can be stated in either differential or integral form, as follows:

- $i(t) = C\frac{dv(t)}{dt}$
- $v(t) = \frac{1}{C}\int_{t_0}^{t} i(\xi)d\xi + v(t_0)$

Example 6.3

If the voltage as a function of time across a capacitor with capacitance $C=1\mu F$ is as shown below, determine the current as a function of time through the capacitor.

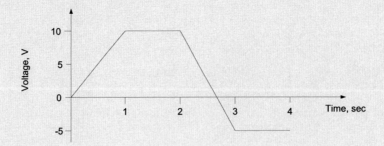

$0 < t < 1$: The voltage rate of change is 10 V/s. Thus, $C\frac{dv(t)}{dt} = (1 \times 10^{-6}F)\left(10\frac{V}{s}\right) = 10\mu A$.

$1 < t < 2$: The voltage is constant. Thus, $C\frac{dv(t)}{dt} = 0A$.

$2 < t < 3$: The voltage rate of change is -15V/s. Thus, $C\frac{dv(t)}{dt} = (1 \times 10^{-6}F)\left(-15\frac{V}{s}\right) = -15\mu A$.

$3 < t < 4$: The voltage is constant. Thus, $C\frac{dv(t)}{dt} = 0A$

A plot of the current through the capacitor as a function of time is shown below.

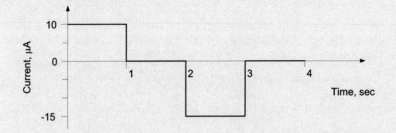

Example 6.4

If the current as a function of time through a capacitor with capacitance $C=10mF$ is as shown below, determine the voltage as a function of time across the capacitor. Assume that the voltage across the capacitor is $0V$ at time $t=0$.

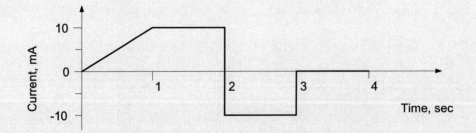

- At time $t=0$, the voltage is given to be $0V$.
- In the time period $0<t<1$ second, the current increases linearly and the voltage will increase quadratically. The total voltage change during this time period is the integral of the current, which is simply the area under the current curve divided by the capacitance: $\frac{1}{2}\frac{(10\times10^{-3}A)(1s)}{0.01F} = 0.5V$.

Chapter 6: Energy Storage Elements

- In the time period *1<t<2* seconds, the current is constant at 10 mA. The voltage change is the area under the current curve divided by the capacitance: $(10 \times 10^{-3} A) \frac{(1s)}{0.01F} = 1V$. The total voltage at *t=2* seconds is, then, $0.5V + 1V = 1.5V$.
- In the time period *2<t<3* seconds, the current is constant at -10 mA. The voltage change is the negative of the voltage change from *1<t<2* sec. The total voltage at *t=3* seconds is, then, $1.5V - 1V = 0.5V$.
- In the time period *3<t<4* seconds, the current is zero. The integral of zero over any time period is zero, so there is no change in voltage during this time range and the voltage remains constant at 0.5V.

A plot of the voltage across the capacitor as a function of time is shown below.

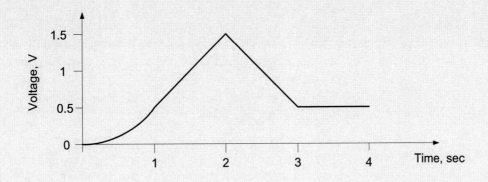

It is often useful, when analyzing circuits containing capacitors, to examine the circuit's response to constant operating conditions and to instantaneous changes in operating condition. We examine the capacitor's response to each of these operating conditions below:

- Capacitor response to constant voltage:
    - If the voltage across the capacitor is constant, equation (6.14) indicates that the current through the capacitor is zero. Thus, if the voltage across the capacitor is constant, the capacitor is equivalent to a open circuit.
    - This property can be extremely useful in determining a circuit's steady-state response to constant inputs. If the inputs to a circuit change from one constant value to another, the transient components of the response will eventually die out and all circuit parameters will become constant. Under these conditions, capacitors can be replaced with open circuits and the circuit analyzed relatively easily. As we will see later, this operating condition can be useful in determining the response of circuits containing capacitors and in double-checking results obtained using other methods.
- Capacitor response to instantaneous voltage changes:
    - If the voltage across the capacitor changes instantaneously, the rate of change of voltage is infinite. Thus, by equation (6.14), if we wish to change the voltage across a capacitor instantaneously, we must supply infinite current to the capacitor. This implies that infinite power is available, which is not physically possible. Thus, in any practical circuit, the voltage across a capacitor cannot change instantaneously.
    - Any circuit that allows an instantaneous change in the voltage across an ideal capacitor is not physically realizable. We may sometimes assume, for mathematical convenience, that an ideal capacitor's voltage changes suddenly; however, it must be emphasized that this assumption requires an underlying assumption that infinite power is available and is thus not an allowable operating condition in any physical circuit.

Important Capacitor Properties:

- Capacitors can be replaced by open-circuits, under circumstances when all operating conditions are constant.
- Voltages across capacitors cannot change instantaneously. No such requirement is placed on currents.

6.3.2 Energy Storage

The power dissipated by a capacitor is:

$$p(t) = v(t) \cdot i(t)$$

Eq. 6.16

Since both voltage and current are functions of time, the power dissipation will also be a function of time. The power as a function of time is called the *instantaneous power*, since it provides the power dissipation at any instant in time.

Substituting equation (6.14) into equation (6.16) results in:

$$p(t) = C \cdot v(t) \frac{dv(t)}{dt}$$

Eq. 6.17

Since power is, by definition, the rate of change of energy, the energy is the time integral of power. Integrating equation (6.17) with respect to time gives the following expression for the energy stored in a capacitor:

$$W_C(t) = \int_{-\infty}^{t} Cv(\xi) \frac{dv(\xi)}{dt} dt = \int_{-\infty}^{t} Cv(\xi) dv(\xi) = \frac{1}{2} Cv^2(\xi) \Big|_{-\infty}^{t}$$

Where we have set our lower limits of integration at $t = -\infty$ to avoid issues relative to initial conditions. We assume that no energy is stored in the capacitor at time $t = -\infty$ so that:

$$W_C(t) = \frac{1}{2} Cv^2(t)$$

Eq. 6.18

From equation (6.18) we see that the energy stored in a capacitor is always a non-negative quantity, so $W_C(t) \geq 0$. Ideal capacitors do not dissipate energy, as resistors do. Capacitors <u>store</u> energy when it is provided to them from the circuit; this energy can later be recovered and returned to the circuit.

Example 6.5

Consider the circuit shown below. The voltage applied to the capacitor by the source is as shown. Plot the power absorbed by the capacitor and the energy stored in the capacitor as functions of time.

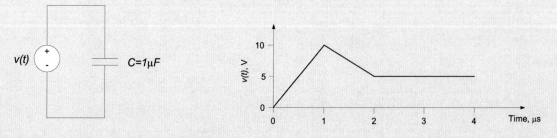

Power is most readily computed by taking the product of voltage and current. The current can be determined from equation (6.14). The current as a function of time is plotted below.

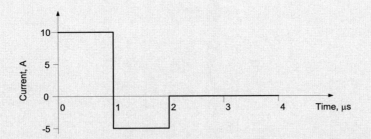

The power absorbed by the capacitor is determined by taking a point-by-point product between the voltage and current.

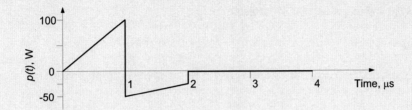

Recall that power is absorbed or generated based on the passive sign convention. If the relative signs between voltage and current agree with the passive sign convention, the circuit element is absorbing power. If the relative signs between voltage and current are opposite to the passive sign convention, the element is generating power. Thus, the capacitor in this example is absorbing power for the first microsecond. It generates power (returns power to the voltage source) during the second microsecond). After the second microsecond, the current is zero and the capacitor neither absorbs nor generates power.

The energy stored in the capacitor can be determined either from integrating the power or from application of equation (6.18) to the voltage curve provided in the problem statement. The energy in the capacitor as a function of time is shown below:

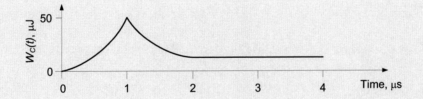

During the first microsecond, while the capacitor is absorbing power, the energy in the capacitor is increasing. The maximum energy in the capacitor is 50 μJ, at 1μs. During the second microsecond, the capacitor is releasing power back to the circuit and the energy in the capacitor is decreasing. At 2μs, the capacitor still has 12.5 μJ of stored energy. After 2μs, the capacitor neither absorbs nor generates energy and the energy stored in the capacitor remains at 12.5μJ.

6.3.3 Capacitors in Series

Consider the series connection of N capacitors shown in Fig. 6.23.

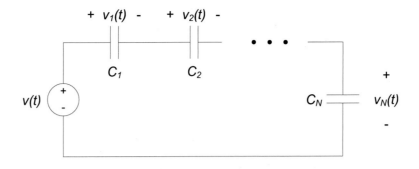

Figure 6.23. Series connection of N capacitors.

Applying Kirchhoff's voltage law around the loop results in:

$$v(t) = v_1(t) + v_2(t) + \cdots v_N(t)$$

Eq. 6.19

Using equation (6.15) to write the capacitor voltage drops in terms of the current through the loop gives:

$$v(t) = \left[\frac{1}{C_1}\int_{t_0}^{t} i(\xi)d\xi + v_1(t_0)\right] + \left[\frac{1}{C_2}\int_{t_0}^{t} i(\xi)d\xi + v_2(t_0)\right] + \cdots + \left[\frac{1}{C_N}\int_{t_0}^{t} i(\xi)d\xi + v_N(t_0)\right]$$

$$= \left[\frac{1}{C_1}\int_{t_0}^{t} i(\xi)d\xi + \frac{1}{C_2}\int_{t_0}^{t} i(\xi)d\xi + \cdots \frac{1}{C_N}\int_{t_0}^{t} i(\xi)d\xi\right] + [v_1(t_0) + v_2(t_0) + \cdots + v_N(t_0)]$$

$$= \left(\frac{1}{C_1} + \frac{1}{C_2} + \cdots + \frac{1}{C_N}\right)\int_{t_0}^{t} i(\xi)d\xi + v(t_0)$$

This can be re-written using summation notation as:

$$v(t) = \left(\sum_{k=1}^{N}\frac{1}{C_k}\right)$$

Eq. 6.21

Thus, the circuits of Fig. 6.23 and Fig. 6.24 are equivalent circuits, if the equivalent capacitance is chosen according to equation (6.21).

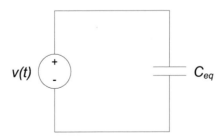

Figure 6.24. Equivalent circuit to Figure 3.

For the special case of two capacitors C_1 and C_2 in series, equation (6.21) simplifies to:

$$C_{eq} = \frac{C_1 C_2}{C_1 + C_2}$$

Eq. 6.22

Equations (6.21) and (6.22) are analogous to the equations, which provide the equivalent resistance of parallel combinations of resistors.

6.3.4 Capacitors in Parallel

Consider the parallel combination of N capacitors, as shown in Fig. 6.25.

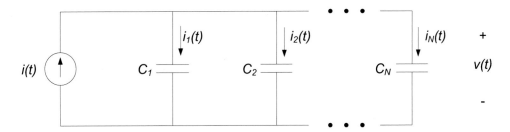

Figure 6.25. Series connection of N capacitors.

Applying Kirchhoff's current law at the upper node results in:

$$i(t) = i_1(t) + i_2(t) + \cdots i_N(t)$$

Eq. 6.23

Using equation (6.14) to write the capacitor currents in terms of their voltage drop gives:

$$i(t) = C_1 \frac{dv(t)}{dt} + C_2 \frac{dv(t)}{dt} + \cdots + C_N \frac{dv(t)}{dt}$$

$$= (C_1 + C_2 + \cdots C_N) \frac{dv(t)}{dt}$$

Using summation notation results in:

$$i(t) = \left(\sum_{k=1}^{N} C_k \right) \frac{dv(t)}{dt}$$

Eq. 6.24

This is the same equation that governs the circuit of Fig. 6.26, if:

$$C_{eq} = \sum_{k=1}^{N} C_k$$

Eq. 6.25

Thus, the equivalent capacitance of a parallel combination of capacitors is simply the sum of the individual capacitances. This result is analogous to the equations, which provide the equivalent resistance of a <u>series</u> combination of resistors.

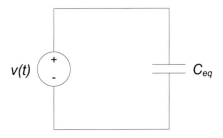

Figure 6.26. Equivalent circuit to Figure 5.

Summary: Series and Parallel Capacitors

- The equivalent capacitance of a <u>series combination of capacitors</u> C_1, C_2, ..., C_N is governed by a relation which is analogous to that providing the equivalent resistance of a <u>parallel</u> combination of resistors:

$$\frac{1}{C_{eq}} = \sum_{k=1}^{N} \frac{1}{C_k}$$

- The equivalent of a <u>parallel combination of capacitors</u> C_1, C_2, …, C_N is governed by a relation which is analogous to that providing the equivalent resistance of a <u>series combination of resistors</u>:

$$C_{eq} = \sum_{k=1}^{N} C_k$$

6.3.5 Practical Capacitors

Commercially available capacitors are manufactured in a wide range of both conductor and dielectric materials and are available in a wide range of capacitances and voltage ratings. The voltage rating of the device is the maximum voltage, which can be safely applied to the capacitor; using voltages higher than the rated value will damage the capacitor. The capacitance of commercially available capacitors is commonly measured in microfarads (μF; one microfarad is 10^{-6} of a Farad) or picofarads (pF; one picofarad is 10^{-12} of a Farad). Large capacitors are available, but are relatively infrequently used. These are generally called "super-capacitors" or "ultra-capacitors" and are available in capacitances up to tens of Farads. For most applications, however, using one would be comparable to buying a car with a 1000 gallon gas tank.

Several approaches are used for labeling a capacitor with its capacitance value. Large capacitors often have their value printed plainly on them, such as "10μF" (for 10 microfarads). Smaller capacitors, appearing as small disks or wafers, often have their values printed on them in an encoded manner. For these capacitors, a three-digit number indicates the capacitor value in pico-farads. The first two digits provides the "base" number, and the third digit provides an exponent of 10 in units of picofarads (so, for example, "104" printed on a capacitor indicates a capacitance value of 10 x 104 or 100000 pF). Occasionally, a capacitor will only show a two-digit number, in which case that number is simply the capacitor value in pF. (For completeness, if a capacitor shows a three-digit number and the third digit is 8 or 9, then the first two digits are multiplied by .01 and .1 respectively).

Capacitors are generally classified according to the dielectric material used. Common capacitor types include mica, ceramic, Mylar, paper, Teflon and polystyrene. An important class of capacitors which require special mention are *electrolytic* capacitors. Electrolytic capacitors have relatively large capacitances relative to other types of capacitors of similar size. However, some care must be exercised when using electrolytic capacitors – they are *polarized* and must be connected to a circuit with the correct polarity. The positive lead of the capacitor must be connected to the positive lead of the circuit. <u>Connecting the positive lead of the capacitor to the negative lead of a circuit can result in unwanted current "leakage" through the capacitor or, in extreme cases, destroy the capacitor.</u> Polarized capacitors either have a dark stripe near the pin that must be kept at the higher voltage, or a "-" near the pin that must be kept at a lower voltage.

Practical capacitors, unlike ideal capacitors, will dissipate some power. This power loss is primarily due to *leakage currents*. These currents are due to the fact that real dielectric materials are not perfect insulators – some small current will tend to flow through them. The overall effect is comparable to placing a high resistance in parallel with an ideal capacitor, as shown in Fig. 6.27. Different types of capacitors have different leakage currents. Mica capacitors tend to have low leakage currents, the leakage currents of ceramic capacitors vary according to the type of capacitor, and electrolytic capacitors have high leakage currents.

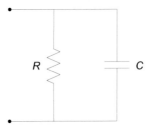

Figure 6.27. Model of practical capacitor including leakage current path.

- Capacitors store electrical energy. This energy is stored in an electric field between two conductive elements, separated by an insulating material.
- Capacitor energy storage is dependent upon the voltage across the capacitor, if the capacitor voltage is known, the energy in the capacitor is known.
- The voltage-current relationship for a capacitor is:

$$i(t) = C\frac{dv(t)}{dt}$$

Where C is the capacitance of the capacitor. Units of capacitance are Farads (abbreviated F). The capacitance of a capacitor, very roughly speaking, gives an indication of how much energy it can store

- The above voltage-current relation results in the following important properties of capacitors:
  - If the capacitor voltage is constant, the current through the capacitor is zero. Thus, if the capacitor voltage is constant, the capacitor can be modeled as an open circuit.
  - Changing the capacitor voltage instantaneously requires infinite power. Thus (for now, anyway) we will assume that capacitors cannot instantaneously change their voltage.
- Capacitors placed in series or parallel with one another can be modeled as a single equivalent capacitance. Thus, capacitors in series or in parallel are not "independent" energy storage elements.

6.3   Exercises

1. Determine the maximum and minimum capacitances that can be obtained from four 1µF capacitors. Sketch the circuit schematics that provide these capacitances.
2. Determine voltage divider relationships to provide v_1 and v_2 for the two uncharged series capacitors shown below. Use your result to determine v_2 if $C_1=C_2=10µF$.

Solutions can be found at digilent.com/real-analog.

6.4   Inductors

We continue our study of energy storage elements with a discussion of *inductors*. Inductors, like resistors and capacitors, are passive two-terminal circuit elements. That is, no external power supply is necessary to make them function. Inductors commonly consist of a conductive wire wrapped around a core material; inductors store energy in the form of a magnetic field set up around the current-carrying wire.

In this section, we describe physical properties of inductors and provide a mathematical model for an <u>ideal</u> inductor. Using this ideal inductor model, we will develop mathematical relationships for the energy stored in an inductor and governing relations for series and parallel connections of inductors. The section concludes with a brief discussion of practical (non-ideal) inductors.

6.4.1   Inductors

Passing a current through a conductive wire will create a *magnetic field* around the wire. This magnetic field is generally thought of in terms of as forming closed loops of *magnetic flux* around the current-carrying element. This physical process is used to create *inductors*. Figure 6.28 illustrates a common type of inductor, consisting of a coiled wire wrapped around a core material. Passing a current through the conducting wire sets up lines of magnetic flux, as shown in Fig. 6.28; the inductor <u>stores energy</u> in this magnetic field. The *inductance* of the inductor is a quantity, which tells us how much energy can be stored by the inductor. Higher inductance means that the inductor can store more energy. Inductance has units of *Henrys*, abbreviated H.

The amount of inductance an inductor has is governed by the geometry of the inductor and the properties of the core material. These effects can be complex; rather than attempt a comprehensive discussion of these effects, we will simply claim that, in general, inductance is dependent upon the following parameters:

- The number of times the wire is wrapped around the core. More coils of wire results in a higher inductance.
- The core material's type and shape. Core materials are commonly ferromagnetic materials, since they result in higher magnetic flux and correspondingly higher energy storage. Air, however, is a fairly commonly used core material – presumably because of its ready availability.
- The spacing between turns of the wire around the core.

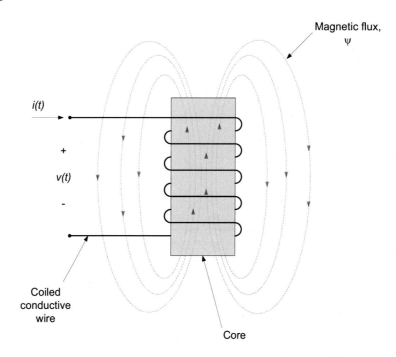

Figure 6.28. Wire-wrapped inductor with applied current through conductive wire.

We will denote the total magnetic flux created by the inductor by ψ, as shown in Fig. 6.28. For a linear inductor, the flux is proportional to the current passing through the wound wires. The constant of proportionality is the inductance, *L*:

$$\psi(t) = Li(t)$$

Eq. 6.26

Voltage is the time rate of change of magnetic flux, so:

$$v(t) = \frac{d\psi(t)}{dt}$$

Eq. 6.27

Combining equations (6.26) and (6.27) results in the voltage-current relationship for an ideal inductor:

$$v(t) = L\frac{di(t)}{dt}$$

Eq. 6.28

The circuit symbol for an inductor is shown in Fig. 6.29, along with the sign conventions for the voltage- current relationship of equation (6.28). The passive sign convention is used in the voltage-current relationship, so positive current is assumed to enter the terminal with positive voltage polarity.

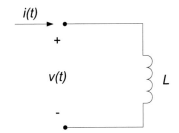

Figure 6.29. Inductor circuit symbol and voltage-current sign convention.

Integrating both sides of equation (6.28) results in the following form for the inductor's voltage-current relationship:

$$i(t) = \frac{1}{L}\int_{t_0}^{t} v(\xi)d\xi + i(t_0)$$

Eq. 6.29

In equation (6.29), $i(t_0)$ is a known current at some initial time t_0 and ξ is used as a dummy variable of integration to emphasize that the only "t" which survives the integration process is the upper limit of the integral.

Important Result

The voltage-current relationship for an ideal inductor can be stated in either differential or integral form, as follows:

- $v(t) = L\frac{di(t)}{dt}$
- $i(t) = \frac{1}{L}\int_{t_0}^{t} v(\xi)d\xi + i(t_0)$

Example 6.6

A circuit contains a 100mH inductor. The current as a function of time through the inductor is measured and shown below. Plot the voltage across the inductor as a function of time.

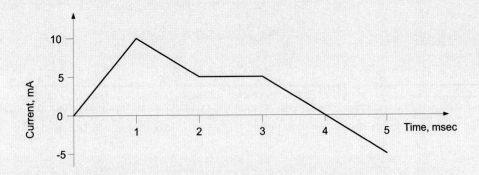

- In the time range 0<t<1ms, the rate of change of current is 10 A/sec. Thus, from equation (3), the voltage is $v(t) = (0.1H)(10A / s) = 1V$.
- In the time range $1ms < t < 2ms$, the rate of change of current is -5A/sec. The voltage is -0.5V.
- In the time range $2ms < t < 3ms$, the current is constant and there is no voltage across the inductor.
- In the time range $3ms < t < 5ms$, the rate of change of current is -5A/sec. The voltage is -0.5V

The plot of voltage vs. time is shown below:

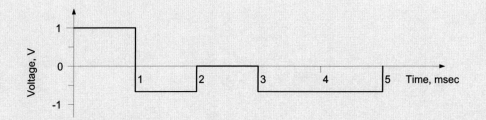

Power is the product of voltage and current. If the signs of voltage and current are the same according to the passive sign convention, the circuit element <u>absorbs</u> power. If the signs of voltage and current are not the same, the circuit element <u>generates</u> power. From the above voltage and current curves, the inductor is absorbing power from the circuit during the times 0<t<1ms and 4ms<t<5ms. The inductor returns power to the circuit during the times 1ms<t<2ms and 3ms<t<4ms.

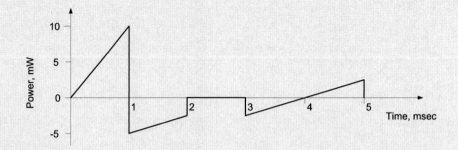

If the voltage as a function of time across an inductor with inductance L = 10 mH is as shown below, determine the current as a function of time through the capacitor. Assume that the current through the capacitor is 0A at time *t=0*.

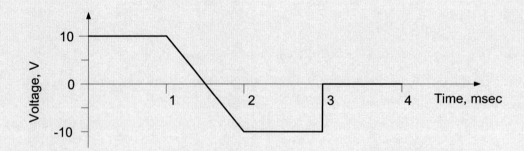

- At time *t=0*, the current is given to be 0A.
- In the time period 0<t<1 msec, the voltage is constant and positive so the current will increase linearly. The total current change during this time period is the area under the voltage curve curve, divided by the inductance: $\frac{1}{0.01}(10V)(1 \times 10^{-3}s) = 1A$
- In the time period *1<t<2* msec, the voltage is decreasing linearly. The current during this time period is a quadratic curve, concave downward. The maximum value of current is 1.25A, at *t=1.5* msec. The current at the end of this time period is 1A.
- In the time period *2<t<3* seconds, the voltage is constant at -10V. The current change during this time period is the area under the voltage curve, divided by the inductance: $\frac{1}{0.01}(-10V)(1 \times 10^{-3}s) = -1A$. The total current at t=3 seconds is, then, 1A − 1A = 0A.
- In the time period 3<t<4 seconds, the voltage is zero. The integral of zero over any time period is zero, so there is no change in current during this time range and the current remains constant at 0A.

A plot of the current through the inductor as a function of time is shown below.

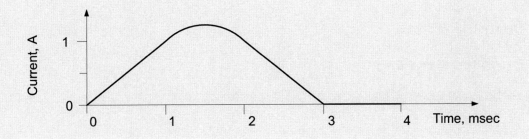

It is often useful, when analyzing circuits containing inductors, to examine the circuit's response to constant operating conditions and to instantaneous changes in operating condition. We examine the inductor's response to each of these operating conditions below:

- Inductor response to constant current:
    - If the current through the inductor is constant, equation (6.28) indicates that the voltage across the inductor is zero. <u>Thus, if the current through the inductor is constant, the inductor is equivalent to a short circuit.</u>
- Inductor response to instantaneous current changes:
    - If the current through the inductor changes instantaneously, the rate of change of current is infinite. Thus, by equation (6.28), if we wish to change the current through an inductor instantaneously, we must supply infinite voltage to the inductor. This implies that infinite power is available, which is not physically possible. <u>Thus, in any practical circuit, the current through an inductor cannot change instantaneously.</u>
    - Any circuit that allows an instantaneous change in the current through an ideal inductor is not physically realizable. We may sometimes assume, for mathematical convenience, that an ideal inductor's current changes suddenly; however, it must be emphasized that this assumption requires an underlying assumption that infinite power is available and is thus not an allowable operating condition in any physical circuit.

Important Inductor Properties

- Inductors can be replaced by short-circuits, under circumstances when all operating conditions are constant.
- Currents through inductors cannot change instantaneously. No such requirement is placed on voltages.

6.4.2 Energy Storage

The instantaneous power dissipated by an electrical circuit element is the product of the voltage and current:

$$p(t) = v(t) \cdot i(t)$$

Eq. 6.30

Using equation (6.28) to write the voltage in equation (6.30) in terms of the inductor's current:

$$p(t) = L \cdot i(t) \frac{di(t)}{dt}$$

Eq. 6.31

As was previously done for capacitors, we integrate the power with respect to time to get the energy stored in the inductor:

$$W_L(t) = \sum_{-\infty}^{t} Li(\xi) \frac{di(\xi)}{dt} dt$$

Which, after some manipulation (comparable to the approach taken when we calculated energy storage in capacitors), results in the following expression for the energy stored in an inductor:

$$W_L(t) = \frac{1}{2}Li^2(t)$$

Eq. 6.32

6.4.3 Inductors in Series

Consider the series connection of N inductors shown in Fig. 6.30.

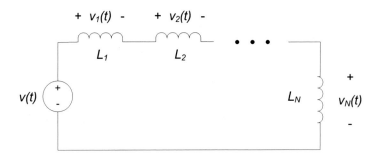

Figure 6.30. Series connection of N inductors.

Applying Kirchhoff's voltage law around the loop results in:

$$v(t) = v_1(t) + v_2(t) + \cdots v_N(t)$$

Eq. 6.33

Using equation (6.28) to write the inductor voltage drops in terms of the current through the loop gives:

$$v(t) = L_1\frac{di(t)}{dt} + L_2\frac{di(t)}{dt} + \cdots + L_N\frac{di(t)}{dt}$$

$$= (L_1 + L_2 + \cdots L_N)\frac{di(t)}{dt}$$

Using summation notation results in:

$$v(t) = \left(\sum_{k=1}^{N} L\_k\right)\frac{di(t)}{dt}$$

Eq. 6.34

This is the same equation that governs the circuit of Fig. 6.31, if:

$$L_{eq} = \sum_{k=1}^{N} L_k$$

Thus, the equivalent inductance of a series combination of inductors is simply the sum of the individual inductances. This result is analogous to the equations which provide the equivalent resistance of a <u>series</u> combination of resistors.

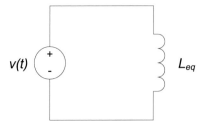

Figure 6.31. Equivalent circuit to Figure 3.

Chapter 6: Energy Storage Elements

6.4.4 Inductors in Parallel

Consider the parallel combination of N inductors, as shown in Fig. 6.32.

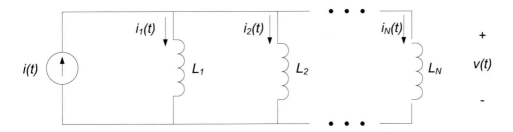

Figure 6.32. Parallel combination of I inductors.

Applying Kirchhoff's current law at the upper node results in:

$$i(t) = i_1(t) + i_2(t) + \cdots i_N(t)$$

Eq. 6.36

Using equation (6.29) to write the inductor currents in terms of their voltage drops gives:

$$i(t) = \left[\frac{1}{L_1}\int_{t_0}^{t} v(\xi)d\xi + i_1(t_0)\right] + \left[\frac{1}{L_2}\int_{t_0}^{t} v(\xi)d\xi + i_2(t_0)\right] + \cdots + \left[\frac{1}{L_N}\int_{t_0}^{t} v(\xi)d\xi + i_N(t_0)\right]$$

$$= \left[\frac{1}{L_1}\int_{t_0}^{t} v(\xi)d\xi + \frac{1}{L_2}\int_{t_0}^{t} v(\xi)d\xi + \cdots \frac{1}{L_N}\int_{t_0}^{t} v(\xi)d\xi\right] + [i_1(t_0) + i_2(t_0) + \cdots + i_N(t_0)]$$

$$= \left(\frac{1}{L_1} + \frac{1}{L_2} + \cdots + \frac{1}{L_N}\right)\int_{t_0}^{t} v(\xi)d\xi + i(t_0)$$

This can be re-written using summation notation as:

$$i(t) = \left(\sum_{k=1}^{N}\frac{1}{L_k}\right)\int_{t_0}^{t} v(\xi)d\xi + i(t_0)$$

Eq. 6.37

This is the same equation that governs the circuit of Fig. 6.31, if:

$$\frac{1}{L_{eq}} = \frac{L_1 L_2}{L_1 + L_2}$$

Eq. 6.39

Equations (6.38) and (6.39) are analogous to the equations which provide the equivalent resistance of <u>parallel</u> combinations of resistors.

Summary: Series and Parallel Inductors

- The equivalent inductance of a <u>series combination of inductors</u> L_1, L_2, ..., L_N is governed by a relation which is analogous to that providing the equivalent resistance of a <u>series combination of resistors</u>:

$$L_{eq} = \sum_{k=1}^{N} L_k$$

- The equivalent inductance of a <u>parallel combination of inductors</u> L_1, L_2, ..., L_N is governed by a relation which is analogous to that providing the equivalent resistance of a <u>parallel</u> combination of resistors:

$$\frac{1}{L_{eq}} = \sum_{k=1}^{N} \frac{1}{L_k}$$

6.5   Practical Inductors

Most commercially available inductors are manufactured by winding wire in various coil configurations around a core. Cores can be a variety of shapes; Fig. 6.28 in this chapter shows a core, which is basically a cylindrical bar. Toroidal cores are also fairly common – a closely wound toroidal core has the advantage that the magnetic field is confined nearly entirely to the space inside the winding.

Inductors are available with values from less than 1 micro-Henry ($1\mu H = 10^{-6}$ Henries) up to tens of Henries. A 1H inductor is very large; inductances of most commercially available inductors are measured in millihenries ($1mH = 10^{-3}$ Henries) or microhenries. Larger inductors are generally used for low-frequency applications (in which the signals vary slowly with time).

Attempts at creating inductors in integrated-circuit form have been largely unsuccessful; therefore many circuits that are implemented as integrated circuits do not include inductors. Inclusion of inductance in the analysis stage of these circuits may however, be important. Since any current-carrying conductor will create a magnetic field, the *stray inductance* of supposedly non-inductive circuit elements can become an important consideration in the analysis and design of a circuit.

Practical inductors, unlike the ideal inductors discussed in this chapter, dissipate power. An equivalent circuit model for a practical inductor is generally created by placing a resistance in series with an ideal inductor, as shown in Fig. 6.33.

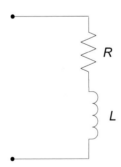

Figure 6.33. Equivalent circuit model for a practical inductor.

Section Summary

- Inductors store magnetic energy. This energy is stored in a magnetic field (typically) generated by a coiled wire wrapped around a core material.
- Inductor energy storage is dependent upon the current through the inductor, if the inductor current is known, the energy in the inductor is known.
- The voltage-current relationship for an inductor is:

$$v(t) = L\frac{di(t)}{dt}$$

Where L is the inductance of the inductor. Units of inductance are Henries (abbreviated H). The inductance of an inductor, very roughly speaking, gives an indication of how much energy it can store.

- The above voltage-current relation results in the following important properties of inductors:
    - If the inductor current is constant, the voltage across the inductor is zero. Thus, if the inductor current is constant, the inductor can be modeled as a short circuit.
    - Changing the inductor current instantaneously requires infinite power. Thus (for now, anyway) we will assume that inductors cannot instantaneously change their current.
- Inductors placed in series or parallel with one another can be modeled as a single equivalent inductance. Thus, inductors in series or in parallel are not "independent" energy storage elements.

6.4   Exercises

1. Determine the equivalent inductance of the network below:

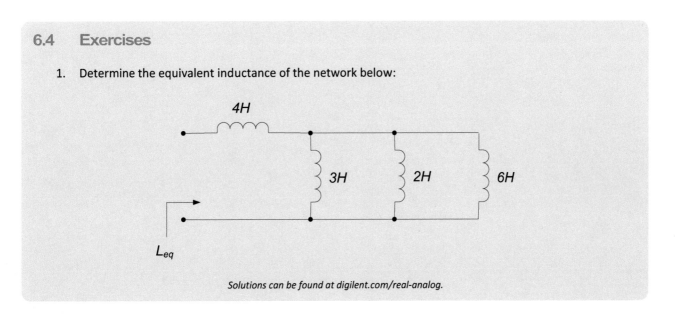

Solutions can be found at digilent.com/real-analog.

Chapter 7:
First Order Circuits

First order systems are, by definition, systems whose input-output relationship is a *first order* differential equation. A first order differential equation contains a *first order derivative* but no derivative higher than first order – the order of a differential equation is the order of the highest order derivative present in the equation.

First order systems contain a *single energy storage element*. In general, the order of the input-output differential equation will be the same as the number of <u>independent</u> energy storage elements in the system. Independent energy storage cannot be combined with other energy storage elements to form a single equivalent energy storage element. For example, we previously learned that two capacitors in parallel can be modeled as a single equivalent capacitor – therefore, a parallel combination of two capacitors forms a single independent energy storage element.

First order systems are an extremely important class of systems. Many practical systems are first order; for example, the mass-damper system and the mass heating examples from section 6.1 are both first order systems. Higher order systems can often be approximated as first order systems to a reasonable degree of accuracy if they have a *dominant first order mode*. (System modes will be discussed later in this text.) Understanding first order systems and their responses is an important aspect to design and analysis of systems in general.

First order electrical circuits are a special class of first order systems – they are first order systems which are composed of electrical components. Since the electrical components which store energy are capacitors and inductors, first order circuits will contain either one (equivalent) capacitor or one (equivalent) inductor.

In this textbook, we are really interested only in the analysis of electrical circuits, so the bulk of this chapter, of course, deals with analysis of first order electrical circuits. However, at this stage of your studies, you probably do not have an intuitive grasp of the mechanisms of energy storage in electrical circuits and the response of electrical circuits with energy storage elements. Therefore, this chapter begins in Section 7.1 with a general discussion of the response of first order systems, using a sliding mass as an example within which to frame the basic concepts. This provides a relatively gentle introduction to the nomenclature and mathematics which will be used throughout this chapter, in the context of an example for which the student should have some physical insight. Section 7.1 can be omitted, however, without loss of clarity of the remaining sections. Sections 7.2 and 7.3 present the natural response of RC and RL circuits, respectively (RC circuits have a capacitor as an energy storage element, while RL circuits contain an inductor). The natural response of a system corresponds to the system response to some initial condition, with no forcing function provided to the system. In section 7.4, we present the force response of first order circuits, and in section 7.5 we examine the response of first order circuits to a specific forcing function – a step input.

After completing this chapter, you should be able to:

- Write the general form of the differential equation governing a first order system
- State, in physical terms, the significance of a differential equation's homogeneous and particular solutions
- Define, from memory, the relationships between a system's unforced response, zero-input response, natural response, and the homogeneous solution to the differential equation governing the system
- Define, from memory, the relationships between a system's forced response, zero-state response, and the particular solution to the differential equation governing the system
- Determine the time constant of a first order system from the differential equation governing the system
- Write mathematical expressions from memory, giving the form of the natural and step responses of a first order system
- Sketch the natural response of a first order system from the differential equation governing the system and the system's initial condition
- Sketch the step response of a first order system from the differential equation governing the system and the amplitude of the input step function
- Write the differential equation governing RC and RL circuits
- Determine the time constant of RC and RL circuits from their governing differential equations
- Determine the time constant of RC and RL circuits directly from the circuits themselves
- Determine initial conditions on arbitrary RC and RL circuits
- Write from memory the form of the natural responses of RC and RL circuits
- Determine the natural response of RC and RL circuits, given the governing differential equation and initial conditions
- Write the form of the differential equations governing forced first order electrical circuits
- Determine the time constant of a forced electrical circuit from the governing differential equation
- Write differential equations governing passive and active first order circuits
- Determine the differential equation governing the step response of a first order electrical circuit
- Write the form of the particular solution of a first order differential equation, to a step input
- Write the form of the step response of a first order electrical circuit
- Determine the final conditions (steady-state response) of a first order electrical circuit, to a step input
- Define DC gain for a circuit and relate it to the steady-state response to a step input
- Determine the step response of a first order electrical circuit from the governing differential equation, the initial conditions, and the final conditions

7.1   Introduction to First Order Systems

In this section, we introduce some basic nomenclature relative to first order system responses and illustrate these terms in the context of an example for which the reader may have an intuitive understanding: a mass sliding on a surface. This example, though not directly relevant to the study of electrical circuits, is intended to allow the reader to develop some physical insight into the terminology and concepts relative to the solution of first order differential equations. The concepts and results obtained with this example are then generalized to apply to any arbitrary first order system. These results are used in later sections to provide insight in the analysis of electrical circuits, for which the reader may not yet have an intuitive understanding.

Before discussing first-order electrical systems specifically, we will introduce the response of general first order systems. A general first order system is governed by a differential equation of the form:

$$a_1 \frac{dy(t)}{dt} + a_0 y(t) = ft, \ t > 0 \qquad \text{Eq. 7.1}$$

Where *f(t)* is the (known) input to the system and *y(t)* is the response of the system. a_1 and a_0 are constants specific to the system being analyzed. We assume in equation (7.1) that the input function is applied only for times *t>t₀*. Thus, from equation (7.1), we can only determine the response of the system for times *t>t₀*.

In order to find the solution to equation (7.1), we require knowledge of the system's *initial condition*:

$$y(t = t_0) = y_0 \qquad \text{Eq. 7.2}$$

The initial condition, *y₀*, defines the state of the system at time *t=t₀*. Since equation (7.1) describes a system which stores energy, the effect of the initial condition is to provide information as to the amount of energy stored in the system at time *t=t₀*.

The system described by equations (7.1) and (7.2) can be illustrated in block diagram form as shown in Fig. 7.1. The output of the system depends upon the initial condition, *y₀*, and the input function *f(t)*. The initial condition provides information relative to the energy stored in the system prior to application of the input function. The input function provides information relative to the energy being applied to the system from external sources. The input-output equation describes how the system transfers the energy initially present in the system and the energy added to the system to the system output.

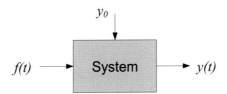

Figure 7.1. System block diagram.

The solution to equation (7.1) consists of two parts – the *homogeneous solution, yₕ(t)*, and the particular solution, *yₚ(t)*, as shown below:

$$y(t) = y_h(t) + y_p(t) \qquad \text{Eq. 7.3}$$

The <u>homogeneous solution</u> is due to the properties of the system and the initial conditions applied to the system; it describes the response of the system if no input is applied to the system, so *f(t)=0*. The homogeneous solution is sometimes called the systems *natural response*, the *unforced response*, or the *zero input response*. Since all physical systems dissipate energy (according to the second law of Thermodynamics) the homogeneous solution must die out with time; thus, $y_h(t) \rightarrow 0$ as $t \rightarrow \infty$.

The <u>particular solution</u> describes the systems response to the <u>particular</u> forcing function applied to the system; the form of the particular solution is dictated by the form of the forcing function applied to the system. The particular solution is also called the *forced response* or the *zero state response*.

Since we are concerned only with linear systems, superposition principles are applicable, and the overall system response is the sum of the homogeneous and particular solutions. Thus, equation (7.3) provides the system's overall response to both initial conditions and the particular forcing function being applied to the system.

The previous concepts are rather abstract, so we provide below an example of the application of the above concepts to a system for whose response the students should have some intuitive expectations. This example is intended to provide some physical insight into the concepts presented above prior to applying these concepts to electrical systems.

7.1.1 Mass-damper System Example

As an example of a system which includes energy storage elements we revisit the mass-damper system of section 6.1. The system under consideration is shown in Fig. 7.2. The applied force *F(t)* pushes the mass to the right. The mass's velocity is *v(t)*. The mass slides on a surface with sliding coefficient of friction *b*, which induces a force which opposes the mass's motion. The mass will have some initial velocity:

$$v(t = 0) = v_0$$

Eq. 7.4

Consistent with section 6.1, we consider the applied force to be the input to our system and the mass's velocity to be the output. Figure 7.3 illustrates the system input-output relationship and initial conditions in block diagram form.

The governing equation for the system was determined in section 4.1 to be the first order differential equation:

$$m\frac{dv(t)}{dt} + bv(t) = F(t)$$

Eq. 7.5

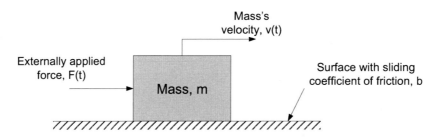

Figure 7.2. Sliding mass on surface with friction coefficient, b.

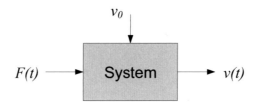

Figure 7.3. Block diagram of system shown in Figure 1.

We consider two cases of specific forcing functions in the following cases. In the first case, the forcing function is zero, and we determine the system's natural response or the homogeneous solution to equation (7.5) above. In the second case, the forcing function is a constant nonzero force applied to the mass with zero initial velocity.

Case i: Natural (Homogeneous) Response

Let us consider first the case in which the mass has some initial velocity but no external force is applied to the mass. Intuitively, we expect that the velocity of the mass will decrease until the mass comes to rest. In this example, we will determine the solution of the differential equation (7.5) and compare this solution with our expectations.

With no applied forcing function, the differential equation governing the system is:

$$m\frac{dv(t)}{dt} + bv(t) = 0$$

Eq. 7.6

The initial condition is given by equation (7.4) above, repeated here for convenience:

$$v(t = 0) = v_0$$

Equation (7.6) is a homogeneous differential equation, since there is no forcing function applied to the system. Thus, the particular solution in this case is $y_p(t)=0$ and our overall solution is simply the homogeneous solution, $y(t)=y_h(t)$.

To solve the above differential equation, we rearrange equation (7.6) to give:

$$\frac{m}{b} \cdot \frac{dv(t)}{dt} = -v(t)$$

Eq. 7.7

Separating variables in equation (7.7) results in:

$$\frac{dv(t)}{v} = -\frac{b}{m} dt$$

Eq. 7.8

Incorporating dummy variables of integration and integrating both sides of (7.8) gives:

$$\int_{v_0}^{v(t)} \frac{d\xi(t)}{\xi} = -\frac{b}{m}\int_0^t d\varsigma$$

Which evaluates to:

$$ln(v)\Big|_{v_0}^{v(t)} = -\frac{b}{m}t \Rightarrow \ln[v(t)] - \ln[v_0] = -\frac{b}{m}t \Rightarrow ln\left[\frac{v(t)}{v_0}\right] = -\frac{b}{m}t$$

Taking the exponent of both sides of the above provides our final result:

$$v(t) = v_0 e^{\frac{-bt}{m}}$$

Eq. 7.9

A plot of the response given in equation (7.9) is shown in Fig. 7.4. This plot matches our previous expectations, the velocity of the mass at time $t=0$ is v_0 and the velocity decreases exponentially until the mass is (essentially) at rest. Referring to section 6.2, we see that the response of equation (7.9) can be written in terms of a time constant as:

$$v(t) = v_0 e^{\frac{-t}{\tau}}$$

Where the time constant $\tau = \frac{m}{b}$. This result also agrees with our intuition: as the friction coefficient decreases, the time constant increases and the mass comes to rest more slowly. Likewise, increasing the mass causes the time constant to increase – a larger mass will tend to "coast" for a longer time.

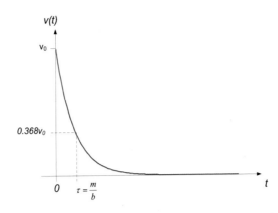

Figure 7.4. Homogeneous response of mass-damper system.

Note: The velocity of the mass tells us how much kinetic energy is being stored by the system. The initial condition provides the energy initially stored in the system. The calculated response describes how this energy is dissipated through the sliding friction. No energy is added to the system in this case, since the external applied force is zero.

Case ii: Response to Step Input

We will now consider the case in which the mass is initially at rest, and a constant force is applied to the mass at time $t=0$. Intuitively, we expect the velocity of the mass to increase to some final value; the final velocity of the mass corresponds to the condition in which the frictional force is equal and opposite to the applied force (recall that in our model, the frictional force is proportional to velocity – as the velocity increases, the frictional force opposing the motion also increases). We now solve the governing differential equation for this system and compare the results to our expectations.

The differential equation governing the system, valid for $t>0$, and initial condition, providing the energy in the system at $t=0$, are:

$$m\frac{dv(t)}{dt} + bv(t) = F$$

$$v(t = 0) = 0 \hspace{4cm} \text{Eq. 7.10}$$

Where F is the magnitude of the (constant) applied force. Note that since F is constant, and only applied for times $t>0$, we have a step input with magnitude F. We want to solve the above differential equation for $t>0$; since the input forcing function can be represented as a step function, this resulting solution is called the step response of the system.

For this case, we have both a nonzero forcing function and an initial condition to consider. Thus, we must determine both the homogeneous and particular solutions and superimpose the result per equation (7.3) above.

The homogeneous solution is determined from:

$$m\frac{dv_h(t)}{dt} + bv_h(t) = 0 \hspace{3cm} \text{Eq. 7.11}$$

Where $v_h(t)$ is the homogeneous solution. This equation has been solved as case *i*; the _form_ of the solution is:

$$v_h(t) = K_1 e^{\frac{-bt}{m}} \hspace{4cm} \text{Eq. 7.12}$$

Where K_1 is (in this case) an unknown constant which will be determined from our initial conditions.

Chapter 7: First Order Circuits

The particular solution is determined from:

$$m\frac{dv_p(t)}{dt} + bv_p(t) = F$$ Eq. 7.13

Where $v_p(t)$ is the particular solution to the differential equation in equation (7.10). Since the right-hand side of equation (7.13) is constant for $t>0$, the left-hand side of the equation must also be constant for $t>0$ and $v_p(t)$ must be constant for $t>0$. If $v_p(t)$ is constant, $\frac{dv_p(t)}{dt}$ is zero and equation (7.13) simplifies to:

$$bv_p(t) = F$$

So that:

$$v_p(t) = \frac{F}{b}$$ Eq. 7.14

Superimposing equations (7.12) and (7.14), per the principle expressed in equation (7.3) results in:

$$v(t) = v_k(t) + v_p(t) = K_1 e^{\frac{-bt}{m}} + \frac{F}{b}$$ Eq. 7.15

We can now use our initial condition, $v(t=0)=0$, to determine the constant K_1. Evaluating equation (7.15) at $t=0$ and applying the initial condition results in:

$$v(t=0) = 0 = K_1 e^{\frac{-b\cdot0}{m}} + \frac{F}{b}$$ Eq. 7.16

Since $e^{-b\cdot0}m = 1$, equation (7.16) results in:

$$K_1 = -\frac{F}{b}$$ Eq. 7.17

Substituting equation (7.17) into equation (7.15) results in the overall solution:

$$v(t) = -\frac{F}{b} e^{\frac{-bt}{m}} + \frac{F}{b} = \frac{F}{b}\left(1 - e^{\frac{-bt}{m}}\right)$$ Eq. 7.18

If, as in case i, we define the time constant $\tau = \frac{m}{b}$, equation (7.13) can be expressed as:

$$v(t) = \frac{F}{b}\left(1 - e^{\frac{-t}{\tau}}\right)$$ Eq. 7.19

A plot of the system response is shown in Fig. 7.5. This plot matches our intuitive expectations: the initial velocity is zero; the applied force causes the mass to move. When the frictional and applied forces balance, the velocity of the mass becomes constant. The time constant is determined by the mass and the frictional coefficient; a larger mass results in a longer time constant – it takes longer to get a large mass to its final velocity than a small mass. The frictional coefficient also affects the system time constant; a smaller friction coefficient results in a longer time constant. This result seems counter-intuitive at first, since a smaller frictional coefficient should allow us to accelerate the mass more rapidly. However, the smaller frictional coefficient also results in a higher final velocity – since the time constant is defined by the time required to reach approximately 63.2% of the final velocity, the higher final velocity causes a longer time constant even though the mass is accelerating more rapidly. (If the damping coefficient is zero, the time constant goes to infinity. However, the final velocity also goes to infinity – it takes an infinite amount of time to get to 63.2% of an infinite velocity!)

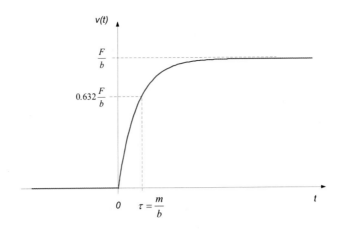

Figure 7.5. Step response of mass-damper system.

Note: The velocity of the mass again describes the energy stored by the system; in this case, the initial velocity is zero and the system has no energy before the force is applied. The applied force adds energy to the system by causing the mass to move. When the rate of energy addition by the applied force and energy dissipation by the friction balance, the velocity of the mass becomes constant and the energy stored in the system becomes constant.

Summary

We use the results of the above examples to re-state some primary results in more general terms. It is seen above that the natural and step responses of first order systems are strongly influenced by the system time constant, τ. The original, general, differential equation – equation (7.1) above – can be re-written directly in terms of the system time constant. We do this by dividing equation (7.1) by the coefficient a_1. This results in:

$$\frac{dy(t)}{dt} + \frac{a_0}{a_1}y(t) = \frac{1}{a_1}f(t), \quad t > t_0$$

Eq. 7.20

Defining $\tau = \frac{a_1}{a_0}$, equation (7.20) becomes:

$$\frac{dy(t)}{dt} + \frac{1}{\tau}y(t) = \frac{1}{a_1}f(t)$$

Eq. 7.21

The initial condition on equation (7.21) is as before:

$$y(t = t_0) = y_0$$

Eq. 7.22

The cases of the system homogeneous response (or *natural* or *unforced* response) and step response are now stated more generally, for the system described by equations (7.21) and (7.22).

1. **Homogeneous response**

   For the homogenous response *f(t) = 0*, and the system response is

   $$y(t) = y_0 e^{\frac{-t}{\tau}} \; for \; t \geq 0$$

   Eq. 7.23

   The response is shown graphically in Fig. 7.6.

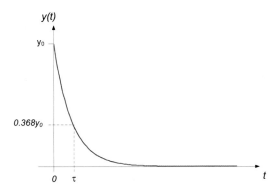

Figure 7.6. First-order system homogeneous response.

2. Step Response

For a step input of amplitude A, $f(t) = Au_0(t)$ where $u_0(t)$ is the unit step function defined in section 6.1. Substituting this input function into equation (7.21):

$$\frac{dy(t)}{dt} + \frac{1}{\tau}y(t) = \frac{A}{a_1}, \quad t > 0$$

Eq. 7.24

Using the approach of case 2. of our previous mass-damper system example, we determine the system response to be:

$$y(t) = \frac{A}{a_0}\left[1 - e^{\frac{-1}{\tau}}\right]$$

Eq. 7.25

This response is shown graphically in Fig. 7.7.

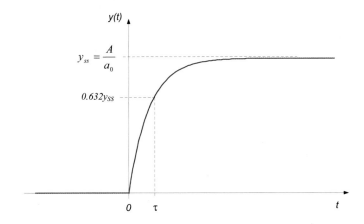

Figure 7.7. First order system response to step input with amplitude A.

Section Summary

- A first order system is described by a first order differential equation. The order of the differential equation describing a system is the same as the number of independent energy storage elements in the system – a first order system has one independent energy storage element. (The number of energy dissipation elements is arbitrary, however.)
- The differential equation governing a first order system is of the form:

$$a_1\frac{dy(t)}{dt} + a_0y(t) = f(t)$$

Where y(t) is the system output, f(t) is the applied input to the system, and a_0 and a_1 are constants.

- The differential equation governing a first order system can also be written in the form:

$$\frac{dy(t)}{dt} + \frac{1}{\tau}y(t) = \frac{f(t)}{a_1}$$

Where $y(t)$ is the system output, $f(t)$ is the applied input to the system, and τ is the system time constant.

- The system time constant is a primary parameter used to describe the response of first order systems.
- In this chapter, we considered two types of forcing functions: a zero-input case, in which $f(t)=0$ and $y(t=0)=y_0$, and a step input case, in which $f(t)=Au_0(t)$ and $y(t=0)=0$. For the zero-input case, the response is:

$$y(t) = y_0 e^{\frac{-t}{\tau}}, \qquad t > 0$$

For the step input case, the so-called *step response* is:

$$y(t) = \frac{A}{a_0}[1 - e^{-t}\tau], \ t > 0$$

- The system response consists of two parts: a *homogeneous solution* and a *particular solution*. The response can also be considered to consist of a *transient response* and a *steady-state response*. The homogeneous solution and the transient response die out with time; they are due to a combination of the system characteristics and the initial conditions. The particular solution and the steady state response have the same form as the forcing function; they persist as $t \to \infty$. It can be seen from the above that, for the zero-input case, the steady state response is zero (since the forcing function is zero). The steady state step response is $\frac{A}{a_0}$; it is a constant value and is proportional to the magnitude of the input forcing function.

7.1 Exercises

1. In Example 6.2, we examined a body which was subjected to external heating. The system is shown in the figure below. The mass of the body is m, the body material has a specific heat, c_P, and is at some temperature T_B. The surroundings are at an ambient temperature T_0. A heat input q_{in} is applied to the body, the heat dissipation between the body and its surroundings is q_{out}. It is common to assume that the heat dissipation q_{out} is proportional to the difference in temperature between the mass and its surrounds, so that $q_{out}=h(T_B-T_0)$. Incorporating this assumption into the governing equation for the system provided in Example 6.2, results in the following differential equation relating q_{in} and T_B:

$$mc_p\frac{d(T_B - T_0)}{dt} + h(T_B - T_0) = q_{in}$$

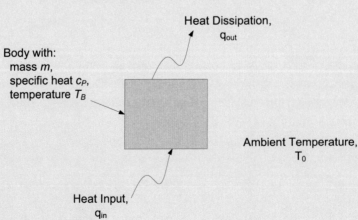

Heat Dissipation, q_{out}

Body with:
mass m,
specific heat c_P,
temperature T_B

Ambient Temperature, T_0

Heat Input, q_{in}

a. If the body has some initial temperature T_i, and no heat is applied to the body (e.g. $q_{in} = 0$),
    i.   What is the final temperature of the body?
    ii. What is the time constant (in terms of m, c_p, and h)?
    iii. If the body mass is doubled, what is the effect on the time constant? Does this agree with your expectations based on your intuition?
    iv. Sketch the response of the body temperature (T_B) vs. time. Label the initial condition and time constant on the sketch.
b. If the body is initially at a temperature T_0 (the same as the ambient surroundings) and a constant heat input q_{in} is applied starting at t = 0,
    i.   What is the final temperature of the body (in terms of m, c_p, q_{in}, and h)
    ii. What is the effect of doubling the heat input q_{in} on the final temperature? Does this agree with your intuition?
    iii. What is the effect of doubling the mass on the final temperature. Does this agree with your intuition?
    iv. What is the effect of doubling the mass on the time constant? Does this agree with your intuition?
    v.   Sketch the response T_B vs. time. Label the initial temperature, final temperature, and time constant on the sketch.

Solutions can be found at digilent.com/real-analog.

7.2 Natural Response of RC Circuits

In this section, we consider source-free circuits containing only resistors and a single capacitor – commonly referred to as RC circuits. Since these circuits contain only a single energy storage element – the capacitor – the governing equations for the circuits will be first order differential equations. Since the circuits are source-free, no input is applied to the system and the governing differential equation will be homogeneous. Thus, in this section we will be examining the *natural response of RC circuits*.

To begin our investigation of the natural response of RC circuits, consider the simple resistor-capacitor combination shown in Figure 7.8. We assume that the capacitor is initially charged to some voltage, V_0, at time *t=0* (so that *v(0)=V_0*). We want to determine the capacitor voltage, *v(t)*, for *t>0*.

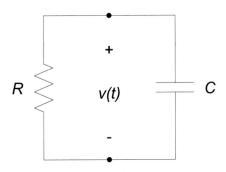

Figure 7.8. RC circuit; $v(t=0) = V_0$.

Applying Kirchhoff's current law at the positive terminal of the capacitor, as shown in Fig. 7.9, results in:

$$i_C(t) + i_R(t) = 0$$

Eq. 7.26

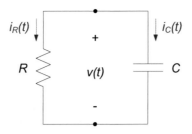

Figure 7.9. Currents in RC circuit.

Since $i_R(t) = \frac{v(t)}{R}$ and $i_C(t) = C\frac{dv(t)}{dt}$, equation (7.26) can be written in terms of the capacitor voltage as:

$$C\frac{dv(t)}{dt} + \frac{v(t)}{R} = 0$$

Separation of variables results in:

$$\frac{dv}{v} = -\frac{1}{RC}dt$$

The integral of the above is:

$$\int_{V_0}^{v(t)}\frac{dv}{v} = -\frac{1}{RC}\int_0^t dt$$

Which evaluates to:

$$\ln[v(t)] - lm[V_0] = -\frac{t}{RC}$$

Or

$$ln\left[\frac{v(t)}{V_0}\right] = -\frac{t}{RC}$$

Since $e^{\ln(x)} = x$, the above becomes:

$$v(t) = V_0 e^{\frac{-t}{RC}}$$

Alternate Approach to Solving the Above Differential Equation:

Since $\frac{dv(t)}{dt} = -\frac{1}{RC}v(t)$ we see that the form of the voltage signal must not change as a result of differentiation. Thus, assume that the voltage signal is of the form:

$$v(t) = Ke^{-st}$$

Where K and s are unknown constants. If we substitute this into the original differential equation, we obtain:

$$-Kse^{-st} = -\frac{K}{RC}e^{-st}$$

This is satisfied if we choose $s = -\frac{1}{RC}$. Employing our initial condition, $v(0) = V_0$, gives:

$$Ke^{\frac{-0}{RC}} = K = V_0$$

Results in:

$$v(t) = V_0 e^{\frac{-t}{RC}}$$

As before.

The capacitor voltage response is shown graphically in Fig. 7.10. The voltage response is a decaying exponential with a time constant:

$$\tau = RC \qquad\qquad\qquad \text{Eq. 7.27}$$

Thus, if we increase the resistance without changing capacitance, the circuit's time constant will increase. Likewise, increasing capacitance while maintaining the resistance constant will also increase the system's time constant. It is important to note that neither the resistance nor the capacitance alone specify the time constant, it is determined by the product of the two – if we simultaneously double the resistance and halve the capacitance, the system's time constant is unchanged.

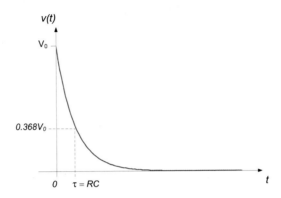

Figure 7.10. RC circuit natural response.

We can also obtain the above result by writing the governing differential equation directly in terms of the time constant. Previously, applying KCL to the circuit of Fig. 7.9, we obtained:

$$C\frac{dv(t)}{dt} + \frac{v(t)}{R} = 0$$

Which can be re-written (by dividing the equation by the capacitance, C, as:

$$\frac{dv(t)}{dt} + \frac{v(t)}{RC} = 0$$

Since the time constant for this circuit is τ=RC, the above can be re-written as:

$$\frac{dv(t)}{dt} + \frac{1}{\tau}v(t) = 0 \qquad\qquad\qquad \text{Eq. 7.28}$$

With initial condition:

$$v(0) = V_0 \qquad\qquad\qquad \text{Eq. 7.29}$$

The solution to equation (7.28), subject to the initial condition of equation (7.29) is (per our results above):

$$v(t) = V_0 e^{-t}\tau \ \text{ for } t \geq 0 \qquad\qquad\qquad \text{Eq. 7.30}$$

Where the time constant is defined per equation (7.27). The above approach matches our previous result. We will use the problem description provided by equations (7.28) and (7.29) and the solution of the form (7.30) most commonly in the subsequent examples. It should be emphasized, however, that the results are not dependent upon the solution approach – either of the other two approaches presented above yield the same conclusions.

7.2.1 Generalization to Multiple Resistors

The resistance in the time constant of equation (7.27) can be more generally defined as the <u>equivalent overall resistance of the circuit as seen by the capacitor</u>. Thus, if we remove the capacitor from the circuit and create a Thevenin equivalent resistance as seen by the capacitor, the time constant will be the product of the capacitance and this equivalent resistance. We illustrate this point with an example.

Example 7.1

Determine the voltage $v(t)$ for the circuit below if $v(0)$=5V.

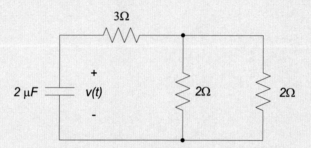

We will first solve the problem by writing the first order differential equation governing the system. To aid this process we re-draw the circuit as shown below, labeling the current through the capacitor, defining node "A", and labeling the voltage at node "A". For simplicity, we label the capacitor as having capacitance "C" in the figure below.

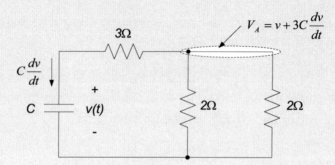

The voltage at node A $V_A = v + (3\Omega)C\frac{dv}{dt}$ is obtained by applying KVL around the outer loop of the circuit.

Applying KCL at node A results in:

$$C\frac{dv}{dt} + \frac{V_A}{2\Omega} + \frac{V_A}{2\Omega} = C\frac{dv}{dt} + V_A = 0$$

Which, when substituting $V_A = v + 3C\frac{dv}{dt}$ results in:

$$4C\frac{dv}{dt} + V_A = 0$$

This can be placed in the "standard form", $\frac{dv(t)}{dt} + \frac{1}{\tau}v(t) = 0$, by dividing through by 4C:

$$\frac{dv}{dt} + \frac{1}{4C}V_A = 0$$

Thus, the time constant $\tau = 4C = 8 \times 10^{-6}$ seconds.

Removing the capacitor and using circuit reduction to determine an equivalent resistance results in the circuit shown to the left below. The parallel combination of two, 2Ω resistors results in an equivalent 1Ω resistor, as shown in the figure to the right below. The resulting series combinations simplifies to a single 4Ω resistance, so $R_{eq}=4\Omega$.

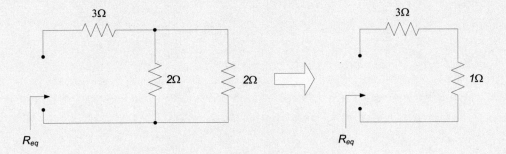

The circuit time constant can now be determined from R_{eq} and C. Thus:

$$\tau = R_{eq}C = (4\Omega)(2 \times 10^{-6}F) = 8 \times 10^{-6} \text{seconds}$$

Since the initial capacitor voltage is given to be 5V, $v(t) = 5e^{\frac{-t}{8 \times 10^{-6}}} = 5e^{1.25 \times 10^5 t}V$.

7.2.2 Determining Initial Conditions

The circuits we have considered so far in this chapter contain no sources, the circuits' initial conditions are given. In general, we will need to determine the initial conditions from a given source and/or switching operation. For example, a conceptual circuit showing how the initial condition for the circuit of Fig. 7.8 can be created is shown in Fig. 7.11(a). The switch in Fig. 7.11(a) has been closed for a long time; thus, just before the switch opens, the voltage across the capacitor is V_0. Opening the switch removes the source from the circuit of interest. Since the voltage across a capacitor cannot change suddenly, the capacitor still has voltage V_0 immediately after the switch opens. (Mathematically, we say that $v(t=0) = v(t=0^+) = V_0$. Where time $t=0$ is an infinitesimal time before the switch opens, and the time $t=0^+$ is an infinitesimal time after the circuit opens.) Thus, for times $t>0$, the shaded portion of the circuit of Fig. 7.11(a) is identical to the circuit of Fig.7.11(b) from the viewpoint of the capacitor voltage. An example of the analysis of an RC circuit with an included source is provided below; note that the circuit being analyzed is still <u>unforced</u> - the source only provides an initial condition.

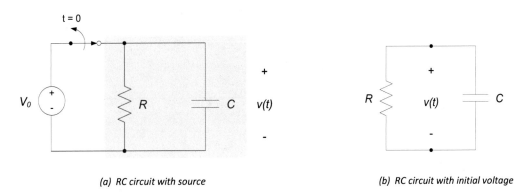

(a) RC circuit with source   (b) RC circuit with initial voltage

Figure 7.11. Capacitor energy storage.

Example 7.2: Switched Circuit Natural Response

Consider the circuit shown below. The switch is originally at position A; at time $t=0$ seconds, the switch moves to position B in the circuit. We wish to determine the capacitor voltage, $v(t)$ for $t>0$.

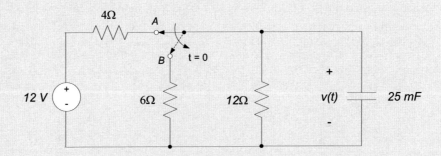

Before time $t=0$, we assume that the switch has been at position A for a long time – all transients have died off, and any voltages and currents in the circuit have become constant. Since the capacitor voltage-current relationship is $i = C\frac{dv}{dt}$, if all parameters are constant the capacitor current is zero and the capacitor looks like an open circuit. Replacing the capacitor with an open circuit, as shown in the figure below, allows us to determine the voltage across the capacitor before the switch moved to position B. It is fairly easy to see that the capacitor voltage is the same as the voltage across the 12Ω resistor. Since no current flows through the 6Ω resistor in the circuit, the voltage across the 12Ω resistor can be determined by a voltage division between the 12Ω resistor and the 4Ω resistor.

$$v(0^-) = 12V\left[\frac{12\Omega}{12\Omega + 4\Omega}\right] = 9V$$

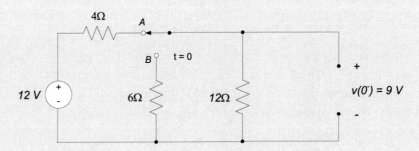

Since a capacitor cannot change its voltage instantaneously, the capacitor voltage just after the switch moves to position B is $v(0^+) = v(0^-) = 9V$, which gives us our initial condition on the capacitor voltage.

The system time constant can be determined from the capacitance and the equivalent resistance seen by the capacitor. The equivalent resistance can be determined by looking into the capacitor terminals with the switch at position B (recall that we are solving the differential equation for $t>0$). The appropriate circuit is shown below. The equivalent resistance consists of a parallel combination of the 12Ω and 6Ω resistors (note that the 4Ω resistor and the voltage source are no longer relevant to the problem – they are isolated from the capacitor after the switch changes to position B). The equivalent resistance is thus:

$$R_{eq} = \frac{(6\Omega)(12\Omega)}{6\Omega + 12\Omega} = 4\Omega$$

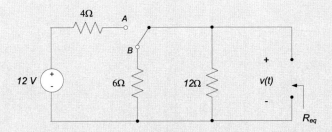

The system time constant is, therefore, $\tau = R_{eq}C = (4\Omega)(25 \times 10^{-3}F) = 100 \times 10^{-3}$ seconds or 0.1 seconds. Appropriate substitution of the initial condition and time constant into equation (7.30) gives:

$$v(t) = 9e^{\frac{-t}{0.1}} = 9e^{-10t}V$$

Section Summary

- The natural response of an RC circuit describes the capacitor voltage in a circuit consisting only of resistors and a single equivalent capacitance. The circuit is source-free; the response is entirely due to energy initially stored in the capacitor.
- The differential equation for an unforced RC circuit is of the form:

$$\frac{dv(t)}{dt} + \frac{1}{R_{eq}C}v(t) = 0$$

Where R_{eq} is the equivalent resistance "seen" by the capacitor.

- The RC circuit natural response is of the form:

$$v(t) = V_0 e^{\frac{-t}{\tau}} \text{ for } t \geq 0$$

Where V_0 is the initial voltage across the capacitor and τ is the circuit time constant.

- The time constant for **any** first order system can be determined from the differential equation governing the system. If the governing differential equation is written in the form:

$$\frac{dv(t)}{dt} + \frac{1}{\tau}v(t) = 0$$

The time constant τ can be determined by inspection. Thus, by comparison with the above differential equation for RC circuits, $\tau = R_{eq}C$.

- Alternatively, for the special case of an RC circuit, the time constant can also be determined by:

$$\tau = R_{eq}C$$

Where R^{eq} is the equivalent resistance "seen" by the capacitor and C is the capacitance in the circuit. (Notice, that to use this relation, we must accurately identify the circuit as a first order RC circuit before proceeding.)

- The capacitor properties can be useful in determining initial conditions for an RC circuit:
  - Capacitors behave like open-circuits when all circuit parameters are constant, and
  - Capacitor voltages cannot change instantaneously

7.2   Exercises

1. The switch in the circuit below moves from position A to position B at time $t = 0$.
    a. Write the differential equation governing $v(t)$, $t > 0$.
    b. Determine the time constant of the circuit from the differential equation of part a.
    c. Use the capacitance and the equivalent resistance seen by the capacitor to check your answer to part b.
    d. Determine the initial condition on the capacitor voltage, $v(t=0^+)$
    e. Determine $v(t)$, $t > 0$.

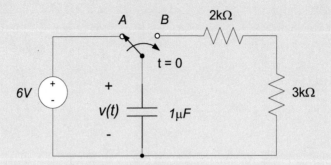

Solutions can be found at digilent.com/real-analog.

7.3   Natural Response of RL Circuits

In this section, we consider source-free circuits containing only resistors and a single inductor – commonly referred to as RL circuits. Like RC circuits, these circuits contain only a single energy storage element – the inductor – and the governing equations for the circuits will be first order differential equations. Since the circuits are source-free, no input is applied to the system and the governing differential equation will be homogeneous; the response of the circuit is due entirely to any energy initially stored in the inductor. We will thus be concerned with the *natural response* of RL circuits.

We will base our discussion of RL circuit natural responses on the series resistor-inductor circuit shown in Figure 7.12. We assume that the inductor has some initial current, I_0, flowing through it at time $t=0$ (so that $i(0)=I_0$). We will determine the inductor current, $i(t)$, for $t>0$.

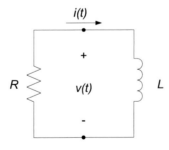

Figure 7.12.   RL circuit with initial condition $i(t=0) = I_0$.

Since the inductor's voltage drop and current are related by $v(t) = L \frac{di(t)}{dt}$, application of Kirchhoff's voltage law around the single loop in the circuit results in:

$$L \frac{di(t)}{dt} + Ri(t) = 0$$

Eq. 7.31

In this chapter, we will solve this differential equation using the "alternate approach" presented in section 7.2 for capacitors. This approach consists of assuming a form of the solution, based on the form of the differential equation being solved. The assumed solution will contain unknown constants; these constants will be determined by plugging the assumed solution into the original differential and forcing the solution to satisfy the original differential equation and initial conditions. Since the differential equation is linear and has constant coefficients, the solution to the differential equation is unique – thus, if we can find <u>any</u> solution, we have found the <u>only</u> solution. This approach is an extremely common differential equation solution method, we will use it regularly in subsequent chapters.

The form of equation (7.31) indicates that i(t) must be a function which does not change form when it is differentiated ($L\frac{di(t)}{dt}$ must cancel out $Ri(t)$). The only function with this property is an exponential function. Thus, we assume that the current is of the form:

$$i(t) = Ke^{-st}$$

Eq. 7.32

Where K and s are unknown constants. Substituting equation (7.32) into equation (7.31) results in:

$$L(-Kse^{-st}) + R(Ke^{-st}) = 0$$

The above simplifies to:

$$(R - Ls)Ke^{-st} = 0$$

Which is satisfied if $s = \frac{R}{L}$ or $Ke^{-st} = 0$. Choosing $Ke^{-st} = 0$ results in the trivial solution *i(t)=0*, which will not, in general, satisfy the initial condition on the circuit. By the process of elimination, we choose $s = \frac{R}{L}$ and the form of our solution becomes:

$$i(t) = Ke^{\frac{-tR}{L}}$$

Eq. 7.33

The unknown constant K is determined by applying the initial condition, *i(0)=I₀*. Evaluating equation (7.33) at time *t=0*, and equating the result to the given initial condition, we obtain:

$$i(0) = Ke^{\frac{-0 \cdot R}{L}} = K = I_0$$

Thus, $K = I_0$, and the solution to the differential equation is:

$$i(t) = I_0 e^{\frac{-tR}{L}} = I_0 e^{\frac{-t}{\tau}}$$

Eq. 7.34

And the circuit time constant is:

$$\tau = \frac{L}{R}$$

Eq. 7.35

Equation (7.35) indicates that increasing L or decreasing R causes the time constant to increase. Conversely, decreasing L or increasing R decreases the time constant. A plot of the response of equation (7.34) is shown in Fig. 7.13.

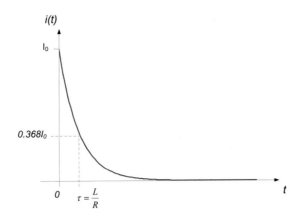

Figure 7.13. RL circuit natural response.

7.3.1 Generalization to Multiple Resistors

As with the RC circuit, the resistance in the time constant of equation (7.35) can be more generally defined as the <u>equivalent overall resistance of the circuit as seen by the inductor</u>. Thus, if we remove the inductor from the circuit and create a Thevenin equivalent resistance as seen by the inductor, the time constant will be the quotient of the inductance and the equivalent resistance.

7.3.2 Determining Initial Conditions

Though the initial condition is given in the above example, in general we will need to determine the initial condition from the application of some source and/or switching condition. For example, the circuit of Fig. 7.14 can be used to generate the initial condition of the example circuit above. In the circuit of Fig. 7.14, we assume that the switch has been closed for a long time and all circuit voltages and currents have become constant. When all circuit operating conditions are constant, the inductor behaves like a short circuit and all the current applied by the current source goes through the inductor and the inductor current is I_0. Since the current through an inductor cannot change suddenly, the inductor still has current I_0 immediately after the switch opens. Mathematically, $i(t=0^-) = i(t=0^+) = I_0$. where time $t = 0^-$ is an infinitesimal time before the switch opens, and the time $t=0^+$ is an infinitesimal time after the circuit opens. Thus, for times $t>0$, the shaded portion of the circuit of Fig. 7.14 is identical to the circuit of Fig. 7.12 from the viewpoint of the inductor current.

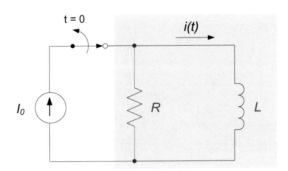

Figure 7.14. Circuit to realize the initial condition of the circuit of Figure 7.12.

An example is provided below to illustrate the points made in this chapter.

Example 7.3: Switched RL Circuit Natural Response

Consider the circuit shown below. The switch has been closed for a long time; at time *t=0* seconds, the switch suddenly opens. Determine the inductor current, *i(t)* for *t>0*.

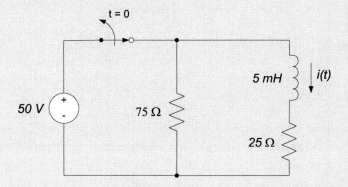

Since we are told that the switch has been closed for a long time, we assume that all voltages and currents in the circuit are constant before we open the switch. Therefore, before the switch is open the inductor behaves like a short circuit and the inductor current at time $t=0^-$ can be determined by analyzing the circuit below:

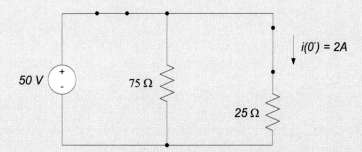

From the above circuit, the inductor current just before the switch is opened is, from Ohm's law, $i(0^-) = \frac{50V}{25\Omega} =$ $2A$. Since an inductor cannot change its current suddenly, the current immediately after the circuit opens is $i(0^+) = i(0^-) = 2A$. This provides our initial condition on the inductor current.

The time constant of the circuit is determined from the inductance and the equivalent resistance of the circuit seen by the inductor, after the switch opens. The equivalent resistance can be determined by analyzing the circuit shown below.

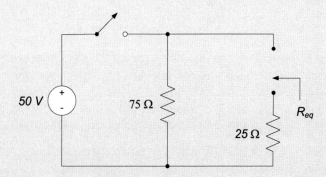

From the circuit above it can be seen that, to the inductor, the 25Ω and 75Ω resistors are in series. Thus, $R_{eq} = 25\Omega + 75\Omega = 100\Omega$. The system time constant is, therefore:

$$\tau = \frac{L}{R_{eq}} = \frac{5 \times 10^{-3} H}{100\Omega} = 5 \times 10^{-5} \text{ seconds}$$

Substitution of the initial condition and time constant into equation (4) gives:

$$i(t) = 2e^{\frac{-t}{5 \times 10^{-5}}} = 2e^{-20,000t} A$$

Section Summary

- The natural response of an RL circuit describes the inductor current in a circuit consisting only of resistors and a single equivalent inductance. The circuit is source-free; the response is entirely due to energy initially stored in the inductor.
- The differential equation for an unforced RL circuit is of the form:

$$\frac{di(t)}{dt} + \frac{R_{eq}}{L} i(t) = 0$$

Where R_{eq} is the equivalent resistance "seen" by the inductor.

- The RL circuit natural response is of the form

$$i(t) = I_0 e^{\frac{-t}{\tau}}, \text{ for } t \geq 0$$

Where I_0 is the initial voltage across the capacitor and τ is the circuit time constant.

- The time constant for a first order system can be determined from the differential equation governing the system. If the governing differential equation is written in the form:

$$\frac{di(t)}{dt} + \frac{1}{\tau} i(t) = 0$$

The time constant τ can be determined by inspection. Thus, by comparison with the above differential equation for RL circuits, $\tau = \frac{L}{R_{eq}}$.

- Alternatively, for the special case of an RL circuit, the time constant can also be determined by:

$$\tau = \frac{L}{R_{eq}}$$

Where R_{eq} is the equivalent resistance "seen" by the inductor and L is the inductance in the circuit. (Notice, that to use this relation, we must accurately identify the circuit as a first order RL circuit before proceeding.)

- The inductor properties can be useful in determining initial conditions for an RL circuit:
  - Inductors behave like short-circuits when all circuit parameters are constant, and
  - Inductors currents cannot change instantaneously

1. The switch in the circuit below moves from position A to position B at time $t = 0$.
   a. Write the differential equation governing $i_L(t)$, $t > 0$.
   b. Determine the time constant of the circuit from the differential equation of part a.
   c. Use the inductance and the equivalent resistance seen by the inductor to check your answer to part b.
   d. Determine the initial condition on the inductor current, $i_L(t=0^+)$
   e. Determine $i_L(t)$, $t > 0$.
   f. Determine the resistor current $i_R(t)$ just before and just after the switch moves. (e.g. determine $i_R(t=0^-)$ and $i_R(t=0^+)$.) Is the resistor current continuous with time? Is the current through the other resistor continuous with time?

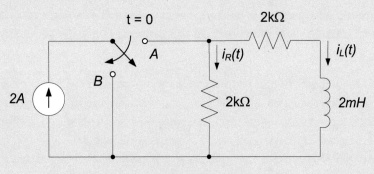

Solutions can be found at digilent.com/real-analog.

7.4 Forced Response of First Order Circuits

In sections 7.2 and 7.3, we were concerned with the natural response of electrical circuits containing a single energy storage element. For the natural response, any sources in the circuit were isolated from the circuit prior to determining the circuit response, so that the circuit being analyzed contained no sources. Thus, the circuit response of interest was entirely due to the energy initially stored in the circuit's capacitors or inductors. In these cases, all voltages and currents in the circuit die out with time.

In this section, we consider the case in which voltage or current sources are present in the first order circuit being analyzed. In this case, we must concern ourselves not only with the initial conditions in the circuit, but also with any *driving* or *forcing* functions applied to the circuit. The response of a system in the presence of an external input such as a voltage or current source is commonly called the *forced response* of the system. A primary difference between the natural response and the forced response of a system is that, although the natural response of a system always decays to zero, the forced response has no such restriction. In fact, the forced response of the system will take the same form as the forcing function, as time goes to infinity.

The differential equations governing the forced response of first order circuits are still, as implied, first order – thus, the circuits presented here will contain only a single energy storage element. Figure 7.15 shows two examples of forced first order circuits; Fig. 7.15(a) is a forced RC circuit and Fig. 7.15(b) is a forced RL circuit. The voltage sources $v_s(t)$ in Fig. 7.15 provide an arbitrary input voltage which can vary as a function of time. Without loss of generality, we will concern ourselves only with determining the forced response of the voltages across capacitors or the currents through inductors. In spite of the simplicity of the circuits shown in Fig. 7.15, their analysis provides a framework within which to place the analysis of an arbitrary first order electrical circuit. These two circuits are, therefore, analyzed below in order to present the forced solution of an arbitrary first order differential equation.

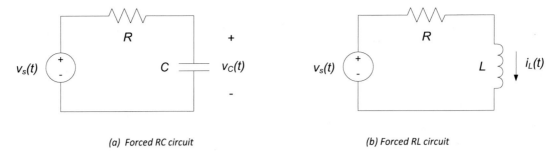

(a) Forced RC circuit   (b) Forced RL circuit

Figure 7.15. Forced first order circuit examples.

Tip: In all circuits we analyze, we will define as unknown variables the voltages across capacitors and the currents through inductors. We will then solve for these variables and determine any other necessary circuit parameters from these variables.

In any electrical circuit, we can determine *any* circuit parameter from the voltages across capacitors and the currents through inductors. The reason for this is that capacitor voltages describe the capacitor energy storage and inductor currents describe the inductor energy storage. If we know the energy stored in all energy storage elements, we have completely characterized the circuit's operating parameters – mathematically, we say that we have defined the *state* of the system. We will formalize this concept later when we discuss *state variable models*.

Examples of this concept, in the context of Fig. 7.15 include:

- The voltage drop across the resistor in Fig. 7.15(a) is: $v_R(t) = v_s(t) - v_c(t)$
- The current through the capacitor in Fig. 7.15(a) is: $i_R(t) = \frac{v_s(t) - v_c(t)}{R}$
- The voltage drop across the resistor in Fig. 7.15(b) is: $V_R(t) = Ri_L(t)$

KCL at the positive terminal of the capacitor of the circuit shown in Fig. 7.15(a) provides:

$$\frac{v_s(t) - v_c(t)}{R} = C\frac{dv_c(t)}{dt}$$

Eq. 7.36

Dividing through by the capacitance, C, and grouping terms results in the governing differential equation for the circuit of Fig. 7.15(a):

$$\frac{dv_c(t)}{dt} + \frac{1}{RC}v_c(t) = \frac{1}{RC}v_s(t)$$

Eq. 7.37

KVL around the loop of the circuit of Fig. 7.15(b) results in:

$$-v_s(t) + Ri_L(t) + L\frac{di_L(t)}{dt} = 0$$

Eq. 7.38

Dividing through by the inductance, L, and rearranging results in the governing differential equation for the circuit of Fig. 7.15(b):

$$\frac{di_L(t)}{dt} + \frac{R}{L}i_L(t) = \frac{1}{L}v_s(t)$$

Eq. 7.39

We notice now that the $\frac{1}{RC}$ term in equation (7.37) corresponds to $\frac{1}{\tau}$ where τ is the time constant of an RC circuit. Likewise, we note that the RL term in equation (7.39) corresponds to $\frac{1}{\tau}$ where τ is the time constant of an RL circuit. Thus, both equation (7.37) and equation (7.39) are of the form:

$$\frac{dy(t)}{dt} + \frac{1}{\tau}y(t) = u(t)$$

Eq. 7.40

Where τ is the time constant of the system, *u(t)* is the input to the system, and *y(t)* is the desired system parameter (a voltage across a capacitor or a current through an inductor, for example). Equation (7.40) can be solved, given knowledge of the initial conditions on *y(t)*, $y(0)=y_0$. A block diagram of the system described by equation (7.40) is shown in Fig. 7.16.

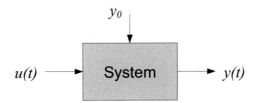

Figure 7.16. Block diagram of general forced first order system.

The solution to any forced differential equation can be considered to be formed of two parts: the *homogeneous solution* or *natural response* (which characterizes the portion of the response due to the system's time constant and initial conditions) and the *particular solution* or *forced response* (which characterizes the system's response to the forcing function *u(t)* after the natural response has died out). Thus, the system response *y(t)* in equation (7.40) and Fig. 7.16 can be expressed as:

$$y(t) = y_h(t) + y_p(t)$$

Eq. 7.41

Where *y_h(t)* is the homogeneous solution and *y_p(t)* is the particular solution.

We will not attempt to analytically determine the solution of equation (7.40) for the general case of an arbitrary forcing function *u(t)*; instead, we will focus on specific types of inputs. Inputs of primary interest to us will consist of:

- Constant (step) input functions
- Sinusoidal input functions

The study of circuit responses to step functions is provided in Section 7.5. Sinusoidal input functions are discussed in later chapters.

7.4.1 Generalization to Multiple Resistors

As in the first order circuit natural response, the resistance in the time constant of equation (7.37) can be more generally defined as the equivalent overall resistance of the circuit as seen by the energy storage element. This conclusion follows directly from Thévenin's theorem. The circuits of Fig. 7.15 consist of energy storage elements (a capacitor and an inductor) which are connected to a circuit which can be considered to be the Thévenin equivalent circuit of a more complex circuit. Thus, the resistance R in the circuits of Fig. 7.15 can be the equivalent (Thévenin) resistance of an arbitrary linear circuit to which an energy storage element is connected. Thus, the resistances in the governing differential equations (7.37) and (7.39) can be considered to be Thévenin equivalent resistances. These equations thus can be written as:

$$\frac{dv_c(t)}{dt} + \frac{1}{R_{eq}C} v_c(t) = \frac{1}{R_{eq}C} v_s(t)$$

Eq. 7.42

For an RC circuit, and :

$$\frac{di_L(t)}{dt} + \frac{R_{eq}}{L} i_L(t) = \frac{1}{L} v_s(t)$$

Eq. 7.43

For an RL circuit, where R_{eq} is the equivalent (Thévenin) resistance seen by the energy storage element. This leads to the conclusion that the time constants for first order forced circuits can be written in terms of the Thevenin resistance seen by the energy storage element. The appropriate relationships are:

$$\tau = R_{eq}C$$

Eq. 7.44

For RC circuits, and:

$$\tau = \frac{L}{R_{eq}}$$

Eq. 7.45

For RL circuits. Note that this conclusion is consistent with our previous results for <u>unforced</u> RC and RL circuits. We conclude this section with several examples in which we determine the differential equations governing first order electrical circuits. Note that we make no attempt to <u>solve</u> these differential equations – in fact, we <u>cannot</u> solve the differential equations, since we have not specified what the forcing functions are in the circuits below.

Example 7.4

Determine the differential equation relating $v_{in}(t)$ and $v_c(t)$ in the circuit below.

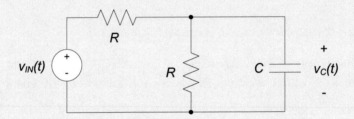

We will apply KCL at node "A", as indicated in the figure below, to begin our analysis.

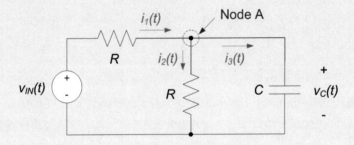

Thus,

$$i_1(t) = i_2(t) + i_3(t)$$

Using the voltage-current relations to write these currents in terms of voltages results in:

$$\frac{v_{in}(t) - v_c(t)}{R} = \frac{v_c(t)}{R} + C\frac{dv_c(t)}{dt}$$

After a little algebra, the above results can be written in our standard first order circuit form as:

$$\frac{dv_c(t)}{dt} + \frac{2}{RC}v_c(t) = \frac{1}{RC}v_{in}(t)$$

And the time constant of the circuit is $\tau = \frac{RC}{2}$.

Example 7.5

Determine the differential equation relating $V_{in}(t)$ and $V_{out}(t)$ in the circuit below.

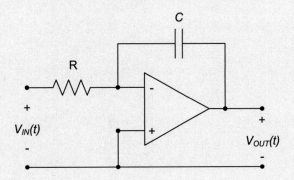

Consistent with our approach of defining variables as voltages across capacitors and currents through inductors, we define the capacitor voltage as $v_c(t)$, as shown in the figure below. Also in the figure below, node A is defined and the rules governing ideal op-amps are used to identify the node voltage $V_A=0V$.

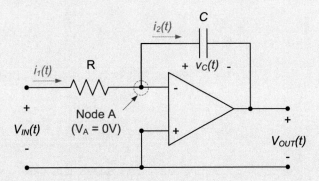

Applying KCL at node A in the circuit above gives:

$$i_1(t) = i_2(t)$$

The currents can be written in terms of the voltages in the circuit to provide:

$$\frac{V_{in}(t) - 0}{R} = C\frac{dv_c(t)}{dt}$$

The capacitor voltage can be written in terms of V_{OUT} (using KVL) as:

$$V_{OUT}(t) = -v_c(t)$$

Thus, the governing differential equation for this circuit can be written as:

$$V_{OUT} = -\frac{1}{RC}\int V_{in}(t)dt$$

Note that this circuit is performing an <u>integration</u>.

Example 7.6

Determine the differential equation relating $V_{in}(t)$ and $V_{out}(t)$ in the circuit below.

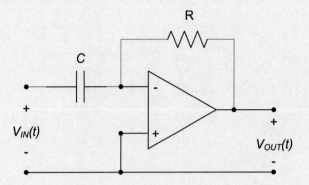

As in example 7.5, we define node A is defined and use the rules governing ideal op-amps to identify the node voltage $V_A=0V$, as shown in the figure below.

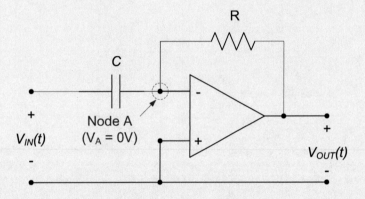

Writing KCL at node A directly in terms of the node voltages results in:

$$C\frac{dV_{in}(t)}{dt} = -\frac{V_{OUT}}{R}$$

So that:

$$V_{OUT} = -RC\frac{dV_{in}(t)}{dt}$$

And the output voltage is proportional to the <u>derivative</u> of the input voltage.

7.4.2   Cross-checking Results

The above examples revolve entirely around determining the governing differential equation for the circuit. The actual circuit response depends upon the governing differential equation, the initial conditions, and the specific forcing function being applied to the circuit. In the above examples, the circuit time constants were inferred from the differential equation coefficients governing the forced response just as they were when we determined the natural response.

It is <u>always</u> desirable to check one's results in as many ways as possible. With this in mind, we would like to check to see if the differential equation we have written for a given electrical circuit makes sense <u>before</u> solving the equation for a specific forcing function. For first order circuits, at least, we can do this by determining a time constant <u>directly from the circuit itself</u> and comparing this time constant with the time constant inferred from the governing differential equation. The time constant of any first order forced circuit can be obtained by calculating the Thévenin resistance seen by the energy storage element and using equations (7.44) and (7.45) to provide the time constant. We will now revisit example 7.4 using this approach to validate the differential equation we previously determined for this circuit.

Example 7.7

Check the time constant for the circuit of Example 7.4 by calculating the equivalent resistance seen by the capacitor.

The circuit of example 7.4 is shown below for reference.

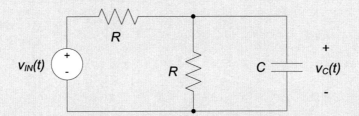

We can determine the equivalent resistance seen by the capacitor by replacing the voltage source with a short circuit and looking at the resistance seen across the capacitors terminals, as shown below:

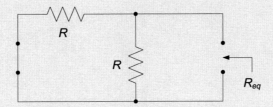

The resistors are now in parallel, so that the equivalent resistance is R/2. The time constant is then $\tau = R_{eq}C = \frac{RC}{2}$, which agrees with the result of example 7.4

Section Summary

- The forced response of a first order circuit describes the response of the circuit in the presence of (in general) both a non-zero initial condition and an arbitrary time-varying input function.
- The differential equation describing the forced response of a first order circuit is of the form:

$$\frac{dy(t)}{dt} + \frac{1}{\tau}y(t) = f(t)$$

Where $f(t)$ is the forcing function applied to the circuit. The time constant, τ, of the circuit is readily obtained from the differential equation when it is written in the above form.

- The time constant for a first order forced system can also be determined directly from the circuit itself. The process is to determine the Thevenin resistance, R_{eq}, seen by the energy storage element and use

---

that resistance in the appropriate time constant formula as introduced in sections 7.2 and 7.3. For an RL circuit, the time constant is $\tau = \frac{L}{R_{eq}}$, while for an RC circuit the time constant is $\tau = R_{eq}C$.

- Although the time constant can be determined from either the governing differential equation or the circuit itself, it is strongly recommended that both approaches be used and the results compared with one another to provide a cross-check of your analysis.

7.4   Exercises

1.   For the circuit below, write the differential equation governing $i_L(t)$. The input is the current source, $u(t)$.

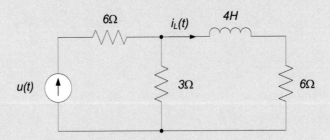

2.   Determine the differential equation governing $i_c(t)$ in the circuit below:

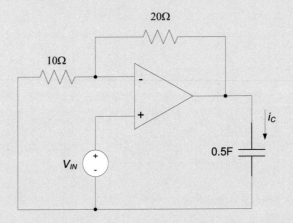

3.   Determine the differential equation governing $V_{out}(t)$ in the circuit below.

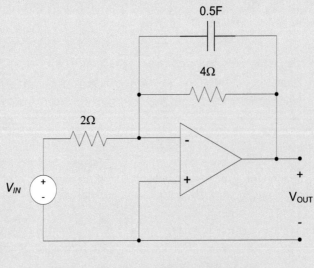

Solutions can be found at digilent.com/real-analog.

7.5   Step Response of First Order Circuits

In section 7.4 we introduced the concept of the response of a first order circuit to an <u>arbitrary</u> forcing function. We will not attempt to <u>solve</u> this problem for an arbitrary forcing function; we will instead restrict our attention to specific forcing functions. In this section, we address the case in which the input consists of the sudden application of a constant voltage or current to a circuit; this type of input is typically modeled as a step function. The response of a system to this type of input, in the absence of any initial conditions, is called the *step response* of the system.

Figure 7.17 shows a conceptual circuit which applies a step input to an RC circuit, and an actual switched circuit which may be used to implement this forcing function.

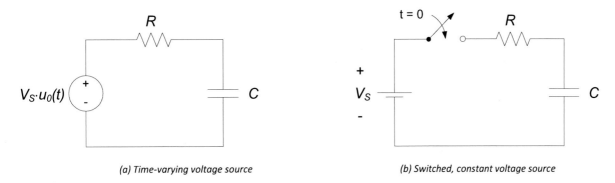

(a) Time-varying voltage source   (b) Switched, constant voltage source

Figure 7.17. Circuits to provide step input to RC circuit.

In section 7.3, we saw that the differential equation governing the forced response of a first order circuit is of the form:

$$\frac{dy(t)}{dt} + \frac{1}{\tau}y(t) = u(t)$$
                                                                                    Eq. 7.46

where τ is the time constant of the system, $u(t)$ is the input to the system, and $y(t)$ is the desired system parameter (for example, the voltage across a capacitor or the current through an inductor). In the case of a step input to the system, the input $u(t)$ to the system is a constant,

$$u(t) = Au_0(t)$$
                                                                                    Eq. 7.47

Where $u_0(t)$ is the unit step function.

We also saw, in section 7.3, that the solution of equation (7.46) can be written as the superposition of a homogeneous solution and the particular solution,

$$y(t) = y_h(t) + y_p(t)$$
                                                                                    Eq. 7.48

The *homogeneous solution, $y_h(t)$,* characterizes the portion of the response due to the system's time constant and initial conditions while the *particular solution, $y_p(t)$,* characterizes the system's response to the forcing function $u(t)$ after the natural response has died out.

The homogeneous response is the solution to the homogeneous differential equation:

$$\frac{dy(t)}{dt} + \frac{1}{\tau}y(t) = 0$$
                                                                                    Eq. 7.49

In Section 7.1, we showed that the form of the solution of the homogeneous response is:

$$y_h(t) = K_1 e^{\frac{-t}{\tau}}$$
                                                                                    Eq. 7.50

However, now we cannot determine K_1 directly at this point. Any conditions we can generate from the circuit with which to determine unknown coefficients apply to the entire forced solution, not the homogeneous or particular solution individually.

Our next step, therefore, is to determine the particular solution by substituting the input of equation (7.47) into the differential equation (7.46) and solving for $y_p(t)$. The appropriate differential equation is, therefore:

$$\frac{dy_p(t)}{dt} + \frac{1}{\tau}y_p(t) = Au_0(t)$$

Eq. 7.51

The particular solution is appropriate after the homogeneous solution dies out. Thus, we evaluate equation (7.51) as $t \rightarrow \infty$. The right-hand side of equation (7.51) is a constant value as $t \rightarrow \infty$, since:

$$Au_0(t) = \begin{cases} 0, t < 0 \\ A, t > 0 \end{cases}$$

If the right-hand side of equation (7.51) is a constant, then the left-hand side of equation (6) must be a constant and the individual terms in the left-hand side of equation (7.51) must be constants. It follows, then, that $y_p(t)$ is a constant and that $\frac{dy_p}{dt} = 0$. Therefore, as $t \rightarrow \infty$, equation (7.51) becomes:

$$\frac{1}{\tau}y_p(t) = A \Rightarrow y_p(t) = K_2$$

Eq. 7.52

The overall solution, then, from equations (7.48), (7.50), and (7.52) is:

$$y(t) = K_1 e^{\frac{-t}{\tau}} + K_2$$

Eq. 7.53

The unknown constants K_1 and K_2 are typically determined from evaluating the circuit's behavior for $t=0$ and $t \rightarrow \infty$.

We illustrate the overall solution process with three examples below. The first two examples are of passive first order circuit responses; the third example is of an active first order circuit.

Example 7.8

Determine the voltage across the capacitor, $v_c(t)$ for $t>0$ in the circuit below. The switch has been open for a long time, and the initial voltage across the capacitor is zero.

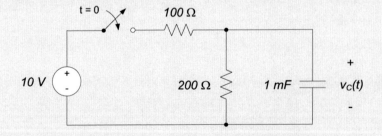

When the switch is closed, the circuit is as shown below. The capacitor current has been labeled for later convenience. Note that the direction of the capacitor current is set to agree with the polarity of the capacitor voltage, according to the passive sign convention.

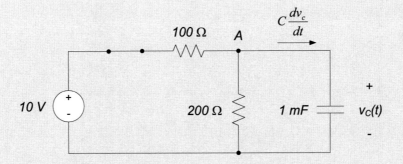

KCL at node "A" of the circuit shown above results in:

$$\frac{10 - v_c}{100\Omega} = \frac{v_c}{200\Omega} + 1 \times 10^{-3}\frac{dv_c}{dt}$$

Placing this in the form of equation (7.46) results in:

$$\frac{dv_c}{dt} + 15v_c = 100$$

Thus, the time constant $\tau = \frac{1}{15}$ seconds. From equation (7.53) above, the form of the solution is:

$$v_c(t) = K_1 e^{\frac{-t}{\tau}} + K_2$$

We now apply the given initial condition, $v_c(0)=0$ to get:

$$0 = K_1 e^{\frac{-t}{\tau}} + K_2 \Rightarrow K_1 + K_2 = 0 \qquad\qquad (*)$$

Another condition for determining the unknown constants is the capacitor voltage as $t \to \infty$. As $t \to \infty$, for a constant input, the capacitor becomes an open circuit. Thus, the circuit above becomes:

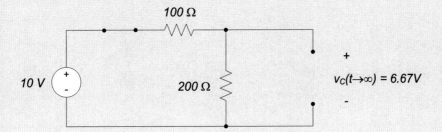

And the capacitor voltage can be determined from voltage division to be:

$$v_c(t \to \infty) = 10V\frac{200\Omega}{100\Omega + 200\Omega} = 6.67V$$

Substituting this result into the expression for the capacitor voltage results in:

$$6.67V = K_1 e^{\frac{-\infty}{\tau}} + K_2 \Rightarrow K_2 = 6.67V \qquad\qquad (**)$$

Equations (*) and (* *) provide two equations in two unknowns. Solving these results in:

$$K_1 = -6.67V$$

$$K_2 = 6.67V$$

And the capacitor voltage becomes:

$$v_C(t) = 6.67(1 - e^{-15t})$$

The value for τ can be checked by determining the equivalent resistance seen by the capacitor. To do this, we kill the sources and look into the capacitor terminals. The appropriate circuit is shown below.

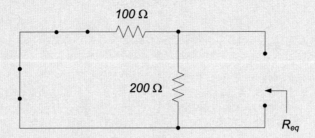

The equivalent resistance is $R_{eq} = \frac{(100\Omega)(200\Omega)}{100\Omega+200\Omega} = 66.67\Omega$ and $\tau = R_{eq}C = (66.67\Omega)(1mF) = \frac{1}{15}$ seconds, which checks our previous result.

Example 7.9

Determine the current through the inductor, $i_L(t)$, in the circuit below. No energy is stored in the circuit prior to $t=0$ seconds. The applied current input consists of a *12A* step input applied at $t=0$.

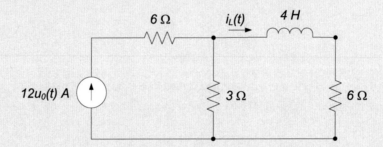

The circuit is shown below for $t>0$, with the inductor current labeled for ease of reference.

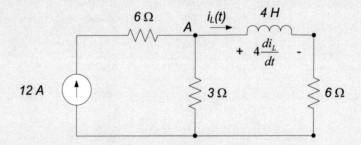

KVL around the rightmost loop in the circuit results in the following voltage across the 3Ω resistor:

$$v_{3\Omega} = 4\frac{di_L}{dt} + 6i_L$$

Employing this result and applying KCL at node A results in:

$$12 = i_L + \frac{1}{3\Omega}\left(4\frac{di_L}{dt} + 6i_L\right)$$

Placing the above equation in the form of equation (7.46) results in:

$$\frac{di_L}{dt} + \frac{9}{4}i_L = 9$$

From this, we see that the circuit time constant is $\tau = \frac{4}{9}$ and the form of $i_L(t)$ is, from equation (7.53):

$$i_L(t) = K_1 e^{\frac{-9}{4}t} + K_2$$

From the given initial condition:

$$i_L(0) = K_1 + K_2 = 0$$

As $t \to \infty$, the inductor becomes a short circuit and the above circuit becomes:

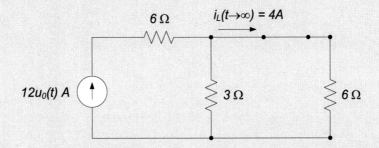

Current division allows us to determine that $i_L(t \to \infty) = 12A\frac{3\Omega}{3\Omega+6\Omega} = 4A$. Substituting this into equation governing $i_L(t)$, we obtain:

$$i_L(t \to \infty) = 4A = K_1 e^{-\infty} + K_2 \Rightarrow K_2 = 4A$$

Thus, the current through the inductor is:

$$i_L(t) = 4\left(1 - e^{\frac{-9}{4}t}\right)$$

Note that, once again, we can check our value for the time constant by killing any sources and determining the equivalent resistance seen by the inductor. The appropriate circuit is shown below:

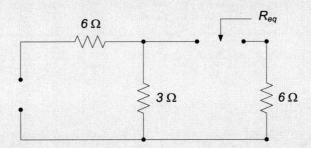

From the above circuit, the equivalent resistance is simply a series combination of the 3Ω and 6Ω resistors. Thus, $R_{eq}=9\Omega$. For an RL circuit, the time constant $\tau = \frac{L}{R} = \frac{4}{9}$ seconds. This agrees with the previous result we obtained from examining the form of the governing differential equation.

Example 7.10

The switch in the circuit below closes at time $t=0$. Find $V_{OUT}(t)$, for $t>0$. The capacitor has no energy stored in it prior to $t=0$.

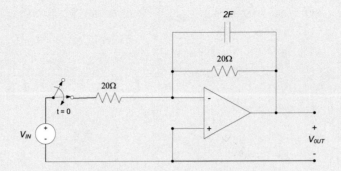

For time $t>0$, the switch is closed and the circuit is as shown on the figure below. Labeling node A on this circuit as shown, we can determine from the ideal operational amplifier rules that $V_A=0V$.

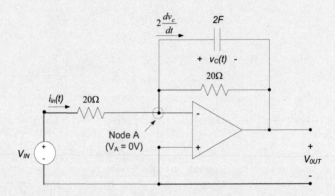

Applying KCL at node A results in:

$$\frac{V_{in} - 0}{20\Omega} = \frac{v_C(t)}{20\Omega} + 2\frac{dv_C(t)}{dt}$$

Since $v_{C(t)} = 0 - V_{OUT}(t)$, the above equation can be written as:

$$\frac{V_{IN}}{20\Omega} = \frac{0 - V_{OUT}(t)}{20\Omega} - 2\frac{dV_{OUT}(t)}{dt}$$

Placing this in the form of equation (7.46) results in:

$$\frac{dV_{OUT}(t)}{dt} + 40V_{OUT}(t) = -V_{IN}$$

Thus, the time constant $\tau = \frac{1}{40}$ sec. From equation (7.53) above, the form of the solution is:

$$V_{OUT}(t) = K_1 e^{\frac{-t}{\tau}} + K_2$$

We now apply the given initial condition, $v_C(0)=0$ to get:

$$0 = K_1 e^{\frac{-0}{\tau}} + K_2 \Rightarrow K_1 + K_2 = 0 \tag{*}$$

The output voltage as $t \to \infty$ can be determined from by open-circuiting the capacitor and analyzing the resulting circuit. The circuit with the capacitor open-circuited is simply an inverting voltage amplifier with a gain of one, so:

$$V_{OUT}(t \to \infty) = -V_{IN}$$

Substituting this result into the expression for the output voltage results in:

$$-V_{IN} = K_1 e^{\frac{-\infty}{\tau}} + K_2 \Rightarrow K_2 = -V_{IN} \qquad (**)$$

Equations (*) and (* *) provide two equations in two unknowns. Solving these results in:

$$K_1 = V_{IN}$$

$$K_2 = -V_{IN}$$

And the output voltage is:

$$V_{OUT}(t) = -V_{IN}(1 - e^{-40t})$$

7.5.1 Cross-checking Results

As in section 7.4, the examples above emphasize writing the governing differential equation for the circuit and determining the time constant from this differential equation. We also noted in section 7.4 that cross-checking results is crucial to producing reliable analyses, and that the time constant can also be determined directly from the circuit by calculating an equivalent resistance seen by the energy storage element. This cross-check was performed in exercises 7.8 and 7.9 above, as it should be.

For the case of a constant (or step) forcing function, we can use the final value of the solution as an additional cross-check of our results. In the above examples, we determined the final value of the response, $y(t \to \infty)$, based on the circuit behavior with capacitors replaced by open circuits and inductors replaced by short circuits. We can also determine the final value directly from the differential equation itself by examining the response of the differential equation as $t \to \infty$. This value is called the *steady-state* response of the circuit.

The general differential equation governing the step response of a first order circuit is given by equation (7.51) above. If we examine the solution to this differential equation as $t \to \infty$, we obtain only the particular solution, $y_p(t)$. (The homogeneous solution must go to zero as $t \to \infty$, leaving only the particular solution.) Thus, as $t \to \infty$ equation (7.51) becomes:

$$\frac{dy_p(t)}{dt} + \frac{1}{\tau}y_p(t) = A \qquad \text{Eq. 7.54}$$

Since the particular solution has the same form as the forcing function, and the forcing function is a constant, the derivative of the particular solution with respect to time is zero, and equation (7.54) becomes:

$$\frac{1}{\tau}y_p = A$$

And the steady state response, y_{ss}, is $y_{ss}=A \cdot \tau$. This value must agree with the final value obtained by short-circuiting inductors, open circuiting capacitors, and determining the final value from the circuit itself.

We apply this cross-check to the circuits of examples 7.8 and 7.9 below.

Example 7.11

In example 7.8, we determined (directly from the circuit behavior) that the final value of the capacitor voltage was:

$$v_C(t \to \infty) = 6.67V$$

And that the governing differential equation for the circuit was:

$$\frac{dv_C}{dt} + 15v_C = 100$$

We wish to check our final value of capacitor voltage relative to the differential equation behavior.

We can determine the final value of capacitor voltage by assuming that the voltage in the differential equation is constant, and setting its derivative to zero. Thus, the steady-state capacitor voltage can be determined from:

$$15v_{ss} = 100$$

So that $v_{ss} = \frac{100}{15} = 6.67V$ and agrees with the final value obtained by replacing the capacitor with an open circuit, as was done in example 7.8.

Example 7.12

In example 7.9, we determined (directly from the circuit behavior) that the final value of the inductor current was:

$$i_L(t \to \infty) = 4A$$

and that the governing differential equation for the circuit was:

$$\frac{di_L}{dt} + \frac{9}{4}i_L = 9$$

So that $i_{ss} = 9 \cdot \frac{4}{9} = 4A$ which agrees with the final value obtained by replacing the inductor with a short circuit, as was done in example 7.9.

7.5.2 DC Gain

The steady-state response of a circuit to a step input provides an important parameter which is often used to characterize the circuit's behavior. This parameter is called the DC gain, and is essentially the steady state response, normalized by the magnitude of the input step function. Mathematically, if the amplitude of the input step is A, the DC gain is given by:

$$DC\ gain = \frac{y_{ss}}{A} \hspace{4cm} \text{Eq. 7.56}$$

So the DC gain is simply the ratio of the output amplitude to the input amplitude, as $t \to \infty$. This parameter is of comparable importance to the characterization of first order circuits as the time constant. If we know the time constant and the DC gain of the circuit, we can immediately sketch the response of the circuit to <u>any</u> step input.

Example 7.13

Determine the DC gain for the circuit of example 7.8.

In example 7.8, the input voltage amplitude was 10V. The steady state output, the capacitor voltage, had an amplitude of:

$$v_C(t \to \infty) = 6.67V$$

Thus, the DC gain is simply the ratio of the input magnitude to the (steady-state) output magnitude:

$$DC\ gain = \frac{6.67V}{10V} = 0.67$$

The DC gain can also be determined from the governing differential equation. This is probably easiest to do if we replace the original 10V source with an arbitrary voltage, V_{in}, as shown below.

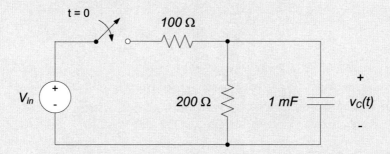

Re-deriving the governing differential equation, as was done in example 7.8, results in:

$$\frac{dv_C}{dt} + 15v_C = 10V_{IN}$$

If we are only concerned with the steady-state response, the derivative term can be set to zero and:

$$15v_{ss} = 10V_{IN}$$

So that $\frac{v_{ss}}{V_{in}} = \frac{10}{15} = 0.667$

Which agrees with the DC gain determined by calculating the steady state response to a specific input voltage and taking the same ratio.

Section Summary

- The step response of a first order circuit describes the response of a first order circuit to an applied step function. Typically, the term "step response" implies that all initial conditions in the circuit are zero, but this is not a requirement for application of any of the concepts presented in this section
- The differential equation describing the forced response of a first order circuit is of the form:

$$\frac{dy(t)}{dt} + \frac{1}{\tau}y(t) = Au_0(t)$$

  Where $u_0(t)$ is the unit step function defined in section 6.2. The time constant, τ, of the circuit is readily obtained from the differential equation when it is written in the above form.

- The form of the step response of a first order system is:

$$y(t) = K_1 e^{\frac{-1}{\tau}} + K_2$$

- The time constant in the solution above can be determined from either the governing differential equation or directly from the circuit itself.
- The unknown constants in the response are determined from initial, $y(0^+)$, and final, $y(t \to \infty)$, conditions. The initial conditions must be determined from the circuit itself. The final conditions can be determined from either the circuit itself or from the governing differential equation.
- Although both the time constant and the final value of the response can be determined from either the governing differential equation or the circuit itself, it is strongly recommended that both approaches be used and the results compared with one another to provide a cross-check of your analysis.
- The DC gain of a circuit provides the ratio of the output amplitude to the input amplitude, as $t \to \infty$, if the input is a constant value. The DC gain and the time constant are often used to characterize the response of a first order circuit.

7.5 Exercises

1. The initial current in the circuit below is zero. (e.g. $i_L(t = 0^-) = 0A$).)
    a. Write the differential equation governing $i_L(t)$.
    b. From your result in part 1, determine the time constant of the circuit.
    c. Write the form of the current $i_L(t)$.
    d. Use conditions at $t=0$ and $t \to \infty$ to determine the unknown constants in the expression for $i_L(t)$ in part 3.
    e. Determine the equivalent resistance seen by the inductor to check your answer from part b.

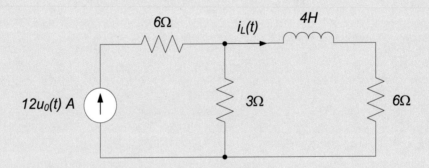

2. An input voltage input, $v(t)$, is applied to a first order electrical circuit. The differential equation governing the resulting current, $i(t)$, through an inductor is determined to be:

$$2\frac{di(t)}{dt} + 3i(t) = 5v(t)$$

What is the DC gain of the circuit? What are the units of DC gain for this circuit? What is the time constant of the circuit?

3. What is the DC gain of the circuit below? $u(t)$ is the voltage input to the circuit and $v(t)$ is the response. What are the units of the DC gain for this circuit?

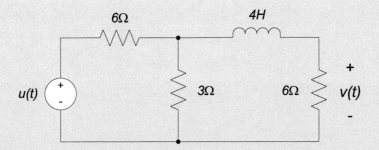

4. The differential equation governing the circuit shown below is determined to be:

$$\frac{dv(t)}{dt} + \frac{1}{9}v(t) = i(t)$$

Where the current *i(t)* is the input to the circuit and the voltage *v(t)* is the circuit response. <u>Without re-deriving the differential equation governing the circuit</u>, do you feel that the given differential equation above accurately describes the circuit response?

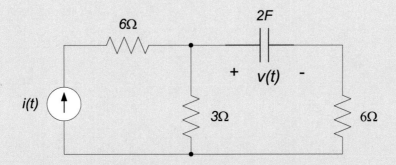

5. The differential equation governing the circuit shown below is determined to be:

$$3\frac{dv_C(t)}{dt} + v_C(t) = v(t)$$

Where the voltage *v(t)* is the input to the circuit and the capacitor voltage *v_C(t)* is the circuit response. <u>Without re-deriving the differential equation governing the circuit</u>, do you feel that the given differential equation above accurately describes the circuit response? Justify your answer.

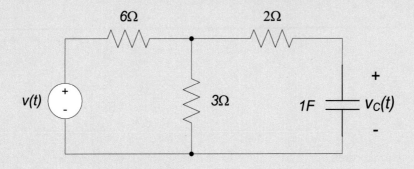

Solutions can be found at digilent.com/real-analog.

Chapter 8:
Second Order Circuits

Second order systems are, by definition, systems whose input-output relationship is a *second order* differential equation. A second order differential equation contains a *second order derivative* but no derivative higher than second order. Second order systems contain *two independent energy storage elements*, per our comments in Chapter 7 pertaining to the relationship between the number of energy storage elements in a system and the system order

Second order systems, like first order systems, are an extremely important class of systems. In previous chapters, we saw that the natural response of first order systems decays exponentially with time – the natural response decays monotonically to zero. The natural response of second order systems can, however, oscillate with time – we will see that a second order systems response can contain sinusoidal components. The motion of a pendulum, for example, can be modeled by a second order system. These oscillations are due to the transfer of energy between the two energy storage mechanisms; a pendulum, for example, oscillates because of the cyclic exchange of potential and kinetic energy of the mass.

Since the natural response of second-order systems can oscillate with time, their response can be fundamentally different than the response of first order systems. In the introduction to chapter 7, we noted that it is common to approximate higher-order systems as first order systems (at the time, we said that such a system has dominant first order modes). This approximation is not possible if the natural response of the higher order system oscillates. However, it may be possible to approximate the response of such a system as a second order system. Systems which behave approximately as second order systems have what are called *dominant second order modes*. In fact, the natural response of <u>any</u> higher order system can be considered in terms of the responses of multiple first and/or second order systems[1]. This is why an understanding of first and second order system responses is so

---

[1] In fact, in this chapter we will see that the responses of <u>some</u> second order systems can be interpreted in terms of two first order system responses.

crucial to the engineer – these responses provide the building blocks for understanding the responses of <u>all</u> linear systems.

In this textbook, of course, we are interested in the response of electrical circuits. Thus, we begin this chapter with a presentation of two simple second order electrical circuits: the series RLC and parallel RLC circuits. In section 8.1, we derive the governing equations for these circuits and use the results to write the general form of the differential equation governing second order systems. This equation is in terms of two very important parameters: the system *natural frequency* and the system *damping ratio*. The homogeneous solution of this general equation is determined in sections 8.2 and 8.4. In section 8.2, we develop the <u>form</u> of the solution (in terms of the natural frequency and damping ratio). Since the response of second order systems contains complex exponential functions, we provide some material (in section 8.3) relative to complex exponentials and sinusoidal signals. This material will provide us the necessary background to allow us to determine the natural response. Section 8.3 is optional for readers who are comfortable with complex exponential and sinusoidal signals. The overall natural response is developed in section 8.4, using the solution form presented in section 8.2 and the background material on complex exponentials in section 8.3.

After completing this chapter, you should be able to:

- Write differential equations governing second order circuits
- Define damping ratio and natural frequency from the coefficients of a second order differential equation
- Express the form of the natural response of an arbitrary second order system in terms of complex exponentials, the damping ratio, and the natural frequency
- Summarize the behavior of the complex exponentials in the system natural response for the damping ratio ranges below:
    - Damping ratio greater than one
    - Damping ratio less than one
    - Damping ratio equal to one
- Write complex numbers in terms of complex exponentials
- Express sinusoidal signals in terms of complex exponentials
- Classify *overdamped*, *underdamped*, and *critically damped* systems according to their damping ratio
- Identify the expected shape of the natural response of over-, under-, and critically damped systems
- State from memory the definition of an underdamped second order system's overshoot, rise time, and steady-state response
- Use the coefficients of a second order system's governing equation to estimate the system's overshoot, rise time, and steady-state response

8.1   Introduction to Second Order Systems

We will develop our discussion of second order systems in the context of two electrical circuits examples.

Example 8.1: Series RLC Circuit

Consider the circuit shown in Fig. 8.1 below, consisting of a resistor, a capacitor, and an inductor (this type of circuit is commonly called an RLC circuit). The circuit contains two energy storage elements: an inductor and a capacitor. The energy storage elements are independent, since there is no way to combine them to form a single equivalent energy storage element. Thus, we expect the governing equation for the circuit to be a second order differential equation. We will develop equations governing both the capacitor voltage, $v_C(t)$ and the inductor current, $i_L(t)$ as indicated in Fig. 8.1.

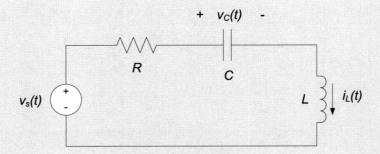

Figure 8.1. Series RLC circuit.

In order to determine the governing equations for $v_C(t)$ and $i_L(t)$ we will attempt to write two first-order differential equations for the system and then combine these equations to obtain the desired second order differential equation. To facilitate this process, the circuit of Fig. 8.1 is repeated in Fig. 8.2 with the node and loop we will use labeled. Note that we also label the current through the capacitor in terms of the capacitor voltage and the voltage across the inductor in terms of the inductor current.

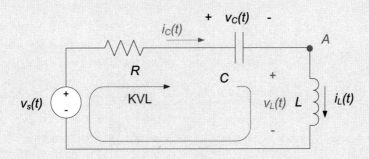

Figure 8.2. Series RLC circuit with node and loop defined.

The voltage-current relationships for inductors and capacitors indicate that, in Fig. 8.2, $i_C(t) = C\frac{dv_C(t)}{dt}$ and $V_L(t) = L\frac{di_L(t)}{dt}$. Using the latter of these relations, KVL around the indicated loop in Fig. 8.2 provides:

$$v_s(t) = Ri_L(t) + v_C(t) + L\frac{di_L}{dt}$$

Eq. 8.1

KCL at node A, along with the voltage-current relation for the capacitor, indicates that:

$$C\frac{dv_C(t)}{dt} = i_L(t)$$

Eq. 8.2

We can determine the equation governing the capacitor voltage by differentiating equation (8.2) with respect to time to obtain an expression for the derivative of the inductor current:

$$C\frac{d^2v_C(t)}{dt^2} = \frac{di_L(t)}{dt}$$

Eq. 8.3

Substituting equations (8.2) and (8.3) into equation (8.1) results in:

$$v_s(t) = RC\frac{dv_C(t)}{dt} + v_C(t) + LC\frac{d^2v_C(t)}{dt^2}$$

Rearranging this slightly results in:

$$\frac{d^2v_C(t)}{dt^2} + \frac{R}{L}\frac{dv_C(t)}{dt} + \frac{1}{LC}v_C(t) = \frac{1}{LC}v_s(t)$$

Eq. 8.4

To determine the relationship governing the inductor current, we can again use equation (8.2) to write the capacitor voltage as:

$$v_C(t) = \frac{1}{C}\int_0^t i_L(t)dt \qquad\qquad \text{Eq. 8.5}$$

Where we assume that the voltage across the capacitor at time *t=0* is zero; e.g. *v_C(0)=0*.

Substituting equation (8.5) into equation (8.1) results in the integro-differential equation:

$$v_s(t) = Ri_L(t) + \frac{1}{C}\int_0^t i_L(t)dt + L\frac{di_L}{dt}$$

In general, we prefer not to work with a mixture of derivatives and integrals in the same equation, so we differentiate the above to obtain our final expression for *i_L(t)*:

$$\frac{d^2 i_L(t)}{dt^2} + \frac{R}{L}\frac{di_L(t)}{dt} + \frac{1}{LC}i_L(t) = \frac{1}{L}\frac{dv_S(t)}{dt} \qquad\qquad \text{Eq. 8.6}$$

Important Tip: Equations (8.1) and (8.2) consist of two coupled first order differential equations in two unknowns: *i_L(t)* and *v_C(t)*. This set of differential equations completely describes the behavior of the circuit – if we are given appropriate initial conditions and the input function *v_s(t)* they can be solved to determine the inductor currents and capacitor voltages. Once the capacitor voltage and inductor current are known, the energy in the system is completely defined and we can determine any other desired circuit parameters. Any manipulations of equations (8.1) and (8.2) we performed subsequently do not fundamentally increase the information we have about the circuit – we were simply rearranging equations (8.1) and (8.2) to create a single equation with the desired unknown.

Example 8.2: Parallel RLC Circuit

Our second exemplary circuit is the parallel combination of a resistor, capacitor, and inductor shown in Figure 8.3. This circuit is called a parallel RLC circuit. The forcing function to the circuit is provided by a current source, *is(t)*. The circuit of Fig. 8.3, like that of Fig. 8.2, contains two independent energy storage elements –we expect the governing equations for the circuit to be second order differential equations. We will again develop equations governing both the capacitor voltage, *vc(t)* and the inductor current, *iL(t)* as indicated in Fig. 8.3.

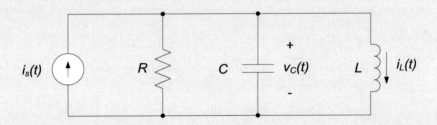

Figure 8.3. Parallel RLC circuit.

Consistent with our approach for the series RLC circuit, we will write first order differential equations using the variables *vc(t)* and *iL(t)* and subsequently combine these equations to eliminate the undesired unknown. Figure 8.4 shows the node and loop we will use to generate these equations. Figure 8.4 also shows the current through the capacitor in terms of the capacitor voltage and the voltage across the inductor in terms of the inductor current.

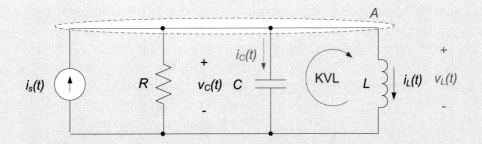

Figure 8.4. Parallel RLC circuit with node and loop defined.

KVL around the indicated loop provides:

$$L\frac{di_L(t)}{dt} = v_C(t)$$

Eq. 8.7

KCL at node A provides:

$$i_S(t) = \frac{v_C(t)}{R} + i_L(t) + C\frac{dv_C(t)}{dt}$$

Eq. 8.8

As in example 8.1, equations (8.7) and (8.8) completely describe the circuit's response. However, to gain additional insight into the individual parameters $v_C(t)$ and $i_L(t)$, we rearrange these equations into second order differential equations in a single dependent variable. For example, we can differentiate equation (8.7) to obtain:

$$L\frac{d^2i_L(t)}{dt^2} = \frac{dv_C(t)}{dt}$$

Eq. 8.9

Equations (8.7) and (8.9) can be substituted into equation (8.8) to obtain a second order differential equation in the variable $i_L(t)$. After some manipulation, the resulting equation is:

$$\frac{d^2i_L(t)}{dt^2} + \frac{1}{RC}\frac{di_L(t)}{dt} + \frac{1}{LC}i_L(t) = \frac{1}{LC}i_S(t)$$

Eq. 8.10

Likewise, we can integrate equation (8.7) and use the result to write equation (8.8) in terms of the capacitor voltage:

$$\frac{d^2v_C(t)}{dt^2} + \frac{1}{RC}\frac{dv_C(t)}{dt} + \frac{1}{LC}v_C(t) = \frac{1}{C}\frac{dv_S(t)}{dt}$$

Eq. 8.11

The important thing to note about the above examples is that equations (8.4), (8.6), (8.10), and (8.11) can all be written in the form:

$$\frac{d^2y(t)}{dt^2} + 2\varsigma\omega_n\frac{dy(t)}{dt} + \omega_n^2 y(t) = f(t)$$

Eq. 8.12

Where $y(t)$ is the system parameter of interest (for example, a voltage or current in an electrical circuit), ω_n is the undamped natural frequency and ζ is the damping ratio; the physical significance of these parameters will be presented later in this series of chapters. The point being made here is that the governing equation for any second order system can be written in the form of equation (8.12); thus, we will focus on this format for our discussion of the solution of second order differential equations.

Section Summary

- Second order systems have two independent energy storage elements. These circuits are governed by second order differential equations.

- Unlike first order circuits, the natural response of second order circuits can oscillate. This oscillation is due to energy exchanges between the two energy storage elements (inductors and/or capacitors, in electrical circuits). The oscillations will die out with time due to energy dissipation elements (resistors, in electrical circuits).
- The general differential equation governing second order circuits is of the form:

$$\frac{d^2y(t)}{dt^2} + 2\varsigma\omega_n \frac{dy(t)}{dt} + \omega_n^2 y(t) = f(t)$$

where y(t) is a voltage or current of interest in the circuit.

- In the equation above, ω_n is called the *undamped natural frequency* and ζ is called the damping ratio. These parameters (along with the DC gain of the circuit, as presented in section 7.5) govern the shape of the circuit natural response.

8.1 Exercises

1. The differential equation governing a circuit's natural response is:

$$\frac{d^2y(t)}{dt^2} + 32\frac{dy(t)}{dt} + 64y(t) = 0$$

Where y(t) is the circuit response. What are:

- The circuit's natural frequency and,
- The circuit's damping ratio

2. The differential equation governing a circuit's natural response is:

$$\frac{d^2y(t)}{dt^2} + 8\frac{dy(t)}{dt} + 64y(t) = 0$$

Where y(t) is the circuit response. What are:

- The circuit's natural frequency and,
- The circuit's damping ratio

3. For the circuit below, determine the differential equation for $i_L(t), t>0$. (Hint: write KCL at node A and KVL around loop 1 to get two equations in two unknowns, $v_c(t)$ and $i_L(t)$. Then combine the equations to eliminate $v_c(t)$.)

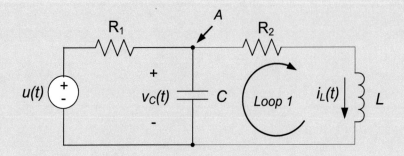

Chapter 8: Second Order Circuits

4. For the circuit shown below, apply KCL at node A and KVL around loop 1 to write two first order differential equations in two unknowns: the current through the inductor and the voltage across the capacitor. Combine these equations to write a single second order differential equation in the voltage *v(t)*.

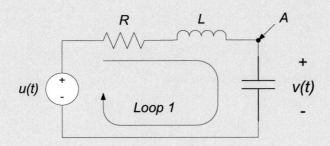

Solutions can be found at digilent.com/real-analog.

8.2 Second Order System Natural Response, Part 1

In section 8.1, we determined that the differential equation governing a second-order system could be written in the form:

$$\frac{d^2y(t)}{dt^2} + 2\varsigma\omega_n\frac{dy(t)}{dt} + \omega_n^2y(t) = f(t)$$

Where *y(t)* is any system parameter of interest (for example, a voltage or current in an electrical circuit), ω_n and ς are the *undamped natural frequency* and the *damping ratio* of the system, respectively, and *f(t)* is a forcing function applied to the system. In general, *f(t)* is an arbitrary function of the <u>physical</u> input to the system. (The physical input to the system can be, for example, a voltage or current source; *f(t)* is a function of these power sources. In section 8.1, we saw examples in which *f(t)* was proportional to an applied voltage or current or proportional to the derivative of an applied voltage or current.)

In this chapter, we will develop the homogeneous solution to the above second order differential equation. For the homogeneous case, the forcing function *f(t)=0*.

In this chapter, we develop the homogeneous solution to the differential equation provided in equation (8.12) of section 8.1. The appropriate differential equation to be solved is thus:

$$\frac{d^2y_h(t)}{dt^2} + 2\varsigma\omega_n\frac{dy_h(t)}{dt} + \omega_n^2y_h(t) = 0 \qquad \text{Eq. 8.13}$$

In equation (8.13), *yₕ(t)* is the solution to the homogeneous, or unforced differential equation given by equation (8.13). A second order differential equation requires two initial conditions in order to solve it; we will take our initial conditions to be the value of the function *y(t)* at *t=0* and the derivative of the function *y(t)* at *t=0*. We will state our initial conditions as:

$$y(t = 0) = y_0$$

$$\frac{dy(t)}{dt}\Big|_{t=0} = y_0' \qquad \text{Eq. 8.14}$$

Our approach to the solution of equation (8.13) will be consistent with our previous approach to the solution of first order homogeneous differential equations: we will assume the <u>form</u> of the differential equation (8.13) plug this assumed solution into equation (8.13) and then use our initial conditions to determine any unknown constants in the solution.

Examination of equation (8.13) leads us to conclude that the solution $y_h(t)$ of equation (8.13) must be a function whose form does not change upon differentiation. Thus, we assume (consistent with our approach in section 7.3) that the solution to equation (8.13) will be of the form:

$$y_h(t) = Ke^{st}$$

Eq. 8.15

Substituting equation (8.15) into equation (8.13) results in:

$$(Ks^2)e^{st} + 2\varsigma\omega_n(Ks)e^{st} + K\omega_n^2 e^{st} = 0$$

The above can be simplified to:

$$[s^2 + 2\varsigma\omega_n s + \omega_n^2]Ke^{st} = 0$$

The solutions to the above equation are $Ke^{st} = 0$ and $s^2 + 2\varsigma\omega_n s + \omega_n^2 = 0$. The first of these results in the trivial solution, $K=0$, which in general will not allow us to satisfy our initial conditions. Thus, in our solution given by equation (8.15), we choose s according to:

$$s^2 + 2\varsigma\omega_n s + \omega_n^2 = 0$$

Eq. 8.16

Since equation (8.16) is quadratic, values of s which satisfy it are given by:

$$s = \frac{-2\varsigma\omega_n \pm \sqrt{(2\varsigma\omega_n)^2 - 4(2\varsigma\omega_n)\omega_n^2}}{2}$$

After simplification, this provides:

$$s = -\varsigma\omega_n \pm \omega_n\sqrt{\zeta^2 - 1}$$

Eq. 8.17

Equations (8.15) and (8.17) indicate that there are two possible solutions to equation (8.13). Since the original differential equation is linear, we know that superposition is valid and our overall solution can be a linear combination of the two solutions provided by equations (8.15) and (8.17). Thus, we take our overall solution to be of the form:

$$y_h(t) = K_1 e^{s_1 t} + K_2 e^{s_2 t}$$

Where s_1 and s_2 are provided by equation (8.17) so that:

$$y_h(t) = K_1 e^{\left(-\varsigma\omega_n + \omega_n\sqrt{\varsigma^2 - 1}\right)t} + K_2 e^{-\left(-\varsigma\omega_n - \omega_n\sqrt{\varsigma^2 - 1}\right)t}$$

Which can be re-written as:

$$y_h(t) = e^{-\varsigma\omega_n t}\left[K_1 e^{\left(\omega_n\sqrt{\varsigma^2 - 1}\right)t} + K_2 e^{-\left(\omega_n\sqrt{\varsigma^2 - 1}\right)t}\right]$$

Eq. 8.18

The initial conditions, given by equations (8.14) can be used to determine the unknown constants, K_1 and K_2.

Let us briefly examine the form of equation (8.18) before providing examples of the homogeneous solution for specific circuit-related examples. We do this by examining individual terms in equation (8.18):

- In equation (8.18), the term $e^{-\varsigma\omega_n t}$ is an exponential function of the form discussed in section 6.2. Thus, we know that this term corresponds to a decaying exponential, as long as the term $\varsigma\omega_n$ is positive.

- There are three possible forms which the term $e^{\pm\left(\omega_n\sqrt{\varsigma^2 - 1}\right)t}$ can take:

- o If $\varsigma > 1$, the terms $e^{\pm\left(\omega_n\sqrt{\varsigma^2-1}\right)t}$ are either growing or decaying exponentials of the form discussed in section 6.2 (if $\varsigma > 1$ $e^{\left(\omega_n\sqrt{\varsigma^2-1}\right)t}$ grows exponentially with time and $e^{-\left(\omega_n\sqrt{\varsigma^2-1}\right)t}$ decays exponentially with time).
- o If $\varsigma = 1$, the terms $e^{\pm\left(\omega_n\sqrt{\varsigma^2-1}\right)t}$ are constant and equal to one ($e^{\pm(0)t} = 1$).
- o If $\varsigma < 1$, the terms $e^{\pm\left(\omega_n\sqrt{\varsigma^2-1}\right)t}$ are *complex exponentials*. (The term $\sqrt{\varsigma^2-1} = j\sqrt{1-\varsigma^2}$, where $j = \sqrt{-1}$. Thus, the term $e^{\pm\left(\omega_n\sqrt{\varsigma^2-1}\right)t} = e^{\pm\left(j\omega_n\sqrt{1-\varsigma^2}\right)t}$ and we have an exponential raised to an imaginary power.

Before examining the above results in more detail and performing some physical, circuit-related examples, we present some material in section 8.3 relative to complex exponentials and sinusoidal signals. This material will provide us a context within which we can place our solution of equation (8.18). Section 8.3 is optional for readers who are comfortable with complex exponential and sinusoidal signals.

Section Summary

- The form of the natural response of a general second order system is:

$$y_h(t) = e^{-\varsigma\omega_n t}\left[K_1 e^{\left(\omega_n\sqrt{\varsigma^2-1}\right)t} + K_2 e^{-\left(\omega_n\sqrt{\varsigma^2-1}\right)t}\right]$$

Where K_1 and K_2 are constants which depend upon the system initial conditions.

- The form of the $e^{\pm\left(\omega_n\sqrt{\varsigma^2-1}\right)t}$ terms in the system response depends strongly upon the damping ratio. If $\varsigma > 1$, these terms become growing or decaying exponentials. If $\varsigma < 1$, these terms are complex exponentials, and the solution will have sinusoidal components. The relationship between complex exponentials is presented in more depth in section 8.3. If $\varsigma = 1$, the $e^{\pm\left(\omega_n\sqrt{\varsigma^2-1}\right)t}$ are simply one.
- The $e^{-\varsigma\omega_n t}$ term in the natural response causes the overall solution to decay as time increases. Thus, the natural response goes to zero as $t \to \infty$.

8.3 Sinusoidal Signals and Complex Exponentials

Sinusoidal signals and complex exponentials are extremely important to any engineer who is concerned with determining the dynamic response of a system. Electrical circuits, in particular, are often characterized by their response to sinusoidal inputs.

This chapter provides some background relative to these signals.

8.3.1 Sinusoidal Signals

Sinusoidal signals are represented in terms of sine and/or cosine functions. In general, we will represent sinusoids as cosine functions. Our general expression for a sinusoidal signal is:

$$v(t) = V_p \cos(\omega t + \theta) \qquad \text{Eq. 8.19}$$

Where V_P is the zero-to-peak amplitude of the sinusoid, ω is the radian frequency of the sinusoid (we will always use radians/second as the units of ω) and θ is the phase angle of the sinusoid (in units of either radians or degrees are used for phase angle – recall that 2π radians = 360°). A representative plot of a sinusoidal signal is provided in Fig. 8.5. In Fig. 8.5, the frequency of the sinusoid is indicated as a <u>period</u> of the signal (the period is defined as the shortest time interval at which the signal repeats itself). The radian frequency of a sinusoid is related to the period by:

$$\omega = \frac{2\pi}{T}$$

Eq. 8.20

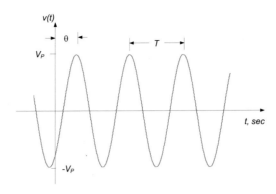

Figure 8.5. Arbitrary sinusoidal signal.

Note: Complex exponential signals have both real and imaginary parts; when we introduce complex exponentials later in this chapter, we will see that the cosine function is the <u>real part</u> of a complex exponential signal. Complex exponentials make dynamic systems analysis relatively simple – thus, we often analyze a signals response in terms of complex exponentials. Since any measurable quantity is real-valued, taking the real part of the analytical result based on complex exponentials will result in a cosine function. Thus, cosines become a natural way to express signals which vary sinusoidally.

The frequency of a sinusoidal signal is alternately expressed in units of Hertz (abbreviated Hz). A Hertz is the number of cycles which the sinusoid goes through in one second. Thus, Hertz correspond to cycles/second. The frequency of a signal in Hertz is related to the period of the signal by:

$$f = \frac{1}{T}$$

Eq. 8.21

Radian frequencies relate to frequencies in Hertz by:

$$f = \frac{2\pi}{\omega} \Leftrightarrow \omega = 2\pi f$$

Eq. 8.22

Although frequencies of signals are often expressed in Hertz, it is not a unit which lends itself to calculations. Thus, all our calculations will be performed in radian frequency – if given a frequency in Hertz, it should be converted to radians/second before any calculations are performed based on this frequency.

8.3.2 Complex Exponentials

In our presentation of complex exponentials, we first provide a brief review of complex numbers. A complex number contains both real and imaginary parts. Thus, we may write a complex number A as:

$$A = a + jb$$

Eq. 8.23

Where:

$$j = \sqrt{-1}$$

Eq. 8.24

The complex number A can be represented on orthogonal axes representing the real and imaginary part of the number, as shown in Fig. 8.6. (In Fig. 8.6, we have taken the liberty of representing A as a vector, although it is really just a number.) We can also represent the complex number in polar coordinates, also shown in Fig. 8.6. The polar coordinates consist of a magnitude $|A|$ and phase angle θ_A, defined as:

$$|A| = \sqrt{a^2 + b^2} \qquad \text{Eq. 8.25}$$

$$\theta_A = \tan^{-1}\left(\frac{b}{a}\right) \qquad \text{Eq. 8.26}$$

Notice that the phase angle is defined counterclockwise from the positive real axis. Conversely, we can determine the rectangular coordinates from the polar coordinates from:

$$a = Re\{A\} = |A|\cos(\theta_A) \qquad \text{Eq. 8.27}$$

$$b = Im\{A\} = |A|\sin(\theta_A) \qquad \text{Eq. 8.28}$$

Where the notation $Re\{A\}$ and $Im\{A\}$ denote the real part of A and the imaginary part of A, respectively.

The polar coordinates of a complex number A are often represented in the form:

$$A = |A|\angle\theta_A \qquad \text{Eq. 8.29}$$

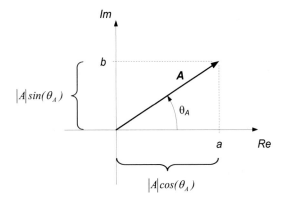

Figure 8.6. Representation of a complex number in rectangular and polar coordinates.

An alternate method of representing complex numbers in polar coordinates employs complex exponential notation. Without proof, we claim that:

$$e^{j\theta} = 1\angle\theta \qquad \text{Eq. 8.30}$$

Thus, $e^{j\theta}$ is a complex number with magnitude 1 and phase angle θ. From Fig. 8.6, it is easy to see that this definition of the complex exponential agrees with Euler's equation:

$$e^{\pm j\theta} = \cos\theta \pm j\sin\theta \qquad \text{Eq. 8.31}$$

With the definition of equation (8.30), we can define any arbitrary complex number in terms of complex exponentials. For example, our previous complex number A can be represented as:

$$A = |A|e^{j\theta_A} \qquad \text{Eq. 8.32}$$

We can generalize our definition of the complex exponential to time-varying signals. If we define a time varying signal $e^{j\omega t}$, we can use equation (8.31) to write:

$$e^{\pm j\omega t} = \cos\omega t \pm j\sin\omega t \qquad \text{Eq. 8.33}$$

The signal $e^{j\omega t}$ can be visualized as a unit vector rotating around the origin in the complex plane; the tip of the vector scribes a unit circle with its center at the origin of the complex plane. This is illustrated in Fig. 8.7. The vector rotates at a rate defined by the quantity ω– the vector makes one complete revolution every $\frac{2\pi}{\omega}$ seconds.

The projection of this rotating vector on the real axis traces out the signal $\cos \omega t$, as shown in Fig. 8.7, while the projection of the rotating vector on the imaginary axis traces out the signal $\sin \omega t$, also shown in Fig. 8.7.

Thus, we interpret the complex exponential function $e^{j\omega t}$ as an alternate "type" of sinusoidal signal. The real part of this function is $\cos \omega t$ while the imaginary part of this function is $\sin \omega t$.

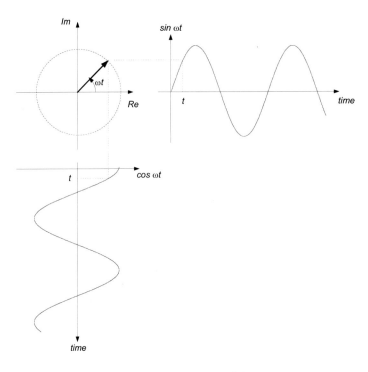

Figure 8.7. Illustration of $e^{j\omega t}$.

Section Summary

- We will represent sinusoidal signal in terms of cosine functions. The general form of our sinusoidal signals is: $v(t) = V_p \cos(\omega t + \theta)$.
- Sinusoidal signals can also be represented as complex exponentials. The relationship is an extension of Euler's equation, and is:

$$e^{\pm j\omega t} = \cos \omega t \pm j \sin \omega t$$

1. By extension, cosine signals can be represented in terms of complex exponentials as:

$$\cos(\omega t) = \frac{e^{j\omega t} + e^{-j\omega t}}{2}$$

2. The above general sinusoidal signal can be expressed as the real part of a complex exponential:

$$V_p \cos(\omega t + \theta) = Re\{V_p e^{j(\omega t + \theta)}\}$$

8.4   Second Order System Natural Response, Part 2

In section 8.2, we developed the <u>form</u> of the solution of the differential equation governing the natural response of second order systems. The form of the solution contained so-called complex exponentials; the background material relative to these signals was provided in section 8.3. We are thus now in a position to re-examine and interpret the solution presented in section 8.2

In section 8.2, we noted that the form of the natural response of a second order system was strongly dependent upon the damping ratio, ζ. If the damping ratio was greater than one, all terms in the response decay exponentially, but if the damping ratio was between zero and one some terms in the response became complex exponentials – in section 8.3, we saw that this corresponded to an oscillating signal. Thus, depending upon the value of damping ratio, the response could decay exponentially or oscillate. In this chapter, we will quantify and formalize these results. This section concludes with an extended example of a second order system natural response.

In section 8.1, the differential equation governing the natural response of a second order system was written as:

$$\frac{d^2 y_h(t)}{dt^2} + 2\varsigma\omega_n \frac{dy_h(t)}{dt} + \omega_n^2 y_h(t) = 0 \qquad \text{Eq. 8.34}$$

Where $y(t)$ is any system parameter of interest, ω_n is the *undamped natural frequency* and ζ is the *damping ratio*. The initial conditions are the value of the function $y(t)$ at $t=0$ and the derivative of the function $y(t)$ at $t=0$:

$$y(t = 0) = y_0$$

$$\frac{dy(t)}{dt}\Big|_{t=0} = y_0' \qquad \text{Eq. 8.35}$$

In section 8.2, we wrote the solution to equation (8.34) in the form:

$$y_h(t) = e^{-\varsigma\omega_n t}\left[K_1 e^{\left(\omega_n\sqrt{\varsigma^2-1}\right)t} + K_2 e^{-\left(\omega_n\sqrt{\varsigma^2-1}\right)t}\right] \qquad \text{Eq. 8.36}$$

Where K_1 and K_2 are unknown coefficients which can be determined by application of the initial conditions provided in equation (8.35). The form of the solution of equation (8.36) will fall into one of three categories, depending on the value of damping ratio. The three possible cases are:

1. If $\varsigma > 1$, all terms in the solution will be either growing or decaying exponentials and the solution will decay exponentially with time. If the damping ratio is large, this decay rate can be very slow. A system with $\varsigma > 1$ is said to be *overdamped*.

2. If $\varsigma < 1$, the terms $e^{\pm\left(\omega_n\sqrt{\varsigma^2-1}\right)t}$ are *complex exponentials*. Thus, have terms in our solution which are exponentials raised to an imaginary power and the solution can oscillate. A system with $\varsigma < 1$ is said to be *underdamped*.

3. $\varsigma = 1$; the form of the solution in this case is approximately that of case 1 above, in that the solution will decay exponentially. However, in this case, the response decay rate will be faster than the response of any overdamped system with the same natural frequency. Systems with $\varsigma = 1$ are said to be *critically damped*.

Details of the responses for each of the above three cases are provided in the subsections below.

1. Overdamped System

For an overdamped system, $\varsigma < 1$, and equation (8.36) becomes as shown in equation (8.37).

$$y_h(t) = e^{-\varsigma\omega_n t}\left[\frac{\dot{y}_0 + \left(\varsigma + \sqrt{\varsigma^2-1}\right)\omega_n y_0}{2\omega_n\sqrt{\varsigma^2-1}}e^{\omega_n t\sqrt{\varsigma^2-1}} + \frac{\dot{y}_0 - \left(\varsigma - \sqrt{\varsigma^2-1}\right)\omega_n y_0}{2\omega_n\sqrt{\varsigma^2-1}}e^{-\omega_n t\sqrt{\varsigma^2-1}}\right]$$ Eq. 8.37

In equation (8.37), the $e^{-\varsigma\omega_n t}$ term is a decaying exponential with time constant $\frac{1}{\varsigma\omega_n}$. The $e^{\omega_n t\sqrt{\varsigma^2-1}}$ is a growing exponential with time constant $\frac{1}{\omega_n\sqrt{\varsigma^2-1}}$. Thus, the overall system response is a sum of two decaying exponential signals, one which is proportional to $e^{-\varsigma\omega_n t} \cdot e^{\omega_n t\sqrt{\varsigma^2-1}}$ and the other which is proportional to $e^{-\varsigma\omega_n t} \cdot e^{-\omega_n t\sqrt{\varsigma^2-1}}$.

The term $e^{-\varsigma\omega_n t} \cdot e^{\omega_n t\sqrt{\varsigma^2-1}}$ is the product of two exponentials: one which grows with time, and the other which decays with time. The decaying exponential time constant, $\frac{1}{\varsigma\omega_n}$, is smaller than the growing exponential time constant, $\frac{1}{\omega_n\sqrt{\varsigma^2-1}}$. Thus, the product of the two will decay with time, though the decay rate may be very slow. (Note that in the limit as $\varsigma \to \infty, \frac{1}{\varsigma\omega_n} \approx \frac{1}{\omega_n\sqrt{\varsigma^2-1}}$, the two time constants are nearly identical, and this term becomes constant with time.)

The term $e^{-\varsigma\omega_n t} \cdot e^{-\omega_n t\sqrt{\varsigma^2-1}}$ is the product of two decaying exponentials; this term will, in general, decay quickly relative to the $e^{\varsigma\omega_n t} \cdot e^{-\omega_n t\sqrt{\varsigma^2-1}}$ term.

An example of the response of an overdamped system is shown in Fig. 8.8, for various values of damping ratio. The two system time constants are readily observable in this example. Note that as the damping ratio increases, the overall time required for the system response to decay to zero increases. The response of overdamped systems cannot oscillate; however, the response can change sign <u>once</u> (e.g. the function is allowed one zero-crossing).

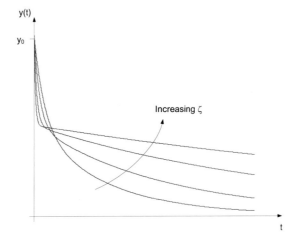

Figure 8.8. Overdamped system response.

2. Underdamped System

For an underdamped system, $\varsigma < 1$, and equation (8.36) becomes as shown in equation (8.38).

$$y_h(t) = e^{-\varsigma \omega_n t} \left[\frac{\dot{y}_0 + \varsigma \omega_n y_0}{\omega_n \sqrt{1-\varsigma^2}} \sin\left(\omega_n t \sqrt{1-\varsigma^2}\right) + y_0 \cos\left(\omega_n t \sqrt{1-\varsigma^2}\right) \right]$$

Eq. 8.38

The solution is a decaying sinusoid. The decay rate is set by the term $e^{-\varsigma \omega_n t}$, while the oscillation frequency of the sinusoid is $\omega_n \sqrt{1-\varsigma^2}$. The oscillation frequency seen in the natural response is thus not identically the natural frequency of the system; it is also influenced by the damping ratio. This leads to the definition of the *damped natural frequency*:

$$\omega_d = \omega_n \sqrt{1-\varsigma^2}$$

Eq. 8.39

Oscillations seen in the system response will have radian frequency ω_d; thus, the period of the oscillations is $\frac{2\pi}{\omega_d}$.

Example responses for underdamped systems are shown in Fig. 8.9; the responses shown are all for the same natural frequency and initial conditions – only the damping ratio varies. Note that smaller damping ratios result in slower decay rates for the response, oscillations persist for longer and are more pronounced for smaller damping ratios.

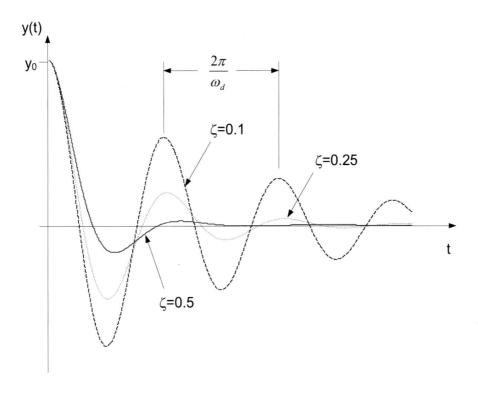

Figure 8.9. Underdamped system response.

3. Critically Damped System

For a critically damped system, $\varsigma = 1$, and equation (8.36) becomes as shown in equation (8.40).

$$y_h(t) = e^{-\varsigma \omega_n t} [y_0 + (\dot{y}_0 + \omega_n y_0 t)]$$

Eq. 8.40

The critically damped system response does not oscillate although, as with the overdamped case, one zero crossing of the function is allowed. The importance of the critically damped system response is that, for a particular natural frequency, it has the shortest decay time <u>without oscillation</u> of any system. An example response of a critically damped system is shown in Fig. 8.10.

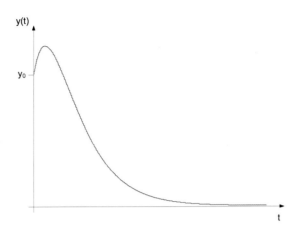

Figure 8.10. Critically damped system response.

Example 8.3

For the circuit shown below:

1. Write the differential equation for $v_c(t)$.
2. If $L=1H$, $R=200\Omega$, and $C=1x10^{-6}F$, find the undamped natural frequency, the damping ratio, and the damped natural frequency.
3. For the conditions in part (2), is the system underdamped, overdamped, or critically damped?
4. For the values of L and C in part (2), determine the value of R that makes the system critically damped.
5. If $v_c(0)=1V$ and $i_L(0)=0.01A$, what are the appropriate initial conditions to solve the differential equation determined in part (1)?

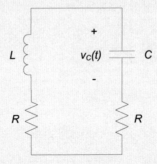

a) As usual, we define the voltage across the capacitor and the current through the inductor as our variables and write KVL and KCL in terms of these variables. The figure below shows these variables, along with the associated currents through capacitors and voltages across inductors.

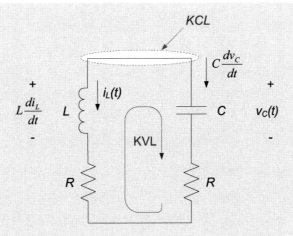

KCL at the indicated node results in:

$$i_L(t) + C\frac{dv_C(t)}{dt} = 0$$

Eq. 8.41

KVL around the indicated loop provides:

$$L\frac{di_L(t)}{dt} + 2Ri_L(t) = v_C(t)$$

Eq. 8.42

The above two equations can be combined to obtain an equation for $v_C(t)$. To do this, we use the first equation to obtain:

$$i_L(t) = -C\frac{dv_C(t)}{dt}$$

Eq. 8.43

Differentiating equation (8.43) provides:

$$\frac{di_L(t)}{dt} = -C\frac{d^2v_C(t)}{dt^2}$$

Eq. 8.44

Substituting equations (8.43) and (8.44) into equation (8.42) results in:

$$-LC\frac{d^2v_C(t)}{dt^2} - 2RC\frac{dv_C(t)}{dt} = v_C(t)$$

Dividing the above by LC and grouping terms gives our final result:

$$\frac{d^2v_C(t)}{dt^2} + \frac{2R}{L}\frac{dv_C(t)}{dt} + \frac{1}{LC}v_C(t) = 0$$

Eq. 8.45

b) Equation (5) is of the form:

$$\frac{d^2y(t)}{dt^2} + 2\varsigma\omega_n\frac{dy(t)}{dt} + \omega_n^2 y(t) = 0$$

Eq. 8.46

Equating coefficients in equations (8.45) and (8.46) and substituting $L=1H$, $R=200\Omega$, and $C=1x10^{-6}F$ results in:

$$2\varsigma\omega_n = \frac{2R}{L} = 400$$

Eq. 8.47

$$\omega_n^2 = \frac{1}{LC} = 1 \times 10^6$$

Eq. 8.38

Solving equation (8) for the natural frequency results in $\omega_n=1000$ rad/sec. Substituting this result into equation (8.47) and solving for the damping ratio gives $\zeta=0.2$. The damped natural frequency is:

$$\omega_d = \omega_n\sqrt{1 - \varsigma^2} = 979.8 \ rad/sec$$

c) The damping ratio determined in part (b) is ζ=0.2; since this is less than one, the system is underdamped.

d) In order for the system to be critically damped, the damping ratio $\varsigma = 1$. From equation (8.47) with $\varsigma = 1$, we obtain:

$$2\varsigma\omega_n = \frac{1R}{L} \Rightarrow 2(1)(1000) = \frac{2R}{1H} \Rightarrow R = 1000\Omega$$

e) Initial conditions on $v_C(t)$ are $v_C(0)$ and $\frac{dv_C(t)}{dt}|_{t=0}$. We are given $v_C(0)$=1V in the problem statement, but we need to determine $\frac{dv_C(t)}{dt}|_{t=0}$; the current through the inductor, $i_L(0)$ can be used to determine this. The current through the inductor is related to the capacitor voltage via equation (8.43) above:

$$i_L(t) = -C\frac{dv_C(t)}{dt}$$

So at time *t=0*,

$$i_L(0) = -(1 \times 10^{-6}F)\frac{dv_C(t)}{dt}|_{t=0} = 0.01A$$

Solving for $\frac{dv_C(t)}{dt}|_{t=0}$:

$$\frac{dv_C(t)}{dt}|_{t=0} = \frac{1}{C}i_L(0) = -\frac{0.01A}{1 \times 10^{-6}F} = -10,000 \ V/sec$$

We conclude this example with plots of the system response for underdamped, critically damped, and overdamped conditions.

Figure 8.11 shows the response of the circuit described by the differential equation determined in part (a) above, for the circuit parameters provided in part (b), to the initial conditions of part (e). Thus, the governing differential equation is:

$$\frac{d^2v_C(t)}{dt^2} + \frac{2R}{L}\frac{dv_C(t)}{dt} + \frac{1}{LC}v_C(t) = 0$$

With *L=1H, R=200Ω*, and *C=1x10⁻⁶F*, the differential equation becomes:

$$\frac{d^2v_C(t)}{dt^2} + 400\frac{dv_C(t)}{dt} + 1 \times 10^6 v_C(t) = 0$$

The initial conditions are, from part (e):

$$v_C(0) = 1V$$

$$\frac{dv_C(t)}{dt}|_{t=0} = -10,000 \ V/sec$$

Using MATLAB to evaluate the differential equation results in Fig. 8.11. Fig. 8.11 agrees with our expectations based on the calculations of part (b). In part (b), we determined that the damping ratio $\zeta=0.2$, so that the system is underdamped – Fig. 8.11 exhibits the oscillations (multiple zero axis crossings) that we would expect from an underdamped system. Likewise, we determined in part (b) that the damped natural frequency of the system is approximately 980 rad/sec. The period of the oscillations we would expect to see in the response is therefore:

$$T = \frac{2\pi}{\omega_d} = 0.0064\ seconds$$

This value is consistent with the period of the oscillations seen in Fig. 8.11.

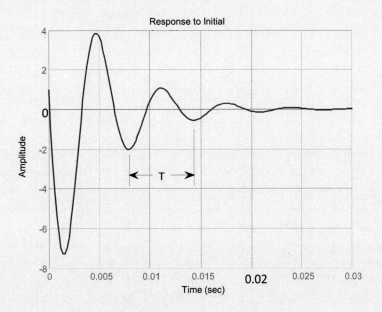

Figure 8.11. Underdamped response to initial conditions.

In part (d) above, we determined that the value of R resulting in a critically damped system is $R=1000\Omega$. Re-evaluating the above governing differential equation with this value for R results in:

$$\frac{d^2v_C(t)}{dt^2} + 2000\frac{dv_C(t)}{dt} + 1 \times 10^6 v_C(t) = 0$$

The initial conditions are as in the above example:

$$v_C(0) = 1V$$

$$\frac{dv_C(t)}{dt}\Big|_{t=0} = -10,000\ ^V/_{sec}$$

The resulting response is shown in Fig. 8.12. This plot also matches our expectations, though we have fewer quantitative results against which to compare it. The response does not oscillate (the response does have one and only one zero crossing, which is allowable for a critically damped or overdamped system. The response also appears to be composed of exponential signals, which is consistent with our expectations.

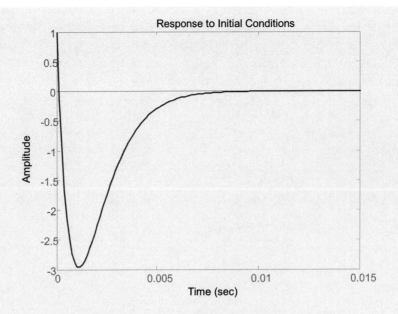

Figure 8.12. Critically damped system response.

In order to obtain a better understanding of critically damped vs. overdamped systems, we increase R to *3000Ω*. The resulting damping ratio is *ζ=3*; increasing R above the critically damped value will result in an overdamped system since the damping ratio is proportional to R. We will expect the response shape to be somewhat like that shown in Fig. 8.12 (it will still be composed of decaying exponential functions) but the overdamped system should decay more slowly. This overdamped system response is shown in Fig. 8.13. This response agrees with our qualitative expectations – the response does not oscillate, and the decay time is longer than that shown in Fig. 8.12.

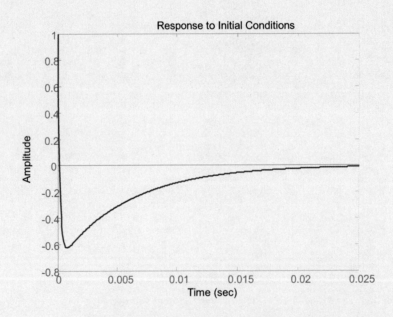

Figure 8.13. Overdamped system response.

Section Summary

- It is common to categorize second order systems by their damping ratio. This also characterizes the shape of their natural response. The three categories are:
    - If $\varsigma > 1$, the system is said to be *overdamped*. For this case, the response will decay exponentially with time with no oscillations. If the damping ratio is large, this decay rate can be very slow.
    - If $\varsigma < 1$, the system is said to be *underdamped*. In this case, the natural response can oscillate. Increasing the damping ratio tends to reduce the amplitude of the oscillations, and cause the oscillations to die out more quickly.
    - $\varsigma = 1$, the solution is said to be critically damped. In this case, the response will not oscillate, and the decay rate of the response will be faster than the response of any overdamped system with the same natural frequency.

For an underdamped system, the oscillations observed in the response have a radian frequency ω_d defined as:

$$\omega_d = \omega_n\sqrt{1 - \varsigma^2}$$

ω_d is called the *damped natural frequency* of the system. The period of the oscillations in the natural frequency (the time between successive peaks) is $\frac{2\pi}{\omega_d}$.

8.3 Exercises

1. The differential equation governing a circuit with output *y(t)* is given by:

$$\frac{d^2y(t)}{dt^2} + 6\frac{dy(t)}{dt} + 144y(t) = 0$$

What are the damping ratio and natural frequency of the circuit? Is the circuit under-, over-, or critically damped?

2. The differential equation governing a circuit's natural response is:

$$\frac{d^2y(t)}{dt^2} + 32\frac{dy(t)}{dt} + 64y(t) = 0$$

Where *y(t)* is the circuit response. What are:

- The circuit's natural frequency,
- The circuit's damping ratio, and
- The <u>two</u> time constants governing the circuit

3. The differential equation governing a circuit's natural response is:

$$\frac{d^2y(t)}{dt^2} + 8\frac{dy(t)}{dt} + 64y(t) = 0$$

Where *y(t)* is the circuit response. What are:

- The circuit's natural frequency,
- The circuit's damping ratio, and
- The circuit's damped natural frequency?

Solutions can be found at digilent.com/real-analog.

8.5　Second Order System Step Response

In this section, we address the case in which the input to a second order system consists of the sudden application of a constant voltage or current to the circuit; this type of input can be modeled as a step function. The response of a system to this type of input is called the *step response* of the system.

The material presented in this section will emphasize the development of <u>qualitative</u> relationship between the damping ratio and natural frequency of a system and the system's time-domain response. We will also see that we can <u>quantitatively</u> relate several specific response parameters to the system's damping ratio and natural frequency. This approach allows us to infer a great deal about the expected system response directly from the damping ratio and natural frequency of the system, without explicitly solving the differential equation governing the system. This approach is also useful in system design, since we can readily determine the damping ratio and natural frequency necessary to provide the desired response shape. Since the damping ratio and natural frequency are typically functions of resistances, capacitances, and inductances, we can readily design a system to produce the desired response.

In section 8.1, we wrote a general differential equation governing a second order system as:

$$\frac{d^2y(t)}{dt^2} + 2\varsigma\omega_n \frac{dy(t)}{dt} + \omega_n^2 y(t) = f(t)$$

Eq. 8.49

Where $y(t)$ is any system parameter of interest (for example, a voltage or current in an electrical circuit), ω_n and ς are the *undamped natural frequency* and the *damping ratio* of the system, respectively, and $f(t)$ is a forcing function applied to the system.

In this chapter section, we restrict our attention to the specific case in which $f(t)$ is a step function. Thus, the forcing function to the system can be written as:

$$f(t) = Au_0(t) = \begin{cases} 0, t < 0 \\ A, t > 0 \end{cases}$$

Eq. 8.50

Thus, the differential equation governing the system becomes:

$$\frac{d^2y(t)}{dt^2} + 2\varsigma\omega_n \frac{dy(t)}{dt} + \omega_n^2 y(t) = Au_0(t)$$

Eq. 8.51

In addition to the above restriction on the forcing function, we will assume that the initial conditions are all zero (we sometimes say that the system is *initially relaxed*). Thus, for the second-order system above, our initial conditions will be:

$$y(t = 0) = 0$$

$$\frac{dy(t)}{dt}\Big|_{t=0} = 0$$

Eq. 8.52

Solving equation (8.51) with the initial conditions provided in equations (8.52) results in the *step response* of the system.

As in our discussion of forced first order system responses in section 8.1, we write the overall solution of the differential equation of equation (8.51) as the sum of a particular solution and a homogeneous solution. Thus:

$$y(t) = y_h(t) + y_p(t)$$

The homogeneous solution of second order differential equations has been discussed in sections 8.1 and 8.4 and will not be repeated here. The particular solution of the differential equation (8.51) can be obtained by examining the solution to the equation after the homogeneous solution has died out. Letting $t \to \infty$ in equation (8.51) and noting that the forcing function is a constant as $t \to \infty$ allows us to set $\frac{d^2y(t\to\infty)}{dt^2} = \frac{dy(t\to\infty)}{dt} = 0$ and thus,

$$\omega_n^2 y_p(t) = A \Rightarrow y_p(t) = \frac{A}{\omega_n^2}$$

Eq. 8.53

Combining the particular and homogeneous solutions, assuming the system is underdamped (ζ<1), and employing the initial conditions results in our final expression for the <u>step response of an underdamped second order system</u>:

$$y(t) = \frac{A}{\omega_n^2}\left\{1 - e^{-\varsigma\omega_n t}\left[\cos(\omega_d t) + \frac{\varsigma}{\sqrt{1-\varsigma^2}}\sin(\omega_d t)\right]\right\}$$

Eq. 8.54

Where $\omega_d = \omega_n\sqrt{1-\varsigma^2}$ is the damped natural frequency of the system, previously defined in chapter 8.4.

It is common to interpret an underdamped second order system's response in terms of the damping ratio and the natural frequency, rather than direct evaluation of equation (8.54). Figure 8.14 shows a typical step response for an underdamped second order system. The system response overshoots to a maximum value y_p and has steady-state response y_{ss}. The maximum overshoot is generally normalized by the steady-state response and is presented in terms of a variable M_P defined as:

$$M_P = \frac{y_p - y_{ss}}{y_{ss}}$$

Eq. 8.55

M_P is often presented as a <u>percent</u>, obtained by multiplying equation (8.55) by 100. Other parameters of interest in characterizing the step response are the period of any oscillations in the response (T in Fig. 8.14) and the rise time, t_r. The rise time is defined as the time required for the system response to go from 10% to 90% of the steady state response. The rise time is often used as an indication of how quickly a second order system responds.

The time domain parameters M_P, t_r, and T are readily related to the parameters ξ, ω_n, and ω_d. We provide the following relations here, without proof:

$$M_P = e^{\frac{-\pi\xi}{\sqrt{1-\xi^2}}}$$

Eq. 8.56

$$t_r \approx \frac{1.8}{\omega_n}$$

Eq. 8.57

Note: for small damping ratios, (ξ<0.6), equation (8.56) is often approximated as:

$$M_P \approx -\frac{\xi}{0.06}$$

Eq. 8.59

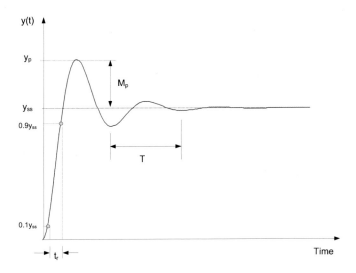

Figure 8.14. Underdamped second order system step response.

Section Summary

- Typical parameters used to characterize the step response of an underdamped system are the rise time, the maximum overshoot, and the frequency of the oscillations in the response. These parameters are defined as follows:
    - The rise time, t_r, is the time required for the response to go from 10% to 90% of its steady-state response
    - The maximum overshoot provides the maximum value achieved by the response. The maximum overshoot is a normalized value, defined as:

$$M_P = \frac{y_p - y_{ss}}{y_{ss}}$$

Where y_p is the peak (or maximum) value of the response and y_{ss} is the steady state system response. M_P is often expressed as a percent, by multiplying the above quantity by 100.

- The radian frequency of the oscillations in the step response is given by the damped natural frequency:

$$\omega_d = \omega_n\sqrt{1 - \varsigma^2}$$

The period of the oscillations in the response is then given by:

$$T = \frac{2\pi}{\omega_d}$$

- The rise time and maximum overshoot can be related to the damping ratio and natural frequency of the system. The appropriate relations are provided below:
    - $t_r \approx \frac{1.8}{\omega_n}$
    - $M_P = e^{\frac{-\pi\xi}{\sqrt{1-\xi^2}}}$ or $M_P - \frac{\xi}{0.6}$ (for small damping ratios, $\xi < 0.6$)

The period of the oscillations can be used to cross-check the above results, since it depends upon both the damping ratio and natural frequency.

Chapter 8: Second Order Circuits

1. The differential equation governing the circuit shown below is:

$$\frac{d^2v(t)}{dt^2} + 12\frac{dv(t)}{dt} + 400v(t) = 400u(t)$$

If $u(t)=2u_0(t)$, what are:

- The circuit's natural frequency,
- The circuit's damping ratio,
- The percent overshoot (M_P), the rise time (t_r), and the steady-state response of the capacitor voltage
- What is the maximum value seen by the capacitor voltage?

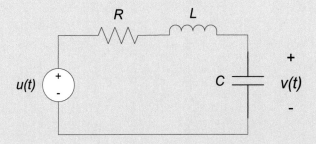

Solutions can be found at digilent.com/real-analog.

Chapter 9:
State Variable Methods

In our analysis approach of dynamic systems so far, we have defined variables which describe the energy in the circuit energy storage elements (voltages across capacitors and currents through inductors). We then used KVL and KCL to write differential equations describing the circuit, in terms of those variables. The resulting equations were then combined into a single differential equation governing the parameter in which we were interested (the *input-output equation* for the system); this equation was solved to determine the response of the circuit. This approach is useful for low-order systems, such as the first or second order systems we have examined so far, but it becomes cumbersome for higher-order systems. An alternate modeling approach, *state variable* (or *state space*) modeling, has a number of advantages over the approach we have been using to date, especially for higher-order systems.

In this chapter, we will provide a very brief introduction to the topic of state variable modeling[1]. The brief presentation provided here is intended simply to introduce the reader to the basic concepts of state variable models, since they are a natural – and relatively painless – extension of the analysis approach we have used in Chapters 7 and 8. Introduction to state variable models at this stage also allows the reader to perform *numerical simulations* of system responses. Numerical simulations are computer-generated solutions to the differential equations governing the system. Most numerical approaches to the solution of differential equations require the equations to be in state variable form[2].

State variable models of dynamic systems consist of several first order differential equations, in several different variables. (These variables are called the *state variables*.) The state variables for a system must completely describe the energy contained in all the energy storage elements in the system, so natural choices of state variables for electrical circuits are the voltages across capacitors and the currents through inductors. If there are N state variables required to describe the circuit, the state variable model is created by applying KVL and KCL to obtain N first-order differential equations in these N variables. Please notice that this approach is exactly the

---

[1] We will provide a fairly in-depth presentation of state variable models later in this chapter when we explicitly address modeling of higher-order systems.

[2] The differential equation solvers in MATLAB and Octave, for example, require the equations to be in state variable form. Circuit simulation software packages such as SPICE create the equations governing the circuit in state variable form before solving them

approach we have used in Chapter 8 to determine the differential equation governing a second order circuit – we are simply eliminating the step in which the individual equations are combined into a single, higher-order differential equation in a single unknown. Since the mathematics associated with combining the individual equations can be tedious, state variable models are actually <u>easier</u> to create than input-output equations!

A brief description of state variable models is provided in section 9.1 of this chapter. An example of the state variable model for a third order system is provided to illustrate development of the model. Section 9.2 provides information relative to numerical simulation of a state variable model using MATLAB, and section 9.3 provides Octave syntax to perform the same processes[3].

If desired, this chapter can be skipped without loss of continuity.

After completing this chapter, you should be able to:

- Define state variables for electrical circuits
- Write differential equations governing electrical circuits in state variable form
- Use MATLAB and/or Octave to simulate the impulse response of an electrical circuit
- Use MATLAB and/or Octave to simulate the step response of an electrical circuit
- Use MATLAB and/or Octave to plot the state trajectory of an electrical circuit

9.1   Introduction to State Variable Models

9.1.1   Background and Introduction

As their name implies, state variable models are based on the concept of a system's state. The state of a system is the minimum amount of information necessary to completely characterize the system at some instant in time. More specifically, if we know the state at any time, and the input to the system for all subsequent times, we can determine the output of the system at any subsequent time[4]. It turns out that the system's state uniquely determines the energy in all the system's energy storage elements and vice-versa. If the energy in any of the energy storage elements changes, the system's state changes.

The *state variables* are the smallest set of variables which completely describe the state (or the energy storage) of the system. The choice of state variables is not unique, but one possible choice of state variable is those variables which describe the energy stored in all of the independent energy storage elements in the system. For example, in electrical circuits, inductors store energy as current and capacitors store energy as voltage. If we choose as state variables the currents in inductors and the voltages across the capacitors, we will have created a legitimate set of state variables for the circuit.

Since the state variables are independent, they can be visualized as a set of orthogonal axes defining a space. The space defined by the state variables is called *state space* of the system. If the system is described by *N* state variables, the state space will be N-dimensional. The state of the system at any given time can be visualized as a point in the state space.

In general, as the system responds to some input, the system's state will change over time. Since the state of the system is a point in state space, the change in the system's state can be visualized as tracing a path over time in the state space. This path is called the *state trajectory*.

---

[3] Information relative to acquiring MATLAB and Octave are provided in the relevant sections.

[4] Thus, the initial conditions of a system constitute the state of the system.

9.1.2 Form of State Variable Models

State variable models, as mentioned previously, represent an Nth order system as N first order differential equations in N unknowns. (The unknowns are the state variables.) For linear, lumped-parameter, time invariant systems, these equations will take the form:

$$\dot{x}_1(t) = a_{11}x_1(t) + a_{12}x_2(t) + \cdots + a_{1N}x_N(t) + b_1u(t)$$
$$\dot{x}_2(t) = a_{21}x_1(t) + a_{22}x_2(t) + \cdots + a_{2N}x_n(t) + b_2u(t)$$
$$\vdots$$
$$\dot{x}_n = a_{N1}x_1(t) + a_{N2}x_2(t) + \cdots + a_{NN}x_N(t) + b_Nu(t) \qquad \text{Eq. 9.1}$$

Where $x_1(t), x_2(t), \cdots, x_N(t)$ are the system states and *u(t)* is the input to the system. The overdot notation denotes differentiation with respect to time; $\dot{x}_k(t) = \frac{dx_k(t)}{dt}$. (We will assume that no derivatives of the input are applied to the system – this is a special case which we will avoid in this introductory chapter.)

It turns out that, if all system states are known, we can determine any other parameter in the system. In fact, any other parameter in the system can be written as a linear combination of the states and the input. Thus, we can write the system output as:

$$y(t) = c_1x_1(t) + c_2x_2(t) \cdots + c_Nx_N(t) + du(t) \qquad \text{Eq. 9.2}$$

Equations (9.1) and (9.2) are commonly written in matrix form as:

$$\underline{x}(t) = A\underline{x}(t) + \underline{b}u(t) \qquad \text{Eq. 9.3}$$

$$y(t) = \underline{c}\underline{x}(t) + du(t) \qquad \text{Eq. 9.4}$$

In equation (9.3), the vector $\underline{x}(t)$ is an *Nx1* column vector containing the system state variables. The matrix *A* is a square *NxN* matrix, and the vector $\underline{b}$ is an *Nx1* column vector. The vector $\underline{\dot{x}}(t)$ is an *Nx1* column vector containing the <u>derivatives</u> of the state variables as a function of time. In equation (9.4), the vector $\underline{c}$ is a *1xN* row vector, and *d* is a scalar. Equation (9.3) provides the *state equations* for the system, and equation (9.4) is called the *output equation* of the system.

It is possible to define more than one output in a system. To define multiple outputs, we simply create a vector of outputs, each row of which is an equation of the form of equation (9.2). For example, if we define P outputs, the set of output equations becomes:

$$y_1 = c_{11}x_1 + c_{12}x_2 + \cdots + c_{1N}x_N + d_1u$$
$$y_2 = c_{21}x_1 + c_{22}x_2 + \cdots + c_{2N}x_N + d_2u$$
$$\vdots$$
$$y_P = c_{P1}x_1 + c_{P2}x_2 + \cdots + c_{PN}x_N + d_Pu \qquad \text{Eq. 9.5}$$

In the case of multiple outputs, we modify our matrix expression of equation (9.4) to:

$$\underline{y}(t) = C\underline{x}(t) + \underline{d}u(t) \qquad \text{Eq. 9.6}$$

Where $\underline{y}(t)$ is a Px1 column vector containing the outputs, C is a PxN matrix, and $\underline{d}$ is a Px1 column vector.

Creation of the state variable model for an electrical circuit is probably best described by example. Examples of creation of state variable models for both second and third order circuits are provided in the examples below. Please notice that the creation of a third order state variable model is not significantly more difficult that creation of a second order state variable model. Creation of a third order input-output equation is, however, generally

---

considerably more difficult than creation of a second order input-output model. (Try, for example, creating an input-output relation for the circuit of example 9.2 below.)

Example 9.1: State Variable Model of Series RLC Circuit

A series RLC circuit is shown below. Appropriate state variables are the current through the inductor and the voltage across the capacitor, as shown.

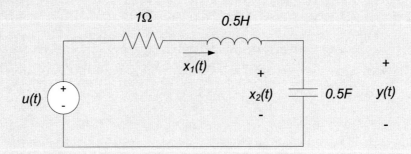

Applying KVL around the circuit loop, we obtain:

$$u = x_1 + 0.5\dot{x}_1 + x_2$$

Applying KCL at the node between the inductor and capacitor results in:

$$x_1 = 0.5\dot{x}_2$$

Rearranging the above equations and placing them in matrix form results in:

$$\begin{bmatrix} \dot{x}_1 \\ \dot{x}_2 \end{bmatrix} = \begin{bmatrix} -2 & -2 \\ 2 & 0 \end{bmatrix} \begin{bmatrix} x_1 \\ x_2 \end{bmatrix} + \begin{bmatrix} 2 \\ 0 \end{bmatrix} u(t)$$

Since the output $y = x_2$, the output equation is:

$$y = \begin{bmatrix} 0 & 1 \end{bmatrix} \begin{bmatrix} x_1 \\ x_2 \end{bmatrix} + 0 \cdot u$$

Example 9.2: State Variable Model of Third Order Circuit

Consider the circuit shown below. The input to the system is the voltage u(t), and the output variable is the voltage across the resistor, y(t). There are three energy storage elements in the system (two inductors and a capacitor) so we will expect the system to be third order with three state variables. These state variables are chosen to be the currents through the inductors and the voltage difference across the capacitor; these are indicated on the figure below.

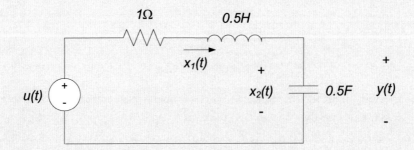

We write the state equations by applying KVL and KCL to the circuit. Since there are three state variables, three state equations must be written. Applying KVL around the leftmost loop results in:

$$u(t) = L_1 \dot{x}_1(t) + x_3(t)$$

Applying KVL around the rightmost loop results in:

$$x_3(t) = L_2 \dot{x}_2(t) + R x_2(t)$$

Note that in the equation above, the voltage across the resistor is written as Rx_2, rather than y. This is consistent with the general state equation format which requires that the derivative of each state variable be written <u>only</u> in terms of the other state variables and the input. Our final state equation is obtained by applying KCL at the node interconnecting the two inductors and the capacitor:

$$x_1(t) = x_2(t) + C \dot{x}_3(t)$$

The above can be re-written in matrix form as:

$$\begin{bmatrix} \dot{x}_1(t) \\ \dot{x}_2(t) \\ \dot{x}_3(t) \end{bmatrix} = \begin{bmatrix} 0 & 0 & \dfrac{-1}{L_1} \\ 0 & \dfrac{-R}{L_2} & \dfrac{1}{L_2} \\ \dfrac{1}{C} & \dfrac{-1}{C} & 0 \end{bmatrix} \begin{bmatrix} x_1(t) \\ x_2(t) \\ x_3(t) \end{bmatrix} + \begin{bmatrix} \dfrac{1}{L_1} \\ 0 \\ 0 \end{bmatrix} u(t)$$

The above state equations allow us to determine <u>any</u> parameter of interest in the circuit. Our output variable is the voltage across the resistor, R. We can use Ohm's law to write the equation describing the desired output in terms of the state variable x_2 to obtain:

$$y(t) = \begin{bmatrix} 0 & R & 0 \end{bmatrix} \begin{bmatrix} x_1(t) \\ x_2(t) \\ x_3(t) \end{bmatrix} + 0 \cdot u(t)$$

Section Summary

- The system's *state* completely describes the system. If we know the state of the system at some time t_0, and the input to the system for all times $t \geq t_0$, we can determine the output of the system for all times $t \geq t_0$. The state of the system must uniquely describe the energy stored in all energy storage elements in the system.

- The *state variables* are a set of system variables which describe the system state. A system's state variables are not unique – there are a variety of variables which can describe the energy in a system. However, the number of state variables must correspond to the number of independent energy storage elements in the system. Since inductors store energy in terms of current and capacitors store energy in terms of voltage, one possible choice of state variables is the voltages across capacitors and the currents through inductors.

- The *state equations* for the system are a set of *N* first order differential equations, in *N* state variables. If the system is linear and time invariant, the state equations can be written in matrix form as:

$$\underline{\dot{x}}(t) = A\underline{x}(t) + \underline{b}u(t)$$

- The state equations are typically obtained by application of Kirchhoff's laws to the circuit.
- The system output at any time can be determined from the states and the input at that time. The *output equation* for a system is a linear combination of the states and the input which provide the desired

output. In the case of a linear, time invariant system with a single output, the output equation can be written in matrix form as:

$$y(t) = \underline{c}\,\underline{x}(t) + du(t)$$

- If multiple outputs are desired, the above matrix form of the output equation can be generalized as:

$$\underline{y}(t) = C\underline{x}(t) + \underline{d}u(t)$$

Where $\underline{y}(t)$ is a column vector of the outputs, C is a matrix, and $\underline{d}$ is a column vector.

9.1 Exercises

1. For the circuit shown below, apply KCL at node A and KVL around loop 1 to write two first order differential equations in two unknowns: the current through the inductor and the voltage across the capacitor. Place the two equations in state variable format.

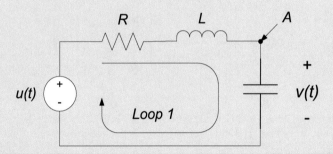

2. Write a state variable model {A,b,c,d} for the circuit of problem 1 if the output is the voltage across the capacitor.
3. Write a state variable model {A,b,c,d} for the circuit of problem 1 if the output is the voltage across the inductor.
4. Write a state variable model {A,b,c,d} for the circuit of problem 1 if the output is the voltage across the resistor.
5. Write a state variable model for the circuit below. u(t) is the input voltage, and y(t) is the output. (Hint: you might want to try applying KCL at node A and KVL around the indicated loop.)

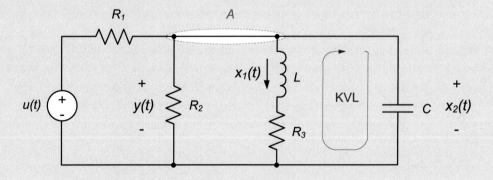

Solutions can be found at digilent.com/real-analog.

Chapter 9: State Variable Methods

9.2 Numerical Simulation of System Responses Using MATLAB

Analytical solutions of the state variable or input-output models is difficult or impossible for higher-order or nonlinear systems. Thus, numerical (or computer-based) solutions of these differential equations have become increasingly popular. This chapter provides a brief outline describing the use of some special-purpose MATLAB commands for simulating the response of linear, time invariant systems (these are systems which are governed by linear differential equations with constant coefficients).

Some MATLAB functions presented in this chapter are available in MATLAB's Control Systems Toolbox. The Control Systems Toolbox comes with the Student Edition of MATLAB. For more information about MATLAB products, see the MathWorks web site at http://www.mathworks.com/.

This section assumes some knowledge of basic MATLAB syntax. For those who are not familiar with MATLAB, a brief overview of the necessary topics is provided in Appendix A.1 of this textbook.

9.2.1 Basic Commands for Simulation of Linear, Time-invariant Systems

MATLAB's Control Systems Toolbox contains a number of special-purpose commands for simulating the response of linear, time-invariant systems. Among these commands are commands specific to determining the step response and natural response of systems; we will restrict our attention to these commands in this chapter. Later courses in your engineering curriculum will most likely present more general-purpose MATLAB commands.

To calculate system responses (e.g. to solve the differential equations of interest), we will use only MATLAB's **step** and **initial** commands in this chapter. The **step** command calculates a unit step response for the system, while the **initial** command calculates the natural response of a system to some set of initial conditions. We will also use the **ss** command to create state space model objects, to send to the **step** and **initial** commands. Basic syntax for these commands is provided below.

step: The command **[y,x,t]=step(sys)** returns the step response of the state variable model described by model object **sys**. The vector **y** contains the system output, the matrix **x** contains the states, and the vector **t** contains the time samples.

- The command **[y,x]=step(sys)** returns the step response as above, but calculated over the specified time vector **t**.
- The command **[y,t]=step(sys)** returns the system output as above, and the times at which the response is calculated, but not the state variables **x**.
- **step(sys)** with no left-hand arguments results in a plot of the step response output.

initial: Response of linear system to an initial condition. **[y,x,t]=initial(sys,x0)** returns the response of the system described by the model object **sys** to an initial condition contained in the vector **x0**. Variations on this command are similar to those provided above for the **step** command.

ss: Create a state space model object. **sys = ss(A, b, c, d)** returns an object named **sys** which provides a state space model corresponding to the matrices provided in **A**, **b**, **c**, and **d**.

Example 9.3: Step Response of Series RLC Circuit

Determine and plot the response of the system of example 9.1 if:

$$u(t) = \begin{cases} 0V, t < 0 \\ 2V, t \geq 0 \end{cases}$$

And the circuit is initially relaxed (i.e. all voltages and currents in the system are initially zero). Also plot the state trajectory for this input. The state equations for the circuit of example 9.1 were previously determined to be:

$$\begin{bmatrix} \dot{x}_1 \\ \dot{x}_2 \end{bmatrix} = \begin{bmatrix} -2 & -2 \\ 2 & 0 \end{bmatrix} \begin{bmatrix} x_1 \\ x_2 \end{bmatrix} + \begin{bmatrix} 2 \\ 0 \end{bmatrix} u(t)$$

While the output equation is:

$$y = \begin{bmatrix} 0 & 1 \end{bmatrix} \begin{bmatrix} x_1 \\ x_2 \end{bmatrix} + 0 \cdot u$$

Thus, the matrices describing the state space model are:

$$A = \begin{bmatrix} -2 & -2 \\ 2 & 0 \end{bmatrix}, \underline{b} = \begin{bmatrix} 2 \\ 0 \end{bmatrix}, \underline{c} = \begin{bmatrix} 0 & 1 \end{bmatrix}, d = 0$$

To simulate the response of the system we first need to input the state variable model. We begin by defining the $\underline{A}, \underline{b}, \underline{c},$ and d matrices as follows:

$$\gg A = [-2 \quad -2; 2 \quad 0];$$
$$\gg b = [2; 0];$$
$$\gg c = [0 \ 1];$$
$$\gg d = 0;$$

The $\gg$ symbols denote the command prompt at MATLAB's command window; they are included here to emphasize MATLAB commands.

It is generally desirable to create a model object in MATLAB to represent the system model[5]. To create a state space system model, the command is **ss**. Arguments to the command are the above matrices; the output is the system model object. To create a model of our system, we type:

$$\gg sys = ss(A, b, c, d);$$

Our workspace now contains a state space model object of our system named "sys".

We can simulate the response of this system to the desired input by using MATLAB's **step** command. The step command assumes that the system is initially relaxed and the input to the system is:

$$u(t) = \begin{cases} 0, t < 0 \\ 1, \geq 0 \end{cases}$$

The input to our system is exactly twice this input, so we can simply scale our output by a factor of two. (This works because the system is linear – don't try this with a nonlinear system!) The appropriate commands are (note that we have to scale both the output and the states, since we will be plotting the output response and the state trajectory):

$$\gg [y, x, t] = step(sys);$$

---

[5] This is not entirely necessary, since the step and initial commands will accept the A, b, c, and d matrices directly as arguments. It is, however, encouraged.

$$\gg y = 2 * y;$$
$$\gg x = 2 * x;$$

The final step is to plot the responses. Plotting the output response can be accomplished with the following commands:

$$\gg figure$$
$$\gg plot(t, y)$$
$$\gg title('System\ output\ vs, time')$$
$$\gg xlabel('Time, sec')$$
$$\gg ylabel('Response, Volts')$$

Which results in the figure below:

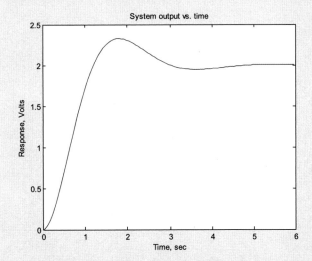

We can plot the state trajectory by plotting the second state vector, $x_1(t)$, vs. the first state vector, $x_2(t)$. MATLAB returns the first state vector as the first column of the x matrix, the second state vector as the second column of the x matrix, and so on. Thus, we can plot the state trajectory with the following commands:

$$\gg plot\big(x(:, 1), x(:, 2)\big)$$
$$\gg grid$$
$$\gg xlabel('X_1(t)')$$
$$\gg ylabel('X_2(t)')$$
$$\gg title('State\ trajectory\ for\ Example\ 1')$$

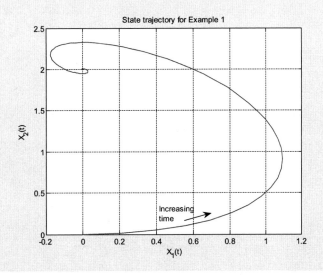

Section Summary:

- If you have access to MATLAB's control system toolbox,
  - A state space model object can be created with the **ss** function. Inputs to the function are the A, b, c, and d matrices of the state space model.
  - The **step** command can be used to calculate the step response of the system.
  - The **initial** command can be used to calculate the natural response of the system.

9.2 Exercises

1. Simulate the response y(t) of the circuit below, if u(t) is a unit step function.

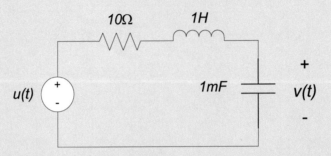

2. Simulate the response y(t) of the circuit below, if u(t) is a unit step function.

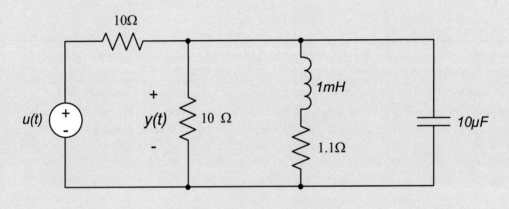

Solutions can be found at digilent.com/real-analog.

9.3 Numerical Simulation of System Responses Using Octave

This chapter provides a brief outline describing the use of some special-purpose Octave commands for simulating the response of linear, time invariant systems (these are systems which are governed by linear differential equations with constant coefficients).

Octave is an open-source software with many of the same capabilities as MATLAB. Unlike MATLAB, however, Octave is available for free. For more information about Octave, see the website at www.gnu.org. Octave syntax is very similar to MATLAB syntax, so the commands in this section are very similar to those provided in section 9.2.

This section assumes some knowledge of basic Octave syntax. For those who are not familiar with Octave, a brief overview of the necessary topics is provided in Appendix A.2 of this textbook.

Chapter 9: State Variable Methods

9.3.1 Basic Commands for Simulation of Linear, Time-invariant Systems

Like MATLAB, Octave provides a number of special-purpose commands for simulating the response of linear, time-invariant systems. Among these commands are commands specific to determining the step response and natural response of systems; we will restrict our attention to these commands in this chapter.

To calculate system responses (e.g. to solve the differential equations of interest), we will use only Octave's **step** and **initial** commands in this chapter. The **step** command calculates a unit step response for the system, while the **initial** command calculates the natural response of a system to some set of initial conditions. We will also use the **ss** command to create state space model objects, to send to the **step** and **initial** commands. Basic syntax for these commands is provided below.

step: The command **[y,t]=step(sys)** returns the step response of the state variable model described by the model object **sys**. The vector **y** contains the system output, the matrix **x** contains the states, and the vector t contains the time samples.

- The command **[y]=step(sys,t)** returns the step response as above, but calculated over the specified time vector **t**.
- The command **[y,t]=step(sys)** returns the system output as above, and the times at which the response is calculated, but not the state variables **x**.
- **step(sys)** with no left-hand arguments results in a plot of the step response output.

initial: Response of linear system to an initial condition. **[y,x,t]=initial(sys,x0)** returns the response of the system described by the state space model {A,b,c,d} to an initial condition contained in the vector x0. Variations on this command are similar to those provided above for the **step** command.

ss: Create a state space model object. **sys = ss(A, b, c, d)** returns an object named **sys** which provides a state space model corresponding to the matrices provided in **A, b, c,** and **d.**

Example 9.4: Step Response of Series RLC Circuit

Determine and plot the response of the system of example 9.1 if:

$$u(t) = \begin{cases} 0V, t < 0 \\ 2V, t \geq 0 \end{cases}$$

and the circuit is initially relaxed (i.e. all voltages and currents in the system are initially zero). Also plot the state trajectory for this input. The state equations for the circuit of example 9.1 were previously determined to be:

$$\begin{bmatrix} \dot{x}_1 \\ \dot{x}_2 \end{bmatrix} = \begin{bmatrix} -2 & -2 \\ 2 & 0 \end{bmatrix} \begin{bmatrix} x_1 \\ x_2 \end{bmatrix} + \begin{bmatrix} 2 \\ 0 \end{bmatrix} u(t)$$

While the output equation is:

$$y = \begin{bmatrix} 0 & 1 \end{bmatrix} \begin{bmatrix} x_1 \\ x_2 \end{bmatrix} + 0 \cdot u$$

Thus, the matrices describing the state space model are:

$$A = \begin{bmatrix} -2 & -2 \\ 2 & 0 \end{bmatrix}, \underline{b} = \begin{bmatrix} 2 \\ 0 \end{bmatrix}, \underline{c} = \begin{bmatrix} 0 & 1 \end{bmatrix}, d = 0$$

To simulate the response of the system we first need to input the state variable model. We begin by defining the $\underline{A}, \underline{b}, \underline{c},$ and d matrices as follows:

$$> A = [-2 - 2; 2\ 0];$$
$$> b = [2; 0];$$
$$> c = [0\ 1];$$
$$> d = 0;$$

The > symbols denote the command prompt at Octave's command window; they are included here to emphasize Octave commands.

Unlike MATLAB, Octave <u>requires</u> you to create a model object to represent the system model. To create a state space system model, the command is **ss**. Arguments to the command are the above matrices; the output is the system model object. To create a model of our system, we type:

$$> sys = ss(A, b, c, d);$$

Our workspace now contains a state space model object of our system named "sys".

We can simulate the response of this system to the desired input by using Octave's step command. The step command assumes that the system is initially relaxed and the input to the system is:

$$u(t) = \begin{cases} 0, t < 0 \\ 1, t \geq 0 \end{cases}$$

The input to our system is exactly twice this input, so we can simply scale our output by a factor of two. (This works because the system is linear – don't try this with a nonlinear system!) The appropriate commands are (note that we have to scale both the output and the states, since we will be plotting the output response and the state trajectory):

$$> [y, t] = step(sys);$$
$$> y = 2 * y;$$

The final step is to plot the response. Plotting the output response can be accomplished with the following commands:

$$> plot(t, y)$$
$$> title('System\ output\ vs. time')$$
$$> xlabel('Time, sec')$$
$$> ylabel('Response, Volts')$$

which results in the figure below:

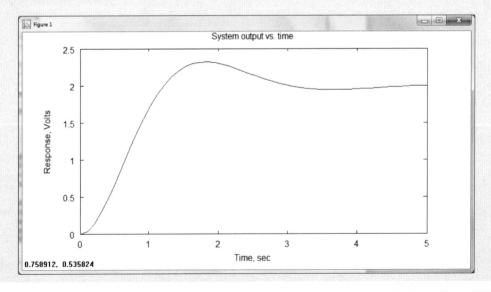

In order to plot the state trajectory using Octave, we must modify our state space model somewhat. Unlike MATLAB, the states themselves are not returned by Octave's **step** command. However, we can alter our c and d matrices so that the output, y, contains <u>both</u> system states. We will set up our output equations as follows:

$$\begin{bmatrix} y_1(t) \\ y_2(t) \end{bmatrix} = \begin{bmatrix} 1 & 0 \\ 0 & 1 \end{bmatrix} \begin{bmatrix} x_1 \\ x_2 \end{bmatrix} + \begin{bmatrix} 0 \\ 0 \end{bmatrix} u$$

This is implemented in Octave by re-setting the c and d matrices, re-calculating the model object, and re-calculating the system response with the following commands:

$$> c = [1\ 0; 0\ 1];$$
$$> d = [0; 0];$$
$$> sys = ss(A, b, c, d);$$
$$> [y, t] = step(sys);$$
$$> y = 2 * y;$$

Now, the output $y_1(t)$ is simply the state $x_1(t)$ and the output $y_2(t)$ is the state $x_2(t)$. Octave returns the first state vector as the first row of the y matrix, and the second state vector as the second row of the y matrix. Thus, we can plot the state trajectory with the following commands:

$$> plot\big(y(1, :), y(:, 2)\big)$$
$$> grid$$
$$> xlabel('X_1(t)')$$
$$> ylabel('X_2(t)')$$
$$> title('State\ trajectory\ for\ Example\ 1')$$

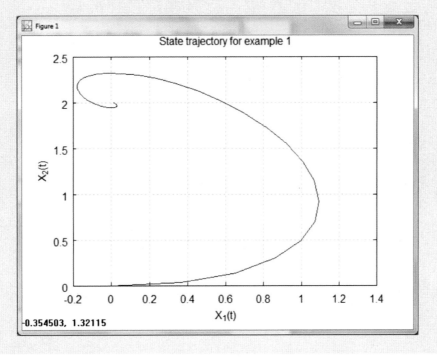

Section Summary

- Octave allows you to simulate linear, time invariant systems with the following commands:
  - A state space model object can be created with the **ss** function. Inputs to the function are the A, b, c, and d matrices of the state space model.
  - The **step** command can be used to calculate the step response of the system.
  - The **initial** command can be used to calculate the natural response of the system.

1. Simulate the response y(t) of the circuit below, if u(t) is a unit step function.

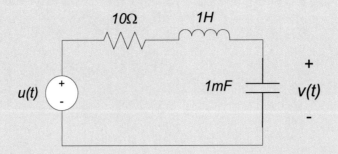

2. Simulate the response y(t) of the circuit below, if u(t) is a unit step function.

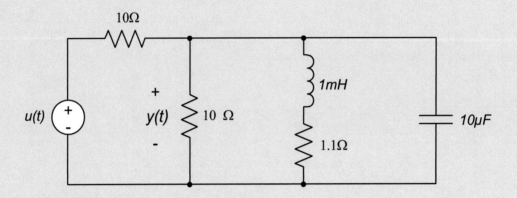

Solutions can be found at digilent.com/real-analog.

Chapter 10:
Steady-State Sinusoidal Analysis

We will now study dynamic systems which are subjected to <u>sinusoidal</u> forcing functions. Previously, in our analysis of dynamic systems, we determined both the *unforced response* (or *homogeneous solution*) and the *forced response* (or *particular solution*) to the given forcing function. In the next several chapters, however, we will restrict our attention to <u>only</u> the system's <u>forced response</u> to a sinusoidal input; this response is commonly called the sinusoidal steady-state system response. This analysis approach is useful if we are concerned primarily with the system's response after any initial conditions have died out, since we are ignoring any transient effects due to the system's natural response.

Restricting our attention to the steady-state sinusoidal response allows a considerable simplification in the system analysis: we can solve algebraic equations rather than differential equations. This advantage often more than compensates for the loss of information relative to the systems natural response. For example it is often the case that a sinusoidal input is applied for a very long time relative to the time required for the natural response to die out, so that the overall effects of the initial conditions are negligible.

Steady-state sinusoidal analysis methods are important for several reasons:

- Sinusoidal inputs are an extremely important category of forcing functions. In electrical engineering, for example, sinusoids are the dominant signal in the electrical power industry. The alternating current (or AC) signals used in power transmission are, in fact, so pervasive that many electrical engineers commonly refer to any sinusoidal signal as "AC". Carrier signals used in communications systems are also sinusoidal in nature.
- The simplification associated with the analysis of steady state sinusoidal analysis is often so desirable that system responses to non-sinusoidal inputs are interpreted in terms of their sinusoidal steady-state response. This approach will be developed when we study Fourier series.
- System design requirements are often specified in terms of the desired steady-state sinusoidal response of the system.

In section 10.1 of this chapter, we qualitatively introduce the basic concepts relative to sinusoidal steady state analyses so that readers can get the "general idea" behind the analysis approach before addressing the mathematical details in later sections. Since we will be dealing exclusively with sinusoidal signals for the next few chapters, section 10.2 provides review material relative to sinusoidal signals and complex exponentials. Recall from chapter 8 that complex exponentials are a mathematically convenient way to represent sinusoidal signals. Most of the material in section 10.2 should be review, but the reader is strongly encouraged to study section 10.2 carefully -- we will be using sinusoids and complex exponentials extensively throughout the remainder of this text, and a complete understanding of the concepts and terminology is crucial. In section 10.3, we examine the forced response of electrical circuits to sinusoidal inputs; in this section, we analyze our circuits using differential equations and come to the important conclusion that steady-state response of a circuit to sinusoidal inputs is governed by algebraic equations. Section 10.4 takes advantage of this conclusion to perform steady-state sinusoidal analyses of electrical circuits without writing the governing differential equation for the circuit! Finally, in section 10.5, we characterize a system's response purely by its effect on a sinusoidal input. This concept will be used extensively throughout the remainder of this textbook.

After completing this chapter, you should be able to:

- State the relationship between the sinusoidal steady state system response and the forced response of a system
- For sinusoidal steady-state conditions, state the relationship between the frequencies of the input and output signals for a linear, time-invariant system
- State the two parameters used to characterize the sinusoidal steady-state response of a linear, time-invariant system
- Define periodic signals
- Define the amplitude, frequency, radian frequency, and phase of a sinusoidal signal
- Express sinusoidal signals in phasor form
- Perform frequency-domain analyses of electrical circuits
- Sketch phasor diagrams of a circuit's input and output
- State the definition of impedance and admittance
- State, from memory, the impedance relations for resistors, capacitors, and inductors
- Calculate impedances for resistors, capacitors, and inductors
- State how to use the following analysis approaches in the frequency domain:
  - KVL and KCL
  - Voltage and current dividers
  - Circuit reduction techniques
  - Nodal and mesh analysis
  - Superposition, especially when multiple frequencies are present
  - Thévenin's and Norton's theorems
- Determine the load impedance necessary to deliver maximum power to a load
- Define the frequency response of a system
- Define the magnitude response and phase response of a system
- Determine the magnitude and phase responses of a circuit

10.1 Introduction to Steady-state Sinusoidal Analysis

In this chapter, we will be almost exclusively concerned with sinusoidal signals, which can be written in the form:

$$f(t) = A\cos(\omega t + \theta)$$

Eq. 10.1

Where *A* is the *amplitude* of the sinusoid, *ω* is the *angular frequency* (in radians/second) of the signal, and θ is the *phase angle* (expressed in radians or degrees) of the signal. *A* provides the peak value of the sinusoid, *ω* governs the rate of oscillation of the signal, and θ affects the translation of the sinusoid in time. A typical sinusoidal signal is shown in Fig. 10.1.

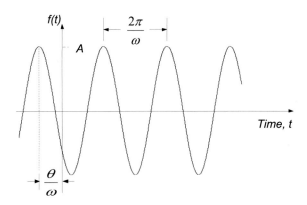

Figure 10.1. Sinusoidal signal.

If the sinusoidal signal of Fig. 10.1 is applied to a linear time invariant system, the response of the system will consist of the system's natural response (due to the initial conditions on the system) superimposed on the system's forced response (the response due to the forcing function). As we have seen in previous chapters, the forced response has the same form as the forcing function. Thus, if the input is a constant value the forced response is constant, as we have seen in the case of the step response of a system. In the case of a sinusoidal input to a system, the forced response will consist of a sinusoid of the same frequency as the input sinusoid. Since the natural response of the system decays with time, the steady state response of a linear time invariant system to a sinusoidal input is a sinusoid, as shown in Fig. 10.2. The amplitude and phase of the output may be different than the input amplitude and phase, but both the input and output signals have the same frequency.

It is common to characterize a system by the ratio of the magnitudes of the input and output signals ($\frac{B}{A}$ in Fig. 10.2) and the difference in phases between the input and output signals (φ−θ) in Fig. 10.2) at a particular frequency. It is important to note that the ratio of magnitudes and difference in phases is dependent upon the frequency of the applied sinusoidal signal.

Figure 10.2. Sinusoidal steady-state input-output relation for a linear time invariant system.

Example 10.1: Series RLC Circuit Response

Consider the series RLC circuit shown in Fig. 10.3 below. The input voltage to the circuit is given by:

$$v_s(t) = \begin{cases} 0, t < 0 \\ \cos(5t), t \geq 0 \end{cases}$$

Thus, the input is zero prior to *t=0*, and the sinusoidal input is suddenly "switched on" at time *t=0*. The input forcing function is shown in Fig. 10.4(a). The circuit is "relaxed" before the sinusoidal input is applied, so the circuit initial conditions are:

$$y(0^-) = \frac{dy}{dt}|_{t=0^-} = 0$$

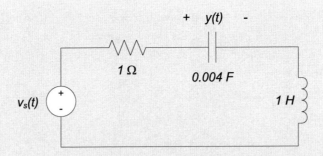

Figure 10.3. Series RLC circuit; output is voltage across capacitor.

This circuit has been analyzed previously in Chapter 8, and the derivation of the governing differential equation will not be repeated here. The full output response of the circuit is shown in Fig. 10.4(b). The natural response of the circuit is readily apparent in the initial portion of the response but these transients die out quickly, leaving only the sinusoidal steady-state response of the circuit. It is <u>only</u> this steady state response in which we will be interested for the next several modules. With knowledge of the frequency of the signals, we can define both the input and (steady-state) output by their amplitude and phase, and characterize the circuit by the <u>ratio of the output-to-input amplitude</u> and the <u>difference in the phases of the output and input</u>.

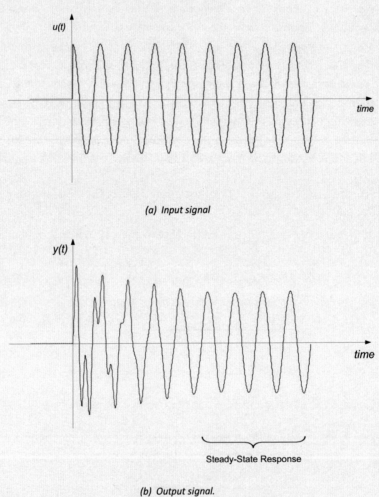

(a) Input signal

(b) Output signal.

Figure 10.4. Input and output signals for circuit of Figure 10.3.

Section Summary

- Sinusoidal signals can be expressed mathematically in the form:

$$f(t) = A \cos(\omega t + \theta)$$

- In the above, A is the amplitude of the sinusoid, it describes the maximum and minimum values of the signal.
- In the above, θ is the phase angle of the sinusoid, it describes the time shift of the sinusoid relative to a pure cosine.
- In the above, ω is the radian frequency of the sinusoid. The sinusoid repeats itself at time intervals of $\frac{2\pi}{\omega}$ seconds.
- A sinusoidal signal is completely described by its frequency, its amplitude, and its phase angle.
- The steady-state response of a linear, time-invariant system to a sinusoidal input is a sinusoid with the same frequency.
- Since the frequencies of the input and output are the same, the relationship between the input and output sinusoids is completely characterized by the relationships between:
  - The input and output amplitudes.
  - The input and output phase angles.

10.1 Exercises

1. In the circuit below, all circuit elements are linear and time invariant. The input voltage $V_{in}(t) = 10 \cos(2t + 40°)$. What is the radian frequency of the output voltage $V_{out(t)}$?

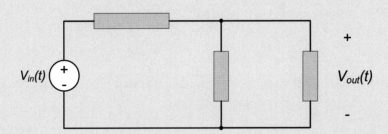

2. In the circuit below, all circuit elements are linear and time invariant. The input voltage is $V_{in}(t) = 10 \cos(2t + 40°)$. The output voltage is of the form $V_{out}(t) = A \cos(\omega t + \phi°)$. If the ratio between the input and output, $\left|\frac{V_{out}}{V_{in}}\right| = 0.5$ and the phase difference between the input and output is 20°, what are:

   a. The radian frequency of the output, ω?
   b. The amplitude of the output, A?
   c. The phase angle of the output, ϕ?

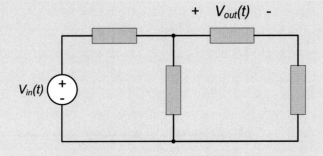

Solutions can be found at digilent.com/real-analog.

10.2 Sinusoidal Signals, Complex Exponentials, and Phasors

In this section, we will review properties of sinusoidal functions and complex exponentials. We will also introduce phasor notation, which will significantly simplify the sinusoidal steady-state analysis of systems, and provide terminology which will be used in subsequent sinusoidal steady-state related modules.

Much of the material presented here has been provided previously in Chapter 8; this material is, however, important enough to bear repetition. Likewise, a brief overview of complex arithmetic, which will be essential in using complex exponentials effectively, is provided at the end of this section. Readers who need to review complex arithmetic may find it useful to peruse this overview <u>before</u> reading the material in this section relating to complex exponentials and phasors.

10.2.1 Sinusoidal Signals

The sinusoidal signal shown in Fig. 10.5 is represented mathematically by:

$$f(t) = V_P \cos(\omega t) \hspace{5cm} \text{Eq. 10.2}$$

The *amplitude* or *peak value* of the function is V_P. V_P is the maximum value achieved by the function; the function itself is bounded by $+V_P$ and $-V_P$, so that $-V_P \le f(t) \le V_P$. The *radian frequency* or *angular frequency* of the function is ω; the units of ω are radians/second. The function is said to be periodic; *periodic* functions repeat themselves at regular intervals, so that:

$$f(t + nT) = f(t) \hspace{5cm} \text{Eq. 10.3}$$

Where n is any integer and T is the *period* of the signal. The sinusoidal waveform shown in Fig. 10.5 goes through one complete cycle or period in T seconds. Since the sinusoid of equation (10.2) repeats itself every 2π radians, the period is related to the radian frequency of the sinusoid by:

$$\omega = \frac{2\pi}{T} \hspace{5cm} \text{Eq. 10.4}$$

It is common to define the frequency of the sinusoid in terms of the number of cycles of the waveform which occur in one second. In these terms, the frequency f of the function is:

$$f = \frac{1}{T} \hspace{5cm} \text{Eq. 10.5}$$

The units of f are cycles/second or Hertz (abbreviated Hz). The frequency and radian frequency are related by:

$$f = \frac{\omega}{2\pi} \hspace{5cm} \text{Eq. 10.6}$$

Or equivalently:

$$\omega = 2\pi f \hspace{5cm} \text{Eq. 10.7}$$

Regardless of whether the sinusoid's rate of oscillation is expressed as frequency or radian frequency, it is important to realize that the argument of the sinusoid in equation (10.2) <u>must be expressed in radians</u>. Thus, equation (10.2) can be expressed in terms of frequency in Hz as:

$$f(t) = \cos(2\pi f t) \hspace{5cm} \text{Eq. 10.8}$$

To avoid confusion in our mathematics, we will almost invariably write sinusoidal functions in terms of radian frequency as shown in equation (10.2), although Hz is generally taken as the standard unit for frequency (experimental apparatus, for example, commonly express frequency in Hz).

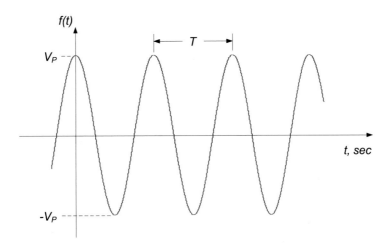

Figure 10.5. Pure cosine waveform.

A more general expression of a sinusoidal signal is:

$$v(t) = V_P \cos(\omega t + \theta)$$

Eq. 10.9

Where θ is the *phase angle* or *phase* of the sinusoid. The phase angle simply translates the sinusoid along the time axis, as shown in Fig. 10.6. A <u>positive phase angle shifts the signal left in time</u>, while a <u>negative phase angle shifts the signal right</u> – this is consistent with our discussion of step functions in section 6.1, where it was noted that subtracting a value from the unit step argument resulted a time delay of the function. Thus, as shown in Figure 10.6, a positive phase angle causes the sinusoid to be shifted left by $\frac{\theta}{\omega}$ seconds.

The units of phase angle should be radians, to be consistent with the units of ωt in the argument of the cosine. It is typical, however, to express phase angle in degrees, with 180° corresponding to π radians. Thus, the conversion between radians and degrees can be expressed as:

$$\text{Number of degrees} = \frac{180}{\pi} x \text{ Number of radians}$$

For example, we will consider the two expressions below to be equivalent, though the expression on the right-hand side of the equal sign contains a mathematical inconsistency:

$$V_P \cos\left(\omega t + \frac{\pi}{2}\right) = V_P \cos(\omega t + 90°)$$

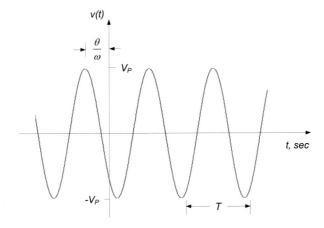

Figure 10.6. Cosine waveform with non-zero phase angle.

For convenience, we introduce the terms *leading* and *lagging* when referring to the sign on the phase angle, θ. A sinusoidal signal $v_1(t)$ is said to *lead* another sinusoid $v_2(t)$ of the same frequency if the phase difference between the two is such that $v_1(t)$ is shifted left (or reverse) in time relative to $v_2(t)$. Likewise, $v_1(t)$ is said to *lag* another sinusoid $v_2(t)$ of the same frequency if the phase difference between the two is such that $v_1(t)$ is shifted right (or forward) in time relative to $v_2(t)$. This terminology is described graphically in Fig. 10.7.

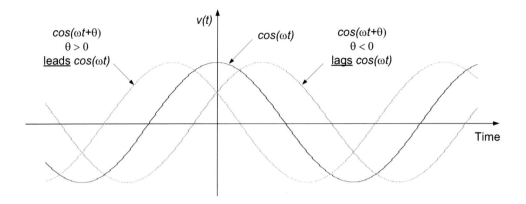

Figure 10.7. Leading and lagging sinusoids.

Finally, we note that the representation of sinusoidal signals as a phase shifted cosine function, as provided by equation (10.9), is completely general. If we are given a sinusoidal function in terms of a sine function, it can be readily converted to the form of equation (10.9) by subtracting a phase of $\frac{\pi}{2}$ (or 90°) from the argument, since:

$$\sin(\omega t) = \cos\left(\omega t - \frac{\pi}{2}\right)$$

Likewise, sign changes can be accounted for by a ±π radian phase shift, since:

$$-\cos(\omega t) = \cos(\omega t \pm \pi)$$

Obviously, we could have chosen either a cosine or sine representation of a sinusoidal signal. We prefer the cosine representation, since a <u>cosine is the real part of a complex exponential</u>. In the next module, we will see that sinusoidal steady-state circuit analysis is simplified significantly by using complex exponentials to represent the sinusoidal functions. The cosine is the <u>real</u> part of a complex exponential (as we saw previously in chapter 8). Since all measurable signals are real valued, we take the real part of our complex exponential-based result as our physical response; this results in a solution of the form of equation (10.9).

Since representation of sinusoidal waveforms as complex exponentials will become important to us in circuit analysis, we devote the following subsection to a review of complex exponentials and their interpretation as sinusoidal signals.

10.2.2 Complex Exponentials and Phasors

Euler's identity can be used to represent complex numbers as complex exponentials:

$$e^{j\theta} = \cos\theta \pm j\sin\theta \hspace{6cm} \text{Eq. 10.10}$$

If we generalize equation (9) to time-varying signals of arbitrary magnitude, we can write:

$$V_p e^{\pm j(\omega t + \theta)} = V_p\cos(\omega t + \theta) \pm jV_p\sin(\omega t + \theta) \hspace{3cm} \text{Eq. 10.11}$$

So that:

$$V_P \cos(\omega t + \theta) = Re\{V_P e^{\pm(\omega t+\theta)}\}$$

Eq. 10.12

And:

$$V_P \sin(\omega t + \theta) = Im\{V_P e^{\pm j(\omega t+\theta)}\}$$

Eq. 10.13

Where $Re\{V_P e^{\pm(\omega t+\theta)}\}$ and $Im\{V_P e^{\pm j(\omega t+\theta)}\}$ denote the real part of $V_P e^{\pm j(\omega t+\theta)}$ and the imaginary part of $V_P e^{\pm j(\omega t+\theta)}$, respectively. The complex exponential of equation (10.11) can also be written as:

$$V_P e^{\pm j(\omega t+\theta)} = V_P e^{j\theta} e^{j\omega t}$$

Eq. 10.14

The term $V_P e^{j\theta}$ on the right-hand side of equation (10.14) is simply a <u>complex number which provides the magnitude and phase information</u> of the complex exponential of equation (10.11). From equation (10.12), this magnitude and phase can be used to express the magnitude and phase angle of a sinusoidal signal of the form given in equation (10.9).

The complex number in polar coordinates which provides the magnitude and phase angle of a time-varying complex exponential, as given in equation (10.14) is called a *phasor*. The phasor representing $V_P \cos(\omega t + \theta)$ is defined as:

$$\underline{V} = V_P e^{j\theta} = V_P \angle \theta$$

Eq. 10.15

We will use a capital letter with an underscore to denote a phasor. Using bold typeface to represent phasors is more common; our notation is simply for consistency between lecture material and written material – boldface type is difficult to create on a whiteboard during lecture!

Note: The phasor representing a sinusoid does <u>not</u> provide information about the frequency of the sinusoid – <u>frequency information must be kept track of separately</u>.

10.2.3 Complex Arithmetic Review

Much the material in this section has been provided previously in section 8.3. It is repeated here to emphasize its importance and to expand slightly upon some crucial topics.

In our presentation of complex exponentials, we first provide a brief review of complex numbers. A complex number contains both real and imaginary parts. Thus, we may write a complex number $\underline{A}$ as:

$$\underline{A} = a + jb$$

Eq. 10.16

Where:

$$j = \sqrt{-1}$$

Eq. 10.17

And the underscore denotes a complex number. The complex number $\underline{A}$ can be represented on orthogonal axes representing the real and imaginary part of the number, as shown in Fig. 10.8. (In Figure 10.8, we have taken the liberty of representing $\underline{A}$ as a vector, although it is really just a number.) We can also represent the complex number in polar coordinates, also shown in Figure 10.8. The polar coordinates consist of a magnitude $|A|$ and phase angle θ_A, defined as:

$$|A| = \sqrt{a^2 + b^2}$$

Eq. 10.18

$$\theta_A = \tan^{-1}\left(\frac{b}{a}\right)$$

Eq. 10.19

Notice that the phase angle is defined counterclockwise from the positive real axis. Conversely, we can determine the rectangular coordinates from the polar coordinates from:

$$a = Re\{\underline{A}\} = |A|\cos(\theta_A)$$

Eq. 10.20

$$b = Im\{\underline{A}\} = |A|\sin(\theta_A)$$

Eq. 10.21

Where the notation $Re\{\underline{A}\}$ and $Im\{\underline{A}\}$ denote the real part of $\underline{A}$ and the imaginary part of $\underline{A}$, respectively.

The polar coordinates of a complex number of $\underline{A}$ are often represented in the form:

$$\underline{A} = |A|\angle\theta_A$$

Eq. 10.22

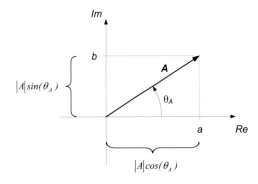

Figure 10.8. Representation of a complex number in rectangular and polar coordinates.

An alternate method of representing complex numbers in polar coordinates employs complex exponential notation. Without proof, we claim that:

$$e^{j\theta} = 1\angle\theta$$

Eq. 10.23

Thus, $e^{j\theta}$ is a complex number with magnitude 1 and phase angle θ. From Fig. 10.8, it is easy to see that this definition of the complex exponential agrees with Euler's equation:

$$e^{\pm j\theta} = cos\theta \pm j\sin\theta$$

Eq. 10.24

With the definition of equation (10.23), we can define any arbitrary complex number in terms of complex numbers. For example, our previous complex number $\underline{A}$ can be represented as:

$$\underline{A} = |A|e^{j\theta_A}$$

Eq. 10.25

We can generalize our definition of the complex exponential to time-varying signals. If we define a time varying signal $e^{j\omega t}$, we can use equation (10.24) to write:

$$e^{j\omega t} = \cos\omega t \pm j\sin\omega t$$

Eq. 10.26

The signal $e^{j\omega t}$ can be visualized as a unit vector rotating around the origin in the complex plane; the tip of the vector scribes a unit circle with its center at the origin of the complex plane. This is illustrated in Fig. 10.9. The vector rotates at a rate defined by the quantity ω– the vector makes one complete revolution every $\frac{2\pi}{\omega}$ seconds.

The projection of this rotating vector on the real axis traces out the signal $\cos\omega t$, as shown in Fig. 10.7, while the projection of the rotating vector on the imaginary axis traces out the signal $\sin\omega t$, also shown in Fig. 10.9.

Thus, we interpret the complex exponential function $e^{j\omega t}$ as an alternate "type" of sinusoidal signal. The real part of this function is $\cos\omega t$ while the imaginary part of this function is $\sin\omega t$.

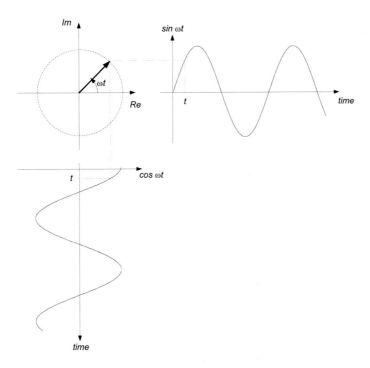

Figure 10.9. Illustration of $e^{j\omega t}$.

Addition and subtraction of complex numbers is most easily performed in rectangular coordinates. Given two complex numbers $\underline{A}$ and $\underline{B}$, defined as:

$$\underline{A} = a + jb$$
$$\underline{B} = c + jd$$

The sum and difference of the complex number can be determined by:

$$\underline{A} + \underline{B} = (a + c) + j(b + d)$$

And:

$$\underline{A} - \underline{B} = (a - c) + j(b - d)$$

Multiplication and division, on the other hand, are probably most easily performed using polar coordinates. If we define two complex numbers as:

$$\underline{A} = |A|e^{j\theta_A} = |A|\angle\theta_A$$

$$\underline{B} = |B|e^{j\theta_B} = |B|\angle\theta_B$$

The product and quotient can be determined by:

$$\underline{A} \cdot \underline{B} = |A|e^{j\theta_A} \cdot |B|e^{j\theta_B} = |A| \cdot |B|e^{j(\theta_A+\theta_B)} = |A| \cdot |B|\angle(\theta_A + \theta_B)$$

And:

$$\frac{\underline{A}}{\underline{B}} = \frac{|A|e^{j\theta_A}}{|B|e^{j\theta_B}} = \frac{\underline{A}}{\underline{B}}\angle(\theta_A - \theta_B)$$

The conjugate of a complex number, denoted by a *, is obtained by changing the sign on the imaginary part of the number. For example, if $\underline{A} = a + jb = |A|e^{j\theta}$, then:

$$A^* = a - jb = |A|e^{-j\theta}$$

Conjugation does not affect the magnitude of the complex number, but it changes the sign on the phase angle. It is easy to show that:

$$\underline{A} \cdot \underline{A}^* = |A|^2$$

Several useful relationships between polar and rectangular coordinate representations of complex numbers are provided below. The reader is encouraged to prove any that are not self-evident.

$$j = 1\angle 90°$$
$$-j = 1\angle -90°$$
$$\frac{1}{j} = -j = 1\angle -90°$$
$$1 = 1\angle 0°$$
$$-1 = 1\angle 180°$$

Section Summary

- Periodic signals repeat themselves at a specific time interval. Sinusoidal signals are a special case of periodic signals.
- A sinusoidal signal can always be written in the form $v(t) = V_P \cos(\omega t + \theta)$.
- It is often convenient, when analyzing a system's steady-state response to sinusoidal inputs, to express sinusoidal signals in terms of complex exponentials. This is possible because of Euler's formula:

$$e^{\pm j\omega t} = \cos \omega t \pm j \sin \omega t$$

- From Euler's formula, a sinusoidal signal can be expressed as the real part of a complex exponential:

$$v(t) = V_P \cos(\omega t + \theta) = Re\{V_P e^{\pm j(\omega t + \theta)}\}$$

- The magnitude and phase angle of a complex exponential signal are conveniently expressed as a phasor:

$$\underline{V} = V_P e^{j\theta}$$

- Using phasor notation, the above complex exponential signal can be written as:

$$V_P e^{\pm j(\omega t + \theta)} = \underline{V} e^{j\omega t}$$

- Phasors can then be operated on arithmetically in the same way as any other complex number. However, when operating on phasors, keep in mind that you are dealing with the amplitude and phase angle of a sinusoidal signal.

10.2 Exercises

1. Express the following complex numbers in rectangular form:
    1.1. $3e^{j45°}$
    1.2. $5\sqrt{2}e^{j135°}$
    1.3. $2.5e^{j90°}$
    1.4. $6e^{j\pi}$

2. Express the following complex numbers in complex exponential form:
   2.1. $2 - j2$
   2.2. $-j3$
   2.3. 6
   2.4. $3 + j$

3. Evaluate the following expressions. Express your results in complex exponential form.
   3.1. $-\dfrac{j}{2(j+1)}$
   3.2. $\dfrac{2-j2}{4+j4}$
   3.3. $2e^{j45°} \cdot \dfrac{2}{j+1}$
   3.4. $j + \dfrac{2}{j}$

4. Represent the following sinusoids in phasor form:
   4.1. $3\cos(5t - 60°)$
   4.2. $-2\cos(300t + 45°)$
   4.3. $\sin(6t)$
   4.4. $7\cos(3t)$

5. Write the signal representing the real part of the following complex exponentials:
   5.1. $5\sqrt{2}e^{j(100t-45°)}$
   5.2. $3e^{j\pi}e^{j3t}$
   5.3. $2e^{j(\pi t-30°)} + 4e^{j(4t+20°)}$

Solutions can be found at digilent.com/real-analog.

10.3 Sinusoidal Steady-state System Response

In this section, the concepts presented in sections 10.1 and 10.2 are used to determine the sinusoidal steady-state response of electrical circuits. We will develop sinusoidal steady-state circuit analysis in terms of examples, rather than attempting to develop a generalized approach à priori. The approach is straightforward, so that a general analysis approach can be inferred from the application of the method to several simple circuits.

The overall approach to introducing sinusoidal steady-state analysis techniques used in this section is as follows:

- We first determine the sinusoidal steady-state response of a simple RC circuit, by solving the differential equation governing the system. This results directly in a solution which is a function of time; it is a *time domain* analysis technique. The approach is mathematically tedious, even for the simple circuit being analyzed.
- We then re-analyze the same RC circuit using complex exponentials and phasors. This approach results in the transformation of the governing time domain differential equation into an algebraic equation which is a function of <u>frequency</u>. It is said to describe the circuit behavior in the *frequency domain*. The frequency domain equation governing the system is then solved using phasor techniques and the result transformed back to the time domain. This approach tends to be mathematically simpler than the direct solution of the differential equation in the time domain, though in later sections we will simplify the approach even further.
- Several other examples of sinusoidal steady-state circuit analysis are then performed using frequency domain techniques in order to demonstrate application of the approach to more complex circuits. It will

be seen that, unlike time-domain analysis, the difficulty of the frequency domain analysis does not increase drastically as the circuit being analyzed becomes more complex.

Example 10.2: RC Circuit Sinusoidal Steady-state Response via Time-domain Analysis

In the circuit below, the input voltage is $u(t) = V_P \cos(\omega t)$ volts and the circuit response (or output) is the capacitor voltage, $y(t)$. We want to find the steady-state response (as $t \to \infty$).

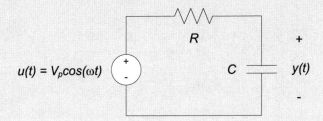

The differential equation governing the circuit is:

$$\frac{dy(t)}{dt} + \frac{1}{RC} y(t) = \frac{VP}{RC \cos(\omega t)} \qquad \text{Eq. 10.27}$$

Since we are concerned only with the steady-state response, there is no need to determine the homogeneous solution of the differential equation (or, equivalently, the natural response of the system) so we will not be concerned with the initial conditions on the system – their effect will have died out by the time we are interested in the response. Thus, we only need to determine the particular solution of the above differential equation (the forced response of the system). Since the input function is a sinusoid, the forced response must be sinusoidal, so we assume that the forced response $y_f(t)$ has the form:

$$y_f(t) = A \cos(\omega t) + B \sin(\omega t) \qquad \text{Eq. 10.28}$$

Substituting equation (10.28) into equation (10.27) results in:

$$-A\omega \sin(\omega t) + B\omega \cos(\omega t) + \frac{1}{RC}[A \cos(\omega t) + B \sin (\omega t)] = \frac{V_P}{RC} \cos(\omega t) \qquad \text{Eq. 10.29}$$

Equating coefficients on the sine and cosine terms results in two equations in two unknowns:

$$-A\omega + \frac{B}{RC} = 0 \quad B\omega + \frac{A}{RC} = \frac{V_P}{RC} \qquad \text{Eq. 10.30}$$

Solving equations (10.30) results in:

$$A = \frac{V_P}{1+(\omega RC)^2} \qquad B = \frac{V_P \omega RC}{1+(\omega RC)^2} \qquad \text{Eq. 10.31}$$

Substituting equations (10.31) into equation (10.28) and using the trigonometric identity $A \cos(\omega t) + B \sin(\omega t) = \sqrt{A^2 + B^2} \cos\left[\omega t - \tan^{-1}\left(\frac{B}{A}\right)\right]$ results in (after some fairly tedious algebra):

$$y_f(t) = \frac{V_P}{\sqrt{1+(\omega RC)^2}} \cos[\omega t - \tan^{-1}(\omega RC)] \qquad \text{Eq. 10.32}$$

Note: In all steps of the above analysis, the functions being used are functions of <u>time</u>. That is, for a particular value of ω, the functions vary with time. The above analysis is being performed in the *time domain*.

Example 10.3: RC Circuit Sinusoidal Steady-state Response via Frequency-domain Analysis

We now repeat Example 10.2, using phasor-based analysis techniques. The circuit being analyzed is shown in the figure to the left below for reference; the input voltage is $u(t) = V_P \cos(\omega t)$ volts and the circuit response (or output) is the capacitor voltage, $y(t)$. We still want to find the steady-state response (as $t \to \infty$). In this example, we replace the physical input, $u(t) = V_P \cos(\omega t)$, with a conceptual input based on a complex exponential as shown in the figure to the right below. <u>The complex exponential input is chosen such that the real part of the complex input is equivalent to the physical input applied to the circuit</u>. We will analyze the conceptual circuit with the complex valued input.

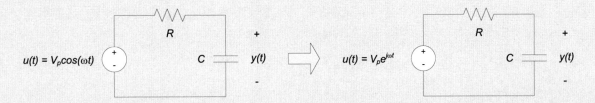

The differential equation governing the circuit above is the same as in example 10.2, but with the complex input:

$$\frac{dy(t)}{dt} + \frac{1}{RC} y(t) = \frac{V_P}{RC} e^{j\omega t} \qquad \text{Eq. 10.33}$$

As in example 10.2, we now assume a form of the forced response. In this case, however, our solution will be assumed to be a complex exponential:

$$y(t) = |Y| e^{j(\omega t + \theta)} \qquad \text{Eq. 10.34}$$

Which can be written in phasor form as:

$$y(t) = \underline{Y} e^{j\omega t} \qquad \text{Eq. 10.35}$$

Where the phasor $\underline{Y}$ is a <u>complex number</u> which can be expressed in either exponential or polar form:

$$y(t) = \underline{Y} e^{j\theta t} \qquad \text{Eq. 10.36}$$

Substituting (10.35) into equation (10.33) and taking the appropriate derivative results in:

$$j\omega \underline{Y} e^{j\omega t} + \frac{1}{RC} \underline{Y} e^{j\omega t} = \frac{V_P}{RC} e^{j\omega t} \qquad \text{Eq. 10.37}$$

We can divide equation (10.37) by $e^{j\omega t}$ to obtain:

$$j\omega \underline{Y} + \frac{1}{RC} \underline{Y} = \frac{V_P}{RC} \qquad \text{Eq. 10.38}$$

Equation (10.38) can be solved for $\underline{Y}$:

$$\left(j\omega + \frac{1}{RC} \right) \underline{Y} = \frac{V_P}{RC} \Rightarrow \underline{Y} = \frac{\frac{V_P}{RC}}{j\omega + \frac{1}{RC}} \qquad \text{Eq. 10.39}$$

So that:

$$\underline{Y} = \frac{V_P}{1 + j\omega RC}$$

Eq. 10.40

The magnitude and phase of the output response can be determined from the phasor $\underline{Y}$:

$$|Y| = \frac{V_P}{\sqrt{1 + (\omega RC)^2}}$$
$$\angle_Y = -\tan^{-1}(\omega RC)$$

Eq. 10.41

The complex exponential form of the system response is then, from equation (10.35):

$$y(t) = \frac{V_P}{\sqrt{1 + (\omega RC)^2}} e^{j(\omega t - \tan^{-1}(\omega RC))}$$

Eq. 10.42

Since our physical input is the real part of the conceptual input, and <u>since all circuit parameters are real valued</u>, our physical output is the real part of equation (10.42) and the forced response is:

$$y_f(t) = \frac{V_P}{\sqrt{1 + (\omega RC)^2}} \cos[\omega t - \tan^{-1}(\omega RC)]$$

Eq. 10.43

Which agrees with our result from the time-domain analysis of example 10.2.

Notes:

- The transition from equation (10.37) to equation (10.38) removed the time-dependence of our solution. The solution is now no longer a function of time! The solution includes the phasor representations of the input and output, as well as (generally) frequency. Thus, equation (10.38) is said to be in the *phasor domain* or, somewhat more commonly, the *frequency domain*. The analysis remains in the frequency domain until we reintroduce time in equation (10.43).
- Equations in the frequency domain are algebraic equations rather than differential equations. This is a significant advantage mathematically, especially for higher-order systems.
- Circuit components must have purely real values for the above process to work. We do not prove this, but merely make the claim that the process of taking the real part of the complex exponential form of the system response is not valid if circuit components (or any coefficients in the differential equation governing the system) are complex valued. Fortunately, this is not a strong restriction – complex values do not exist in the physical world.
- The complex exponential we use for our "conceptual" input, $V_P e^{j\omega t}$, is not physically realizable. That is, we cannot create this signal in the real world. It is a purely mathematical entity which we introduce solely for the purpose of simplifying the analysis. The complex form of the output response given by equation (10.42) is likewise not physically realizable.

Example 10.4: Numerical Example and Phasor Diagrams

We now examine the circuit shown below. This circuit is simply the circuit of Example 10.3, with $R = 1k\Omega, C = 1\mu F, V_P = 5V$, and $\omega = 1000$ rad/second.

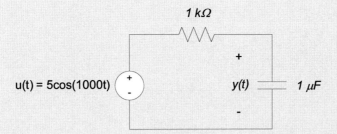

In phasor form, the input is $u(t) = \underline{U}e^{j1000t}$, so that the phasor $\underline{U}$ is $\underline{U} = 5e^{j0°} = 5\angle 0°$.

The phasor form of the output is given by equations (10.41):

$$|Y| = \frac{V_P}{\sqrt{1 + (\omega RC)^2}} = \frac{5}{\sqrt{1 + (1000 \cdot 1000 \cdot 1 \times 10^{-6})}} = \frac{5}{\sqrt{2}}$$

$$\angle\theta_T = -\tan^{-1}(\omega RC) = -\tan^{-1}(1000 \cdot 1000 \cdot 1 \times 10^{-6}) = -\frac{\pi}{4} = -45°$$

And the phasor $\underline{Y}$ can be written as $\underline{Y} = \frac{5}{\sqrt{2}}e^{-j45°} = \frac{5}{\sqrt{2}}\angle -45°$

We can create a phasor diagram of the input phasor $\underline{U}$ and the output phasor $\underline{Y}$

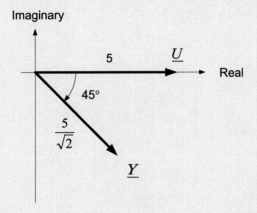

The phasor diagram shows the input and output phasors in the complex plane. The magnitudes of the phasors are typically labeled on the diagram, as is the phase <u>difference</u> between the two phasors. Note that since the phase difference between $\underline{Y}$ and $\underline{U}$ is negative, the output y(t) <u>lags</u> the input u(t).

The time-domain form of the output is:

$$y(t) = \frac{5}{\sqrt{2}}\cos(1000t - 45°)$$

A time-domain plot of the input and output are shown below. This plot emphasizes that the output lags the input, as indicated by our phasor diagram. The plot below replicates what would be seen from a measurement of the input and output voltages.

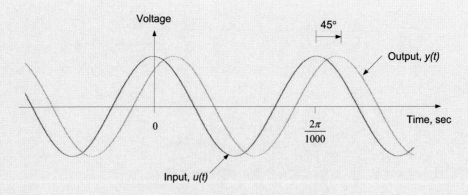

Example 10.5: RL Circuit Sinusoidal Steady-state Response

In the circuit to the left below, the input voltage is $V_P \cos(\omega t + 30°)$ volts and the circuit response (or output) is the inductor current, $i_L(t)$. We want to find the steady-state response $i_L(t \to \infty)$.

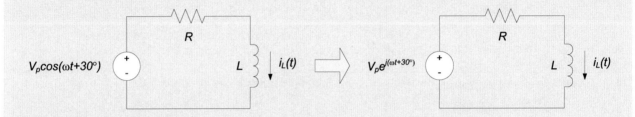

The differential equation governing the circuit can be determined by applying KVL around the single loop:

$$L\frac{di_L(t)}{dt} + Ri_L(t) = u(t)$$

Eq. 10.44

We apply the conceptual input, $u(t) = V_P e^{j(\omega t + 30°)}$ as shown in the figure to the right above to this equation. We can represent this input in phasor form as:

$$u(t) = \underline{U}e^{j\omega t}$$

Eq. 10.45

Where the phasor $\underline{U} = V_P \angle 30°$. Likewise, we represent the output in phasor form:

$$i_L(t) = \underline{I_L}e^{j\omega t}$$

Eq. 10.46

Where the phasor $\underline{I_L} = |I_L|\angle\theta$.

Substituting our assumed input and output in phasor form into equation (10.44) results in:

$$Lj\omega\underline{I_L}e^{j\omega t} + R\underline{I_L}e^{j\omega t} = \underline{U}e^{j\omega t}$$

Eq. 10.47

As in Example 10.4, we divide through by $e^{j\omega t}$ to obtain the frequency domain governing equation:

$$Lj\omega\underline{I_L} + R\underline{I_L} = \underline{U}$$

Eq. 10.48

So that:

$$\underline{I_L} = \frac{\underline{U}}{R + j\omega L} = \frac{V_P \angle 30°}{R + j\omega L}$$

Eq. 10.49

So that the phasor $\underline{I_L}$ has magnitude and phase:

$$|I_L| = \frac{V_P}{\sqrt{R^2+(\omega L)^2}}$$
$$\theta = 30° - \tan^{-1}\left(\frac{\omega L}{R}\right)$$

Eq. 10.50

The exponential form of the inductor current is therefore:

$$i_L(t) = \frac{V_P}{\sqrt{R^2+(\omega L)^2}}e^{j\left[\omega t+30°-\tan^{-1}\left(\frac{\omega L}{R}\right)\right]}$$

Eq. 10.51

And the actual physical inductor current is:

$$i_L(t) = \frac{V_P}{\sqrt{R^2+(\omega L)^2}}\cos\left[\omega t + 30° - \tan^{-1}\left(\frac{\omega L}{R}\right)\right]$$

Eq. 10.52

Example 10.6: Series RLC Circuit Sinusoidal Steady-state Response

Consider the circuit shown below. The input to the circuit is $v_s(t) = 2\cos(\omega t)$ volts. Find the output $v(t)$.

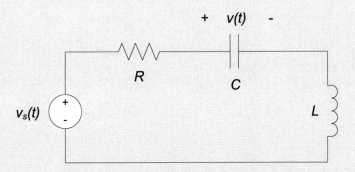

In section 8.1, it was determined that the differential equation governing the system is:

$$\frac{d^2v(t)}{dt^2} + \frac{R}{L}\frac{dv(t)}{dt} + \frac{1}{LC}v(t) = \frac{1}{LC}v_S(t)$$

Eq. 10.53

Assuming that the input is a complex exponential whose real part is the <u>given</u> $v_S(t)$ provides:

$$v_S(t) = 2e^{j\omega t}$$

Eq. 10.54

The output is assumed to have the phasor form:

$$v(t) = \underline{V}e^{j\omega t}$$

Eq. 10.55

Where $\underline{V}$ contains the (unknown) magnitude and phase of the output voltage. Substituting equations (10.54) and (10.55) into equation (10.53) results in:

$$-(j\omega)^2\underline{V}e^{j\omega t} + \frac{R}{L}(j\omega)\underline{V}e^{j\omega t} + \frac{1}{LC}\underline{V}e^{j\omega t} = \frac{1}{LC}2e^{j\omega t}$$

Eq. 10.56

Dividing through by $e^{j\omega t}$ and noting that $j^2 = -1$, results in:

$$\left[\frac{1}{LC} - \omega^2 + j\frac{R}{L}\omega\right]\underline{V} = \frac{2}{LC}$$

So that:

$$V = \frac{\frac{2}{LC}}{\frac{1}{LC} - \omega^2 + j\frac{R}{L}\omega}$$

Eq. 10.57

The magnitude and phase of V are:

$$|V| = \frac{\frac{2}{LC}}{\sqrt{\left(\frac{1}{LC} - \omega^2\right)^2 + \left(\frac{R}{L}\omega\right)^2}}$$

$$\angle V = -\tan^{-1}\left(\frac{\frac{R\omega}{L}}{\frac{1}{LC} - \omega^2}\right)$$

And the capacitor voltage is:

$$v(t) = \frac{\frac{2}{LC}}{\sqrt{\left(\frac{1}{LC} - \omega^2\right)^2 + \left(\frac{R}{L}\omega\right)^2}} \cos\left\{\omega t - \tan^{-1}\left(\frac{\frac{R\omega}{L}}{\frac{1}{LC} - \omega^2}\right)\right\}$$

Eq. 10.58

The complex arithmetic in this case becomes a bit tedious, but the complexity of the frequency-domain approach is nowhere near that of the time-domain solution of the second-order differential equation.

Section Summary

- The steady-state response of a linear time invariant system to a sinusoidal input is a sinusoid with the same frequency as the input sinusoid. Only the amplitude and phase angle of the output sinusoid can be different from the input sinusoid, so the solution is entirely characterized by the magnitude and phase angle of the output sinusoid.

- The steady-state response of a system to a sinusoidal input can be determined by assuming a form of the solution, substituting the input signal and the output signal into the governing differential equation and solving for the amplitude and phase angle of the output sinusoid.

- The solution approach is simplified if the sinusoidal signals are represented as complex exponentials. The approach is further simplified if these complex exponentials are represented in phasor form – the phasor is a complex number which provides the amplitude and phase angle of the complex exponential.

- The above solution approaches convert the governing differential equation into an algebraic equation. If complex exponentials in phasor form are used to represent the signals of interest, the governing algebraic equation can have complex coefficients.

- The relationships between the steady state sinusoidal inputs and outputs are described by a relationship between the amplitudes (generally a ratio between the output amplitude and the input amplitude) and the phase angles (generally a difference between the output and input phase angles).
  - These relationships are often displayed graphically in a phasor diagram.

10.3   Exercises

1. The differential equation governing a circuit is:

$$2\frac{dy(t)}{dt} + 6y(t) = u(t)$$

Where *u(t)* is the input and *y(t)* is the output. Determine the steady-state response of the circuit to an input $u(t) = 2\cos(3t)$.

2. For the circuit shown below, *u(t)* is the input and *y(t)* is the output.
   a. Write the differential equation relating *u(t)* and *y(t)*.
   b. Determine $y(t), t \to \infty$, if $u(t) = 3\cos(2t)$

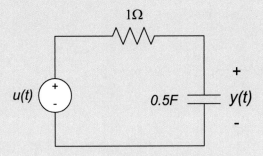

Solutions can be found at digilent.com/real-analog.

10.4 Phasor Representations of Circuit Elements

In section 10.3, we determined the sinusoidal steady-state response of an electrical circuit by transforming the circuit's governing differential equation into the *frequency domain* or *phasor domain*. This transformation converted the differential equation into an algebraic equation. This conversion significantly simplified the subsequent circuit analysis, at the relatively minor expense of performing some complex arithmetic. In this module, we will further simplify this analysis by transforming the <u>circuit itself</u> directly into the frequency domain and <u>writing the governing algebraic equations directly</u>.

This approach eliminates the necessity of ever writing the differential equation governing the circuit (as long as we are only interested in the circuit's sinusoidal steady-state response). This approach also allows us to apply analysis techniques previously used only for purely resistive circuits to circuits containing energy storage elements.

10.4.1 Phasor Domain Voltage-current Relationships

In section 10.2, we introduced phasors as a method for representing sinusoidal signals. Phasors provide the magnitude and phase of the sinusoid. For example, the signal $v(t) = V_P\cos(\omega t + \theta)$ has amplitude V_P and the phase angle θ. This information can be represented in phasor form as:

$$\underline{V} = V_P e^{j\theta}$$

In which complex exponentials are used to represent the phase. Equivalently, the phase can be represented as an angle, and the phasor form of the signal can be written as:

$$\underline{V} = V_P\angle\theta$$

Note that the phasor does not provide the frequency of the signal, ω. To include frequency information, the signal is typically written in complex exponential form as:

$$v(t) = \underline{V}e^{j\omega t}$$

In section 10.3, we used phasor representations to determine the steady-state sinusoidal response of electrical circuits by representing the signals of interest as complex exponentials in phasor form. When signals in the governing differential equation are represented in this form, the differential equation becomes an algebraic equation, resulting in a significant mathematical simplification. In section 10.3, it was also noted that the mathematics could be simplified further by representing the circuit itself directly in the phasor domain. In this section, we present the phasor form of voltage-current relations for our basic circuit elements: resistors, inductors, and capacitors. The voltage-current relations for these elements are presented individually in the following sub-sections.

10.4.2 Resistors

The voltage-current relationship for resistors is provided by Ohm's Law:

$$v(t) = R \cdot i(t)$$

Eq. 10.59

If the voltage and current are represented in phasor form as:

$$v(t) = \underline{V}e^{j\omega t}$$

Eq. 10.60

And:

$$i(t) = \underline{I}e^{j\omega t}$$

Eq. 10.61

Equation (10.59) can be written:

$$\underline{V}e^{j\omega t} = R \cdot \underline{I}e^{j\omega t}$$

Eq. 10.62

Cancelling the $e^{j\omega t}$ term from both sides results in:

$$\underline{V} = R \cdot \underline{I}$$

Eq. 10.63

The voltage-current relationship for resistors (Ohm's Law) is thus identical in the time and frequency domains. Schematically, the time- and frequency-domain representations of a resistor are as shown in Fig. 10.10.

(a) Time domain   (b) Frequency domain

Figure 10.10. Voltage-current relations for a resistor.

Equation (10.63) shows that, in the frequency domain, the voltage and current in a resistor are related by a <u>purely real, constant</u> multiplicative factor. Thus, the sinusoidal voltage and current for a resistor are simply scaled versions of one another – there is no phase difference in the voltage and current for a resistor. This is shown graphically in Fig. 10.11.

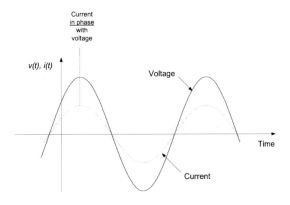

Figure 10.11. Voltage and current waveforms for a resistor.

A representative phasor diagram of the resistor's voltage and current will appear as shown in Fig. 10.12 – the phasors representing voltage and current will always be in the same direction, though their lengths will typically be different.

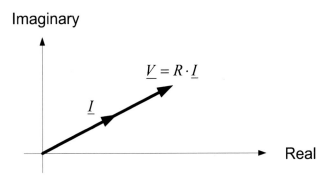

Figure 10.12. Voltage-current phasor diagram for resistor.

10.4.3 Inductors

The voltage-current relationship for inductors is:

$$v(t) = L \cdot \frac{di(t)}{dt}$$

Eq. 10.64

As with the resistive case presented above, we assume that the voltage and current are represented in phasor form as $v(t) = \underline{V}e^{j\omega t}$ and $i(t) = \underline{I}e^{j\omega t}$, respectively. Substituting these expressions into equation (10.64) results in:

$$\underline{V}e^{j\omega t} = L \cdot \frac{d}{dt}\left[\underline{I}e^{j\omega t}\right] = L(j\omega)\underline{I}e^{j\omega t}$$

Eq. 10.65

Dividing equation (10.65) by $e^{j\omega t}$ and re-arranging terms slightly results in the phasor domain or frequency domain representation of the inductor's voltage-current relationship:

$$\underline{V} = j\omega L \cdot \underline{I}$$

Eq. 10.66

In the frequency domain, therefore, the inductor's phasor voltage is proportional to its phasor current. The constant of proportionality is, unlike the case of the resistor, an <u>imaginary number</u> and is a <u>function of the frequency</u>, ω. It is important to note that the differential relationship of equation (10.64) has been replaced with an algebraic voltage-current relationship. Schematically, the time- and frequency-domain representations of an inductor are as shown in Fig. 10.13.

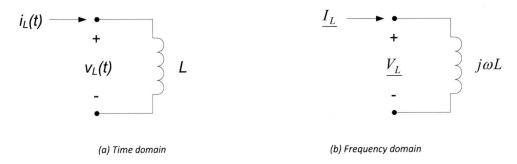

(a) Time domain   (b) Frequency domain

Figure 10.13. Inductor voltage-current relations.

The factor of j in the voltage-current relationship of equation (10.66) introduces a 90° phase shift between inductor voltage and current. Since $j = e^{j90°}$, the voltage across an inductor <u>leads</u> the current by 90° (or, equivalently, the current <u>lags</u> the voltage by 90°). The relative phase difference between inductor voltage and current are shown graphically in the time domain in Fig. 10.14. A representative phasor diagram of the inductor's voltage and current will appear as shown in Fig. 10.15 – the voltage phasor will always lead the current phasor by 90°, and the length of the voltage phasor will be a factor of ωL times the length of the current phasor.

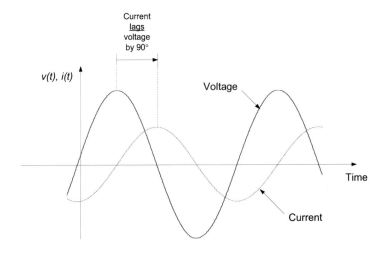

Figure 10.14. Voltage and current waveforms for an inductor.

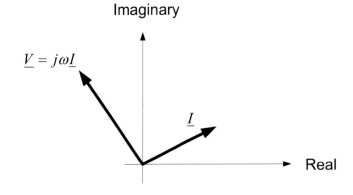

Figure 10.15. Voltage-current phasor diagram for inductor.

10.4.4 Capacitors

The voltage-current relationship for capacitors is:

$$i(t) = C \cdot \frac{dv(t)}{dt}$$

Eq. 10.67

As with the previous cases, we assume that the voltage and current are represented in phasor form as $v(t) = \underline{V}e^{j\omega t}$ and $i(t) = \underline{I}e^{j\omega t}$, respectively. Substituting these expressions into equation (10.67) results in:

$$\underline{I}e^{j\omega t} = C \cdot \frac{d}{dt}\left[\underline{V}e^{j\omega t}\right] = C(j\omega)\underline{V}e^{j\omega t}$$

Eq. 10.68

Dividing the above by $e^{j\omega t}$ results in the phasor domain or frequency domain representation of the capacitor's voltage-current relationship:

$$\underline{I} = j\omega C \cdot \underline{V}$$

Eq. 10.69

To be consistent with our voltage-current relationship for resistors and capacitors, we write the voltage in terms of the current. Thus,

$$\underline{V} = \frac{1}{j\omega C} \cdot \underline{I}$$

Eq. 10.70

In the frequency domain, therefore, the capacitor's phasor voltage is proportional to its phasor current. The constant of proportionality is an <u>imaginary number</u> and is a <u>function of the frequency</u>, ω. As with inductors, the differential voltage-current relationship has been replaced with an algebraic relationship. Schematically, the time- and frequency-domain representations of a capacitor are as shown in Fig. 10.16.

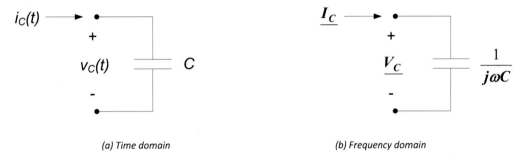

(a) Time domain   (b) Frequency domain

Figure 10.16. Capacitor voltage-current relations.

The factor of $\frac{1}{j}$ in the voltage-current relationship of equation (10.70) introduces a 90° phase shift between inductor voltage and current. Since $\frac{1}{j} = e^{-j90°} = 1\angle-90°$, the voltage across a capacitor <u>lags</u> the current by 90° (or, equivalently, the current <u>leads</u> the voltage by 90°). The relative phase difference between capacitor voltage and current are shown graphically in the time domain in Fig. 10.17. A representative phasor diagram of the capacitor's voltage and current will appear as shown in Fig. 10.18 – the voltage phasor will always lag the current phasor by 90°, and the length of the voltage phasor will be a factor of $\frac{1}{\omega C}$ times the length of the current phasor.

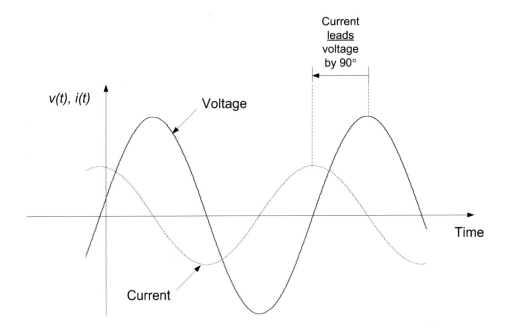

Figure 10.17. Voltage and current waveforms for a capacitor.

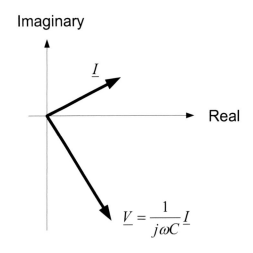

Figure 10.18. Voltage-current phasor diagram for capacitor.

10.4.5 Impedance and Admittance

The frequency domain voltage-current characteristics presented in the previous subsections indicate that the voltage difference across a circuit element can be written in terms of a multiplicative factor (which can be a complex number) times the current through the element. In order to generalize and formalize this concept, we define *impedance* as the ratio of phasor voltage to phasor current. Impedance is typically denoted as $\underline{Z}$ and is defined mathematically as:

$$\underline{Z} = \frac{\underline{V}}{\underline{I}}$$

Eq. 10.71

Therefore, if the phasor voltage and current for a circuit element are given by:

$$\underline{V} = V_P e^{j\theta}$$

And:

$$\underline{I} = I_P e^{j\phi}$$

Then the impedance is:

$$\underline{Z} = \frac{\underline{V}}{\underline{I}} = \frac{V_P}{I_P} e^{j(\theta_Z)} \qquad\qquad \text{Eq. 10.72}$$

Or alternatively,

$$\underline{Z} = \frac{V_P}{I_P} \angle \theta_Z \qquad\qquad \text{Eq. 10.73}$$

Where θ_Z is the angle of $\underline{Z}$. The magnitude of the impedance is the ratio of the magnitude of the voltage to the magnitude of the current:

$$|\underline{Z}| = \frac{V_P}{I_P} = \frac{|\underline{V}|}{|\underline{I}|} \qquad\qquad \text{Eq. 10.74}$$

And the angle of the impedance is the difference between the voltage phase angle and the current phase angle:

$$\theta_Z = \angle \underline{Z} = \angle \underline{V} - \angle \underline{I} = \theta - \phi \qquad\qquad \text{Eq. 10.75}$$

The impedance can also be represented in rectangular coordinates as:

$$\underline{Z} = R + jX \qquad\qquad \text{Eq. 10.76}$$

Where R is the real part of the impedance (called the *resistance* or the *resistive component* of the impedance) and X is the imaginary part of the impedance (called the *reactance* or the *reactive part* of the impedance). R and X are related to $|\underline{Z}|$ and $\angle\underline{Z}$ by the usual rules relating rectangular and polar coordinates, so that:

$$|\underline{Z}| = \sqrt{R^2 + X^2}$$
$$\angle \underline{Z} = \tan^{-1}\left(\frac{X}{R}\right)$$

And:

$$R = Re\{\underline{Z}\} = |\underline{Z}| \cos\theta_Z$$
$$X = Im\{\underline{Z}\} = |\underline{Z}| \sin\theta_Z$$

Impedance is an extremely useful concept, in that it can be used to represent the voltage-current relations for any two-terminal electrical circuit element in <u>the frequency domain</u>, as indicated in Fig. 10.19.

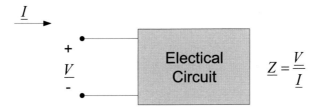

Figure 10.19. Impedance representation of two-terminal electric circuit.

The *admittance*, $\underline{Y}$, is defined as the reciprocal of impedance:

$$\underline{Y} = \frac{1}{\underline{Z}} \qquad\qquad \text{Eq. 10.77}$$

Admittance is also a complex number, and is written in rectangular coordinates as:

$$\underline{Y} = G + jB$$

Eq. 10.78

Where G is called the *conductance* and B is the *susceptance*.

Impedances and admittances for the three electrical circuit elements presented previously in this section are provided in Table 10.1 below. These results are readily obtained from the previously presented phasor domain voltage-current relationships and the definitions of impedance and admittance. The relations provided in Table 10.1 should be committed to memory.

Element	Impedance	Admittance
Resistor	R	$\dfrac{1}{R}$
Inductor	$j\omega L$	$\dfrac{1}{j\omega L}$
Capacitor	$\dfrac{1}{j\omega C}$	$j\omega C$

Table 10.1. Impedances and admittances for passive circuit elements.

Example 10.7: Provide the Phasor-domain Representation of the Circuit Below

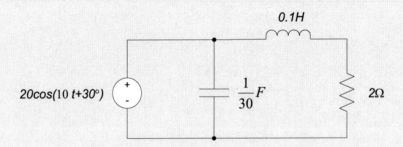

The input amplitude is 20 volts, and the input phase is 30°, so the phasor representation of the input voltage is 20∠30°.

The frequency of the input voltage is *ω=10rad/sec*. Thus, the impedances of the passive circuit elements are as follows:

- Resistor: $\underline{Z} = R = 2\Omega$
- Inductor: $\underline{Z} = j\omega L = j(10\,rad/sec)(0.1H) = j1\Omega$
- Capacitor: $\underline{Z} = \dfrac{1}{j\omega C} = \dfrac{1}{j(10rad/sec)(\frac{1}{30}F)} = \dfrac{3}{j}\Omega = -j3\Omega$

The phasor-domain circuit is shown below.

Chapter 10: Steady-State Sinusoidal Analysis

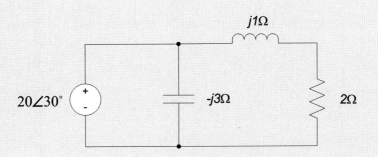

Section Summary

- Voltage-current relations for our passive circuit elements in the frequency domain are:
  - Resistor: $\underline{V} = R\underline{I}$
  - Inductor: $\underline{V} = j\omega L \cdot \underline{I}$
  - Capacitor: $\underline{V} = \frac{1}{j\omega C} \cdot \underline{I}$
- The impedance of a circuit element is the ratio of the phasor voltage to the phasor current in that element:
  - Resistor: $\underline{Z} = R$
  - Inductor: $\underline{Z} = j\omega L$
  - Capacitor: $\underline{Z} = \frac{1}{j\omega C}$
- Impedance is, in general, a complex number. Units of impedance are ohms (Ω). The real part of impedance is the *resistance*. The imaginary part of impedance is *reactance*. Impedance, for general circuit elements, plays the same role as resistance does for resistive circuit elements. In fact, for purely resistive circuit elements, impedance is simply the resistance of the element.
- Admittance is the inverse of impedance.
- Admittance is, in general, a complex number. The real part of admittance is *conductance*. The imaginary part of admittance is *susceptance*. For purely resistive circuits, admittance is the same as conductance.
- Impedance and admittance are, in general, functions of frequency.
- Impedance and admittance are not phasors. They are complex <u>numbers</u> – there is no sinusoidal time domain function corresponding to impedance or admittance. (Phasors, by definition, are a way to describe a time-domain sinusoidal function.)

10.4 Exercises

1. For the circuit shown below, u(t) is the input and y(t) is the output. Determine y(t), t→∞, if u(t) = 3cos(2t).

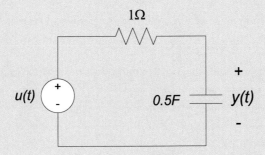

2. Sketch a diagram of the input and output phasors for exercise 1 above.
3. Determine the impedance of the circuit elements shown below if $V_{in}(t)$ = 2cos(4t).

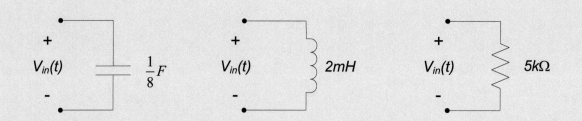

4. Determine the impedance of the circuit elements in exercise 3 if $V_{in}(t) = 3\cos(8t)$

Solutions can be found at digilent.com/real-analog.

10.5 Direct Frequency Domain Circuit Analysis

In section 10.3, we determined the steady-state response of electrical circuits to sinusoidal signals using phasor representations of the signals involved, and time-domain representations of the circuit element voltage-current relations. Applying KVL and KCL in this manner resulted in governing equations in which the time dependence had been removed, which converted the governing equations from differential equations to algebraic equations. Unknowns in the resulting algebraic equations were the phasor representations of the signals. These equations could then be solved to determine the desired signals in phasor form; these results could then be used to determine the time-domain representations of the signals.

In section 10.4, we replaced the time-domain voltage-current relations for passive electrical circuit elements with impedances, which provide voltage-current relations for the circuit elements directly in the frequency domain. At the end of section 10.4, we used these impedances to schematically represent a circuit directly in the frequency domain.

In this section, we will use this frequency-domain circuit representation to perform circuit analysis directly in the frequency domain using phasor representations of the signals and impedance representations of the circuit elements. This will allow us to write the algebraic equations governing the phasor representation of the circuit directly, without any reference to the time domain behavior of the circuit. As in section 10.3, these equations can be solved to determine the behavior of the circuit in terms of phasors, and the results transformed to the time domain.

Performing the circuit analysis directly in the frequency domain using impedances to represent the circuit elements can result in a significant simplification of the analysis. In addition, many circuit analysis techniques which were previously applied to resistive circuits (e.g. circuit reduction, nodal analysis, mesh analysis, superposition, Thevenin's and Norton's Theorems) are directly applicable in the frequency domain. Since these analysis techniques have been presented earlier for resistive circuits, in this section we will simply:

1. Provide examples of applying these analysis methods to frequency-domain circuits, and
2. Note any generalizations relative to using phasors in these analysis methods

Throughout this section, the reader should firmly keep in mind that we are dealing only with the steady-state responses of circuits to sinusoidal forcing functions. It is sometimes easy to lose track of this fact, since the sinusoidal nature of the signal is often not explicitly stated, but any time we deal with impedances and phasors, we are working with sinusoidal signals.

10.5.1 Kirchhoff's Voltage Law

Kirchhoff's Voltage Law states that the sum of the voltage differences around any closed loop is zero. Therefore, if $v_1(t), v_2(t), …, v_N(t)$ are the voltages around some closed loop, KVL provides:

$$\sum_{k=1}^{N} v_k(t) = 0 \qquad\qquad \text{Eq. 10.79}$$

Substituting the phasor representation of the voltages results in:

$$\sum_{k=1}^{N} \underline{V}_k e^{j\omega t} = 0 \qquad\qquad \text{Eq. 10.80}$$

Dividing equation (10.80) by $e^{j\omega t}$ results in:

$$\sum_{k=1}^{N} \underline{V}_k = 0 \qquad\qquad \text{Eq. 10.81}$$

So that KVL states that the sum of the phasor voltages around any closed loop is zero.

10.5.2 Kirchhoff's Current Law

Kirchhoff's Current Law states that the sum of the currents entering any node is zero. Therefore, if $i_1(t), i_2(t), \cdots, i_N(t)$ are the currents entering a node, KCL provides:

$$\sum_{k=1}^{N} i_k(t) = 0 \qquad\qquad \text{Eq. 10.82}$$

Substituting the phasor representation of the currents results in:

$$\sum_{k=1}^{N} \underline{I}_k e^{j\omega t} = 0 \qquad\qquad \text{Eq. 10.83}$$

Dividing equation (10.83) by $e^{j\omega t}$ results in:

$$\sum_{k=1}^{N} \underline{I}_k = 0 \qquad\qquad \text{Eq. 10.84}$$

So that KCL states that the sum of the phasor currents entering (or leaving) a node is zero.

Important Result: KVL and KCL apply directly in the frequency domain.

Example 10.8: RC Circuit Steady-state Sinusoidal Response

In this example, we will revisit example 10.3. In that example, we determined the capacitor voltage in the circuit to the left below, using phasor analysis techniques applied to the circuit's time-domain governing equation. In this example, we will represent the circuit itself directly in the frequency domain, using impedance representations of the circuit element. The frequency-domain representation of the circuit is shown to the right below.

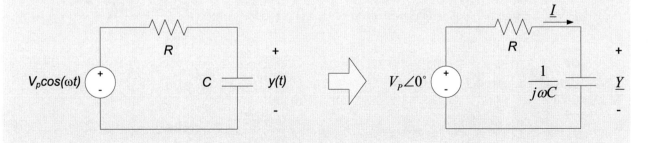

By the definition of impedance, we can determine the current through the capacitor to be:

$$\underline{I} = \frac{\underline{Y}}{\underline{Z}_C} = \frac{\underline{Y}}{\frac{1}{j\omega C}} = j\omega C \underline{Y}$$

The voltage across the resistor can now, by the definition of impedance, be written as $\underline{V_R} = R \cdot \underline{I} = R(j\omega C\underline{Y})$. We now apply KVL for phasors to the circuit to the right above, which leads to:

$$V_P \angle 0° = R(j\omega C\underline{Y}) + \underline{Y}$$

Solving for $\underline{Y}$ in this equation provides $\underline{Y} = \frac{V_P \angle 0°}{1 + j\omega RC}$

By the rules of complex arithmetic, we can determine the magnitude and phase angle of $\underline{Y}$ to be:

$$|\underline{Y}| = \frac{V_P}{\sqrt{1 + (\omega RC)^2}}$$
$$\angle \underline{Y} = -\tan^{-1}(\omega RC)$$

And the time-domain solution for y(t) is thus:

$$y(t) = \frac{V_P}{\sqrt{1 + (\omega RC)^2}} \cos[\omega t - \tan^{-1}(\omega RC)]$$

10.5.3 Parallel and Series Impedances & Circuit Reduction

Consider the case of N impedances connected in series, as shown in Fig. 10.20. Since the elements are in series, and since we have seen that KCL applies to phasors, the phasor current $\underline{I}$ flows through each of the impedances. Applying KVL for phasors around the single loop, and incorporating the definition of impedance, we obtain:

$$\underline{V} = \underline{I}(\underline{Z}_1 + \underline{Z}_2 + \cdots + \underline{Z}_N) = 0 \qquad \text{Eq. 10.85}$$

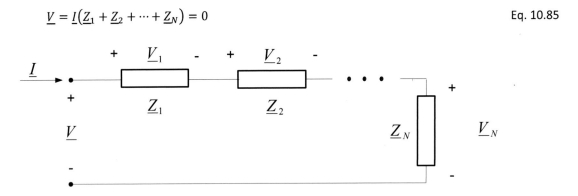

Figure 10.20. Series combination of impedances.

If we define $\underline{Z}_{eq}$ as the equivalent impedance of the series combination, we have $\underline{V} = \underline{I} \cdot \underline{Z}_{eq}$, where:

$$\underline{Z}_{eq} = \underline{Z}_1 + \underline{Z}_2 + \cdots + \underline{Z}_N \qquad \text{Eq. 10.86}$$

So that impedances in series sum directly. Thus, impedances in series can be combined in the same way as resistances in series.

By extension of the above result, we can develop a voltage divider formula for phasors. Without derivation, we state that the phasor voltage across the kth impedance in a series combination of N impedances as shown in Fig. 10.20 can be determined as:

$$\underline{V_k} = \underline{V}(\underline{Y}_1 + \underline{Y}_2 + \cdots + \underline{Y}_N) \qquad \text{Eq. 10.88}$$

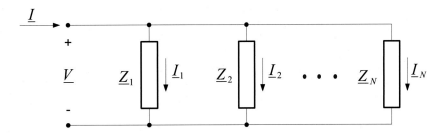

Figure 10.21. Parallel combination of impedances.

If we define $\underline{Y}_{eq}$ as the equivalent impedance of the series combination, we have:

$$\underline{I} = \underline{V} \cdot \underline{Y}_{eq}$$

Eq. 10.89

Where:

$$\underline{Y}_{eq} = \underline{Y}_1 + \underline{Y}_2 + \cdots + \underline{Y}_N$$

Eq. 10.90

So that <u>admittances in series sum directly</u>. Converting our admittances to impedances indicates that the equivalent impedance of a parallel combination of N impedances as shown in Fig. 10.21 is:

$$\underline{Z}_{eq} = \frac{1}{\frac{1}{\underline{Z}_1} + \frac{1}{\underline{Z}_2} + \cdots + \frac{1}{\underline{Z}_N}}$$

Eq. 10.91

Thus, impedances in parallel can be combined in the same way as resistances in parallel.

By extension of the above result, we can develop a current divider formula for phasors. Without derivation, we state that the phasor current through the kth impedance in a series combination of N impedances as shown in Fig. 10.21 can be determined as:

$$\underline{I}_k = \underline{I} \frac{\frac{1}{\underline{Z}_k}}{\frac{1}{\underline{Z}_1} + \frac{1}{\underline{Z}_2} + \cdots + \frac{1}{\underline{Z}_N}}$$

Eq. 10.92

So that our <u>current division relationships for resistors in parallel apply directly in the frequency domain for impedances in parallel</u>.

Important Result: All circuit reduction techniques for resistances apply directly to the frequency domain for impedances. Likewise, voltage and current divider relationships apply to phasor circuits in the frequency domain exactly as they apply to resistive circuits in the time domain.

Example 10.9

Use circuit reduction techniques to determine the current phasor $\underline{I}$ leaving the source in the circuit below. (Note: the circuit below is the frequency domain circuit we obtained in example 10.7.)

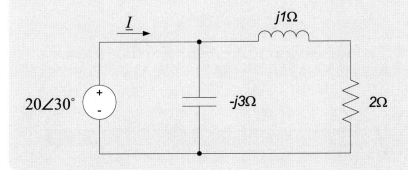

Since <u>impedances in series add directly</u>, the inductor and resistor can be combined into a single equivalent impedance of $(2 + j1)\Omega$, as shown in the figure to the left below. The capacitor is then in parallel with this equivalent impedance. Since impedances in parallel add in the same way as resistors in parallel, the equivalent impedance of this parallel combination can be calculated by dividing the product of the impedances by their sum, so $\underline{Z}_{eq} = \frac{(-j3)(2+j1)}{(-j3)+(2+j1)} \Omega = \frac{3-j6}{2-j2}\Omega$. Converting this impedance to polar form results in $\underline{Z}_{eq} = 2.37\angle -18°\Omega$; the final reduced circuit is shown in the figure to the right below.

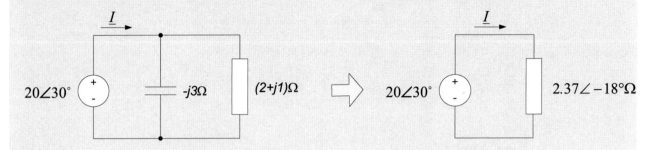

Using the reduced circuit to the right above and the definition of impedance, we can see that:

$$I = \frac{20\angle 30°}{2.37\angle -18°\Omega} = \frac{20}{2.37}\angle[30° - (-18°)]A$$

So that:

$$\underline{I} = 8.44\angle 48°A$$

Example 10.10

Use circuit reduction techniques to determine the current, *i(t)* through the inductor in the circuit below.

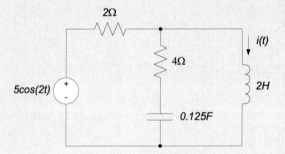

With *ω = 2 rad/sec*, the frequency domain representation of the circuit is as shown in the figure to the left below; in that figure, we have also defined the current phasor $\underline{I}_S$ leaving the source.

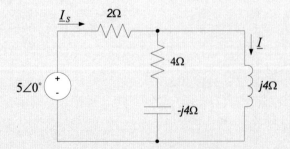

We now employ circuit reduction techniques to determine the phasor $\underline{I}$. To do this, we first determine the circuit impedance seen by the source; this impedance allows us to determine the source current $\underline{I}_S$. The current $\underline{I}$ can be determined from a current divider relation and $\underline{I}_S$.

The impedances of the series combination of the capacitor and the 4Ω resistor is readily obtained by adding their individual impedances, as shown in the figure to the left below. This equivalent impedance is then in parallel with the inductor's impedance; the equivalent impedance of this parallel combination is as shown in the circuit to the right below.

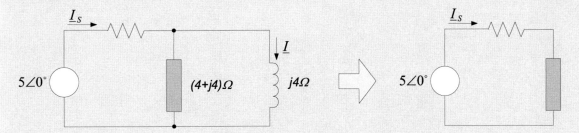

The source current is then, by the definition of impedance, $\underline{I_S} = \frac{5\angle 0°}{(4+j4)\Omega + 2\Omega} = 0.69\angle - 33.7°$.

The circuit to the left above, along with our voltage divider formula, provides:

$$\underline{I} = \frac{(4+j4)\Omega}{(4+j4)\Omega + j4\Omega} \cdot \underline{I_S} = \left(\frac{3}{5} - \frac{j1}{5}\right)\Omega \cdot 0.69\angle - 33.7° = 0.44\angle - 52.13°$$

And the current $i(t) = 0.44\cos(2t - 52.13°)$

10.5.4 Nodal and Mesh Analysis

Nodal analysis and mesh analysis techniques have been previously applied to resistive circuits in the time domain. In nodal analysis, we applied KCL at independent nodes and used Ohm's Law to write the resulting equations in terms of the node voltages. In mesh analysis, we applied KVL and used Ohm's Law to write the resulting equations in terms of the mesh currents.

In the frequency domain, as we have seen in previous sub-sections, KVL and KCL apply directly to the phasor representations of voltages and currents. Also, in the frequency domain, impedances can be used to represent voltage-current relations for circuit elements in the frequency domain in the same way that Ohm's Law applied to resistors in the time domain (the relation $\underline{V} = \underline{I} \cdot \underline{Z}$ in the frequency domain corresponds exactly to the relation $v(t) = R \cdot i(t)$ in the time domain). Thus, nodal analysis and mesh analysis apply to frequency domain circuits in exactly the same way as to time domain resistive circuits, with the following modifications:

- The circuit excitations and responses are represented by phasors
- Phasor representations of node voltages and mesh currents are used
- Impedances are used in the place of resistances

Application of nodal and mesh analysis to frequency-domain circuit analysis is illustrated in the following examples.

Example 10.11

Use nodal analysis to determine the current $i(t)$ in the circuit of example 10.10.

The desired frequency-domain circuit was previously determined in Example 10.10. Nodal analysis of the frequency-domain circuit proceeds exactly as was done in the case of resistive circuits. The reference voltage, $V_R = 0$, and our single node voltage, V_A, for this circuit are defined on the circuit below.

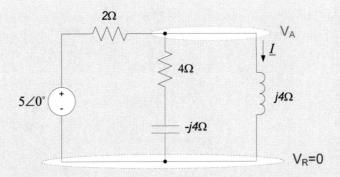

Applying KCL in phasor form at node A provides:

$$\frac{5\angle 0° - \underline{V}_A}{2\Omega} - \frac{\underline{V}_A}{(4 - j4)\Omega} - \frac{\underline{V}_A}{j4\Omega} = 0$$

Solving for $\underline{V}_A$ gives $\underline{V}_A = 3.92\angle 11.31°V$. By the definition of impedance, the desired current phasor $\underline{I} = \frac{\underline{V}_A}{j4\Omega} = \frac{3.92\angle 11.31°}{4\angle 90°} = 0.98\angle - 78.7°$ so that $i(t) = 0.98\cos(2t - 78.7°)$, which is consistent with our result obtained via circuit reduction in Example 3.

Example 10.12

Use mesh analysis to determine the current $i(t)$ in the circuit of examples 10.10 and 10.11.

The desired frequency-domain circuit was previously determined in Example 10.10. Mesh analysis of the frequency-domain circuit proceeds exactly as for resistive circuits. The figure below shows our choice of mesh loops; the series resistor-capacitor combination has been combined into a single equivalent resistance in the figure below, for clarity.

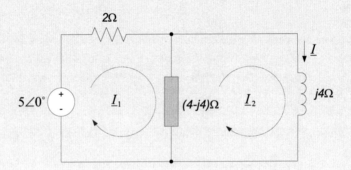

KVL around the mesh loop $\underline{I}_1$ provides:

$$5\angle 0° - 2 \cdot \underline{I}_1 - (4 - j4)(\underline{I}_1 - \underline{I}_2) = 0$$

KVL around the mesh loop $\underline{I}_2$ provides:

$$(4 - j4)(\underline{I}_2 - \underline{I}_1) + j4 \cdot \underline{I}_2 = 0$$

The second equation above can be simplified to provide: $\underline{I}_2 = (1 - j)\underline{I}_1$. Using this result to eliminate $\underline{I}_1$ in the mesh equation for loop $\underline{I}_1$ and simplifying provides:

$$5\angle 0° = \left[\frac{(6 - j4)}{1 - j} + (j4 - 4)\right]\underline{I}_2$$

So that $\underline{I_2} = 0.98\angle - 78.7°$. The mesh current $\underline{I_2}$ is simply the desired current $\underline{I}$, so in the time domain:

$$i(t) = 0.98\cos(2t - 78.7°)$$

Which is consistent without results from examples 10.10 and 10.11.

Important Result: Nodal and mesh analysis methods apply to phasor circuits exactly as they apply to resistive circuits in the time domain. Impedances simply replace resistances, and quantities of interest become complex valued.

10.5.5 Superposition

The extension of superposition to the frequency domain is an extremely important topic. Several common analysis techniques you will encounter later in this course and in future courses (frequency response, Fourier Series, and Fourier Transforms, for example) will depend heavily upon the superposition of sinusoidal signals. In this sub-section, we introduce the basic concepts involved.

In all of our steady-state sinusoidal analyses, we have required that the circuit is linear. (The statement that the steady state response to a sinusoidal input is a sinusoid at the same frequency requires the system to be linear. Nonlinear systems do not necessarily have this characteristic.) Thus, all phasor circuits are linear and superposition must apply. Thus, if a phasor circuit has multiple inputs, we can calculate the response of the circuit to each input individually and sum the results to obtain the overall response. It is important to realize, however, that the final step of summing the individual contributions to obtain the overall response can, in general, only be done in the time domain. Since the phasor representation of the circuit response implicitly assumes a particular frequency, the phasor representations cannot be summed directly. The time domain circuit response, however, explicitly provides frequency information, allowing those responses to be summed.

In fact, because the frequency-domain representation of the circuit depends upon the frequency of the input (in general, the impedances will be a function of frequency), the frequency domain representation of the circuit itself is, in general, different for different inputs. Thus, the only way in which circuits with multiple inputs at different frequencies can be analyzed in the frequency domain is with superposition.

In the special case in which all inputs share a common frequency, the circuit response can be determined by any of our previous analysis techniques (circuit reduction, nodal analysis, mesh analysis, superposition, etc.) In this case, if superposition is used, the circuit response to individual inputs can be summed directly in the frequency domain if desired.

Examples of the application of superposition to analysis of frequency-domain circuits are provided below.

Important Result: In the case of multiple frequencies existing in the circuit, superposition is the only valid frequency-domain analysis approach.

Superposition applies directly in the frequency domain, insofar as contributions from individual sources can be determined by killing all other sources and analyzing the resulting circuit. In general, however, superimposing (summing) the contributions from the individual sources must be done in the time domain.

Superposition of responses to individual sources can be summed directly in the frequency domain (e.g. addition of the phasors representing the individual responses) is only appropriate if all sources have the same frequency. In this case (all source having the same frequency) any of our other modeling approaches are also valid.

Example 10.13

Determine the voltage *v(t)* across the inductor in the circuit below.

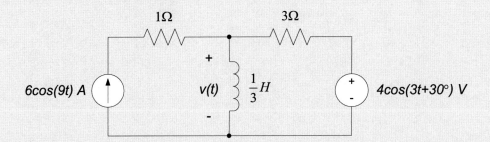

Since two different input frequencies are applied to the circuit, we <u>must</u> use superposition to determine the response. The circuit to the left below will provide the phasor response $\underline{V}_1$ to the <u>current source</u>; the frequency is $\omega = 9$ rad/sec and the voltage source is killed. The circuit to the right below will provide the phasor response $\underline{V}_2$ to the <u>voltage source</u>; the frequency is $\omega = 3$ rad/sec and the current source is killed.

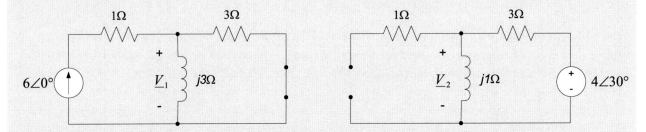

To determine the voltage phasor resulting from the current source ($\underline{V}$ in the circuit to the left above), we note that the inductor and the 3Ω resistor form a current divider. Thus, the current through the inductor resulting from the current source is $\underline{I}_1 = \frac{3\Omega}{(3+j3)\Omega} \cdot 6\angle 0° = \frac{3\angle 0° \cdot 6\angle 0°}{3\sqrt{2}\angle 45°} = \frac{6}{\sqrt{2}}\angle -45°$. The voltage phasor $\underline{V}$ can then be determined by multiplying this current times the inductor's impedance:

$$\underline{V}_1 = j3\Omega \cdot \frac{6}{\sqrt{2}}\angle -45° = 3\angle 90° \cdot \frac{6}{\sqrt{2}}\angle -45°V$$

And the time-domain voltage across the inductor due to the current source is:

$$v_1(t) = 9\sqrt{2}\cos(9t + 45°)V$$

To determine the voltage phasor resulting from the voltage source ($\underline{V}_2$ in the circuit to the right above), we note that the inductor and the 3Ω resistor now form a voltage divider. Thus, the voltage $\underline{V}_2$ can be readily determined by:

$$\underline{V}_2 = \frac{j1\Omega}{(3+j1)\Omega} \cdot 4\angle 30° = \frac{1\angle 90° \cdot 4\angle 30°}{\sqrt{10}\angle 18.4°} = \frac{4}{\sqrt{10}}\angle 101.6°$$

So that the time-domain voltage across the inductor due to the voltage source is:

$$v_2(t) = \frac{4}{\sqrt{10}}\cos(3t + 101.6°)V$$

The overall voltage is then the sum of the contributions from the two sources, in the time domain, so:

$$v(t) = v_1(t) + v_2(t)$$

And:

$$v(t) = 9\sqrt{2}\cos(9t + 45°) + \frac{4}{\sqrt{10}}\cos(3t + 101.6°)V$$

Example 10.14

Determine the voltage *v(t)* across the inductor in the circuit below.

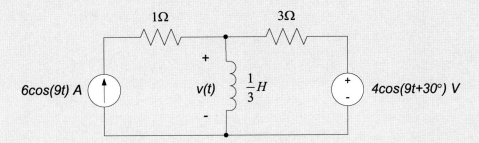

This circuit is essentially the same as the circuit of Example 10.13, with the important difference that the frequency of the <u>voltage</u> input has changed – the voltage source and current source both provide the same frequency input to the circuit, 9 rad/sec. We will first do this problem using superposition techniques. We will then use nodal analysis to solve the problem, to illustrate that multiple inputs at the same frequency do not require the use of superposition.

Individually killing each source in the circuit above results in the two circuits shown below. Note that the impedance of the inductor is now the same in both of these circuits.

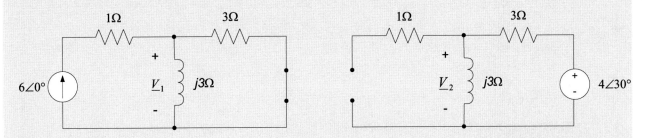

The two circuits shown above will now be analyzed to determine the individual contributions to the inductor voltage; these results will then be summed to determine the overall inductor voltage.

The circuit to the left above has been analyzed in Example 6. Therefore, the voltage phasor $\underline{V}_1$ is the same as determined in Example 10.13:

$$\underline{V}_1 = 9\sqrt{2}\angle 45°V$$

The voltage $\underline{V}_2$ in the circuit to the right above can be determined from application of the voltage divider formula for phasors:

$$\underline{V}_2 = \frac{j3\Omega}{(3 + j3)\Omega} \cdot 4\angle 30° = \frac{3\angle 90° \cdot 4\angle 30°}{3\sqrt{2}\angle 45°} = 2\sqrt{2}\angle 75°$$

Since both inputs have the same frequency, we can superimpose the phasor results directly (we could, of course, also determine the individual time domain responses and superimpose those responses if we chose):

$$\underline{V} = \underline{V}_1 + \underline{V}_2 = 9\sqrt{2}\angle 45° + 2\sqrt{2}\angle 75° = 15.24\angle 50.3°V$$

So that the time domain inductor voltage is $v(t) = 15.24\cos(9t + 50.3°)V$. Notice that the circuit response has only a single frequency component, since both inputs have the same frequency.

The superposition approach provided above is entirely valid. However, since both sources have the same input, we can choose any of our other analysis approaches to perform this problem. To emphasize this fact, we choose to do this problem using nodal analysis.

The frequency-domain circuit, with our definition of reference voltage and independent node, is shown in the figure below.

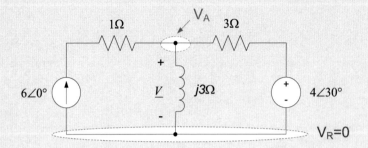

KCL at node A provides:

$$6\angle 0° = \frac{V_A - 0}{j3\Omega} + \frac{V_A - 4\angle 30°}{3\Omega}$$

Solving the above equation for $\underline{V_A}$ provides $\underline{V_A} = 15.24\angle 50.3V$ so that the inductor voltage as a function of time is:

$$v(t) = 15.24\cos(9t + 50.3°)V$$

Which is consistent with our result using superposition.

10.5.6 Thévenin's & Norton's Theorems, Source Transformations, and Maximum Power Transfer

Application of Thévenin's and Norton's Theorems to frequency domain circuits is identical to their application to time domain resistive circuits. The only differences are:

- The open circuit voltage (V_{OC}) and short circuit current (i_{SC}) determined for resistive circuits is replaced by their phasor representations, $\underline{V_{OC}}$ and $\underline{I_{SC}}$.
- The Thévenin resistance, R_{TH}, is replaced by a Thévenin impedance, $\underline{Z_{TH}}$.

Thus, the Thévenin and Norton equivalent circuits in the frequency domain are as shown in Fig. 10.22.

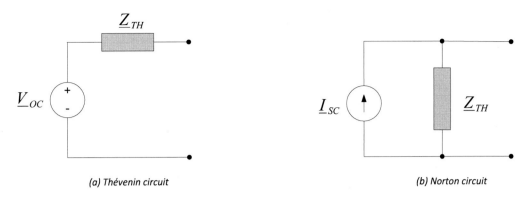

(a) Thévenin circuit   (b) Norton circuit

Figure 10.22. Thévenin and Norton equivalent circuits.

Since Thévenin's and Norton's Theorems both apply in the frequency domain, the approaches we used for source transformations in the time domain for resistive circuits translate directly to the frequency domain, with impedances substituted for resistances and phasors used for voltage and current terms.

In order to determine the load necessary to draw the maximum power from a Thévenin equivalent circuit, we must re-derive the maximum power result obtained previously for resistive circuits, substituting impedances for admittances and using phasors for source terms. We will not derive the governing relationship, but will simply state that, in order to transfer the maximum power to a load, the load impedance must be the complex conjugate of the Thévenin impedance of the circuit being loaded. Thus, if a Thévenin equivalent circuit has some impedance $\underline{Z}_{TH}$ with a resistance R_{TH} and a reactance X_{TH}, the load which will draw the maximum power from this circuit must have resistance R_{TH} and a reactance $-X_{TH}$. The appropriate loaded circuit is shown in Fig. 10.23 below.

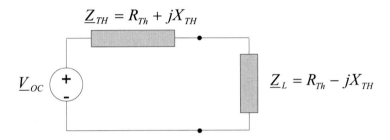

Figure 10.23. Load impedance to draw maximum power from a Thévenin circuit.

Example 10.15

Determine the Thévenin equivalent circuit seen by the load in the circuit below

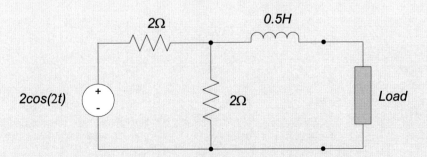

In the circuit below, we have used the input frequency, $\omega=2$ rad/sec, to convert the circuit to the frequency domain.

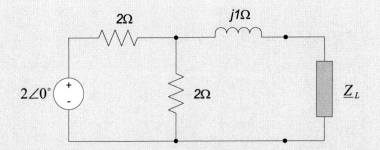

Removing the load and killing the source allows us to determine the Thévenin resistance of the circuit. The appropriate circuit is:

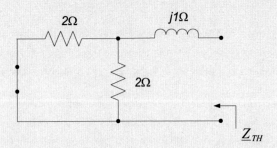

The parallel combination of two, 2Ω resistors have an equivalent resistance of 1Ω. This impedance, in series with the $j1\Omega$ impedance, results in a Thévenin impedance $\underline{Z}_{TH} = (1 + j1)\Omega$. Replacing the source, but leaving the load terminals open-circuited, as shown in the figure below, allows us to determine the open-circuit voltage $\underline{V}_{OC}$.

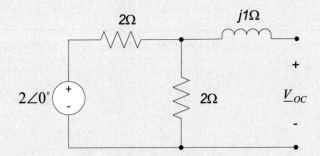

Since there is no current through the inductor, due to the open-circuit condition, $\underline{V}_{OC}$ is determined from a simple resistive voltage divider formed by the two, 2Ω resistors. Thus, the open-circuit voltage is:

$$\underline{V}_{OC} = \frac{2\Omega}{2\Omega + 2\Omega} \cdot 2\angle 0° = 1\angle 0°$$

The resulting Thévenin equivalent circuit is shown below:

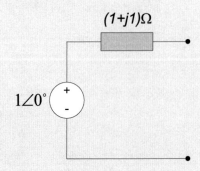

Example 10.16

Determine the Norton equivalent circuit of the circuit of example 10.15.

Since we determined the Thévenin equivalent circuit in Example 10.15, a source transformation can be used to determine the Norton equivalent circuit. Consistent with our previous source transformation rules, the short-circuit current, I_{SC}, is equal to the open-circuit voltage divided by the Thévenin impedance:

$$ I_{SC} = \frac{V_{OC}}{Z_{TH}} = \frac{1\angle 0°}{(1+j1)\Omega} = \frac{1\angle 0°}{\sqrt{2}\angle 45°} = \frac{1}{\sqrt{2}}\angle -45° $$

Since the impedance doesn't change during a source transformation, the Norton equivalent circuit is therefore as shown below:

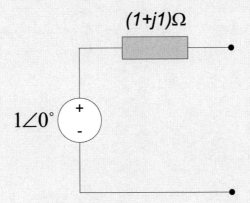

Example 10.17

Determine the load impedance for the circuit of Example 10.15 which will provide the maximum amount of power to be delivered to the load. Provide a physical realization (a circuit) which will provide this impedance.

The maximum power is delivered to the load when the load impedance is the complex conjugate of the Thévenin impedance. Thus, the load impedance for maximum power transfer is:

$$ Z_L = (1-j)\Omega $$

And the loaded Thévenin circuit is:

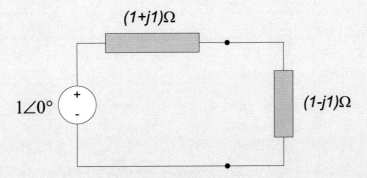

To implement this load, let us look at a parallel RC combination. With the frequency $\omega=2$ rad/sec, the frequency domain load looks like:

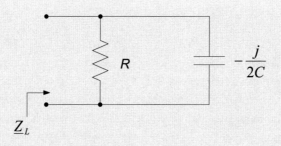

Combining parallel impedances results in:

$$\underline{Z}_L = \frac{-j\left(\frac{R}{2C}\right)}{R - \frac{j}{2C}}\,\Omega = \frac{\frac{R}{4C^2} - j\frac{R^2}{2C}}{R^2 + \frac{1}{4C^2}}\,\Omega$$

Setting $R = 2\Omega$ and $C = 0.25F$ makes $\underline{Z}_L = (1 - j)\Omega$, as desired, so the physical implementation of our load is as shown below:

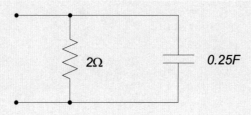

Section Summary

- The following analysis methods apply in the frequency domain exactly as they do in the time domain for purely resistive circuits
    - KVL and KCL
    - Voltage and current dividers
    - Circuit reduction techniques
    - Nodal and mesh analysis
    - Superposition, especially when multiple frequencies are present
    - Thévenin's and Norton's theorems

One simply uses phasor representations for the voltages and/or currents in the circuit and impedances to represent the circuit element voltage-current relationships. The analysis techniques presented in Chapters 1 through 4 are then applied exactly as they were for resistive circuits.

- One minor exception to the above statement is that, in order to draw maximum power from a circuit, the load impedance should be the complex conjugate of the impedance of the circuit's Thévenin equivalent.

10.5 Exercises:

1. Determine the impedance seen by the source for the circuit below if $u(t) = 4cos(t+30°)$.

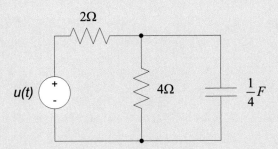

2. Determine the impedance seen by the source for the circuit below if $u(t) = 2cos(4000t)$.

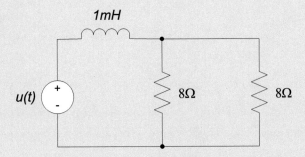

3. For the circuit of exercise 1, determine the current delivered by the source.
4. For the circuit of exercise 2, determine the voltage across the 8Ω resistors.

Solutions can be found at digilent.com/real-analog.

10.6 Frequency Domain System Characterization

In Chapters 7 and 8, we wrote the differential equation governing the relationship between a circuit's input and output (the input-output equation) and used this differential equation to determine the response of a circuit to some input. We also characterized the time-domain behavior of the system by examining the circuit's natural and step responses. We saw that the behavior of a first order circuit can be characterized by its time constant and DC gain, while the response of a second order circuit is characterized by its natural frequency, damping ratio and DC gain. It is important to recognize that these characterizations were independent of specific input parameters; they depended upon the type of response (e.g. a step function or a natural response), but were <u>independent of detailed information</u> such as the amplitude of the step input or the actual values of the initial conditions.

We will now use the steady state sinusoidal response to characterize a circuit's behavior. As in the case of our time-domain characterization, this characterization will allow the system's behavior to be defined in terms of its response to sinusoidal inputs, but the characterization will be independent of details such as the input sinusoid's amplitude or phase angle. (The input sinusoid's frequency will, however, still be of prime importance.)

When a sinusoidal input is applied to a linear system, the system's <u>forced</u> response consists of a sinusoid with the same frequency as the input sinusoid, but in general having a different amplitude and phase from the input sinusoid. Figure 10.24 shows the general behavior, in block diagram form. Changes in the amplitude and phase angle between the input and output signals are often used to characterize the circuit's input-output relationship at the input frequency, ω. In this chapter, we will demonstrate how this characterization is performed for inputs with discrete frequencies (as in the case of circuits with one or several inputs, each with a single frequency component). Later chapters will extend these concepts to the case in which frequency is considered to be a <u>continuous</u> variable.

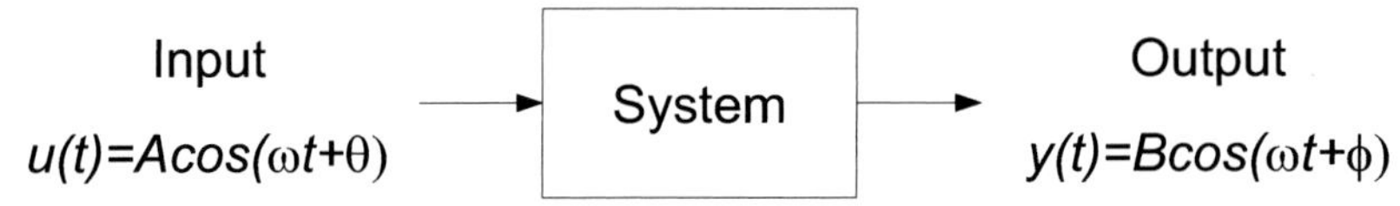

$$u(t)=A\cos(\omega t+\theta) \quad \rightarrow \quad \boxed{\text{System}} \quad \rightarrow \quad y(t)=B\cos(\omega t+\phi)$$

Input → System → Output

Figure 10.24. Sinusoidal steady-state input-output relation for a linear time invariant system.

Previously in this chapter, we have (bit-by-bit) simplified the analysis of a system's steady state sinusoidal response significantly. We first represented the sinusoidal signals as complex exponentials in order to facilitate our analysis. We subsequently used phasors to represent our complex exponential signals, as shown in Fig. 10.25; this allowed us to represent and analyze the circuit's steady state sinusoidal response directly in the frequency domain.

$$\underline{U} = A\angle\theta \quad \rightarrow \quad \boxed{\text{System}} \quad \rightarrow \quad \underline{Y} = B\angle\phi$$

Input → System → Output

Figure 10.25. Phasor representation of sinusoidal inputs and outputs.

In the frequency domain analyses performed to date, we have generally determined the system's response to a <u>specific</u> input signal with a given frequency, amplitude, and phase angle. We now wish to characterize the system response to an input signal with a given frequency, but an arbitrary amplitude and phase angle. As indicated previously in section 10.1, we will see that the input-output relationship governing the system reduces to a relationship between the output and input signal <u>amplitudes</u> and the output and input signal <u>phases</u>. The circuit can thus be represented in phasor form as shown in Fig. 10.26. The system's effect on a sinusoidal input consists of an <u>amplitude gain</u> between the output and input signals ($\frac{B}{A}$ in Fig. 10.26) and a <u>phase difference</u> between the output and input signals ($\phi - \theta$ in Fig. 10.26).

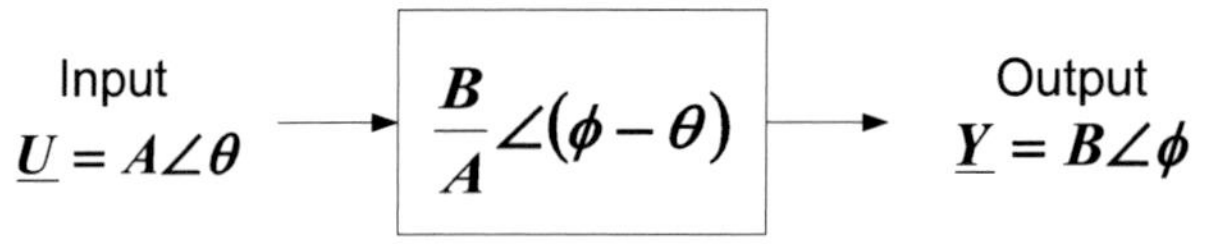

$$\underline{U} = A\angle\theta \quad \rightarrow \quad \boxed{\frac{B}{A}\angle(\phi - \theta)} \quad \rightarrow \quad \underline{Y} = B\angle\phi$$

Input → Output

Figure 10.26. Frequency domain representation of circuit input-output relationship.

Rather than perform a rigorous demonstration of this property at this time, we will simply provide some simple examples to illustrate the basic concept.

Example 10.18

A sinusoidal voltage, $v_{in}(t)$, is applied to the circuit to the left below. Determine the frequency-domain relationship between the phasor representing $v_{in}(t)$ and the phasor representing the output voltage $v_{out}(t)$.

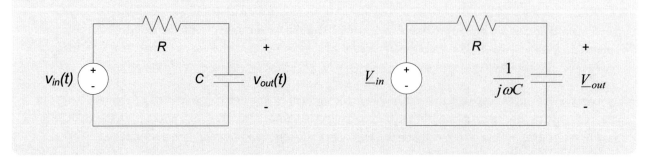

Since the frequency is unspecified, we leave frequency as an independent variable, ω, in our analysis. In the frequency domain, therefore, the circuit can be represented as shown to the right above. The frequency domain circuit is a simple voltage divider, so the relation between input and output is:

$$\underline{V}_{out} = \frac{\frac{1}{j\omega C}}{R + \frac{1}{j\omega C}} \cdot \underline{V}_{in} = \frac{1}{1 + j\omega RC} \cdot \underline{V}_{in}$$

The factor $\frac{1}{1+j\omega RC}$ is a complex number, for given values of ω, R, and C. It constitutes a multiplicative factor which, when applied to the input, results in the output. This multiplicative factor is often used to <u>characterize</u> the system's response at some frequency, ω. We will call this multiplicative factor the frequency response function, and denote it as $H(j\omega)$. For a particular frequency, $H(j\omega)$ is a complex number, with some amplitude, $|H(j\omega)|$, and phase angle, $\angle H(j\omega)$. For our example, the magnitude and phase of our frequency response function are:

$$|H(j\omega)| = \frac{1}{\sqrt{1 + (\omega RC)^2}}$$

$$\angle H(j\omega) = -\tan^{-1}(\omega RC)$$

According to the rules of multiplication of complex numbers, when two complex numbers are multiplied, the magnitude of the result is the product of the magnitudes of the individual numbers, and the phase angle of the result is the sum of the individual phase angles. Thus, if the input voltage is represented in phasor form as $\underline{V}_{in} = |V_{in}| \angle\theta$ and the output voltage is $\underline{V}_{out} = |V_{out}|\angle\phi$, it is easy to obtain the output voltage from the input voltage and the frequency response function:

$$|V_{out}| = |V_{in}| \cdot |H(j\omega)|$$

$$\angle V_{out} = \angle V_{in} + \angle H(j\omega)$$

Example 10.19

Use the frequency response function determined in Example 10.18 above to determine the response $v_{out}(t)$ of the circuit shown below to the following input voltages:

- $v_{in}(t) = 3\cos(2t + 20°)$
- $v_{in}(t) = 7\cos(4t - 60°)$

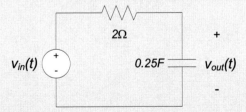

When $v_{in}(t) = 3\cos(2t + 20°)$, $\omega = 2$ rad/sec, $|V_{in}| = 3$ and $\angle V_{in} = 20°$. For this value of ω, and the given values of R and C, the magnitude and phase of the frequency response function are:

$$|H(j2)| = \frac{1}{\sqrt{1 + (\omega RC)^2}} = \frac{1}{\sqrt{1 + (2 \cdot 2\Omega \cdot 0.25F)^2}} = \frac{1}{\sqrt{1 + 1^2}} = \frac{1}{\sqrt{2}}$$

$$\angle H(j2) = -\tan^{-1}(\omega RC) = -\tan^{-1}(2 \cdot 2\Omega \cdot 0.25F) = -\tan^{-1}(1) = -45°$$

The output amplitude is then the product of $|V_{in}|$ and $|H(j2)|$ and the output phase in the sum of $\angle V_{in}$ and $\angle H(j2)$, so that:

$$|V_{out}| = |V_{in}| \cdot |H(j2)| = 3 \cdot \frac{1}{\sqrt{2}} = \frac{3}{\sqrt{2}}$$

$$\angle V_{out} = \angle V_{in} + \angle H(j2) = 20° + (-45°) = -25°$$

And the time-domain output voltage is:

$$v_{out}(t) = \frac{3}{\sqrt{3}} \cos(2t - 25°)$$

When $v_{in} = 7\cos(4t - 60°)$, $\omega = 4\,rad/sec$, $|V_{in}| = 7$ and $\angle V_{in} = -60°$. For this value of ω, and the given values of R and C, the magnitude and phase of the frequency response function are:

$$|H(j4)| = \frac{1}{\sqrt{1 + (\omega RC)^2}} = \frac{1}{\sqrt{5}}$$

And:

$$\angle H(j4) = -\tan^{-1}(\omega RC) = -63.4°$$

The output amplitude is then the product of $|V_{in}|$ and $|H(j4)|$ and the output phase is the sum of $\angle V_{in}$ and $\angle H(j4)$ so that the time-domain output voltage in this case is:

$$V_{out}(t) = \frac{7}{\sqrt{5}} \cos(4t - 123.4°)$$

From the above examples we can see that, once the frequency response function is calculated for a circuit <u>as a function of frequency</u>, we can determine the circuit's steady-state response to <u>any</u> input sinusoid directly from the frequency response function, <u>without re-analyzing the circuit itself</u>.

We conclude this section with one additional example, to illustrate the use of the frequency response function and superposition to determine a circuit's response to multiple inputs of different frequencies.

Example 10.20

Use the results of examples 10.18 and 10.19 above to determine the response $v_{out}(t)$ of the circuit shown below if the input voltage is $v_{in}(t) = 3\cos(2t+20°) + 7\cos(4t-60°)$. Plot the input and output waveforms.

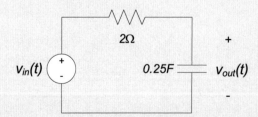

Recall, from section 10.5, that superposition is the <u>only</u> valid approach for performing frequency domain analysis of circuits with inputs at multiple frequencies. Also recall that each frequency can be analyzed separately in the frequency domain, but that the superposition process (the summation of the individual contributions) must be done in the time domain. For this problem, we have contributions at two different frequencies: 2 rad/sec and 4 rad/sec. Luckily, we have determined the individual responses of the circuit to these two inputs in Example 10.19. Therefore, in the time domain, the two contributions to our output will be:

$$v_1(t) = \frac{3}{\sqrt{2}}\cos(2t - 25°)$$

And:

$$v_2(t) = \frac{7}{\sqrt{5}}\cos(4t - 123.4°)$$

The overall response is then:

$$v_{out}(t) = v_1(t) + v_2(t) = \frac{3}{\sqrt{2}}\cos(2t - 25°) + \frac{7}{\sqrt{5}}\cos(4t - 123.4°)$$

A plot of the input and output waveforms is shown below:

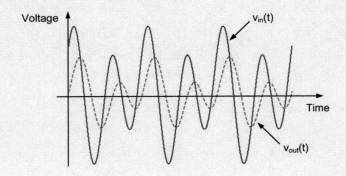

Section Summary

- The frequency response function or *frequency response* describes a circuit's input-output relationship directly in the frequency domain, <u>as a function of frequency</u>.
- The frequency response is a complex function of frequency *H(jω)* (that is, it is a complex number which depends upon the frequency). This complex function is generally expressed as a magnitude and phase, $|H(j\omega)|$ and $\angle H(j\omega)$, respectively. $|H(j\omega)|$ is called the *magnitude response* of the circuit, and $\angle H(j\omega)$ is called the *phase response* of the circuit. The overall idea is illustrated in the block diagram below:

Input $\boxed{H(j\omega) = |H(j\omega)|\angle H(j\omega)}$ Output

$\underline{U} = A\angle\theta$ $\underline{Y} = B\angle\phi$

- The magnitude response of the circuit is the ratio of the output amplitude to the input amplitude. This is also called the gain of the system. Thus, in the figure above, the output amplitude $B = |H(j\omega)| \cdot A$. Note that the magnitude response or gain of the system is a function of frequency, so that inputs of different frequencies will have different gains.
- The phase response of the circuit is the difference between the output phase angle and the input phase angle. Thus, in the figure above, the output phase $\phi = \angle H(j\omega) + \theta$. Like the gain, the phase response is a function of frequency – inputs at different frequencies will, in general, have different phase shifts.
- Use of the frequency response to perform circuit analyses can be particularly helpful when the input signal contains a number of sinusoidal components at different frequencies. In this case, the response of the circuit to each individual component can be determined in the frequency domain using the frequency response and the resulting contributions summed in the time domain to obtain the overall response.

10.6 Exercises

1. Determine the voltage across the capacitor in the circuit below if $u(t) = 4cos(t+30°) + 2cos(2t-45°)$. (Hint: this may be easier if you find the response to the input as a function of frequency, evaluate the response for each of the above frequency components, and superimpose the results.)

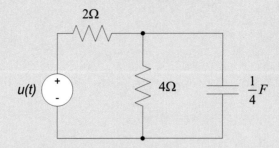

2. Determine the voltage across the resistors in the circuit below if $u_1(t) = 4cos(2t)$ and if $u_2(t) = cos(4t)$. (Hint: this may be easier if you find the response to the input as a function of frequency, evaluate the response for each of the above frequency components, and superimpose the results.)

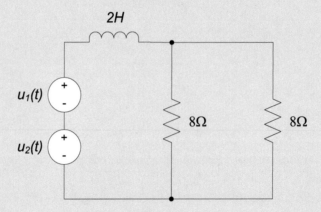

Solutions can be found at digilent.com/real-analog.

Chapter 11:
Frequency Response and Filtering

In section 10.6, we saw that a system's frequency response provided a steady-state input-output relationship for a system, as a function of frequency. We could apply this frequency response to the phasor representation of the input signal in order to determine the system's steady-state sinusoidal response – we simply evaluated the frequency response at the appropriate frequencies to determine the effect of the system on the input sinusoids. This approach had the potential for simplifying our analysis considerably, particularly for the case in which the input signal contained multiple sinusoids with different frequencies.

In Chapter 10, the signals we considered consisted only of individual sinusoids. It is more useful, however, in some ways to think in terms of the inputs and outputs of the system as functions of frequency, in the same way in which we considered the frequency response of the system to be a function of frequency in section 10.6. We can then perform our analysis of the system entirely in terms of the frequencies involved. This leads to the use of the system's frequency response directly as a design and analysis tool. In many cases, this means that the actual time-domain behavior of the system or signal is of limited interest (or in some cases, not considered at all). Some examples of frequency domain analyses are:

1. *Determining dominant sinusoidal frequency components in a measured signal*. Complex signals can often be represented as a superposition of several sinusoidal components with different frequencies. Identifying sinusoidal components with large amplitudes (the so-called dominant frequencies) can help with many design problems. One application of this is in the area of combustion instability – combustion processes in rocket engines can become unstable due to a variety of reasons, any of which can result in catastrophic failure of the engine. The type of instability which occurs is generally linked to a particular frequency; identification of the frequency of the pressure oscillations associated with the combustion instability is generally the first step in determining the cause of the instability.

2. *Designing systems to provide a desired frequency response*. Audio components in stereo systems are generally designed to produce a desired frequency response. A graphic equalizer, for example, can be used to boost (or amplify) some frequency ranges and attenuate other frequency ranges. When adjusting

the settings on an equalizer, you are essentially directly adjusting the system's frequency response to provide a desired system response.

This chapter begins in section 11.1 with a brief review of frequency responses and an overview of the use of the frequency response in system analysis and design. In section 11.2, we discuss representation of signals in terms of their frequency content. At this time, we will also represent the frequency content of the input and output signals and the frequency response of the system in graphical format – this helps us visualize the frequency content of the signals and system. This leads us to think in terms of using a system to create a signal with a desired frequency content – this process is called filtering and is discussed in section 11.3. Using logarithmic scales to represent the signal and system frequency responses can – in many cases – simplify the analysis or design process; this format of presentation is called a Bode plot, and they are very briefly introduced in section 11.4. We will discuss Bode plots in more depth in later chapters.

It is important to keep in mind that, when we are performing frequency domain analyses, we are restricting our attention to the <u>steady-state sinusoidal response</u> of the system. Frequency domain design and analysis methods are so pervasive that they are often used to <u>infer</u> the system's transient response and/or its response to non-sinusoidal signals, so it is sometimes possible to forget the origins and limitations of the original concepts!

After completing this chapter, you should be able to:

- Use the frequency response of a system to determine the frequency domain response of a system to a given input
- State from memory the definition of *signal spectrum*
- Create plots of given signal spectra
- Plot a circuit's magnitude and phase responses
- Check a circuit's amplitude response at low and high frequencies against the expected physical behavior of the circuit
- Graphically represent a system's frequency domain response from provided signal spectra plots and plots of the system's frequency response
- Identify low pass and high pass filters
- Calculate a system's cutoff frequency
- Determine the DC gain of an electrical circuit
- Write, from memory, the equation used to convert gains to decibel form
- Sketch straight-line amplitude approximations to Bode plots
- Sketch straight-line phase approximations to Bode plots

11.1 Introduction to Steady-state Sinusoidal Analysis

In section 10.6, we defined the frequency response $H(j\omega)$ of a system as a <u>complex function of frequency</u> which describes the relationship between the steady state sinusoidal response of a system and the corresponding sinusoidal input. Thus, if a sinusoidal input with some frequency ω_0 is applied to a system with frequency response $H(j\omega)$, the amplitude of the output sinusoid is the input sinusoid's amplitude multiplied by the magnitude response of the system, evaluated at the frequency ω_0. The phase angle of the output sinusoid is the sum of the input sinusoid's phase and the phase response of the system, evaluated at the frequency ω_0. The overall idea is presented in block diagram form in Fig. 11.1 below.

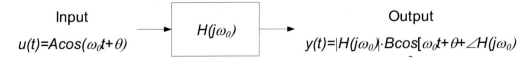

Figure 11.1. *Frequency response used to determine steady state sinusoidal system response.*

The true power of the frequency response is, however, if we consider both the system's input and output phasors to be <u>complex functions of frequency</u>, in the same way that the frequency response is a complex function of frequency. In this case, the block diagram of Fig. 11.1 can be represented as shown in Fig. 11.2.

Input $\quad$ Output

$\underline{U}(j\omega)$ $\qquad$ $H(j\omega)$ $\qquad$ $\underline{Y}(j\omega) = \underline{U}(j\omega) \cdot H(j\omega)$

Figure 11.2. Frequency response used to determine system response as a function of frequency.

In Fig. 11.2, the output is determined by multiplying the phasor representation of the input by the system's frequency response. It is important to keep in mind that the arguments of this multiplication are complex functions of frequency – both the input and the frequency response at any frequency are complex numbers, so the output at any frequency is also a complex number. We typically use polar form to represent these complex numbers, so the <u>amplitude of the output signal is the product of the amplitude of the input signal and the magnitude response of the system</u> and the <u>phase of the output signal is the sum of the phase of the input and the phase response of the system</u>. Mathematically, these are expressed as:

$$|\underline{Y}(j\omega)| = |\underline{U}(j\omega)| \cdot |H(j\omega)|$$

Eq. 11.1

And:

$$\angle\underline{Y}(j\omega) = \angle\underline{U}(j\omega) + \angle H(j\omega)$$

Eq. 11.2

We now present two examples of the process defined by equations (11.1) and (11.2) above.

Example 11.1

Determine the phasor representation for $v_{out}(t)$ in the circuit shown below as a function of frequency, if the input voltage is $v_{in}(t) = 3\cos(2t+20°) + 7\cos(4t-60°)$. (Note: this problem is the same as that of Example 10.19 of chapter 10.6; the difference is primarily philosophical.)

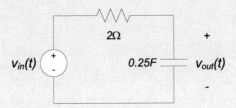

The frequency response of this circuit, for arbitrary resistance and capacitance values, was determined in example 10.18 of chapter 10.6. For our specific resistor and capacitor values, this becomes:

$$H(j\omega) = \frac{1}{1+j\omega RC} = \frac{1}{1+j\omega(2\Omega)(0.25F)} = \frac{1}{1+j\omega(0.5)} = \frac{2}{2+j\omega}$$

We can represent the input as a piecewise function of frequency:

$$\underline{V}_{in} = \begin{cases} 3\angle 20°, & \omega = 2rad/sec \\ 7\angle -60°, & \omega = 4rad/sec \\ 0, & otherwise \end{cases}$$

The input phasor is now considered to be a function of frequency, whose only nonzero components are at frequencies of 2 rad/sec and 4 rad/sec.

The phasor output is simply the product of the input phasor as a function of frequency and the frequency response. For frequencies, other than 2 rad/sec and 4 rad/sec, the input is zero and the frequency response is finite, so the output is zero. We determined the output phasor at frequencies of 2 and 4 rad/sec in example 10.19 in section 10.6; using those results allows us to write the output phasor directly as:

$$\underline{V}_{out} = \begin{cases} \dfrac{3}{\sqrt{2}} \angle -25°, & \omega = 2\,rad/sec \\ \dfrac{7}{\sqrt{5}} \angle -123.4°, & \omega = 4\,rad/sec \\ 0, & otherwise \end{cases}$$

Example 11.2

The frequency response of a system, H(jω), and the frequency domain input to the system, $\underline{U}(j\omega)$, are given below. The frequency response is dimensionless, the input has units of volts, and the units of frequency are rad/sec. Determine the system output $\underline{Y}(j\omega)$.

$$\underline{U}_{j\omega} = \begin{cases} j\omega, & 0 < \omega \leq 1 \\ j(2 - \omega), & 1 < \omega < 2 \\ 0, & otherwise \end{cases}$$

$$\underline{U}_{j\omega} = \begin{cases} 0, & 0 < \omega \leq 5 \\ 1, & 0.5 < \omega \leq 1.5 \\ 0, & otherwise \end{cases}$$

The system output is determined from a point-by-point multiplication of the input and the frequency response. In this case, both the input to the system and the system frequency response are defined as piecewise functions of frequency, so we must perform a piecewise multiplication to obtain the output. The output, for various ranges of frequency, is obtained below:

$0 < \omega \leq 0.5$:

- In this range, $H(j\omega) = 0$ and the input is finite, so $\underline{Y}(j\omega) = 0$.

$0.5 < \omega \leq 1$:

- In this range, $H(j\omega) = 1$ and $\underline{U}(j\omega) = j\omega$, so the output is: $\underline{Y} = (1)(j\omega) = j\omega$.

$1 < \omega \leq 1.5$:

- In this range, $H(j\omega) = 0$ and the input is finite, so $\underline{Y}(j\omega) = 0$.

For any other value of frequency, the frequency response is zero, so the output is obviously zero.

The above results allow us to define the system output in a piecewise fashion as:

$$\underline{Y}_{j\omega} = \begin{cases} j\omega, & 0.5 < \omega \leq 1 \\ j(2 - \omega), & 1 < \omega \leq 1.5 \\ 0, & otherwise \end{cases}$$

Example 11.3

For the signals of example 11.2, plot: the magnitude and phase responses of the system and the magnitude and phase of both the input and output signals. The magnitude and phase response of the system are shown to the left and right below. The phase of the input is indicated as zero for all frequencies, since the input is real-valued for all frequencies. Strictly speaking, however, the phase is not well defined when the magnitude response is zero. (The phase angle provides the direction of a number from the origin of the complex plane, it is difficult to tell what direction "zero" is from itself!)

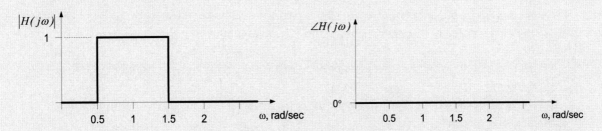

The magnitude and phase of the frequency domain input are shown below. The 90° phase shift over the range of 0 to 2 rad/sec is due to the factor of "j" in the frequency response. The phase is not indicated where the input amplitude is zero; this is again because the phase angle of "zero" is not well defined.

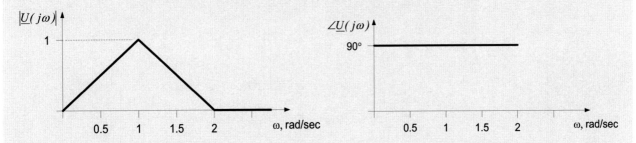

The magnitude and phase of the output are shown below. It is easy to see from the above figures that the magnitude of the output is the product of the input magnitude and the magnitude response and the phase of the output is the sum of the input phase and the phase response.

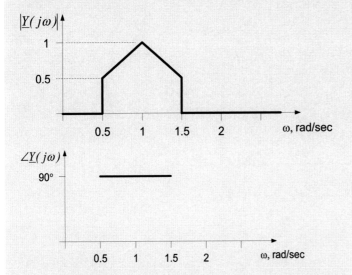

The above system is performing a potentially useful operation. Any sinusoidal signals with frequencies between

0.5 and 1.5 rad/sec are passed through the system (they appear at the output, unchanged). Sinusoids with frequencies outside this range are eliminated by the system – they are not present in the system's output. This system is performing what is called a *band-pass operation*; frequencies within a certain frequency band are passed through the system, while all other frequencies are stopped. This type of operation can be useful, for example, in communication systems – signals from different radio stations should not overlap or they will interfere with one another.

Section Summary

Design techniques and a very powerful analysis for linear systems consists of considering the input and output signals to be phasors which are functions of frequency, so that the amplitude and phase of the input and output signals are both defined at each value of frequency. If this viewpoint is taken,

- The amplitude of the output signal is the frequency-by-frequency product of the amplitude of the input signal and the magnitude response of the system, and
- The phase of the output signal is the frequency-by-frequency sum of the phase of the input and the phase response of the system.
- Calculate the frequency response for the circuit below, if $u(t)$ is the input and $y(t)$ is the output.

11.1 Exercises

1. Calculate the frequency response for the circuit below, if $u(t)$ is the input and $y(t)$ is the output.

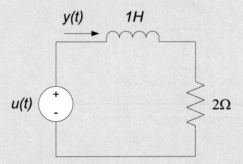

2. The input to a system is $u(t) = 3cos(2t\text{-}60°) + 4cos(4t+30°) + 7cos(6t+45°)$. The system frequency response is given by the piecewise function:

$$H(j\omega) = \begin{cases} 0, 0 < \omega < 3 \\ 1, 3 \le \omega \le 5 \\ 0, \omega > 5 \end{cases}$$

What is the system output, $y(t)$?

Solutions can be found at digilent.com/real-analog.

11.2 Signal Spectra and Frequency Response Plots

In previous sections, we used the frequency response of a system to determine the system output, when the input to the system consists of signals comprised of one or more sinusoidal components. This analysis approach is extremely powerful, since it turns out that nearly any signal can be represented as a superposition of sinusoids[1]. We will ultimately, therefore, use our frequency domain analysis approaches on a very broad range of input signals, many of which may have very little resemblance to sinusoidal signals.

Often, a graphical representation of the system's frequency response and the frequency content of the signals of interest can facilitate analysis and provide insight into the overall system behavior. We have seen an example of this in example 10.3. In this chapter, we introduce the concept of a signal's *spectrum* – the frequency content of a signal – and we will look more closely at the representation of frequency responses in graphical form. We will conclude this section with an example of the use of signal spectra and frequency response plots to obtain a qualitative representation of a system's frequency domain response to some input.

11.2.1 Signal Spectra

The signals currently of interest to us are sinusoidal. Any sinusoidal signal can be written in the form:

$$f(t) = A cos(\omega_0 t + \theta)$$

Eq. 11.3

The signal is completely defined by its amplitude, A, its frequency, ω_0, and its phase angle, θ. Our primary interest in these signals is as inputs and outputs to systems. As indicated in section 10.1, we can characterize systems by their magnitude and phase responses as functions of frequency. To be consistent with this frame of mind, we will consider sinusoidal <u>signals</u> of the type shown in equation (11.3) to be functions of frequency as well. We will thus begin to consider the frequency, ω, to be an independent variable, much in the same way that time was treated as an independent variable when we determined time domain responses of first and second order systems.

With frequency treated as an independent variable, the sinusoidal signal of equation (11.3) can be re-written in terms of ω:

$$F(j\omega) = \begin{cases} A\angle\theta, \omega = \omega_0 \\ 0, otherwise \end{cases}$$

Eq. 11.4

The frequency domain representation of a sinusoidal signal has two dependent variables: the amplitude and the phase. Our immediate goal is to represent the frequency content of signals graphically – we will, therefore, need to use two plots: amplitude as a function of frequency and phase as a function of frequency.

A signal's amplitude and phase as functions of frequency is called the *spectrum* of the signal. If we are provided with the spectrum of the signal, we have all the information necessary to completely define the signal. Signal spectra are often presented graphically in terms of two plots; we will refer to the plot of amplitude as a function of frequency as the *magnitude spectrum*, while the plot of phase as a function of frequency will be called the *phase spectrum*. As an example, the magnitude and phase spectra of the signal provided in equation (11.4) are shown in Fig. 11.3 below.

---

[1] Later in this textbook, we will use *Fourier Series* to represent arbitrary periodic signals and Fourier Transforms to represent non-periodic signals. Computer methods, based on these analysis approaches, are commonly used to determine the frequency components present in measured signals. A detailed discussion of these approaches is currently beyond our capabilities; at the moment, we simply ask that you believe that nearly any time domain signal can be represented to some extent in the frequency domain. For the immediate future, we will assume that the frequency domain representation of any signals of interest is directly available.

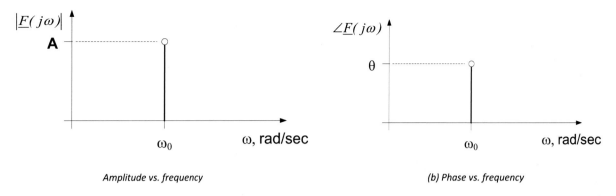

Amplitude vs. frequency | (b) Phase vs. frequency

Figure 11.3. Spectrum for the sinusoidal signal of equation (11.4).

Notes:

- The term spectrum is most commonly applied to the plot of amplitude and phase vs. frequency of signals in complex exponential form. For example, the signal of equation (11.1) can be written in terms of complex exponentials as: $f(t) = \frac{Ae^{j(\omega_0 t+\theta)}+Ae^{-j(\omega_0 t+\theta)}}{2} = \frac{A}{2}e^{j\theta}e^{j\omega_0 t} + \frac{A}{2}e^{-j\theta}e^{-j\omega_0 t}$. The spectral plot of the signal in this form is shown below. Note that spectra in this form have both positive and negative frequencies. In our discussions in this chapter, we will present spectra only in terms of having positive frequencies.

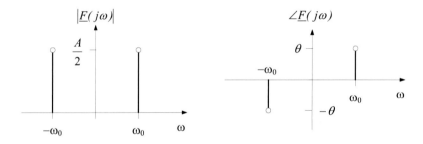

- The time domain representation of a signal has only one dependent variable – the value of the signal at any time. Time domain representations are therefore represented graphically as a <u>single plot</u> with time on the horizontal axis. This difference is, fundamentally, due to the fact that we do not work with complex functions of time; if we could measure a signal with both real and imaginary parts, two plots would be required.)

Example 11.4

Plot the spectrum of the voltage signal $v_{in}(t) = 3\cos(2t + 20°) + 7\cos(4t - 60°)$. (Note: this is the same signal as that used in Example 10.20; for a time-domain plot of the signal, see that example.)

The phasor form of this signal can be expressed as a function of frequency as:

$$V_{in}(j\omega) = \begin{cases} 3\angle 20°, & \omega = 2rad/sec \\ 7\angle -60°, & \omega = 4rad/sec \\ 0, & otherwise \end{cases}$$

The spectrum is shown below:

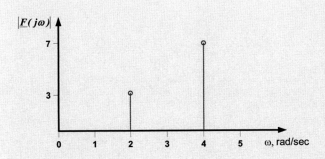

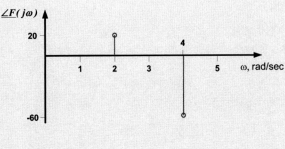

Example 11.5

Plot the voltage signal $v(t) = 2 - 3\cos(4t) + 5\cos(6t + 45°) + \cos(8t - 75°)$ and its spectrum.

A plot of the time domain signal is shown below.

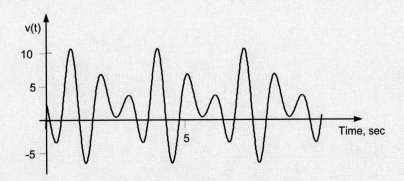

A couple of notes should be made about the spectrum of this signal. (1) The constant (DC) value of two corresponds to a frequency of zero rad/sec, since we can write $2 = 2\cos(0t)$. (2) Sinusoidal amplitudes are by definition positive, so the negative sign in the $-3\cos(4t)$ term must be accounted for in the phase. Therefore, we re-write this term as $+3\cos(4t + 180°)$. The spectrum of the signal can then be plotted as shown below:

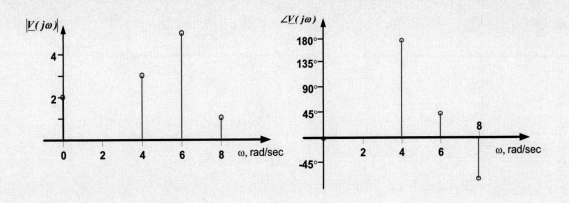

11.2.2 Frequency Response Plots

We have previously seen that the frequency response of a system consists of the system's magnitude response and phase response. The magnitude response provides the <u>gain</u> of the system (the ratio between the amplitudes of the output and input sinusoids) as a function of frequency, while the phase response provides the <u>change in phase</u> between the input and output sinusoids, as a function of frequency. In this section, we will emphasize the presentation of this information graphically. We do this by plotting the frequency response of two simple first order circuits in the examples below.

Example 11.6

Plot the frequency response for the circuit shown below. The voltage $v_{in}(t)$ is the input and the *capacitor voltage $v_{out}(t)$* is the *desired response*.

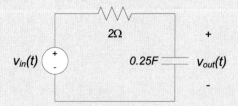

A mathematical expression for the frequency response of this circuit was determined in example 11.1 to be:

$$H(j\omega) = \frac{2}{2 + j\omega}$$

The magnitude and phase responses, as functions of frequency are, therefore:

$$|H(j\omega)| \frac{2}{\sqrt{4 + \omega^2}}$$

And:

$$\angle H(j\omega) = -\tan^{-1}\left(\frac{\omega}{2}\right)$$

Plotting these functions results in the graphical frequency response shown below:

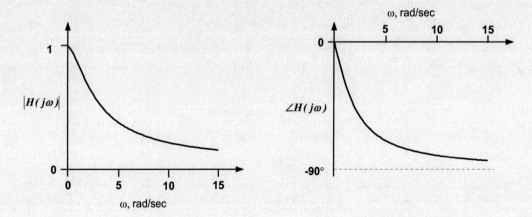

Example 11.7

Plot the frequency response for the circuit shown to the left below. The source voltage $v_S(t)$ is the input and the inductor voltage $v(t)$ is the output.

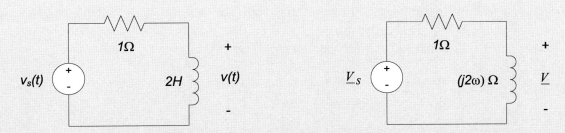

We begin by converting the circuit to the frequency domain. Representing the input and output signals as phasors and the circuit elements as impedances results in the circuit to the right above. This circuit suggests that the output voltage can be determined from the input voltage via a voltage divider formula:

$$V = \frac{j2\omega}{1 + j2\omega} \cdot V_S$$

The circuit frequency response, $H(j\omega)$, is the ratio of the output phasor to the input phasor:

$$H(j\omega) = \frac{V}{V_S} = \frac{j2\omega}{1 + j2\omega}$$

So that the magnitude and phase response of the circuit are:

$$|H(j\omega)| = \frac{2\omega}{\sqrt{1^2 + (2\omega)^2}}$$

And:

$$\angle H(j\omega) = 90° - \tan^{-1}(2\omega)$$

Plots of these functions are shown below.

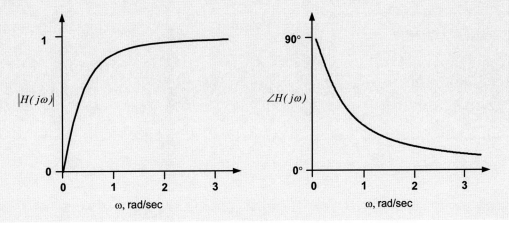

11.2.3 Checking the Frequency Response

A circuit's <u>amplitude response</u> is relatively easy to determine at low and high frequencies. For very low ($\omega \to 0$) and very high ($\omega \to \infty$) frequencies, the circuit can be modeled as a purely resistive network. Since resistive networks are relatively easy to analyze (no complex arithmetic is required), this can provide a valuable tool for checking results or predicting expected behavior.

- <u>Capacitors at low and high frequencies</u>: A capacitor's impedance is $Z_C = \frac{1}{j\omega C}$. At low frequencies ($\omega \to 0$), the impedance $Z_C \to \infty$, and the capacitor behaves as an open circuit. At high frequencies ($\omega \to \infty$) the impedance $Z_C \to 0$ and the capacitor behaves like a short circuit.

- Inductors at low and high frequencies: an inductor's impedance is $Z_L = j\omega L$. At low frequencies ($\omega \rightarrow 0$), the impedance $Z_L \rightarrow 0$, and the inductor behaves as a short circuit. At high frequencies ($\omega \rightarrow \infty$) the impedance $Z_L \rightarrow \infty$ and the inductor behaves like an open circuit.

Please note that the above statements are relative only to the amplitude response.

Example 11.8

Use the circuits' low and high frequency behavior to check the amplitude response plots for example 11.6.

The circuit of interest is shown below.

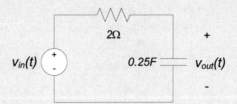

- At low frequencies, the capacitor becomes an open circuit, no current flows through the resistor, and $v_{out}=v_{in}$. Thus, the amplitude of the output is the same as the amplitude of the input and the gain as $\omega \rightarrow 0$ is one.
- At high frequencies, the capacitor becomes a short circuit, so that $v_{out}=0$. Since the output amplitude is zero, for a non-zero input, the gain of the circuit as $\omega \rightarrow \infty$ is zero.

The expected behavior at low and high frequencies agrees with the amplitude response of example 11.6; the amplitude response is one at $\omega=0$, and approaches zero as frequency increases.

Example 11.9

Use the circuits' low and high frequency behavior to check the amplitude response plots for example 11.7. The circuit of interest is shown below:

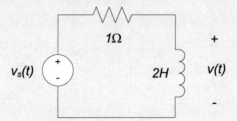

- At low frequencies, the inductor becomes a short circuit, so that $v=0$. Since the output amplitude is zero, for a non-zero input, the gain of the circuit as $\omega \rightarrow 0$ is zero.
- At high frequencies, the inductor becomes an open circuit, no current flows through the resistor, and $v=v_s$. Thus, the amplitude of the output is the same as the amplitude of the input and the gain as $\omega \rightarrow \infty$ is one.

The expected behavior at low and high frequencies agrees with the amplitude response of example 11.7; the amplitude response is zero at $\omega=0$, and approaches one as frequency increases.

Example 11.10

What is the gain of the circuit shown below as $\omega \rightarrow 0$ and $\omega \rightarrow \infty$? The input is $v_{in}(t)$ and the output is $v_{out}(t)$.

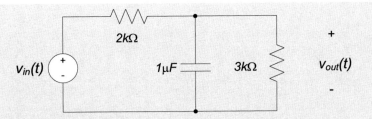

As $\omega \to 0$, the capacitor becomes an open circuit, and the overall circuit becomes as shown to the left below.
As $\omega \to \infty$, the capacitor is replaced by a short circuit and the overall circuit becomes as shown to the right below.

As $\omega \to 0$, the circuit becomes a voltage divider, and $v_{out} = \frac{3k\Omega}{2k\Omega+3k\Omega} \cdot v_{in}$, so that the circuit's gain is $\frac{3}{5}$. As $\omega \to \infty$, v_{out} is measured across a short circuit, and the gain is zero.

11.2.4 Graphical Representation of System Response

We can use graphical depictions of the input signal spectrum and the frequency response of the system to obtain a graphical representation of a system's response. This representation can be especially useful in interpreting and understanding the effect of a system on an input signal. This qualitative interpretation of a system's response can be an invaluable aid in system design.

The frequency-domain representation of a system's response is shown in Fig. 11.4. The frequency-domain output is simply a point-by-point multiplication between the input signal and the system's frequency response. Thus, the amplitude spectrum of the output is simply the point-by-point product of the input signal's amplitude spectrum with the system's magnitude response. The phase spectrum of the output is the sum of the input signal's phase spectrum and the system's phase response. An example of this process and its use in interpreting a system's response is provided in the example below.

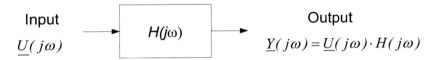

Figure 11.4. Frequency-domain system block diagram.

Example 11.11

Use graphical methods to interpret the response of the circuit of example 11.6 to an input voltage $v_{in}(t) = 3\cos(t + 20°) + 8\cos(8t - 60°)$. The input voltage time-domain signal is shown below. The signal consists of a relatively small amplitude, low frequency sinusoid superimposed with a large amplitude, higher frequency signal.

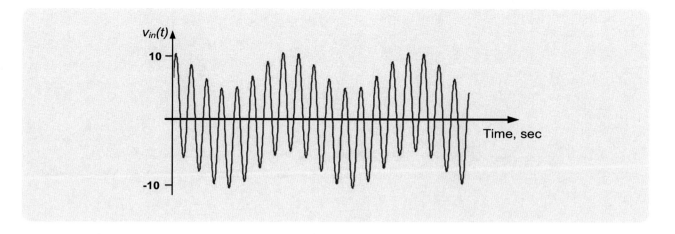

The frequency response of the circuit was determined in example 11.6; the frequency response plots are repeated below:

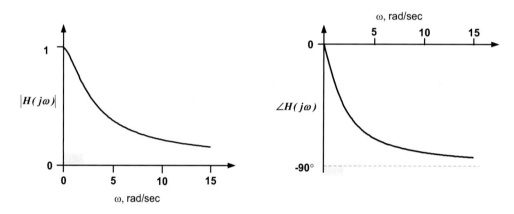

The input signal spectrum, $\underline{V}(j\omega)$ is shown below.

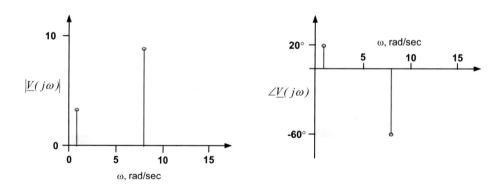

We can obtain the spectrum of the output signal from a frequency-by-frequency product of the input amplitude and the circuit's amplitude response and a frequency-by-frequency sum of the input phase and the circuit's phase response. Keep in mind that when the input amplitude is zero, the output amplitude is also zero and the phase is undetermined.

This process results in the output spectrum shown below. Notice that the circuit attenuates the magnitude of the high frequency component of the signal relative to the low frequency component. The low frequency component is said to be "passed through" the circuit, while the higher frequency component is "stopped" by the circuit.

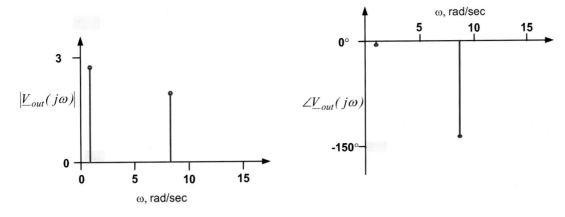

The time-domain signal of the output signal is shown below, superimposed over the input signal. It is clear that the amplitudes of the higher frequency component of the output signal has been reduced relative to the amplitude of the lower frequency component. This circuit is said to be *frequency selective* – it selects low frequencies to pass and high frequencies to stop.

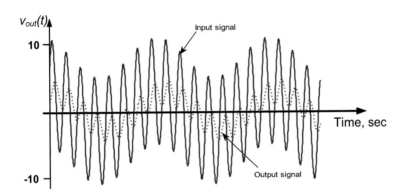

Section Summary

- *Signal spectra* are a primarily a graphical representation of the frequency content of a <u>signal</u>. The spectrum consists, in general, of two plots: amplitude as a function of frequency and phase as a function of frequency.
- The signal spectrum is useful, since many signals of interest can be expressed as a superposition of sinusoidal components. This allows signals which do not appear "sinusoidal" to be analyzed using steady-state sinusoidal analysis techniques.
- *Frequency response plots* are a graphical representation of the frequency response of a <u>system</u>. Frequency response plots also consist of two parts: the system's magnitude response as a function of frequency and the system's phase response as a function of frequency.
- The combination of the signal spectrum and the frequency response plots can provide valuable insight into a system's operation. The amplitude of the output signal is the <u>point-by-point product</u> of the input signal's amplitude and the system's magnitude response. The phase of the output signal is the <u>point-by-point sum</u> of the input signal's phase and the system's phase response.
  - Perhaps even more importantly, the signal spectra and frequency response plots can be used as an effective design tool: if the frequency content of the input signal and the *desired* frequency content of the output signal are both known, we can determine the system frequency response

necessary to provide the desired output signal. This allows us to design our system to perform the desired task

- When calculating a system's frequency response, it is always important to check your result relative to the expected behavior of the system. This can be done by determining the magnitude response at very low ($\omega \to 0$) and very high ($\omega \to \infty$) frequencies. In these extreme conditions the circuit can be approximated as a purely resistive circuit, since energy storage elements can be replaced by either short-circuits or open-circuits as follows:

  o Capacitors at low and high frequencies: A capacitor's impedance is $Z_C = \frac{1}{j\omega C}$. At low frequencies ($\omega \to 0$), the impedance $Z_C \to \infty$, and the capacitor behaves as an open circuit. At high frequencies ($\omega \to \infty$) the impedance $Z_C \to 0$ and the capacitor behaves like a short circuit.

  o Inductors at low and high frequencies: A inductor's impedance is $Z_L = j\omega L$. At low frequencies ($\omega \to 0$), the impedance $Z_L \to 0$, and the inductor behaves as a short circuit. At high frequencies ($\omega \to \infty$) the impedance $Z_L \to \infty$ and the inductor behaves like an open circuit.

11.2 Exercises

1. The input to a system is $u(t) = 3\cos(2t - 60°) + 4\cos(4t + 30°) + 7\cos(6t + 45°)$. The system frequency response is given by the piecewise function:

$$H(j\omega) = \begin{cases} 0, 0 < \omega < 3 \\ 1, 3 \le \omega \le 5 \\ 0, \omega > 5 \end{cases}$$

Sketch:

- The spectrum of the input signal (magnitude and phase)
- The frequency response of the system (magnitude response and phase response)
- And the output signal spectrum.

Compare your sketches to your results of exercise 2 in section 11.1.

2. Sketch the spectrum for the signal $v(t) = 4 + 3\cos(2t - 45°) + 2\cos(4t + 45°)$.
3. Use the circuit behavior at high and low frequencies to check the frequency response you calculated for the circuit of exercise 1 in section 11.1.
4. Determine the steady-state response of the output $y(t)$ for the circuit below at very low and very high frequencies.

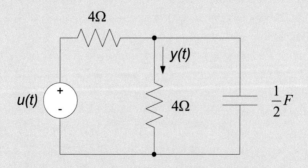

Solutions can be found at digilent.com/real-analog.

11.3 Frequency Selective Circuits and Filters

It is common to categorize circuits by the overall "shape" of their magnitude response. As we saw in example 11.11, in some frequency ranges the output amplitude may be high relative to the input amplitude, while in other frequency ranges the output amplitude will be low relative to the input amplitude. If the output amplitude at some frequency is high relative to the input amplitude, the magnitude response at that frequency is "large" and that frequency is said to be *passed* by the circuit. Conversely, if the output amplitude at some frequency is low relative to the input amplitude, the magnitude response at that frequency is "small" and that frequency is said to be *stopped* by the circuit.

Circuits which select certain frequencies to pass and other frequencies to stop are called *frequency selective* circuits or *filters* (since they tend to "filter out" certain frequency ranges of the input signal). The range of frequencies which are passed are called the *passband* of the filter, and the range of frequencies which are stopped are called the *stopband* of the filter. There are four primary categories of filters:

- *Low-pass filters* pass low frequencies and stop high frequencies
- *High-pass filters* pass high frequencies and stop low frequencies
- *Band-pass filters* pass a range of frequencies between two ranges of stopped frequencies
- *Band-reject filters* stop a range of frequencies between two ranges of passed frequencies

Filters are also categorized by their *order*. The order of the filter is simply the order of the differential equation governing the filter. Thus a first-order filter is governed by a first-order differential equation, a second-order filter is governed by a second-order differential equation, and so on. Low-pass and high-pass filters can be any order, while band-pass and band-stop filters must be <u>at least</u> second order.

In this chapter, we restrict out attention to first order filters, so we will consider <u>only</u> low pass and high pass filters.

11.3.2 Ideal Low-pass and High-pass Filters

We will first introduce the basic concepts relative to first order filters in the context of ideal filters. It must be clearly understood that ideal filters are not *physically realizable* – that is, we cannot construct a physical system which can perform this way[2]. Ideal filters entirely stop all input signals in the stopband and completely pass all signals in the passband. Thus, the magnitude response of an ideal filter is exactly one in the passband and exactly zero in the stop band. First order filters can be either high-pass or low-pass filters.

An ideal low pass filter has a magnitude response as shown in Fig. 11.5. The passband is shown as the shaded area under the magnitude response. The magnitude response is discontinuous – it goes from one to zero instantaneously. The *cutoff frequency*, ω_c, defines the boundary between the passband and the stopband. Any signal with a frequency below ω_c is passed through the filter without any attenuation; any signal with a frequency above ω_c is entirely stopped by the filter – it is not present in the output signal.

---

[2] In order to implement an ideal filter, the circuit would need to know values of the input signal before the values are applied – that is, the circuit would need to be able to see into the future. The technical term is that the filter would need to be non-causal. It is, of course, impossible to build a device that predicts the future.

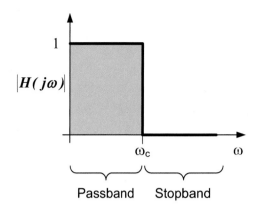

Figure 11.5. Magnitude response of an ideal low-pass filter.

An ideal high-pass filter has a magnitude response as shown in Fig. 11.6. The passband is again shown as the shaded area under the magnitude response. The magnitude response is discontinuous – it goes from zero to one instantaneously. The *cutoff frequency*, ω_c, again defines the boundary between the passband and the stopband. Any signal with a frequency below ω_c is entirely stopped by the filter while any signal with a frequency above ω_c is passed through the filter with no amplitude change.

As previously noted, it is impossible to physically implement an ideal filter. Thus, all electrical circuits implement non-ideal filters. Non-ideal filters do not provide an instantaneous transition between the pass band and the stop band. Non-ideal first order filters are discussed in the following subsections.

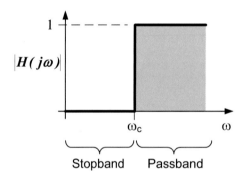

Figure 11.6. Magnitude response of an ideal high-pass filter.

11.3.3 First Order Low-pass Filters

The form of the governing differential equation for a first order low pass filter can be written as:

$$\frac{dy(t)}{dt} + \omega_c y(t) = K \cdot u(t)$$

Eq. 11.5

The frequency response of the filter can be determined to be:

$$H(j\omega) = \frac{K}{j\omega + \omega_c}$$

Eq. 11.6

The magnitude response of the filter is thus:

$$|H(j\omega)| = \frac{K}{\sqrt{\omega^2 + \omega_c^2}}$$

Eq. 11.7

The maximum magnitude response is $\frac{K}{\omega_c}$ when $\omega=0$ and the magnitude response is zero as $\omega \to \infty$. Thus, the filter is passing low frequencies and stopping high frequencies. The differential equation describes a low-pass filter.

The magnitude response of the filter is shown in Fig. 11.7. The frequency response is a smooth curve, rather than the discontinuous function shown in Fig. 11.5. There is no single frequency that obviously separates the passband from the stopband, so we must choose a relatively arbitrary point to define the boundary between the passband and the stopband. By consensus, the cutoff frequency for a low-pass filter is defined as the frequency at which the magnitude response is $\frac{1}{\sqrt{2}}$ times the magnitude response at $\omega=0$. For the magnitude response given by equation (11.7), the cutoff frequency is $\omega=\omega_c$. This point is indicated on Fig. 11.7.

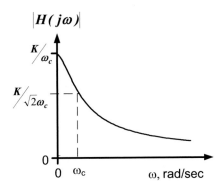

Figure 11.7. Magnitude response of first order low-pass filter.

11.3.4 First Order High-pass Filters

The form of the governing differential equation for a first order low pass filter can be written as:

$$\frac{dy(t)}{dt} + \omega_c y(t) = K \cdot \frac{du(t)}{dt}$$

Eq. 11.8

The frequency response of the filter can be determined to be:

$$H(j\omega) = \frac{jK\omega}{j\omega+\omega_c}$$

Eq. 11.9

The magnitude response of the filter is thus:

$$|H(j\omega)| = \frac{K\omega}{\sqrt{\omega^2+\omega_c^2}}$$

Eq. 11.10

The maximum magnitude response is approximately K when $\omega \to \infty$ and the magnitude response is zero at $\omega=0$. Thus, the filter is passing high frequencies and stopping low frequencies. <u>The differential equation describes a high-pass filter.</u>

The magnitude response of the filter is shown in Fig. 11.8. As with the non-ideal low-pass filter, the frequency response is a smooth curve, rather than the discontinuous function shown in Fig. 11.6. Again, there is no single frequency that obviously separates the passband from the stopband, so we must choose a relatively arbitrary point to define the boundary between the passband and the stopband. Consistent with our choice of cutoff frequency for the low-pass filter, the cutoff frequency for a high-pass filter is defined as the frequency at which the magnitude response is $\frac{1}{\sqrt{2}}$ times the magnitude response at $\omega \to \infty$. For the magnitude response given by equation (1.10), the cutoff frequency is $\omega=\omega_c$. This point is indicated on Fig. 11.8.

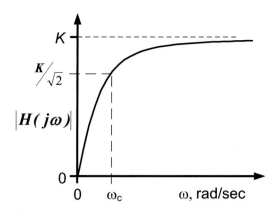

Figure 11.8. Magnitude response of first order high-pass filter.

Notes:

- The cutoff frequency is also called the corner frequency, the 3dB frequency, or the half-power point.
- The cutoff frequency for <u>both</u> low-pass and high-pass filters is defined as the frequency at which the magnitude is $\frac{1}{\sqrt{2}}$ times the <u>maximum</u> value of the magnitude response.
- It can be seen from examples in section 11.2 that the phase response of a first order low-pass filter is 0° at $\omega=0$ and decreases to –90° as $\omega \to \infty$. The phase response is –45° at the cutoff frequency.
- It can be seen from examples in section 11.2 that the phase response of a first order high-pass filter is 90° at $\omega=0$ and decreases to 0° as $\omega \to \infty$. The phase response is 45° at the cutoff frequency.
- For both low-pass and high-pass filters, the cutoff frequency is the inverse of the time constant for the circuit, so that $\omega_c = \frac{1}{\tau}$.
- The circuit's response at zero frequency is generally an important parameter to consider. This is called the DC gain, and is the ratio of the output amplitude to the input amplitude for a constant input. A constant input corresponds to a cosine with zero frequency. Low pass filters have a relatively high DC gain and a correspondingly large response to a constant input. High pass filters have a low DC gain; they have little or no response to constant inputs.

We conclude this section with examples of circuits from section 10.2 which implement low-pass and high-pass filter operations.

Example 11.12: First Order Low-pass Filter

The circuit below is the circuit from example 11.6. The input is $v_{in}(t)$ and the output is $v_{out}(t)$.

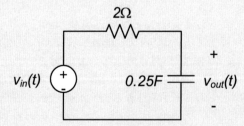

In example 11.6, the frequency response was determined to be:

$$H(j\omega) = \frac{2}{2 + j\omega}$$

The maximum value of the magnitude response is one at a frequency of zero radians/second and the magnitude response goes to infinity as $\omega \to \infty$, so the circuit acts as a low-pass filter. Comparing the amplitude response above with equation (2) above, it can be seen that the cutoff frequency is $\omega_c = 2$ rad/sec. The amplitude response, with the cutoff frequency labeled, is shown below.

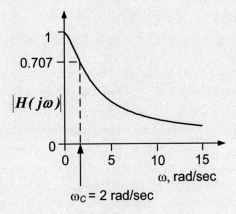

Example 11.13: First Order High-pass Filter

The circuit below is the circuit from example 11.7. The input is $v_s(t)$ and the output is $v(t)$.

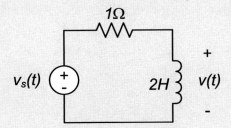

The frequency response of the circuit was previously determined to be:

$$H(j\omega) = \frac{V}{\underline{V_S}} = \frac{j2\omega}{1 + j2\omega}$$

The maximum value of the magnitude response is one as $\omega \to \infty$ and goes to zero at a frequency of zero radians/second, so the circuit acts as a low-pass filter. Comparing the amplitude response above with equation (4) above, it can be seen that the cutoff frequency is $\omega_c = 0.5$ rad/sec. The amplitude response, with the cutoff frequency labeled, is shown below.

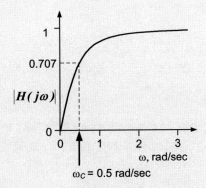

Section Summary

- Filters are frequency-selective systems. These systems provide a desired relationship between the input signal spectrum and the output signal spectrum. The filter does this by *passing* certain frequencies from the input to the output and *stopping* some frequencies from propagating from the input to the output. Nomenclature is as follows:
  - The range of frequencies which are passed is called the *passband* of the filter
  - The range of frequencies which are stopped is called the *stopband* of the filter
- Filters are broadly categorized as follows:
  - *Low-pass filters* pass low frequencies and stop high frequencies
  - *High-pass filters* pass high frequencies and stop low frequencies
  - *Band-pass filters* pass a range of frequencies between two ranges of stopped frequencies
  - *Band-reject filters* stop a range of frequencies between two ranges of passed frequencies
- In this chapter, we were concerned only with first-order low-pass and high-pass filters. These filters are primarily characterized by the following parameters:
  - Cutoff frequency: the cutoff is defined as the frequency at which the magnitude is $\frac{1}{\sqrt{2}}$ times the <u>maximum</u> value of the magnitude response.
  - *DC gain*: the DC gain is the ratio of the output amplitude to the input amplitude for a <u>constant</u> input (a cosine function with zero frequency). Low pass filters have a relatively high DC gain and a correspondingly large response to a constant input. High pass filters have a low DC gain; they have little or no response to constant inputs.

11.3 Exercises

1. What is the cutoff frequency of the circuit below? (You may want to use your results from exercise 1 of section 11.1.)

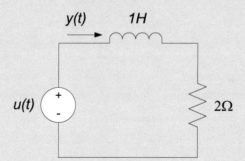

2. Use the circuit behavior at high and low frequencies and your time constant calculated in exercise 1 above to sketch the frequency response of the circuit of exercise 1. Label your frequency response to include DC gain and cutoff frequency. Is the circuit a high-pass or low-pass filter?

3. Calculate the time constant and the cutoff frequency for the circuit below, if *u(t)* is the input and y(t) is the output. Verify that the cutoff frequency is the inverse of the time constant. Use the circuit behavior at high and low frequencies to determine whether the circuit is a high-pass or low-pass filter.

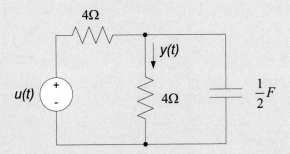

4. Calculate the frequency response of the circuit of exercise 3. Compare your frequency response to your results of exercise 3. Resolve any differences between the two.

Solutions can be found at digilent.com/real-analog.

11.4 Introduction to Bode Plots

Plotting a systems' frequency response on a linear scale, as done in sections 11.2 and 11.3, has a number of drawbacks, especially for higher-order systems[3]. An alternate format for plotting frequency responses, called a Bode plot, is therefore commonly used[4]. On Bode plots, the amplitude response is essentially presented as a log-log plot, while the phase response is a semi-log plot. Some reasons for this are:

- Use of logarithms converts the operation of multiplication and division to addition and subtraction. This can simplify the creation of frequency response plots for higher order systems.
- Frequencies and amplitudes of interest commonly span many orders of magnitude. Logarithmic scales improve the presentation of this type of data.
- Human senses are fundamentally logarithmic. The use of logarithmic scales is therefore more "natural". (This is the reason for use of the Richter scale in measuring earthquake intensity, and the decibel scale in measuring sound levels. It is also the reason that increasing a musical tone by one octave corresponds to doubling its frequency.)

11.4.1 Properties of Logarithms

Since Bode plots employ logarithms extensively, we will briefly review some of the basic properties of logarithms before proceeding further. Bode plots rely upon base-10 logarithms (log_{10}), so we will restrict our attention to base-10 logarithms.

A plot of $log_{10}(x)$ vs. x is shown in Fig. 11.9 below. A few important features to note are:

- $log_{10}(x)$ is a real number only for positive values of x.
- $log_{10}(x)$ asymptotically approaches $-\infty$ as x→0. The slope of $log_{10}(x)$ becomes very large as x→0.
- The slope of $log_{10}(x)$ becomes small as x→∞.
- From the comments above relative to the slope of $log_{10}(x)$, it can be seen that the sensitivity of $log_{10}(x)$ to variations in x decreases as x increases (this is the reason why logarithmic scales are used when large variations in x are encountered – as in Richter scales and musical scales).

---

[3] Higher order systems are often modeled as a series of lower-order systems (or in the technical parlance, *cascaded* lower-order systems). A combination of cascaded frequency responses is multiplicative. Multiplying several frequency responses together can be tedious

[4] Bode plots use logarithmic scales. Logarithms convert multiplication to addition. Thus, a cascaded set of frequency responses in a logarithmic scale add – adding frequency responses is significantly simpler than multiplying them.

- $\log_{10}(1) = 0$

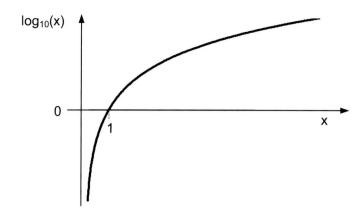

Figure 11.9. Plot of log₁₀(x) vs. x

The basic defining property of a base-10 logarithm is that *x=10ʸ*, then *y=log₁₀x*. This property leads to the following rules governing logarithmic operations:

1. Logarithms convert multiplication and division to addition and subtraction, respectively. Thus,

$$\log_{10}(xy) = \log_{10} x + \log_{10} y$$

And:

$$\log_{10}\left(\frac{x}{y}\right) = \log_{10} x - \log_{10} y$$

This property is especially useful for us, since determining the spectrum of an output signal results from the product of an input signal's spectrum with the frequency response. Thus, the output spectrum on a logarithmic scale can be obtained from a simple addition.

2. Logarithms convert exponentiation to multiplication by the exponent, so that:

$$\log_{10}(x^n) = n\log_{10}x$$

11.4.2 Decibel Scales

Magnitude responses are often presented in terms of decibels (abbreviated dB). Decibels are a logarithmic scale. A magnitude response is presented in units of decibels according to the following conversion:

$$|H(j\omega)|_{dB} = 20\log_{10}(|H(j\omega)|) \hspace{3cm} \text{Eq. 11.11}$$

Strictly speaking, magnitudes in decibels are only appropriate if the amplitude response is unitless (e.g. the units of the input and output must be the same in order for the logarithm to be a mathematically appropriate operation). However, in practice, magnitude responses are often presented in decibels regardless of the relative units of the input and output – thus, magnitude responses are provided in decibels even if the input is voltage and the output is current or vice-versa.

Brief Historical Note

Decibel units are related to the unit "bel", which are named after Alexander Graham Bell. Units of bels are, strictly speaking, applicable only to power. Power in bels is expressed as $\log_{10}\left(\frac{P}{P_{ref}}\right)$, where P_{ref} is a "reference" power.

Bels are an inconveniently large unit, so these were converted to decibels, or tenths of a bel. Thus, power in decibels is $10 \log_{10}\left(\frac{P}{P_{ref}}\right)$. Since the units of interest to electrical engineers are generally voltages or currents, which must be squared to obtain power, we obtain $20 \log_{10}(|H(j\omega)|)$. The significant aspect of the decibel unit for us is not, however, the multiplicative factor of "20"), but the fact that the unit is <u>logarithmic</u>.

We conclude this subsection with a table of common values for $|H(j\omega)|$ and their associated decibel values.

$|H(j\omega)|$	$|H(j\omega)|$ in decibels
10	20
1	0
0.1	-20
$1/\sqrt{2}$	-3
$1/2$	-6

11.4.3 Bode Plots

Bode plots are simply plots of the magnitude and phase response of a system using a particular set of axes. For Bode plots,

- Units of frequency are on a base-10 logarithm scale.
- Amplitudes (or magnitudes) are in decibels (dB)
- Phases are presented on a linear scale

Notes

- Since frequencies are on a logarithmic scale, frequencies separated by the same multiplicative factor are evenly separated on a logarithmic scale. Some of these multiplicative factors have special names. For example, frequencies separated by a factor of two are said to be separated by *octaves* on a logarithmic scale and frequencies separated by a factor of 10 are said to be separated by *decades*.
- Since decibels are intrinsically a logarithmic scale, magnitudes which are separated by the same multiplicative factor are evenly separated on a decibel scale. For example, magnitudes which are separated by a factor of 10 are separated by 20dB on a decibel scale.

One convenient aspect of the presentation of frequency responses in terms of Bode plots is the ability to generate a reasonable sketch of a frequency response very easily. In general, this approach consists of approximating the Bode plot of a system by its asymptotic behavior as a set of straight lines. This is called a "straight line approximation" of the Bode plot; the approach is illustrated for a typical low-pass filter in the following subsection.

11.4.4 Bode Plots for First Order Low-pass Filters

The frequency response of a general first order low-pass filter is provided in section 11.3 as:

$$H(j\omega) = \frac{K}{j\omega + \omega_c}$$

Eq. 11.12

Thus, magnitude response of the circuit is:

$$|H(j\omega)| = \frac{K}{\sqrt{\omega^2 + \omega_c^2}}$$

Eq. 11.13

And the phase response of the circuit is:

$$\angle H(j\omega) = -\tan^{-1}\left(\frac{\omega}{\omega_c}\right)$$

Eq. 11.14

To estimate the asymptotic behavior of the frequency response, we consider the behavior of equations (11.13) and (11.14) for the low frequency and high frequency cases. In general, we consider "low" frequencies to be frequencies which are <u>less than a factor of 10 below the cutoff frequency</u> (i.e. $\omega < \frac{\omega_c}{10}$, or frequencies more than a decade below the cutoff frequency). High frequencies are typically assumed to be frequencies which are <u>more than a factor of 10 above the cutoff frequency</u> (i.e. $\omega > 10\omega_c$, or more than a decade above the cutoff frequency). We consider the high and low frequency cases separately below.

- Low frequencies:
    - The magnitude response given by equation (2) is $|H(j\omega)| = \frac{K}{\sqrt{\omega^2 + \omega_c^2}}$. If $\omega \ll \omega_c$, the denominator is approximately $\sqrt{\omega_c^2} = \omega_c$ and the magnitude response $|H(j\omega)| \approx \frac{K}{\omega_c}$. If $\omega \ll \omega_c$, $\frac{\omega}{\omega_c} \approx 0$ and the phase is approximately $\angle H(j\omega) \approx -\tan^{-1}(0) = 0°$.

- High Frequencies:
    - If $\omega \gg \omega_c$, the denominator of the amplitude response is $\sqrt{\omega^2 + \omega_c^2} \approx \sqrt{\omega^2} = \omega$. Therefore, for high frequencies, the magnitude response $|H(j\omega)| \approx \frac{K}{\omega}$. If, for high frequencies, we increase the frequency by a factor of 10, we reduce the magnitude response by 20dB (since $|H(j \cdot 10\omega)| \approx \frac{K}{10\omega} = 0.1\frac{K}{\omega}$ and the multiplicative factor of 0.1 corresponds to -20dB). Thus, for frequencies well above the cutoff frequency, the magnitude response, presented in Bode plot form, decreases by 20dB/decade. When $\omega \gg \omega_c$, the phase response is given by $\angle H(j\omega) = -\tan^{-1}\left(\frac{\omega}{\omega_c}\right) \approx -\tan^{-1}(\infty) = -90°$.

Summary: Low-pass Filter Straight-line Bode Plot Approximations

The straight line approximation to the magnitude response is constant below the cutoff frequency, with a value (in decibels) of $20\log_{10}\left(\frac{K}{\omega_c}\right)$. Above the cutoff frequency, the Bode plot straight-line approximation has a constant slope of -20 dB/decade.

The straight-line approximation to the phase response is zero degrees up to a frequency of $\frac{\omega_c}{10}$ and is -90° above a frequency of $10\omega_c$. A straight line is used to connect the $\frac{\omega_c}{10}$ and $10\omega_c$ frequencies.

A straight-line approximation to the Bode plot for a typical low-pass circuit, with $K = \omega_c$ (so that the frequency response is $H(j\omega) = \frac{\omega_c}{j\omega + \omega_c}$ and the DC gain is 1, or 0dB) along with an exact curve is provided below in Fig. 11.10.

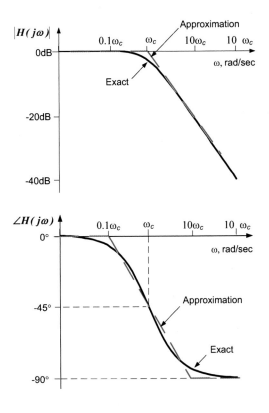

Figure 11.10. Low pass filter straight-line approximation and exact Bode plot.

We conclude this section with a numerical example of the straight-line approximation to a Bode plot for a specific circuit.

Example 11.14

Sketch a straight-line approximation to the Bode plot for the circuit below. The input is $v_{in}(t)$ and the output is $v_{out}(t)$.

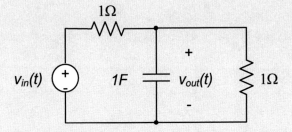

The frequency response for this circuit is $H(j\omega) = \frac{1}{j\omega+2}$. Therefore, the cutoff frequency is $\omega_c=2$ rad/sec and the gain in decibels at low frequencies is $|H(j0)|_{dB} = 20\log_{10}\left(\frac{1}{2}\right) \approx -6dB$. Thus, the straight-line magnitude response is -6dB below the cutoff frequency and decreases by 20dB/decade above the cutoff frequency. The straight-line phase response is 0° below 0.2rad/sec, –90° above 20 rad/sec and a straight line between these frequencies. The associated plots are shown below.

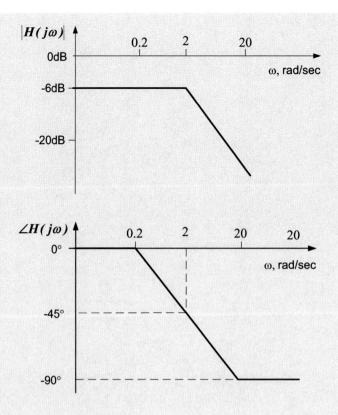

Section Summary

- Bode plots are a very useful format for plotting frequency responses. Bode plots provide magnitude responses and phase responses in the following format:
    - Units of frequency are on a base-10 logarithm scale.
    - Amplitudes (or magnitudes) are in decibels (dB)
    - Phases are presented on a linear scale.
    - Magnitude responses in decibels are calculated according to:

$$|H(j\omega)|_{dB} = 20\log_{10}(|H(j\omega)|)$$

- The use of logarithmic scales in Bode plots has a number of advantages. Logarithms convert multiplication and division into addition and subtraction, respectively. This provides a significant mathematical simplification in the analysis of higher-order systems. Logarithms are also, in some sense, more "natural" to interpret, since human senses are fundamentally logarithmic.
- Bode plots also have the advantage of being approximated fairly well by straight-line approximations. This allows the engineer to sketch a fairly accurate frequency response plot with only a minimal number of calculations.

Chapter 12:
Steady-State Sinusoidal Power

In this chapter we will address the issue of power transmission via sinusoidal (or AC) signals. This topic is extremely important, since the vast majority of power transmission in the world is performed using AC voltages and currents.

For the most part, the topic of AC power transmission focuses on the <u>average</u> power delivered to a load over time. In general, it is not productive to focus on the power transmission at a particular time since, if the load contains energy storage elements (such as capacitors and inductors), it is possible that at times the load will absorb power and at other times the load will release power. This characteristic leads to the concepts of *average power* and *reactive power* – average power is typically the power that is converted by the load to useful work, while reactive power is the power that is simply exchanged by energy storage elements. Power companies cannot really charge customers for power which is not absorbed by the load, so one primary goal in AC power transmission is to reduce the reactive power that is sent to the load.

In this chapter we introduce the basic topics relative to calculation of AC power. In section 12.1, we introduce the basic concepts associated with AC power, including the notion that a load containing energy storage elements may alternately absorb <u>and</u> release power. This discussion will lead to the concepts of average power and reactive power, which are discussed in section 12.2. Power calculations are often presented in terms of RMS values; these are introduced in section 12.3. The relative roles of average and reactive power are often characterized by the apparent power and the power factor, which are presented in section 12.4. In section 12.5, we will use complex numbers to simultaneously quantify the average power, the reactive power, the apparent power, and the power factor. Finally, in section 12.6, we examine approaches to reduce the reactive power which is exchanged between the power company and the user. This technique is called power factor correction.

After completing this chapter, you should be able to:

- Define instantaneous power, average power, and reactive power
- Define real power, reactive power, and complex power
- Define RMS signal values and calculate the RMS value of a given sinusoidal signal
- State, from memory, the definition of power factor and calculate the power factor from a given combination of voltage and current sinusoids
- Draw a power triangle
- Correct the power factor of an inductive load to a desired value

12.1 Instantaneous Power

We will begin our study of steady-state sinusoidal power by examining the power delivered by a sinusoidal signal as a function of time. We will see that, since all the signals involved are sinusoidal, the delivered power varies sinusoidally with time. This time-varying power is called instantaneous power, since it describes the power delivered to the load at every instant in time. The instantaneous power will not, in general, be directly useful to us in later sections but it does provide the basis for understanding the concepts presented throughout this chapter.

In chapter 1, we saw that power is the product of voltage and current, so that power as a function of time is:

$$p(t) = v(t) \cdot i(t)$$
Eq. 12.1

Power as a function of time is often called *instantaneous power*, since it provides the power at any instant in time. So far, this is the only type of power with which we have been concerned. If our voltages and currents are sinusoidal, as is the case for AC power, we can write *v(t)* and *i(t)* as:

$$v(t) = V_m \cos(\omega t + \theta_v)$$
Eq. 12.2

And:

$$i(t) = I_m \cos(\omega t + \theta_i)$$
Eq. 12.3

Where, of course, V_m and θ_v are the amplitude and phase angle of the voltage signal while I_m and θ_i are the amplitude and phase angle of the current signal. It should be noted at this point that the voltage and current signals of equations (12.2) and (12.3) are <u>not</u> independent of one another. Figure 12.1 shows the overall system being analyzed – the voltage *v(t)* and the current *i(t)* are the voltage and current applied to some load. If the load has some impedance, Z_L, the voltage and current are related through this impedance. Thus, if we represent v(t) and i(t) in phasor form as v(t) = $\underline{V}e^{j\omega t}$ and $i(t) = \underline{I}e^{j\omega t}$, then $\underline{V} = Z_L \cdot \underline{I}$.

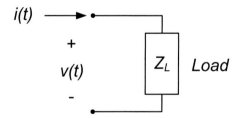

Figure 12.1. Voltage and current applied to a load.

Substituting equations (12.2) and (12.3) into equation (12.1) results in:

$$p(t) = V_m I_m \cos(\omega t + \theta_v)\cos(\omega t + \theta_i)$$
Eq. 12.4

Equation (12.4) can be re-written, using some algebra and trigonometric identities, as:

$$p(t) = \frac{V_m I_m}{2}\{\cos(\theta_v - \theta_i) + \cos(2\omega t + \theta_v + \theta_i)\}$$

Eq. 12.5

Since V_m, θ_v, I_m, and θ_i are all constants, we can see that equation (12.5) is the sum of two terms: a constant value, $\frac{V_m I_m}{2}\cos(\theta_v - \theta_i)$, and a sinusoidal component, $\frac{V_m I_m}{2}\cos(2\omega t + \theta_v + \theta_i)$. The time-domain relationship of equation (12.5) is plotted in Fig. 12.2. The signal's average value is $\frac{V_m I_m}{2}\cos(\theta_v - \theta_i)$ and has a sinusoidal component with an amplitude of $\frac{V_m I_m}{2}$.

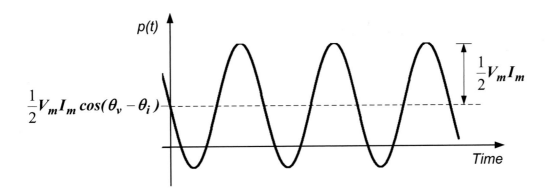

Figure 12.2. Plot of instantaneous power vs. time.

Section Summary:

- The power delivered to a load by a sinusoidal (or AC) signal has two components: an average value and a sinusoidal component.
- Both the average value and the sinusoidal component are dependent upon the amplitude and phase angles of the voltage and current delivered to the load. These values are, in turn, set by the impedance of the load.
- The average power is dissipated or absorbed by the load. This power is electrical power which is converted to heat or useful work.
- The sinusoidal component of the power is due to energy storage elements in in the load; this power is exchanged (in some sense) between the load and the system supplying power. It is purely electrical energy which the load is not using to perform useful work.

12.1 Exercises

1. The current and voltage delivered to a load are i(t) = 2cos(100t) and v(t) = 120cos(100t+65°), respectively. Calculate the average power delivered to the load and the amplitude of the sinusoidal component of the power.

Solutions can be found at digilent.com/real-analog.

12.2 Average and Reactive Power

Examination of equation (12.5) and Fig. 12.2 indicates that the instantaneous power can be either positive or negative, so the load is alternately absorbing or releasing power. The overall amount of power absorbed vs. power released is dependent primarily upon the $\cos(\theta_v - \theta_i)$ term. If the voltage and current are in phase, $\theta_v - \theta_i$,

$\cos(\theta_v - \theta_i) = 1$ and the instantaneous power is <u>never</u> negative. The voltage and current have the same phase if the load is purely resistive – a resistor <u>always</u> absorbs power. If the voltage and current are 90° out of phase, as is the case for a purely capacitive or purely inductive load, $\cos(\theta_v - \theta_i) = 0$. In this case, the instantaneous power curve is a pure sinusoid with no DC offset, so <u>on average</u> no power is delivered to the load. This is consistent with our models of capacitors and inductors as energy storage elements, which do not dissipate any energy.

The concepts presented in the paragraph above can be mathematically presented by rearranging equation (12.5) yet again. Application of additional trigonometric identities and performing more algebra results in:

$$p(t) = \frac{V_m I_m}{2}\cos(\theta_v - \theta_i)\left[1 + \cos(2\omega t)\right] + \frac{V_m I_m}{2}\sin(\theta_v - \theta_i)\left[\sin(2\omega t)\right] \qquad \text{Eq. 12.6}$$

The two terms in equation (12.6) are plotted separately in Fig. 12.3. The first term, $\frac{V_m I_m}{2}\cos(\theta_v - \theta_i)\left[1 + \cos(2\omega t)\right]$, has an average value of $\frac{V_m I_m}{2}\cos(\theta_v - \theta_i)$, while the second term, $\frac{V_m I_m}{2}\sin(\theta_v - \theta_i)[\sin(2\omega t)]$, has an average value of <u>zero</u>. Thus, the <u>average</u> power delivered to a load is:

$$P = \frac{V_m I_m}{2}\cos(\theta_v - \theta_i) \qquad \text{Eq. 12.7}$$

The amplitude of the term $\frac{V_m I_m}{2}\sin(\theta_v - \theta_i)[\sin(2\omega t)]$, which provides no average power to the load, is termed the *reactive* power, Q:

$$Q = \frac{V_m I_m}{2}\sin(\theta_v - \theta_i) \qquad \text{Eq. 12.8}$$

The reactive power is a measure of the amount of power which is delivered to the load, but is <u>not absorbed</u> by the load – the load returns this power to the source!

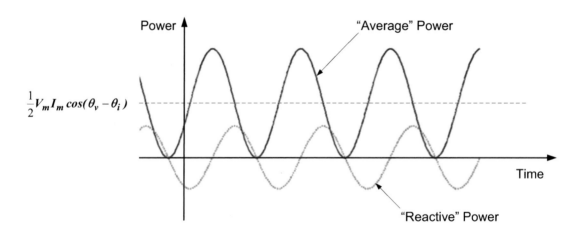

Figure 12.3. Components of instantaneous power vs. time.

Section Summary:

- The *average* power delivered to a load is:

$$P = \frac{V_m I_m}{2}\cos(\theta_v - \theta_i)$$

where V_m and θ_v are the amplitude and phase angle of the voltage while I_m and θ_i are the amplitude and phase angle of the current. The average power is often also called the *real* power. The average power is also the power dissipated by any resistive elements in the load. Units of average power are Watts (abbreviated W).

- The *reactive* power delivered to a load is:

$$Q = \frac{V_m I_m}{2} \sin(\theta_v - \theta_i)$$

The reactive power is not actually absorbed by the load; it is stored by the energy storage elements in the load and then returned to the source. The units of reactive power are taken to be Volt-Amperes Reactive (abbreviated VAR). Note that technically watts are the same as volt-amps, but the terminology is distinct to avoid any confusion between real and reactive power.

12.2 Exercises:

1. The current and voltage delivered to a load are i(t) = 2cos(100t) and v(t) = 120cos(100t+65°), respectively. Calculate the average power delivered to the load and the reactive power delivered to the load.

Solutions can be found at digilent.com/real-analog.

12.3 RMS Values

In sections 12.1 and 12.2, we introduced some basic quantities relative to delivery of power using sinusoidal signals. We saw that power <u>dissipated</u> by a load (essentially, any energy which is converted to non-electrical energy such as heat or work) is the *average power*. *Reactive power* results from energy which is stored by capacitors and inductors in the load and is then returned to the source without dissipation.

In this chapter, we continue our study of AC power analysis. We will introduce the concept of the root-mean-square (RMS) value of a signal as a way to represent the power of a time-varying signal. We will also introduce *complex power* as a way to conveniently represent both average and reactive power as a single complex number. We also introduce power factor as a way to represent the efficiency of the transfer of power to a load.

It is often desirable to compare different types of time-varying signals (for example, square waves vs. triangular waves vs. sinusoidal waves) using a very simple metric. Different types of signals are often compared by their RMS (root-mean-squared) values. The general idea behind the RMS value of a time-varying signal is that we wish to determine a <u>constant</u> value, which delivers the same <u>average</u> power to a resistive load.

The average value, *P*, of an instantaneous power *p(t)* is defined to be:

$$P = \frac{1}{T} \int_{t\_0}^{t_0+T} p(t)dt \qquad\qquad \text{Eq. 12.9}$$

The power delivered to a resistive load by a constant voltage or current source is:

$$P = R \cdot I_{eff}^2 = \frac{v_{eff}^2}{R} \qquad\qquad \text{Eq. 12.10}$$

I$_{eff}$ and V$_{eff}$ are the effective (or <u>constant</u>) current and voltage, respectively, applied to the resistive load, *R*. It is our goal to equate equations (12.9) and (12.10) to determine the effective voltage or current values, which deliver the same average power to a resistive load as some time-varying waveform.

Assuming that a current is applied to a resistive load, the instantaneous power is $p(t) = R \cdot i^2(t)$. Substituting this into equation (12.9) and equating to equation (12.10) results in:

$$R \cdot I_{eff}^2 = \frac{1}{T} \int_{t_0}^{t_0+T} R \cdot i^2(t) dt$$

Eq. 12.11

Solving this for I_{eff} results in:

$$I_{eff} = I_{RMS} = \sqrt{\frac{1}{T} \int_{t_0}^{t_0+T} i^2(t) dt}$$

Eq. 12.12

And the effective current is the square root of the mean of the square of the time-varying current. This is also called the RMS (or root-mean-square) value, for rather obvious reasons.

A similar process can be applied to the voltage across a resistive load, so that $p(t) = \frac{v^2(t)}{R}$. Equating this epression to equation (12.9) results in:

$$V_{eff} = V_{RMS} = \sqrt{\frac{1}{T} \int_{t_0}^{t_0+T} v^2(t) dt}$$

Eq. 12.13

So that the definition of an RMS voltage is equivalent to the definition of an RMS current.

Equations (12.12) and (12.13) are applicable to any time-varying waveform; the waveforms of interest to us are sinusoids, with zero average values (per equations (12.10) and (12.11)). In this particular case, the RMS values can be calculated to be:

$$V_{eff} = V_{RMS} = \frac{V_m}{\sqrt{2}}$$

Eq. 12.14

And

$$I_{eff} = I_{RMS} = \frac{I_m}{\sqrt{2}}$$

Eq. 12.15

Where V_m and I_m are the peak (or maximum) values of the voltage and current waveforms, per equations (12.10) and (12.11). Please note that equations (12.14) and (12.15) are applicable only to sinusoidal signals with zero average values.

The average and reactive powers given by equations (12.16) and (12.17) can be written in terms of the RMS values of voltage and current as follows:

$$P = V_{RMS} I_{RMS} \cos(\theta_v - \theta_i)$$

Eq. 12.16

And

$$Q = V_{RMS} I_{RMS} \sin(\theta_v - \theta_i)$$

Eq. 12.17

Section Summary:

- The RMS value of a sinusoidal signal $f(t) = F_m \cos(\omega t + \theta)$ is given by:

$$f_{RMS} = \frac{F_m}{\sqrt{2}}$$

- The above formula cannot be used for any signal other than a pure sinusoid with no offset.

1. The current and voltage delivered to a load are $i(t) = 2\cos(100t)$ And $v(t) = 120\cos(100t + 65°)$, respectively. What are the RMS values of voltage and current?

Solutions can be found at digilent.com/real-analog.

12.4 Apparent Power and Power Factor

In the previous subsections, we have seen that average power can be represented in terms of either the magnitudes of the voltage and current or the RMS values of the voltage and current and a multiplicative factor consisting of the cosine of the difference between the voltage phase and the current phase:

$$P = \frac{V_m I_m}{2} \cos(\theta_v - \theta_i) = V_{RMS} I_{RMS} \cos(\theta_v - \theta_i)$$

It is sometimes convenient to think of the average power as being the product of *apparent power* and a *power factor* (abbreviated *pf*). These are defined below:

- The <u>apparent power</u> is defined as either $\frac{V_m I_m}{2}$ or $V_{RMS} I_{RMS}$. (the two terms are, of course, equivalent.) Units of apparent power are designated as volt-amperes (abbreviated VA) to differentiate apparent power from either average power or reactive power.
- The <u>power factor</u> is defined as $\cos(\theta_v - \theta_i)$. Since cosine is an even function (the sign of the function is independent of the sign of the argument), the power factor does not indicate whether the voltage is leading or lagging the current. Thus, power factor is said to be either *leading* (if current <u>leads</u> voltage) or *lagging* (if current <u>lags</u> voltage).

It should be emphasized again at this point that the voltage and current are not independent quantities; they are related by the load impedance. For the system of Figure 12.1, for example, the voltage and current phasors are:

$$\underline{V} = Z_L \cdot \underline{I}$$ Eq. 12.18

where $\underline{V}$ is the voltage phasor across the load, $\underline{I}$ is the current phasor through the load, and Z_L is the load impedance. Thus, the difference between the voltage and current phase angles is simply the phase angle of the load impedance: $\theta_v - \theta_i = \angle\theta_{ZL}$. Therefore, the load impedance sets the power factor. If the load is purely resistive, $\theta_v = \theta_i$, the power factor is one, and the average power is the same as the apparent power. If the load is purely imaginary (as with purely inductive or purely capacitive loads) the power factor is zero and there is no average or real power absorbed by the load.

Section Summary

- *Apparent power* and *power factor* provide an alternate method for characterizing the average power delivered to the load. If the average power is:

$$P = \frac{V_m I_m}{2} \cos(\theta_v - \theta_i),$$

The apparent power is $\frac{V_m I_m}{2}$ and the power factor is $\cos(\theta_v - \theta_i)$.

12.4 Exercises

1. The current and voltage delivered to a load are i(t) = 2cos(100t) and v(t) = 120cos(100t+65°), respectively. What are the apparent power and power factor of the power delivered to the load?

2. A load consumes 100kW with a power factor pf = 0.85 (lagging). If the load current is 256A (RMS), find the load voltage.

3. An industrial plant has a load which consumes 20kW of power from a 220V$_{RMS}$ line. If the power factor is 0.9 (lagging), what is the difference in angle between the load voltage and the load current?

Solutions can be found at digilent.com/real-analog.

12.5 Complex Power

Apparent power, average power, reactive power, and power factor can all be represented simultaneously in a single parameter called complex power. If we define complex power as:

$$S = \frac{\underline{V}\,\underline{I}^*}{2}$$

Eq. 12.19

Where $\underline{V}$ is the phasor representing the voltage, $\underline{I}$ is the phasor representing the current, and the superscript * denotes complex conjugation (simply changing the sign on the imaginary part of the phasor).

If we substitute the magnitude and phase angle representations for the phasors in equation (12.19), we obtain (since complex conjugation simply changes the sign of the phase angle of a complex number):

$$S = \frac{1}{2}(V_m \angle \theta_v)(I_m \angle -\theta_i) = \frac{V_m I_m}{2} \angle (\theta_v - \theta_i)$$

Eq. 12.20

So that the complex power S is a complex number with magnitude $\frac{V_m I_m}{2}$ (or, equivalently, $V_{RMS}I_{RMS}$) and phase angle $\theta_v - \theta_i$. It is easy to see that the magnitude of the complex power is simply the apparent power. If we represent S in rectangular coordinates, we obtain:

$$S = P + jQ$$

Eq. 12.21

Where P is the average power,

$$P = \frac{V_m I_m}{2} \cos(\theta_v - \theta_i) = V_{RMS}I_{RMS}\cos(\theta_v - \theta_i)$$

as before, and Q is the reactive power,

$$Q = \frac{V_m I_m}{2} \sin(\theta_v - \theta_i) = V_{RMS}I_{RMS} \sin(\theta_v - \theta_i)$$

also as before.

The complex power, real power, reactive power, and apparent power can be represented graphically in the complex plane as a *power triangle,* as shown in Fig. 12.4 below.

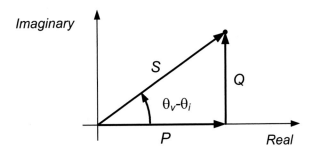

Figure 12.4. Power triangle.

One important thing to note about Fig. 12.4 is that this figure differs from a phasor diagram – the components shown on the power triangle are not phasors, since they do not provide magnitude and phase information about sinusoidal signals. The vectors shown in Fig. 12.4 are simply complex numbers.

We conclude this section with an example.

Example 12.1

For the circuit below,
   a. find the average power delivered by the source
   b. find the power absorbed by the resistor
   c. find the apparent, real, and reactive powers delivered by the source
   d. sketch a power triangle for the source

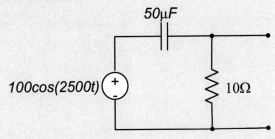

The frequency domain circuit is shown below.

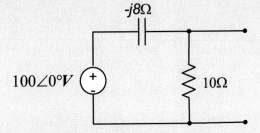

The current delivered by the source is therefore:

$$\underline{I} = \frac{100\angle 0°}{(10 - j8)\Omega} = 7.8 \angle 38.66°A$$

   a. The average power delivered by the source is therefore:

$$P = \frac{(100V)(7.8A)}{2}\cos(0° - 38.66°) = 305W$$

   b. The power absorbed by the resistor is the same as the average power delivered by the source, so $P_{10\Omega} = 305W$, which is the same as $R \cdot I_{RMS}^2$.

---

c. The apparent power is $\frac{(100V)(7.8A)}{2} = 391\ VA$, the reactive power is $Q = \frac{(100V)(7.8A)}{2}\sin(0° - 38.66°) = -244$ VAR, and the real power is simply the average power, $P = 305W$.

d. The power triangle is shown below:

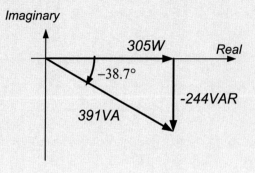

Section Summary:

- It is often convenient to express power as a complex number, S. This quantity expresses, simultaneously, the average power, the reactive power, the apparent power, and the power factor. Complex power can be determined from the voltage and current phasors as:

$$S = \frac{VI^*}{2},$$

Where * denotes complex conjugation.

- As with any other complex number, complex power can be expressed in either rectangular or polar coordinates.
    - In rectangular coordinates, the complex power readily provides the real power (P) and reactive power (Q):

    $$S = P + jQ$$

    - In polar coordinates, the complex power readily provides the apparent power and power factor:

    $$S = \frac{V_m I_m}{2} \angle(\theta_v - \theta_i)$$

    Where the apparent power is $\frac{V_m I_m}{2}$ and the power factor is given by $\cos(\theta_v - \theta_i)$.

12.5 Exercises

1. The current and voltage delivered to a load are $i(t) = 2\cos(100t - 30°)$ and $v(t) = 120\cos(100t + 65°)$, respectively. What is the complex power delivered to the load?
2. For the circuit shown, $i(t) = 2\cos(100t)$ and $v(t) = 120\cos(100t + 65°)$. Find:
    a. The complex power delivered by the source
    b. The average power delivered by the source
    c. The power dissipated by the resistor

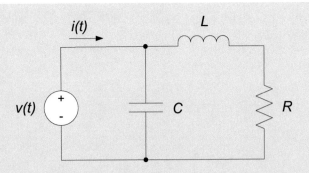

3. For the circuit shown, find
    a. i(t)
    b. The complex power delivered by the source
    c. The average power delivered by the source

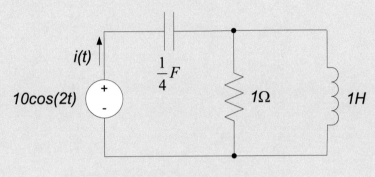

Solutions can be found at digilent.com/real-analog.

12.6 Power Factor Correction

In previous sections, we saw that power can be considered to be real (average power) or imaginary (reactive power). Reactive power is power which is provided to energy storage elements such as inductors or capacitors; this power is returned to the power source, since inductors and capacitors have no energy dissipation mechanism. The power factor provides a metric for assessing the amount of real power relative to the reactive power delivered to a load. The higher the power factor, the larger the amount of real power relative to reactive power – ideally, a power factor of one means that no reactive power is provided to the load.

Power companies in general cannot charge customers for power which is returned to the power company, so delivering reactive power to a customer is not productive from a power company's standpoint. In fact, since transmission losses will typically result in real power losses due to transmission of reactive power, the power company actually <u>loses</u> power when transmitting reactive power, for which no one pays! Unsurprisingly, this is not popular with power companies.

Large power users, such as factories, may have requirements placed upon them by the power company to provide a minimum power factor for their loads. If the factory cannot meet the required power factor, the power company can refuse to supply power or charge an increased rate for the power they do provide. This chapter illustrates how to re-design an inductive load to increase its power factor.

Most large power users' loads are inductive in nature. Therefore, in this section, we will only consider power factor correction for inductive loads. We illustrate the overall process in the context of an example.

Example 12.2

Determine the power factor for the circuit below if v$_s$(t)=100cos(377t). Re-design the load so that the power factor is one.

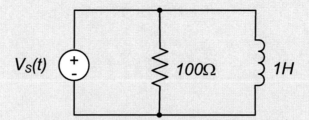

The load in this case consists of a 100Ω resistor in parallel with a 1H inductor. To determine the power factor, we need to determine the current delivered by the source; we do this by determining the equivalent impedance of the load, Z_L:

$$Z_L = \frac{(100\Omega)(j377\Omega)}{100\Omega + j377\Omega} = 96.67°\angle 14.86°$$

Therefore, the current phasor delivered by the source is:

$$\underline{I_S} = \frac{\underline{V_S}}{\underline{Z_L}} = \frac{100\angle 0°}{96.67\angle 14.86°} = 1.03\angle - 14.86°$$

The power factor is:

$$pf = \cos(\theta_v - \theta_i) = \cos(0° - (-14.86°)) = 0.967 \text{ (lagging)}$$

Note that the power factor is lagging, since current lags voltage, this is because the load is inductive in nature.

We can change the power factor of the load by adding a capacitor in parallel with the inductive load. The impedance of the capacitor can be used, in essence, to cancel out the inductive impedance of the load. The re-designed circuit is as shown below. The capacitance, C, must be chosen to provide the desired power factor.

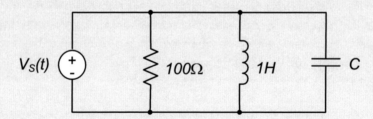

In order to determine the necessary size of the capacitor, we first determine the reactive power of the uncompensated system. Without the capacitor, the reactive power is:

$$Q = \frac{V_m I_m}{2}\sin(\theta_v - \theta_i) = \frac{(100V)(1.03A)}{2}\sin(14.86°) = 13.26 \, VAR$$

Our goal is to use the capacitor to change this reactive power so that the resulting power factor is as desired, without <u>changing the real power delivered to the load</u>. The capacitor will induce a negative reactive power; in order to achieve a power factor of exactly one, the reactive power introduced by the capacitor must exactly cancel the reactive power of the original load. Thus, the capacitor's reactive power must be:

$$Q_C = -13.26 \, VAR$$

For the parallel combination of the resistor, capacitor, and inductor, we can claim:

$$|Q_C| = \frac{V_{RMS}^2}{|Z_C|} = \frac{V_{RMS}^2}{\left|\frac{1}{\omega C}\right|} = \omega C V_{RMS}^2$$

Where $|Q_C|$ is the magnitude of the desired reactive power, and $|Z_C|$ is the magnitude of the capacitor's impedance. Solving the above expression for the desired capacitance provides:

$$C = \frac{|Q_C|}{\omega V_{RMS}^2} = \frac{13.26 \, VAR}{(377 \, rad/sec)(\frac{100}{\sqrt{2}})} = 7 \, \mu F$$

And a $7\mu F$ capacitor placed in parallel with the load will give the desired *pf=1*.

Section Summary:

- A small power factor means that a large portion of the power delivered by the power company to a user is in the form of reactive power. The user does not pay for reactive power, since it is essentially returned to the power company. The power company, however, incurs costs in exchanging reactive power with the user, since <u>transmission</u> of the reactive power results in power dissipation. Power companies, therefore, may require that a user meet a minimum power factor requirement.
- The power factor of an inductive load can be increased. The goal is to increase the power factor without changing the average power delivered to the load.

11.4 Exercises

1. Sketch a Bode plot (straight-line approximation) for the circuit below.

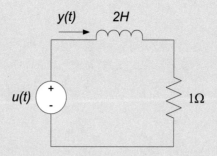

2. Sketch a Bode plot (straight-line approximation) for the circuit below.

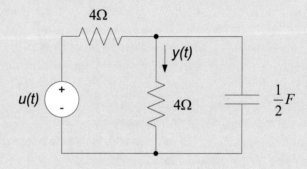

Solutions can be found at digilent.com/real-analog.